WRONGFUL ALLEGATIONS OF SEXUAL AND CHILD ABUSE

WRONGFUL ALLEGATIONS OF SEXUAL AND CHILD ABUSE

EDITED BY
ROS BURNETT

OXFORD
UNIVERSITY PRESS

OXFORD
UNIVERSITY PRESS

Great Clarendon Street, Oxford, OX2 6DP,
United Kingdom

Oxford University Press is a department of the University of Oxford.
It furthers the University's objective of excellence in research, scholarship,
and education by publishing worldwide. Oxford is a registered trade mark of
Oxford University Press in the UK and in certain other countries

© Oxford University Press 2016

The moral rights of the author have been asserted

Impression: 1

All rights reserved. No part of this publication may be reproduced, stored in
a retrieval system, or transmitted, in any form or by any means, without the
prior permission in writing of Oxford University Press, or as expressly permitted
by law, by licence or under terms agreed with the appropriate reprographics
rights organization. Enquiries concerning reproduction outside the scope of the
above should be sent to the Rights Department, Oxford University Press, at the
address above

You must not circulate this work in any other form
and you must impose this same condition on any acquirer

Crown copyright material is reproduced under Class Licence
Number C01P0000148 with the permission of OPSI
and the Queen's Printer for Scotland

Published in the United States of America by Oxford University Press
198 Madison Avenue, New York, NY 10016, United States of America

British Library Cataloguing in Publication Data

Data available

Library of Congress Control Number: 2016939530

ISBN 978-0-19-872330-1

Printed and bound by
CPI Group (UK) Ltd, Croydon, CR0 4YY

Links to third party websites are provided by Oxford in good faith and
for information only. Oxford disclaims any responsibility for the materials
contained in any third party website referenced in this work.

This volume is dedicated to the memory of Richard Webster:
il miglior fabbro

FOREWORD

This is a book that will have a resonance and an importance beyond the academy. It focuses on criminology and public policy at the cutting edge, taking the topical issue of sexual and child abuse and raising myriad issues that have been under-researched and under-discussed. Without seeking to deny the suffering of victims or the shortcomings of the criminal justice system in responding to their complaints, these twenty-one essays turn the spotlight on wrongful allegations and the people who become wrongly accused and, in some instances, wrongly convicted. As with complainants, so with alleged perpetrators, two key questions are how the criminal justice system has dealt with them and how it should deal with them. In relation to the former, prosecutors have been urged to start from the assumption that the complainant is telling the truth. This may be acceptable as a working hypothesis—but equally they should start from the presumption of innocence, looking for objective evidence (admittedly hard to find) and, as emphasized in various chapters, showing an awareness of the possible fallibility of the memory, particularly recovered memory. In relation to both groups, complainants and alleged perpetrators, changes to criminal procedure and the rules of evidence at trial should be considered. It is now fourteen years since the Home Affairs Committee called for 'special safeguards' for alleged perpetrators to ensure that the presumption of innocence is properly respected. The same report called for a more robust approach by the Criminal Cases Review Commission (CCRC) to the review of suspected wrongful convictions of this kind. The chapters in this book demonstrate the wide range of issues that need urgent resolution.

Righting past wrongs (to those victims of sexual and child abuse whose complaints were not taken seriously until recent years) should not be allowed to produce more wrongs (to alleged perpetrators who are innocent of the accusations). One major challenge for the ongoing Independent Inquiry into Child Sexual Abuse (chaired by the Hon. Lowell Goddard DNZM) is to ensure that it deals fairly with the injustices that have been done both to complainants and to alleged perpetrators. This book should be essential reading for all involved.

Professor Andrew Ashworth
CBE, QC (Hon), LLB, MA, PhD, DCL, DJur (Hon), LLD (Hon), FBA
Emeritus Vinerian Professor of English Law
University of Oxford

PREFACE

This book is in no way meant to deny the extent of child sexual abuse and rape, or to dismiss the suffering of victims and the difficulties that these cases present for police and prosecutors, and for public protection and victim support practitioners. There is no question that victims of abuse need support, and that perpetrators of heinous sexual crimes and child abuse should be brought to justice. Essentially, this book concerns a different population: innocent people who have been vilified and criminalized by untrue accusations, and who, as a result and to varying degrees, have had their own and their families' lives damaged because of those allegations.

For many, this is an uncomfortable subject: one that is seen as threat to the good progress made in recent years in facilitating the reporting of abuse and the ability of victims to play a part in bringing perpetrators to justice. The subject of 'false allegations' of rape or of child sexual abuse—under the rubric of 'wrongful allegations of sexual and child abuse' in this volume—is provocative of moral outrage and hostility in some child protection and feminist sectors. It is also difficult to address because some doubt that the problem exists or that false accusations are made often enough for them to be an issue. Partly, this may be the result of narrow definitions of 'false' as intentionally fabricated, whereas it is in the more inclusive sense of 'false' as 'untrue' that such allegations impact on those wrongly accused and that we apply the concept here. In the context of battles to close the justice gap for victims of rape, whereby women through the ages have faced the added ordeal of being called liars if they try to secure justice for themselves, objections to discussion of false allegations are understandable. However, correcting one form of injustice can have the effect of proliferating others, and the antipathy shown towards discussion of false allegations, the failure in key reports to acknowledge that not all allegations are true, or the dismissal of them as negligible are indicative of the need to bring the issue into clearer focus. Indeed, it is a measure of how little attention has been given to the issue of untrue allegations of abuse that a scientifically rigorous and representative survey of its prevalence has not so far been conducted.

My own interest in this form of injustice arose from discovering the writings of Richard Webster (to whom this volume is dedicated) and then seeing a BBC *Panorama* programme 'In the Name of the Children', produced by David Rose (who is a contributor to this volume), examining claims of extensive abuse in children's residential care homes around the end of the last century. A subsequent Home Office inquiry into the methods of investigating alleged historical child abuse had concluded that overzealous police operations working in conjunction with personal injury lawyers to seek out claimants, combined with the promise of compensation, had resulted in a 'new genre of miscarriages of justice'. Yet it continued to be an area of injustice that was discounted politically, overridden in legislation and policy, and passed over in academic research, scarcely featuring in textbooks about miscarriages of justice.

After commencing my own research into wrongful allegations of abuse, I offered voluntary assistance to a support group for falsely accused carers and teachers (FACT), and became familiar with the issues from the perspective of the individuals affected—and I saw for myself the toll taken on them and their families. The founding members had been targeted in earlier police operations that had led to wrongful arrests and, in some cases, convictions of which they were eventually exonerated. Some twelve years later, in the wake of the Jimmy Savile scandal and complaints that organized paedophile rings had been covered up, the same people were again facing the horrific prospect of dawn raids by police officers and the threat of prosecution, while the National Crime Agency solicited victims to come forward and accuse them. From this longer-term perspective, it is alarming that the lessons and insights drawn from those earlier moral panics have either been forgotten or are being ignored.

During the last decade, there has been a cultural shift in responses to complaints of sexual abuse. There is no question that policies needed to change so that complaints of abuse will be taken seriously and properly investigated. But moral crusades to protect children, to achieve more convictions for rape, and to bring more delayed prosecutions for alleged abuse in the last century have resulted in what many regard as overcorrection. The ascendancy of victim survivor groups and the politicization of their demands, along with the impact of high-profile cases, have created a new sense of urgency, prompting tighter policies and legislation to restrict and convict offenders, but also a widening of the net and erosion of legal principles that risks pre-crime penalties for innocent suspects, as well as wrongful convictions.

At the time of writing, mainstream and social media are saturated with news of abusers being tried and sentenced, of adult survivors of historical child abuse breaking their silence and seeking justice, of police operations to uncover paedophile rings and shore up unsupported allegations, and of inquiries and commissions being set up to seek evidence and give a voice to victims. There have been some well-publicized exonerations, but much more coverage is given to guilty verdicts. In the UK, the prisons are filling up with elderly white men convicted for historical institutional abuse, younger Asian men convicted for sexual exploitation of under-age girls, and an increasing number of ex-service personnel convicted for sexual assault. We are all shocked and troubled by the sheer scale of sexual abuse that has been revealed, and the public consensus is that far too many have gone undetected and unprosecuted for far too long—and that all obstacles to supporting victims and prosecuting offenders must now be removed. Yet it is in this climate, sometimes referred to as a 'moral panic' or 'war', that mistakes are more likely to be made and that people become vulnerable to baseless accusations that could destroy their lives if believed. When the default belief is that those accused are guilty, then the risk of more people being traduced and punished by specious claims inevitably rises.

I had initially planned that the title for this book would be 'The Lowest Circle of Hell'. It is an expression that was used to describe the experience of the late Lord McAlpine when, in the final years of his life, he was thrust into the media spotlight, having been mistakenly identified as a child abuser. The epithet encapsulates the Dante-esque nightmare of being plunged into a dark place and being looked upon as the lowest of the low, forever condemned. But the proposed title was taken to task for seeming to imply that wrongly accused people suffer more than victims of abuse, while the book proposal was criticized for its omission of chapters on victims of sexual abuse. Those mild rebukes are well taken. It is characteristic of the diametrical relationship between true and false allegations, and between the rights of victims of abuse and the rights of victims of erroneous, serious criminal charges, that both sides are seen as precariously pitted against the other. Ideally, a large enough volume would discuss both, including meetings points and grey areas. It remains the case, though, that both forms of suffering coexist as overlapping, yet distinct, wrongs.

There are numerous academic books that focus exclusively on victims of child abuse and victims of rape and sexual assault. To fill a gap in the literature, the present volume focuses exclusively on the misfortunes of those who are wrongly accused. The contributors draw on expertise from various disciplines to address issues relevant to understanding the context, causes, and outcome of wrongful allegations of abuse. Although the majority of the chapters pertain to policies and legal developments in either the UK or the United States, the emerging themes and conclusions have wider relevance. This is appropriate because the drumbeat against sex offenders and child abusers is international, as is the need to recognize the threat that such crusading imposes on presumptions of innocence and on communities that prefer to be built more on trust than on suspicion.

ACKNOWLEDGEMENTS

During the time it has taken to write and produce this book, the subject matter has become increasingly controversial, resulting in some unanticipated delays. My thanks are owed to contributing authors who delivered their chapters early for their uncomplaining patience between submission and publication. I am grateful to my commissioning editors at OUP, Peter Daniell and Lucy Alexander, who supported my initial proposal and determination to produce a multi-authored volume dedicated to the subject of wrongful allegations, and who gave useful guidance during the stages of working with contributing authors. Thank you to Clare Jones, senior production editor, Vanessa Plaister, copy-editor, and Chris Wogan, marketing manager, for their vital roles during the production process. Many books have an unsung hero: this one would not have been completed without the unfailing support of my husband, Peter Burnett.

CONTENTS

Contributors   xvii

PART I THE REALITY OF WRONGFUL ALLEGATIONS OF ABUSE: WHAT KIND OF ALLEGATIONS AND WHY DO THEY MATTER?

1 Wrongful Allegations of Sexual and Child Abuse: A Neglected and Expanding Category of Injustice   3
Ros Burnett

2 Experiencing False Allegations of Abuse: First-Person Accounts   16
Edited by Ros Burnett

PART II CULTURE; IDEOLOGY; POLITICS: WHAT IS THE TERRAIN THAT GIVES RISE TO FALSE ALLEGATIONS?

3 Demons, Devils, and Ritual Abuse: Interdisciplinary Perspectives   31
Mary deYoung

4 Moral Crusades, Child Protection, Celebrities, and the Duty to Believe   42
Frank Furedi

5 Telling Stories?: Adults' Retrospective Narratives of Abuse in Residential Child Care   54
Mark Smith

6 'Rape Culture' Narrative, State Feminism, and the Presumption of Guilt   66
John Brigham

7 Making Accusations: Precautionary Logic and Embedded Suspicion in an Insecure and Uncertain World   82
Bill Hebenton and Toby Seddon

PART III THE ALLEGATION: CAUSES; MOTIVATIONS; CASE STUDIES: WHY WOULD ANYONE MAKE A FALSE ACCUSATION?

8 Why and How False Allegations of Abuse Occur: An Overview   99
Felicity Goodyear-Smith

9 The Compensations of Being a Victim   118
   Barbara Hewson

10 His Story; Her Story: Sexual Miscommunication, Motivated
   Remembering, and Intoxication as Pathways to Honest False
   Testimony Regarding Sexual Consent   129
   J. Guillermo Villalobos, Deborah Davis, and Richard A. Leo

11 Beliefs about Memory, Childhood Abuse, and Hypnosis among
   Clinicians, Legal Professionals, and the General Public   143
   Christopher C. French and James Ost

12 To Catch a Sex Offender: Police, Trawls, and Personal Injury Solicitors   155
   David Rose

PART IV INTERROGATION; PROSECUTION; CONVICTION; APPEAL: HOW COULD THE JUSTICE SYSTEM GET IT SO WRONG?

13 When Exoneration Seems Hopeless: The Special Vulnerability
   of Sexual Abuse Suspects to False Confession   175
   Deborah Davis and Richard A. Leo

14 Complaints of Sexual Abuse and the Decline of Objective Prosecuting   191
   Luke Gittos

15 'In Denial': The Hazards of Maintaining Innocence after Conviction   204
   Daniel S. Medwed

16 When Juries Find Innocent People Guilty: Strengths and Limitations
   of the Appellate System in England and Wales   215
   Michael Zander QC

PART V FINDING WAYS FORWARD: WHAT'S TO BE DONE?

17 Reducing Harm Resulting from False Allegations of Child Sexual
   Abuse: The Importance of Corroboration   227
   Steve Herman

18 Advances in Lie Detection: Limitations and Potential for Investigating
   Allegations of Abuse   242
   Galit Nahari

19 Toward Reconciliation of the True and False Recovered Memory Debate   255
   Robert F. Belli

20	The Defendant's Plea of Innocent in Sexual Abuse Cases *Tim Bakken*	271
21	Reducing the Incidence and Harms of Wrongful Allegations of Abuse *Ros Burnett*	282

Index 297

CONTRIBUTORS

Tim Bakken is Professor of Law at the US Military Academy at West Point, NY. He served previously as a homicide prosecutor in New York City (Brooklyn), where he also practised law with private firms. In 2007, he created the first law department at the National Military Academy of Afghanistan. His article 'Innocence Procedures for Innocent Persons' (2008) proposed for the first time the plea of innocence. Professor Bakken has lectured and published in journals throughout the world in the areas of constitutional, criminal, and international law.

Robert F. Belli is Professor of Psychology at the University of Nebraska, Lincoln, NE. An applied experimental cognitive psychologist, Belli's research interests centre on the neuroscience of applied cognition, autobiographical memory, and the impact of suggestion on autobiographical memory quality. His research also includes exploring methods that improve the quality of retrospective reports in survey questionnaires. Belli's work has resulted in more than seventy publications, and he has acquired approximately US$3.3 million in research funding from both public- and private-sector organizations, including the National Institutes of Health, the National Science Foundation, the State of Nebraska, and Gallup.

John Brigham is Professor of Political Science at the University of Massachusetts, Amherst, MA. He is the author of *The Cult of the Court* (1987), *The Constitution of Interests: Beyond the Politics of Rights* (2000), and *Material Law: A Jurisprudence of What's Real* (2009). He has been a Fellow at the International Institute for the Sociology of Law and a member of the board of trustees of the Law and Society Association, and he is currently president of the New England Political Science Association.

Ros Burnett, DPhil, is a senior research associate, formerly Reader in Criminology, at the Centre for Criminology, University of Oxford. She gained her doctorate in social psychology at Oxford. Previously a probation officer and relationship counsellor, she has published books on personal relationships, youth justice, the role of probation services, and offender desistance from crime. Her most recent book was *Where Next for Criminal Justice?* (2011, with David Faulkner). Her voluntary roles include research consultant to FACT, the support group for falsely accused carers, teachers and other professionals, and associate editor of the *International Journal of Offender Therapy and Comparative Criminology.*

Deborah Davis, PhD, is Professor of Psychology at the University of Nevada, Reno, NV, and a member of the faculty of the National Judicial College. She has published more than 100 book chapters and journal articles in the areas of witness memory, interrogations and confessions, and issues of communication of sexual consent, among others. Her research on interrogations has been supported by a grant from the US Federal Bureau of Investigation (FBI). She has given continuing legal education (CLE) seminars on each of these topics for attorney organizations in the United

States and Canada, and has testified as an expert witness in more than 100 trials across the United States.

Mary deYoung, PhD, is Professor of Sociology at Grand Valley State University in Allendale, MI. The author of *The Day Care Ritual Abuse Moral Panic* (2006), she has written extensively on that topic, and has presented papers at national and international conferences. She is also the author of *Madness: An American History of Mental Illness and Its Treatment* (2010) and the *Encyclopedia of Asylum Therapeutics: 1750–1950s* (2015).

Christopher C. French is Professor of Psychology at Goldsmiths, University of London, where he is also head of the Anomalistic Psychology Research Unit and a member of the Forensic Psychology Unit. He is a chartered psychologist and a Fellow of the British Psychological Society. He is also a member of the Scientific Advisory Board of the British False Memory Society (BFMS), a member of the Advisory Group for Falsely Accused Carers, Teachers and Other Professionals (FACT), and an honorary member of the Centre for Memory and Law at City University. He has published more than 120 scientific papers and chapters (including several on memory), as well as a number of books.

Frank Furedi is Emeritus Professor of Sociology at the University of Kent in Canterbury. His studies have been devoted to an exploration of the cultural developments that influence the construction of contemporary risk consciousness. His research has been oriented towards the way in which risk and uncertainty is managed by contemporary culture. He has published widely about the construction of social problems and panics relating to issues such as health, parenting children, food, and new technology. In recent years, Furedi's research has focused on the historical sociology of cultural authority. Currently, he is working on a comparative study of the construction of the reading wars in the UK and the United States.

Luke Gittos is a solicitor practising criminal law at Hughmans Solicitors. After being called to the Bar and gaining extensive experience in the criminal department, he cross-qualified as a solicitor in 2013. He is legal editor for the online magazine *Spiked*, where he writes on defendant's rights. His articles have also been published in the *Criminal Bar Quarterly* and in the *Independent Online*, and his first book is *Why Rape Culture is a Dangerous Myth: From Steubenville to Ched Evans* (2015). Gittos regularly appears in the media to comment on legal issues. Recent appearances include *Channel 4 News*, *Channel 5 News*, *Russia Today*, and numerous BBC radio stations.

Felicity Goodyear-Smith is Professor and head of the Department of General Practice and Primary Health Care, University of Auckland, New Zealand. She is a vocationally trained general practitioner (FRNZCGP) and forensic physician (FFFLM). She has published more than 200 scientific papers, book chapters, and books, a number of which address false abuse allegations. Her latest book, *Murder that Wasn't: The Case of George Gwaze* (2015), explores the factors that led to Gwaze being twice falsely charged and twice acquitted of the rape and murder of his 10-year-old niece.

Bill Hebenton, PhD, lectures and researches at the Centre for Criminology and Criminal Justice, School of Law, at the University of Manchester. He undertook the early assessment for the Home Office of US policies on sexual offenders in the community and the pilot study introducing lay members into multi-agency public protection panels. He has written on the implications of precautionary thinking for the management of dangerous and sexual offenders, and also on developing the situational perspective in prevention of sexual violence. His other interests lie in comparative research. Hebenton co-edited the *Handbook of Asian Criminology* (2013) and the *Routledge Handbook of Chinese Criminology* (2014). He is also co-editor of the Palgrave-Macmillan book series *Palgrave Advances in Criminology and Criminal Justice in Asia*.

Steve Herman is Associate Professor of Psychology at the University of Hawaii at Hilo, HI. His research focuses on evaluating the accuracy of professionals' judgements about the validity of allegations of child sexual abuse. He has published articles in *Law and Human Behavior*, *Child Abuse and Neglect*, and other professional journals. He has presented workshops on the science and practice of forensic child sexual abuse evaluations to psychologists, judges, attorneys, prosecutors, law enforcement personnel, child protection caseworkers, social workers, and forensic interviewers in the United States, Canada, South Korea, Japan, Brazil, Norway, Finland, and Australia.

Barbara Hewson is a barrister in private practice at 1 Gray's Inn Square. She was called to the Bar of England and Wales in 1985. She is also a member of the Bar of Ireland (called 1991) and Northern Ireland (called 2000). She is a public lawyer, whose practice spans human rights, judicial review, mental capacity law, and professional regulation in the healthcare sector. In 2012, she was made an Honorary Fellow of the University of Westminster. She has a special interest in false allegations and false memory, and is an expert adviser to FACT.

Richard A. Leo is Hamill Family Professor of Law and Social Psychology at the University of San Francisco, San Francisco, CA. He is one of the leading experts in the world on police interrogation practices, false confessions, and the wrongful conviction of the innocent. He has authored more than 100 articles and book chapters on these subjects, as well as several books, including the multiple award-winning *Police Interrogation and American Justice* (2008). Leo has won numerous individual and career achievement awards, and his research has been cited by numerous appellate courts, including the US Supreme Court on multiple occasions.

Daniel S. Medwed is Professor of Law at Northeastern University School of Law in Boston, MA, and recipient of the 2013 Robert D. Klein University Lectureship, which is awarded annually to a faculty member at the university who has obtained distinction in his or her field of study. His critically acclaimed book *Prosecution Complex: America's Race to Convict and Its Impact on the Innocent* (2012) explores how even well-meaning prosecutors may contribute to wrongful convictions because of cognitive biases and an overly deferential regime of legal and ethical rules.

Galit Nahari, PhD, is a senior lecturer and the head of the MA research track in the Department of Criminology at Bar-Ilan University, Ramat Gan, Tel Aviv, Israel. Her main research interests are legal and investigative decision-making, applied memory, detection of deception, and witnesses' credibility assessments. As part of this, she develops interrogation and lie-detection methods, then examines their validity and suitability in different contexts, and their vulnerability to judgemental biases. A major part of her research further focuses on the cognitive processes underlying credibility and veracity assessments, as well as on individual differences that impact on these assessments. She is involved in developing training methodology and tools for police officers, and has presented workshops to practitioners.

James Ost, PhD, is a Reader in Applied Cognitive Psychology at the Department of Psychology, University of Portsmouth. His research interests focus on the inherently context-dependent nature of memory and remembering, and he has published work using a variety of paradigms to investigate 'false memories' and memory errors.

David Rose is an award-winning investigative journalist and author, who has worked on miscarriages of justice for many years, for several national newspapers and the BBC. There he made and presented 'In the Name of the Children', a 2000 *Panorama* programme about false allegations of historical abuse. He has returned to this subject in print on many subsequent occasions. His many awards include the One World human rights journalism prize and the David Watt memorial prize. His seven books include *Guantánamo: The War on Human Rights* (2004) and *Violation* (2007), an investigation into a wrongful capital conviction in the US state of Georgia, which was shortlisted for the Golden Dagger award. His first novel, *Taking Morgan*, was published in 2014.

Toby Seddon is Professor of Criminology in the School of Law at the University of Manchester. Within the School, he is a member of the Manchester Centre for Regulation and Governance (ManReg) and of the Centre for Criminology and Criminal Justice (CCCJ). As well as a long-term interest in risk as a technology of governance, his main research focus is currently on developing a new paradigm for global illicit drug policy by recasting it as a regulatory problem.

Mark Smith, PhD, is a senior lecturer and head of social work at the University of Edinburgh. He worked in residential child care over a period of almost twenty years before moving to the University of Strathclyde in 2000, where he developed a Masters in Residential Child Care. He returned to the University of Edinburgh in 2005. He has written extensively on residential child care, including two books. He developed an interest in historical abuse allegations having witnessed former colleagues being investigated and, in some cases, convicted. He is currently working on a project funded by the Economic and Social Research Council (ESRC) examining the residential school context of the initial allegations of abuse made against former BBC entertainer Jimmy Savile. Smith is a member of the expert advisory panel to FACT.

J. Guillermo Villalobos is a student in the Interdisciplinary Social Psychology doctoral programme at University of Nevada, Reno, NV. He migrated from Northwest Mexico to the United States in 2003. He received a BA in psychology from University of California, Riverside, in 2009 and a MA in general-experimental psychology from California State University, San Bernardino, in 2011. He has conducted research in, and published on topics related to, psychology and the law, such as language and communication during law-enforcement procedures and sexual consent interactions, criminal interrogations and confession, and the experiences and legal outcomes of socially disadvantaged populations.

Michael Zander QC, Emeritus Professor, taught at the London School of Economics (LSE) between 1963 and 1998. For twenty-five years (1963–88), he was also legal correspondent for *The Guardian*. He was a member of the Royal Commission on Criminal Justice (1991–93) and also conducted the Crown Court Study, the Royal Commission's biggest research study. He is a member of the Home Office PACE Strategy Board. The seventh edition of *Zander on PACE*, with a foreword by Lord Judge (Lord Chief Justice 2008–13), was published in 2015. He has published a dozen books and more than 300 articles in legal journals.

PART I
THE REALITY OF WRONGFUL ALLEGATIONS OF ABUSE
WHAT KIND OF ALLEGATIONS AND WHY DO THEY MATTER?

1

WRONGFUL ALLEGATIONS OF SEXUAL AND CHILD ABUSE
A NEGLECTED AND EXPANDING CATEGORY OF INJUSTICE

Ros Burnett

> The discovery of truth is prevented more effectively, not by the false appearance things present and which mislead into error, not directly by weakness of the reasoning powers, but by preconceived opinion, by prejudice.
>
> (Schopenhauer, 1890)

> It was in California in the 1970s and 1980s that a new culture of child protection gradually emerged. [. . .] One of the distinctive features was the manner in which it set out to combat the systematic disbelief with which allegations of sexual abuse were all too frequently met. The development was in many ways both necessary and overdue. But the rigid ideology which lay behind this view meant that in too many cases, an attitude of systematic disbelief was replaced not by an open minded willingness to investigate, but by a systematic credulity.
>
> (Webster, 1998: 36–7)

There is a special repugnance reserved for sexual and violent abuse of children, women, and other vulnerable adults. These offences of physical violation and traumatizing psychological degradation are so contemptible that many would refuse to be in the same room as a named child abuser or rapist; even those who support paradigms of rehabilitation and forgiveness would not trust former sex offenders to be alone with children or vulnerable adults. Such offences have become a *crimen exceptum* (Larner, 1980) of modern times—arguably more so than even terrorism—on a par with witchcraft in historical Europe. They are regarded as sufficiently endemic and evil as to necessitate exceptional measures to root them out and to penalize them. Other heinous crimes, such as murder, do not necessarily call forth the same moral opprobrium or populist punitiveness as sexual offences (Roberts et al., 2002). In a prison setting, where there is more tolerance for the criminal wrongdoing of other prisoners, sexual offenders are 'the cultural bogey-men in relation to whom anyone could claim moral superiority' (Crewe, 2009: 277) and hatred of 'nonces' means that they generally need protection from other prisoners.

All the greater, therefore, the calamity visited upon those who are wrongly accused of such offences. They are no less likely to share those same feelings of revulsion against sex offenders and child abusers, and yet are forced to live with being identified as capable of and culpable for such deeds. For an innocent person who has led a law-abiding and decent life, it is hard to imagine a 'crueler tyranny' (Rabinowitz, 2004) than being found guilty of child sexual abuse and sentenced to perhaps decades in prison, with lifelong registration as a sex offender and restricted access to children in his or her family—and having 'every good that [they] put into the world turned around for bad' (Greene, 2011: 2).

Those are worst-case scenarios. It is important to recognize, though, that while many—perhaps most—who are wrongly accused of abuse are not charged, their lives may nonetheless be blighted (Pendergrast, 1998; Webster, 2005; Brand, 2007). Catastrophic life changes can begin from the point of being wrongly accused if that is followed by separation from one's children, suspension from work, and withdrawal of friends while a complaint is being investigated. Adverse publicity could lead to hate mail, vandalism of property, and a ruined reputation. The late Lord McAlpine, whose death may have been hastened by a wrongful allegation, described the existential pain as one that 'gets into your bones' (Smith, 2012), and those who go through court trials before being cleared typically draw on the concept of 'hell' to describe what they have endured. The accused are never declared innocent when acquitted and typically there is no exculpatory evidence to remove suspicion.

THE CRUSADE AGAINST SEXUAL ABUSE

During the second decade of the twenty-first century, following a series of high-profile sex abuse scandals and official inquiries, globalized concern about sexual abuse of children and vulnerable adults has ballooned into one of the foremost issues of our time. This is the latest manifestation of an ongoing social movement during the last fifty-plus years to protect children and women from physical abuse and sexual exploitation by those more powerful than themselves, to prosecute and convict offenders, and to provide reparation to those who were victims of historical abuse. Preventive and retributive measures against sex offenders are now omnipresent in modern society, with multi-agency approaches integrated within official policies, and concerted efforts to combat sexual offending and improve victims' experiences of the criminal justice.

In contrast to a past culture of disbelief, which made it very difficult for victims of abuse to report offences against them with a realistic expectation that offenders would be prosecuted, progress has been made in recognizing the extent of victimization and in improving the experience of victims who report offences. For practitioners and academics who have worked towards reducing the attrition rate between estimated levels of offending and convictions, not enough progress has been made (see, for example, Kelly, Lovett, and Regan, 2005; Wheatcroft and Walklate, 2014). That the aim of this book is not to detract from the importance of protecting children, women, and men from grievous crimes cannot be overemphasized; without question, people who have been sexually abused should be treated with the utmost care and sensitivity. The same care should be extended to those who present themselves as victims and their complaints should be treated as believable during the course of investigation. Our concern is that previous systematic disbelief in victims has, to some extent, been replaced by systematic disbelief that innocent people could be wrongly targeted in the commendable goal of bringing rapists and child abusers to justice. A movement that is morally right can be swept along by moral righteousness (Webster, 2005) and confirmation bias (Medwed, 2012; Tavris and Aronson, 2015) to become overly suspicious and single-minded, and thus, in the course of rounding up the villains, risk persecuting the innocent.

Cultural anthropologists have observed that a preoccupation with dark forces and evil conspiracies is evident through human history, and is part of human nature (Frankfurter, 2006; Webster, 2005). In modern times, the moral crusade to shield what is sacred and inviolable—notably, childhood—has become normative and institutionalized (Furedi, 2013). While the instinct to protect those who are vulnerable and valued cannot simply be attributed to moral panics, the reactions of interest groups, media, and politicians to arising scandals can result in a febrile atmosphere and extreme measures that do more harm than good. The harmful role of moral panics is well documented (see, for example, Nathan and Snedeker, 1995; Jenkins, 1996; Webster, 1998, 2005; Furedi, 2013). Lessons were learned from the moral panics about satanic ritual abuse and organized paedophile rings in residential child care that led to wrongful convictions and broken families (see, for example, La Fontaine, 1998; Home Affairs Select Committee, 2002). But, following the recent scandals about celebrity sexual predators and historical institutional abuse, the daily diet of news about the latest prosecutions and convictions, and a huge increase in reported sexual offences and recent sexual exploitation, those underlying allegations were never put to rest and have resurfaced in various ways (see, for example, Cheit, 2014; Children's Commissioner for Wales, 2015).

The new wave of moral crusading—to root out paedophiles, to beat 'rape culture', to bring closure to victims of non-recent abuse, to 'get to the bottom of' alleged cover-ups, and so forth—is being characterized by many commentators as the 'new Salem' or 'neo-McCarthyism'. Official announcements about the scourge of child abuse and sexual violence against women, the rollout of legislation and policies to tackle the problem, and the amount of government money being poured into inquiries convey a certainty about the extent and seriousness of abuse, presume victimhood and therewith the guilt of the accused, and brook no discussion about the differential nature of abuse and the resulting harms.

Whether the need for such developments really has been inflated and overextended by exaggerated or untrue claims is debatable, given the hidden nature of such crimes, the absence of objective physical evidence to indicate non-recent abuse, and the extent to which much more (admitted and proven) abuse is coming to light. Justice must be for victims, as well as defendants. However, in an atmosphere of moral outrage about rape and child abuse, with slogans such as 'Don't Wait until You're Certain'[1] urging people to report suspected abuse and calling for victims to come forward under the banner of 'Believe the Victim', miscarriages of justice are inevitable. Those accused of sexual offences are particularly vulnerable to errors of justice because their cases turn on whose testimony is most believed.

A SOCIAL CAUSE THAT IS PRONE TO ERROR

To the extent that social problems, including 'abuse', are constructed by the concepts and narratives used to communicate about them (Jenkins, 1996; Hoyano and Keenan, 2007; Daly, 2014), public opinion can be influenced by new labels (such as 'grooming', 'paedophile rings', 'rape culture'), and by shocking revelations in the media and 'hard news' stories (Greer and McLaughlin, 2013; Sköld, 2013). While media reports of child sexual abuse and rape evoke heated responses, an added element in societal calls for something to be done is information about the failures of officials in preventing or dealing with reported abuse—and particularly suggestions that the problems have been covered up (Daly, 2014). This shameful scenario is made more convincing by vivid examples from people who are prepared to stand up and tell their story of victimization. Powerful stories are utilized by activists to promote their causes and to influence public opinion. The danger is that shining the spotlight on a shocking catalogue of offences and their victims leaves other injustices in the dark.

Because sexual abuse is typically unwitnessed and leaves no physical marker, responses to claims made are dependent on believing that the reported abuse has occurred and on believing the accounts of complainants. This is therefore an area in which the criminal justice system is particularly liable to make errors of judgement, and in which prior assumptions and mindset will influence outcomes. Where there is scope for doubt, and choice, in the absence of decisive information, it is inevitable that personal passions, groupthink, and cognitive biases will come into play (Tavris and Aronson, 2015). Most critical, therefore, are the theories held by policymakers that guide practice and legal developments. Slowly over the last few decades, but with crescendo over the last few years, a major shift has taken place in responding to sexual crime. That shift, explained succinctly by Webster (1998: 36–7) in the quote with which this chapter opened, is from systematic disbelief to systematic credulity. As a backlash to an era during which the accused was given the benefit of the doubt, the 'default belief' now is that the accused is guilty (Burnett, 2013). In the absence of objective biometric evidence, judgements become more an act of faith and choosing to err on the side of the perceived greater injustice.

This reinforced credo to believe the accuser comes with belittling of the 'false allegations' problem, with officials and victims' advocates regularly claiming that they are

---

[1] In the UK, the National Society for the Prevention of Cruelty to Children (NSPCC) launched its 'Don't Wait until You're Certain' campaign in January 2013.

'rare', and disapproving of publicity given to them in case they deter victims from 'coming forward'. The very existence of false allegations is challenged or the concept is regarded as offensive—particularly in the narrow sense of 'false' as deliberately fabricated, and therefore as representing women as dishonest, while failing to acknowledge their suffering (see, for example, Kelly, 2010; Wheatcroft and Walklate, 2014). Ironically, this minimizing, and even mythologizing, of false allegations adds to the danger that they will occur, because it sets up ideal conditions for them to be made maliciously or recklessly and nevertheless to be believed.

THIS VOLUME: SCOPE AND DEFINITIONS

There are several books that cover diverse aspects of child sexual abuse (CSA) including false allegations, and which provide practical guidance and 'state of knowledge and the art' reviews for forensic psychologists and other practitioners working on suspected CSA cases (in particular, see Ney, 1995; Kuehnle and Connell, 2009); numerous books are also concerned with the interrogation, policing, and sentencing of sex offenders, and with the victims of sexual abuse and their recovery. The present volume is distinctive in that its focus is on only wrongful allegations (alternately described as 'false', 'untrue', or 'wrongful'), it includes alleged abuse of adults as well as of children, and its scope ranges over such allegations in civil, as well as criminal, justice contexts. It is not intended to be a guide to practice, but rather a multidisciplinary exploration of the causes, processes, and effects that explain the ontology and process by which wrongful allegations take hold and damage lives.

'False', with and without intent The adjective 'wrongful' is used interchangeably with 'false' to provide a less pejorative alternative. The concept of 'false' is problematic when pinned to allegations of abuse, because it is likely to be understood in its narrower sense and perceived as a character attack on the individual making the accusation. From a historical perspective, it will forever be associated with biblical and literary narratives wherein women falsely cry rape in order to achieve their own ends. Unless the context indicates otherwise, the broader dictionary definition of 'false' as 'untrue' is applicable in this volume and alludes to accusations made in error, as well as those that are deliberate fabrications or distortions of the truth. This is an important distinction in meaning, because a claim that is intentionally false could be treated as a crime in itself if it were to waste police time or lead to perjury in a trial, or it may result in a lawsuit for defamation.

Allegations We are dealing in this volume primarily with those alleged cases in which it is difficult to establish whether or not a crime occurred, because the only evidence is verbal. Other challenged allegations, however, may have regard to whether admitted sexual contact was a crime or may assert that the accused has been mistakenly identified as the offender. Reports of such crimes that are accompanied by physical evidence of the crime (such as injuries, DNA, or incidents caught on camera or with third-party witnesses) and which unambiguously link the accused to that crime are obviously far less problematic.

In surveying the harms of wrongful allegations, it would be short-sighted to ignore those that never become the subject of court proceedings or police investigation, but in which cases the accused endures verbal abuse, vandalism, and sometime violent assaults. The scope of the present volume is across this continuum, from untrue allegations that do not lead to official action, through to those that progress to wrongful conviction followed by registration as sex offender, sometimes for life. The allegations include those that refer to current offences, as well as retrospective complaints of non-recent abuse.

What kinds of abuse? While distinct subject specialisms have evolved around each of 'child sexual abuse' and 'rape or sexual assault of women', leading to separate literatures, charities, and advocacy groups, in practice the legal and punitive responses overlap; from the perspective of the accused, the implications are similar. This volume addresses allegations relating to both specialisms, sometimes referring to them generically as 'sexual abuse' or 'person abuse'. Some of the contributors focus on one rather than the other, as befits their own research. Sexual offences against children and women are among the most reviled of crimes, although any kind of physical abuse against vulnerable victims meets with similar moral outrage. Insofar as physical violence, cruelty, and degradation may be alleged in the absence of visible evidence, that too is included within the reach of this volume. It is only recently that sexual and domestic abuse of men has begun to be recognized, but the evidence for this and the harm caused is similarly devastating for victims, and obviously they too should also be included as potential victims in this field of abusive crimes against the person.

The common ground in the abuse brought together here is that such offences are perpetrated against children or vulnerable adults by someone more powerful than themselves, leading to lasting trauma, but in circumstances in which the evidence is hidden or non-existent, making the alleged offence difficult to prove or disprove. Moreover, charges for all of these crimes are susceptible to errors of judgement: applying the language of statistical theory, they are liable to lead to 'false positives' (treating an innocent person as guilty) and 'false negatives' (letting a guilty person go free). It is these errors that make trials for such alleged offences so disturbing for those who know or are convinced that the wrong decision has been reached.

BOOK STRUCTURE AND OUTLINE OF CHAPTERS

This book addresses a particular form of human adversity: that of a person being vilified for sexual assaults and violations that he or she did not commit. The phenomenon of untrue allegations of abuse and their harms is introduced in Part I: The Reality of Wrongful Allegations of Abuse. The present chapter identifies and defines the related categories brought together under the heading of wrongful allegations—or, synonymously, false allegations—of abuse, and introduces the structure of the volume and (broadly) the content or a key argument of each of its chapters. The editor acknowledges in the Preface and in the present chapter the high level of disclosed and undisclosed sexual and child abuse, and the importance of balancing the book's focus with continuing concern for victims of abuse. That this book devotes its chapters to the former with much less attention to the latter is intended to address a gap in knowledge, but in no way is it meant to dispute the seriousness of sexual and child abuse or to belittle the challenge in addressing them—issues that are, thankfully, already the subject of a large body of research and governmental attention.

A regrettable omission from the book is a chapter to address the prevalence of wrongful allegations. An intention to undertake such a chapter was abandoned because of the unusual scope of the book: embracing child physical and sexual abuse, rape and sexual assault of adults, both recent and 'non-recent' abuse, and, importantly, allegations that do not become police matters and are not necessarily on record, but which are nonetheless a significant proportion of those addressed in the book. Without a rigorous self-report survey, any attempt to estimate prevalence would be wildly speculative; most surveys that have been completed of categories of abuse have not been conducted according to reliable methodological standards and are difficult to compare, because they have inconsistent definitions of what exactly is being measured (Rumney, 2006; Saunders, 2012). Because wrongful allegations are frequently not intentionally false and, even when they are, are not a crime unless they have involved a deliberate perversion of justice or a reckless waste of police time, only a very small subset would qualify to be included in recorded crime. A range of factors, addressed in the following chapters, make it likely that the true prevalence of wrongful abuse allegations is much greater than is typically claimed in discourse on child abuse and rape. In any case, allowing for a low estimate of the prevalence of wrongful allegations, the grievous harm done to individuals and families and the dearth of studies dedicated to those wrongly accused would still warrant the present dedicated volume.

Chapter 2 provides anonymous first-person accounts of the experience and consequences of being falsely accused, illustrating some dimensions of the damage caused by wrongful allegations of abuse. While people can be traduced by false allegations without there being any tangible evidence beyond someone's word, the same absence of physical evidence prevents them from negating that slur. Two powerful themes in these accounts are a lasting sense of injustice and a sense that the person's life has been irretrievably damaged. Both of these will have resonance too with victims of abuse who have not been believed.

Following the introductory chapters in Part I, the book is structured across four further sections, each of which is broadly concerned with a key question that will inevitably be raised for anyone encountering this category of injustice

- Why would anyone falsely accuse someone of such terrible crimes?
- How could our justice system, with all of its safeguards, result in innocent people languishing in prison as convicted child abusers or rapists?
- How can we limit the damage of untrue allegations—or, expressed another way, how can we ensure justice for victims of true allegations and better protection for those at risk of sexual and child abuse *without ruining innocent lives*?

The chapters in Part II: Culture; Ideology; Politics discuss some historical, social, and political movements that have provided the backcloth for the rise of both true and false allegations. In Chapter 3, Mary deYoung explores the human tendency to conceptualize evil cults and demons, depicting this master-narrative with analysis of the 1980s moral panic in which day care preschools became the focus for wildfire claims of satanic ritual abuse. In Chapter 4, Frank Furedi provides a penetrating analysis of the belief system and political ascendance of moral crusaders who, under the banner of child protection, have become a moral authority able to prioritize moral weight over empirical truth and to impose a duty to believe accusations of abuse. Mark Smith, in Chapter 5, explores the cultural context that gave rise to moral panics about rampant sexual abuse in residential child care institutions. In Chapter 6, John Brigham discusses the ascendancy of radical feminist ideology and its promotion of the 'rape culture' meme into a political force that has influenced US policy and has facilitated prejudicial sexual assault tribunals across university campuses wherein the accused is denied a defence. Bill Hebenton and Toby Seddon, in Chapter 7, address the politico-cultural backcloth that has led to a framework of 'precautionary logic' aimed at protecting citizens from sexual offenders and other harms. They analyse how the precautionary principle is being played out in socially embedded suspicion, and in pre-crime and counter-law measures that prioritize protection of potential victims over legal principles to protect the innocent and to prevent wrongful prosecutions and convictions.

Part III: The Allegation: Causes; Motivations; Case Studies, focuses on explaining why and how false allegations of abuse are made and accepted as true. As in the volume as a whole, the five chapters in this part apply the broader definition of 'false' to include allegations mistakenly believed to be true as well those that are knowingly false. In between are allegations that refer to true events, but which may not merit the criminal imputations placed on them. Scepticism about prevalence of false allegations and objections that attention to them detracts from bringing offenders to justice have been barriers to investigation of the causes and motivations underlying allegations that are untrue. Correspondingly, assertions about the rarity of false allegations increase the risk of specious reports of abuse allegations being accepted on face value. In light of scepticism about their prevalence, it is vital to show the diverse causal factors that give rise to allegations of non-existent events or which distort and criminalize innocuous events.

In the opening chapter to Part III, Felicity Goodyear-Smith provides a useful typology that organizes diverse causes and motivations under two broad categories: *external factors*, including cultural beliefs, ideologies, legal and policy developments, and investigative methods and biases; and *individual factors*, including self-serving lies, false memories, mistaken identification, custody disputes and parental alienation, and psychiatric disorders. Examples of cases that exemplify one or more of these causal and motivation factors are drawn from the UK, the United States, and New Zealand.

While it may be politically incorrect to look beyond the suffering of victims of abuse, a more nuanced and questioning analysis of victimhood is necessary if we are to understand the motivation for false claims of victimhood. It is undoubtedly the case that many victims find it onerous to report that they have been sexually abused, fearing the invasion of their privacy, the additional trauma of being questioned, and possible repercussions from the person who abused them. That is why advances have been made to make it easier for them to do so, building in safeguards such as anonymity and sometimes reassurances that they will be believed. Barbara Hewson, in Chapter 9, confronts the sensitive issue of victim culture to consider the silver linings in the cloud of being a victim, which may play into a surging culture of victimhood, a contagion effect, and the incidence of false allegations. As well as reviewing the benefits of victimhood status (including possible financial compensation, attention, sympathy, and a new sense of identity and self-importance), she provides an incisive analysis of how the rise of victimhood is supported by a culturally sanctioned narrative that attributes personal failures and behavioural problems to the trauma of abuse and facilitates a new identity as a 'survivor' with moral authority to testify in crusades against sexual offenders.

It is important for a more objective response to wrongful allegations and more balanced discourse that those falsely accused fully recognize the occurrence of what Villalobos, Davis, and Leo call 'honest false testimony'. In Chapter 10, they provide a much-needed fresh look at contested allegations of sexual assault in which they convincingly explain key factors—the ambiguity of non-verbal communication; the unreliability of memory; the effects of intoxication—that can account for conflicting versions of an interaction, both of which are accurate from the perspective of each party. While the authors' analysis is restricted to cases that involve disputes over sexual consent and so necessarily excludes alleged child abuse, the factors discussed could also be valid in explaining 'honest' false allegations relating to child sexual abuse, whether shortly after an encounter or years later in a delayed complaint. By extension, there are multiple meanings in many interactions that might have involved touch, horseplay, or expressions of affection, which one party experienced as abusive, or later construed as abusive, but without there having been any sexual or violent intention in the mind of the accused.

In Chapter 11, Christopher French and James Ost review research findings that reveal a marked difference between the views of memory researchers, on the one hand, and the views held by the general public (that is, potential and actual jurors) and practitioners (clinicians, therapists, legal professionals) about how memory works, on the other. Compared to memory researchers, members of the general public and practitioners are far more likely to believe that memories of serious abuse can be 'repressed' and then recovered at a later date. The views of memory experts are, however, supported by a vast amount of sound empirical data.

David Rose, in Chapter 12, provides an eye-opening account of the role of investigation methods used by police services and personal injury lawyers in creating the ideal conditions for false allegations to be made, in the course of doing their utmost to facilitate genuine victims to come forward. Inspired by the research of Richard Webster (1998, 2005), Rose's chapter discusses what he uncovered in his own in-depth investigations following the 1990s children's care homes scandal in England and Wales, and the evidence that he, Richard Webster, and Bob Woffinden gave to the subsequent parliamentary inquiry (Home Affairs Select Committee, 2002) that acknowledged that such methods had helped to produce a 'new genre of miscarriages of justice'. In particular, he identifies risks of witness evidence being contaminated in the course of information exchange by those running police operations and solicitors' class actions, of the zealous pursuit of convictions by individuals who see themselves engaged in a Manichean struggle between good and evil, and of confirmation bias among those who have more to gain professionally and financially by an increased number of convictions.

Whereas an appreciable proportion of those vilified by false accusations do not become subject to criminal proceedings, the chapters in Part IV: Interrogation; Prosecution; Conviction; Appeal each centre on one or more of the stages in the criminal justice process: arrest; prosecution; trial; sentencing, including imprisonment; and appeals. While it may, prima facie, seem improbable that the innocence of a wrongly accused person will not be recognized, sooner or later, as he or she progresses through the stages of the criminal justice process, once a wrongful allegation has traction, it becomes difficult to dislodge. The chapters in this section, taken together, illustrate the ways in which the process can trap a person into an erroneous 'sex offender' identity and 'guilty' verdict from which he or she cannot escape.

Although it may seem implausible that anyone innocent would admit to such vile crimes, in Chapter 13, Davis and Leo provide a compelling account of why those wrongly accused of sexual offences are particularly vulnerable to the making of false confessions during interrogation. They argue that the reasons lie in the nature of the crimes: the evidentiary situation that often faces suspects is that the only evidence is the complainant's account versus his or her own and, without the means to provide substantive contradictory information, it then becomes a contest of credibility. Add to this the prolonged questioning and numerous persuasive tactics used by interrogators, and it becomes clearer why (false) admission might come to be seen as the best option during the stress of interrogation.

Luke Gittos, in Chapter 14, discusses a shift away from traditional legal principles and due process towards civil and criminal justice procedures prioritizing therapeutic closure for presumed victims. He illustrates this with discussion of changes in prosecution policy in England and Wales that are victim-centred, which give complainants a greater say in whether to bring a prosecution and provide protections for them during trial. As further indication of the prioritizing of presumed victims in lieu of the rule of law, he also discusses the increased use of tribunals, such as the growth of campus rape tribunals in the United States that exist to support the victim, and the establishment of an Independent Inquiry into Child Sexual Abuse in Britain that will name accused persons and which begins from the premise that child sexual abuse has been rife. These developments will be welcomed by the many genuine victims and those who have correctly identified perpetrators of offences against them, but they effectively reverse the presumption of innocence and are particularly dangerous for wrongly accused persons, who can be convicted on uncorroborated testimony.

While it is horrendous enough when an innocent person is sentenced to imprisonment, thereafter he or she is further penalized for maintaining his or her innocence. Daniel Medwed, in Chapter 15, discusses the dilemmas and double-binds faced by innocent prisoners, dubbed 'in denial', and the cognitive biases of justice officials that serve to perpetuate a perception of prisoners as not only guilty, but also lacking in remorse. With examples from the correctional system in US prisons, he illustrates how maintaining their innocence restricts these prisoners' opportunities for parole and how relenting to pressure to (falsely) admit guilt subsequently damages opportunities to be exonerated even when new evidence emerges.

That juries might sometimes convict an innocent person is the issue at the heart of Michael Zander's chapter. In his meticulous analysis of the appellate system in England and Wales as it pertains to erroneous guilty verdicts, he identifies the potential and limitations within the system for addressing this matter. He argues that it is the failure of the Court of Appeal to exercise its power to assess whether the jury 'got it wrong on the facts', rather than flaws in the approach used by the Criminal Cases Review Commission, which causes the blockage in reversing such miscarriages of justice. Given this impasse, he assesses other recourses available to the Commission, but which are rarely applied.

Contributors to Part V: Finding Ways Forward were invited to draw lessons from their subject domain or to advance theories that could be valuable in preventing miscarriages of justice when innocent people are wrongly accused of abuse. Focusing on child sexual abuse allegations, in Chapter 17, Steve Herman argues that the low evidentiary thresholds that are applied—as well as risking the conviction of innocent people—risk harming non-abused children who are wrongly thought to be victims of sexual abuse. Following a cogent analysis of the extent of uncorroborated (and weakly corroborated) allegations of child sexual abuse in the United States, he argues for the reinstatement of corroboration requirements and prioritizing of the search for corroboration in cases of suspected child sexual abuse.

The next two chapters review research findings in two subject domains of acute relevance to prosecution and conviction following claims of abuse. To a large extent, allegations of abuse turn on whether the memories of complainants or the statements that they make are true or false. Galit Nahari, in Chapter 18, reviews the methods used in laboratory and practice settings to assess deception and the veracity of accounts. She presents findings on accuracy rates, identifies the challenges and limitations of interrogation strategies and tools, and makes proposals for improving our ability to detect lies. With regard to memory, the task for Robert Belli, in Chapter 19, was to review the most reliable research on recovered memories, with a view to reconciliation of extreme positions taken in the continuing 'war' between those who claim that buried memories of abuse can be recovered in therapy and those who maintain such recovered 'memories' are false. While he discusses findings from laboratory research supportive on both sides of the divide, he concludes that ascertaining the truth-value of recovered memories in individual cases often will not be possible.

From the perspective of actual innocence, in Chapter 20, Timothy Bakken brings fresh air into the Kafkaesque nightmare of being wrongly accused and placed on trial. He proposes the introduction of a 'plea of innocence' wherein the defendant forgoes the right to remain silent and agrees to a higher standard of proof than 'beyond reasonable doubt', but is then given the opportunity to introduce exonerating facts into the evidence at trial. He details how innocence procedures would be applied in ways that would deter guilty persons from taking this route and which would alleviate the pressure on complainants.

Finally, in Chapter 21, we review the findings and proposals made throughout the book that point to ways forward in reducing the incidence and harms of wrongful allegations of abuse.

REFERENCES

BRAND, N. (2007) *Fractured Families: The Untold Anguish of the Falsely Accused*, Bradford-on-Avon: British False Memory Society.

BURNETT, R. (2013) 'The Default Belief in Allegations of Child and Sexual Abuse', in J. Robins (ed.) *No Defence: Lawyers and Miscarriages of Justice*, London: The Justice Gap.

CHEIT, R. E. (2014) *The Witch-Hunt Narrative: Politics, Psychology, and the Sexual Abuse of Children*, New York: Oxford University Press.

Children's Commissioner for Wales (2015) *Learning the Lessons: Operation Pallial*. Available online at <https://www.childcomwales.org.uk/uploads/publications/528.pdf> [accessed May 2016].

CREWE, B. (2009) *The Prisoner Society: Power, Adaptation and Social Life in an English Prison*, Oxford: Oxford University Press.

DALY, K. (2014) 'Conceptualising Responses to Institutional Abuse of Children', *Current Issues in Criminal Justice*, 26(1): 5–28.

FRANKFURTER, D. (2006) *Evil Incarnate: Rumors of Demonic Conspiracy and Satanic Abuse in History*, Princeton, NJ: Princeton University Press.

FUREDI, F. (2013) *Moral Crusades in an Age of Mistrust: The Jimmy Savile Scandal*, Basingstoke: Palgrave Macmillan.

GREENE, N. (2011) *False Accusations: Guilty until Proven Innocent*, Durham, CT: Strategic Book Group.

GREER, C., and MCLAUGHLIN, E. (2013) 'The Sir Jimmy Savile Scandal: Child Sexual Abuse and Institutional Denial at the BBC', *Crime, Media, Culture*, 9(3): 243–63.

Home Affairs Select Committee (2002) *The Conduct of Investigations into Past Cases of Abuse in Children's Homes: Fourth Report of Session 2001–02*, London: HMSO.

HOYANO. L., and KEENAN, C. (2007) *Child Abuse: Law and Policy across Boundaries*, Oxford: Oxford University Press.

JENKINS, P. (1996) *Pedophiles and Priests: Anatomy of a Contemporary Crisis*, New York: Oxford University Press.

KELLY, L. (2010) 'The (In)Credible Words of Women: False Allegations in European Rape Research', *Violence against Women*, 16(12): 1345–55.

KELLY, L., LOVETT, J., and REGAN, L. (2005) *A Gap or a Chasm? Attrition in Reported Rape Cases*, London: Home Office Research, Development and Statistics Directorate.

KUEHNLE, K., and CONNELL, M. (2009) *The Evaluation of Child Sexual Abuse Allegations: A Comprehensive Guide to Assessment and Testimony*, Hoboken, NJ: John Wiley & Sons.

LA FONTAINE, J. (1998) *Speak of the Devil: Tales of Satanic Abuse in Contemporary England*, Cambridge: Cambridge University Press.

LARNER, C. (1980) '*Crimen Exceptum*? Witchcraft in Europe', in V. A. C. Gatrell, B. Lenman, and G. Parker (eds) *Crime and the Law: The Social History of Crime in Western Europe since 1500*, London: Europa.

MEDWED, D. S. (2012) *Prosecution Complex: America's Race to Convict, and Its Impact on the Innocent*, New York: New York University Press.

NATHAN, D., and SNEDEKER, M. (1995) *Satan's Silence: Ritual Abuse and the Making of a Modern American Witch Hunt*, New York: Basic Books.

NEY, T. (ed.) (1995) *True and False Allegations of Child Sexual Abuse: Assessment and Case Management*, New York: Brunner/Mazel.

PENDERGRAST, M. (1998) *Victims of Memory: Incest Accusations and Shattered Lives*, London: HarperCollins.

RABINOWITZ, D. (2004) *No Crueler Tyrannies: Accusation, False Witness, and Other Terrors of Our Times*, New York: Simon & Schuster.

ROBERTS, J. V., STALANS, L. J., INDERMAUR, D., and HOUGH, M. (2002) *Penal Populism and Public Opinion: Lessons from Five Countries*, New York: Oxford University Press.

RUMNEY, P. N. (2006), 'False Allegations of Rape', *The Cambridge Law Journal*, 65(1): 128–58.

SAUNDERS, C. L. (2012) 'The Truth, the Half-Truth, and Nothing Like the Truth: Reconceptualizing False Allegations of Rape', *British Journal of Criminology*, 52(6): 1152–71.

SCHOPENHAUER, A. (1890/2007) *Counsels and Maxims*, trans. T. Bailey Saunders, New York: Cosimo Classics.

SKÖLD, J. (2013) 'Historical Abuse: A Contemporary Issue—Compiling Inquiries into Abuse and Neglect of Children in Out-of-Home Care Worldwide', *Journal of Scandinavian Studies in Criminology and Crime Prevention*, 14(1): 15–23.

SMITH, L. (2012) ' "It Rots Your Life": Lord McAlpine Speaks out over "Terrifying" Experience of Being Falsely Accused of Paedophilia', *The Independent*, 16 November. Available online at <http://www.independent.co.uk/news/uk/crime/it-rots-your-life--lord-mcalpine-speaks-out-over-terrifying-experience-of-being-falsely-accused-of-paedophilia-8320510.html> [accessed December 2015].

TAVRIS, C., and ARONSON, E. (2015) *Mistakes Were Made (But Not by Me): Why We Justify Foolish Beliefs, Bad Decisions, and Hurtful Acts*, rev'd edn, Boston, MA: Mariner Books.

WEBSTER, R. (1998) *The Great Children's Home Panic*, Oxford: The Orwell Press.

WEBSTER, R. (2005) *The Secret of Bryn Estyn: The Making of a Modern Witch Hunt*, Oxford: The Orwell Press.

WHEATCROFT, J. M., and WALKLATE, S. (2014) 'Thinking Differently about "False Allegations" in Cases of Rape: The Search for Truth', *International Journal of Criminology and Sociology*, 4(1): 239–48.

2

EXPERIENCING FALSE ALLEGATIONS OF ABUSE

FIRST-PERSON ACCOUNTS

Edited by Ros Burnett

Making a false allegation in itself is not a crime, but those on the receiving end experience the pains of being a victim. They are not, however, offered the support given to victims and, if they ask for assistance, are more likely to be ostracized, even if 'no further action' was taken or they were acquitted. Being seen as responsible for such serious crimes has inevitable consequences for these people, in many cases including the ruin of their careers, damage to their mental and physical health, immense psychological suffering both of the accused and their families, and potentially poverty following loss of their jobs or the huge expense of legal fees. Whether convicted or cleared, the accused's reputations are tainted by the lingering suspicion, and they and their families can feel contaminated by the imposed association with such repugnant offences.

While there are many trivial accusations that can be readily brushed off as nonsense or mistaken, in the present paranoid and punitive climate of exaggerated fears for the safety of children (Lancaster, 2011), no chances are taken, and a malicious phone call or a gossipy rumour can lead to full-scale investigation and a record of having been under suspicion. The suffering caused is therefore by no means confined to those who are prosecuted and convicted; it also has a ruinous and long-lasting impact on the lives of those who are *not* prosecuted.

The worst-case scenario is that the accused will be wrongly convicted and imprisoned, usually for many years, without having committed the alleged crimes and quite possibly having never broken the law in his or her entire life. Those convicted and unable to 'clear their name' are unlikely to receive the same support that other prisoners are eligible to receive for their families or their resettlement, because maintaining innocence is perceived as indicative of a lack of remorse and unpreparedness to change.

There has been a movement over the last few decades to take much more notice of victims' perspectives. In respect of inquiries into historical child sexual abuse, victims' accounts are increasingly being accepted on face value as accurate accounts and the alleged guilt of the accused person is accepted uncritically. A prime example of that is *Giving Victims a Voice* (Gray and Watt, 2013), the report into allegations of abuse by

Jimmy Savile. Another is the Independent Inquiry in Child Sexual Abuse (IICSA) in England and Wales, which has invited proven or putative victims and survivors to share their experiences in what is designated the 'Truth Project'.[1] Proven or putative victims of wrongful allegations in the same contexts, whose experiences are also relevant to the overarching goals of the Inquiry, have not been similarly so invited.[2] When, occasionally, cases of false allegations of sexual assault and rape have been profiled in the media, these tend to raise objections from campaigners on behalf of rape victims, wary that the publicity will deter victims from reporting abuse for fear they will not be believed. At a time when giving victims a voice is regarded as of central importance to justice and recovery from trauma, it is inequitable that the voices of victims of wrongful allegations of abuse are rarely heard.

Towards filling this gap, a qualitative study of the impact of being falsely accused has recently been undertaken at Oxford (Hoyle, Speechley, and Burnett, 2016). The written accounts that follow were obtained especially for this volume before the advent of that study, via the editor's contacts with voluntary support groups for individuals claiming to be wrongly accused.[3] Respondents were invited to submit written accounts of approximately 600 words, focused on their experience of being wrongly accused and the harms done thereby to themselves and their loved ones. Apart from some minor grammatical amendments and requests for occasional points to be clarified or elaborated, these accounts are presented here in the respondents' own words.

No one is better placed to explain the pain and damage caused by untrue allegations than those directly affected, and the following is therefore a compilation of six anonymized, first-person accounts of the psychological and social experience, and consequences, for the individuals accused and their families.

ACCOUNT ONE: TERRORIZED AND BETRAYED

It is sometimes said that there is only one thing worse than being sexually assaulted or raped—that is, being falsely accused of having done so.[4] Not having been raped, I don't know whether this is true or not. What I do know is that being falsely accused of a sexual abuse, or any other form of abuse, is likely to be a terrifying experience. For me, it is not that far removed from being terrorized. You live in fear—don't know who to trust or what is coming next.

---

[1] See <https://www.iicsa.org.uk/share-your-experience>   [2] At the time of writing.

[3] Those groups being: FACT, online at <http://www.factuk.org>; the British False Memory Society (BFMS), online at <http://bfms.org.uk>; and the False Allegations Support Organisation (FASO), online at <http://www.false-allegations.org.uk>

[4] The author of this first account was first accused of historical abuse in the early 1990s concerning allegations relating to the period 1972–82. Initially, he was dismissed from his employment, but later reinstated on appeal; he then took early retirement on health grounds. He was interviewed by the police when first accused and no criminal proceeding were taken. At the time of writing, he had recently been re-interviewed about the same matters and was on police bail pending further inquiries. He was later informed by the police that no charges would be brought.

Not surprisingly, many of those falsely accused report high anxiety levels, severe depression, ill health, and associated trauma. Being falsely accused and being disbelieved when you are innocent is life-changing. It eats into your very being; it permanently alters your relationships with loved ones and people in general, and rarely goes away. Even when you find some respite from the anxiety caused, the moment is ruined by the realization that you haven't thought about 'it' for a while. Even in recovery, such flashbacks can be very powerful. Social events, celebrations, and routine family life are spoilt by such intrusive thoughts, and the special occasion becomes tainted. Withdrawal doesn't help either; it only compounds the problem. You no longer really enjoy yourself. You have to show courage and keep trying.

For most people, it is possible to draw a line under past trauma, but when you have been falsely accused, it is virtually impossible to do so. You are left with the feeling that unless the person recants, there *will* still be people who believe them. There is no escape—your hard-earned reputation and sense of worth is totally destroyed. The effect is keenly felt particularly by those who have been accused of abuse in occupational settings. When the motive to follow a particular career has been driven by a desire, on the one hand, for self-improvement and, on the other, to 'help' others, you are made to feel guilty about having a dream and following your vocation. You feel shamed by your involvement even though you are innocent. Even the prospect of death brings no relief. The same false claims are just as likely to be made against you and your name, and loved ones hounded, after you have died just as before. There can be no closure for you—or your family.

For me, the overwhelming feeling is of one of betrayal. I feel betrayed by the people I looked after. I no longer trust children (which is very sad) and no longer trust the system. I feel let down by my employer[s], who, fearing for their reputations, not mine, abandoned any sense of duty of care to me. I feel abandoned by trade unions, who, almost without exception, abandon members accused of abuse, afraid that any association with someone who, as they see it, potentially *might* be guilty is to be avoided at all costs. Like employers, trade unions fully understand that being falsely accused is likely to be very stressful, may cause significant mental health issues, and [may] even be life-threatening, with a risk of suicide, yet they have no appetite to see this issue as genuine health and safety matter. For them, there is no zero tolerance of being falsely accused; it is just an occupational hazard, which has to be tolerated, and we are the victims.

I feel let down by professionals, who seem completely unaware that their approach might in many (but not all) cases unwittingly generate false allegations, and that child protection agencies seem not to appreciate that the damage this causes and the effect it has on society is affecting men's relationships with children in a wholly negative way.

I feel let down by the police, who, it seems, are on a charm offensive to win over much-needed public support by making abuse cases, whether tried in court or not, a cause célèbre. Their mantra that complainants 'will be believed' is frankly very disturbing. No one, it seems, asks the question, 'Why?' Complainants should only be believed if they are telling the truth. No longer can we regard the police as truth seekers. It is not the job of the police to follow some ideological position or to even to accept at face value assertions that those making delayed complaints genuinely believed they would *not* be listened to, or that they were unaware that what was done to them (allegedly) at the time was wrong.

I feel let down by the press, who, with some exceptions, feed an unjustified moral panic regarding current and historical abuse in occupational settings simply to sell copy. I feel let down by politicians, who, in the main, have abandoned their role as bastions of justice and replaced it with a need for vengeance, and by the judiciary, who seem unable to appreciate the very real difficulty [that] those falsely accused of abuse—especially historical abuse—have in proving their innocence. Proving something did not happen—especially years ago—is virtually impossible.

I will feel betrayed also if anyone reading this book does not realize that we have a very serious problem on our hands: an unjustified moral panic that has become a moral crusade bordering on cultural terrorism.

I feel let down; I have been let down.

ACCOUNT TWO: MY WORLD TURNED UPSIDE DOWN

It has been seven years since I was falsely accused. Although the case was eventually thrown out of court, the damage to me and my family has been long-term, and I am still prone to panic attacks. I was a classroom assistant, enjoying my work. A child, who climbed on to a chair and fell off, said I'd pushed him. A member of staff, whose practice I had previously criticized, decided to believe him. I was suspended and ordered to isolate myself from anyone connected to the school, including parents. The police were informed and I was told to anticipate a visit from social services, with a view to taking our own child away from us. It was a huge shock to be accused and to have my family unit threatened this way. The response to the untrue allegation, and the events that followed, went to the very core of my self-belief and sense of justice, and turned my world upside down.

It hurts me most that other people were harmed, not just me. Most seriously, our daughter faced threatening experiences in her infant school. It has taken years for her to regain her confidence and get back on track towards attaining her full educational potential. My wife needed to suspend her PhD in order to support me—putting back her own career development. And it was all so unnecessary. I was innocent and the accusing child had, shortly afterwards, confirmed that his allegation was false. Administrators have opportunities to apply common sense, consider evidence, and nip a false allegation in the bud. Failure to apply these 'safety gates' has dire consequences.

Unfortunately, one small lie can be built up into a more damning character assassination. The school gave the police 'bad character' evidence, which was fabricated, and some did not even refer to me. Against procedural guidelines, the school took steps towards a disciplinary hearing simultaneously with the police investigation. The threat of all this hanging over me, the restraints against whom I could contact, and being suspended from my work all affected my health. I hardly slept, and when I did, my nightmares were so vivid that I confused them with reality. My digestion became abnormal, with unpleasant side effects; I suffered painful spasms. I couldn't feel any emotion when my mother died. I contemplated suicide.

Before the case was thrown out, I had to make several preliminary court appearances from what can only be described as a bulletproof glass cage. It was horrifying for my wife to see me that way. It was stifling, frightening, and I couldn't hear or breathe properly.

Eventually, the trial was vacated on the grounds of abuse of process. The judge could not rule out that all witnesses had been briefed and agreed that evidence against me could not be relied upon, and his reasoning pointed to me being innocent on the balance of probability. Yet the education administrators still attempted to progress to a disciplinary hearing using the same evidence and witnesses. They seemed to have an agenda that ignored truth. I felt they saw me as a non-person, as an object to be abused and ridiculed at their whim. The abuse continued for twenty months before they seemed to tire and dismissed me from my post without a hearing. My attempts at whistleblowing have been covered up, and the rejection, ridiculing, and belittling continue.

We, as a family, can never fully recover from this. I feel alarmed if my child asks if a friend can sleep over. I am reluctant to engage with whole families in recreation activities. I was exonerated, have a clean record, and am not on any barring list. Yet I can't get the jobs I want. I suffer symptoms of PTSD [post-traumatic stress disorder] and have undergone years of therapy. I am lost to children's education and am an ongoing cost to the health service. I wonder if I'll ever be the contributor to society I once was. I still have three more years until I reach retirement age. The way things are panning out, the false allegation, and the way I was abused by the education administrators after it have destroyed the last ten years of my productive life.

ACCOUNT THREE: BOLT FROM THE BLUE

My experience of being falsely accused of so-called historic institutional sexual abuse began very dramatically. I was arrested at the immigration desk at the airport, having just arrived back in the UK. I hadn't been living or working in Britain for a number of years, but this was just a routine trip of the kind I'd made many times before.

My first instinct was that there had been a terrible mistake. After I had answered all the police officers' questions as fully and honestly as I could, I genuinely believed that there could be no case to answer. When I was eventually charged with historic indecent assault of a former pupil, I was stunned.

None of my family or friends was aware of the situation, but gradually I felt I had to confide in my partner and others. I was initially genuinely surprised and moved at the strong support I was offered. I felt that no one who really knew me, including a very large number of ex-students (most now married with families of their own), really believed a word of these totally false allegations.

As I now understand is common in these cases, I threw myself into preparing my defence. Despite the uphill battle of trying to prove a negative—that something had *not* happened twenty-five years ago—my legal team contacted dozens of former pupils, who almost all volunteered to attend court and give evidence in my favour. In consequence, I found it very difficult to believe I could be found guilty. Perhaps, not being aware of the current 'moral panic' over historic allegations of sexual abuse, I was delusional. At that point, I still had a genuine belief in British justice.

When I was convicted (by a majority verdict), I was stunned. My whole life had just imploded. Although my friends and supporters rallied round, I really felt that there was nothing left worth living for. Had it not been for my partner of thirteen years, I'm certain I would have found a way to commit suicide in my prison cell. What I didn't know was that my partner had already made plans to kill himself after my solicitor had informed him of my conviction. Once the jury had given its verdict, I was denied bail and, ironically, this probably saved two lives, as I'm sure that my partner and I would have opted to die together at home whilst I was awaiting sentencing.

Being accused of a sexual crime—regardless of whether it is 'historic' or recent—is such a traumatic experience that I can fully empathize with others who feel that their lives are over. As a qualified counsellor, I had worked with people facing bereavement and I think that there is much to be said for the theory of the 'five stages of grief' proposed by Elisabeth Kübler-Ross in her 1969 book *On Death and Dying*. Conviction for a heinous criminal offence has marked parallels. You—the falsely accused and wrongly convicted—have effectively died: socially, professionally, financially—and, in many cases, emotionally. What you are mourning for is the death of yourself. It is a type of bereavement and I definitely went through similar stages: denial, anger, bargaining, depression, and acceptance.

I served just over two years of a four-year prison sentence. In comparison with the guilty verdict, the impact on my family and the very public collapse of my professional life, my actual time in prison was relatively easy. However, there is a common expression used by prisoners: 'It's your family that actually does the time.' I believe this to be true. The negative implications for one's family are incalculable.

I'm very lucky that my partner was supported by our close friends, who kept him going, including assisting him financially. I still have a home to go to, unlike so many people convicted of similar offences. Most of our real friends have remained loyal, although a few have fallen by the wayside. The real challenge now is to persevere with my continuing appeal, even though the restrictions placed upon me by the Probation Service and the police mean it is virtually impossible for me to find paid employment in the UK.

ACCOUNT FOUR: SUFFOCATING CLOUD THAT NEVER RISES

Why and how did I get here? At first, it didn't sink in. I half expected Jeremy Beadle[5] to jump out with his microphone and tell me that it had all been a very bad joke made at

---

[5] Probably Britain's best-known television prankster, now deceased, who used a hidden camera, disguises, and role play to set up unwary members of the public, making them the butt of cruel jokes.

my expense. I couldn't comprehend what was happening. I remember feeling very, very scared, on my way in the so-called meat wagon to the very unattractive black walls of our local jail. I had been convicted of an offence that I am not capable of committing and which I view with revulsion. My conviction meant that not only was I going to spend the next nine months in prison, [but also] I would be classed as a sex offender and, for my own protection, would be going on the vulnerable prisoners wing. I had to live and socialize with 'nonces'.

Found guilty of the most heinous crime in my opinion, how was I going to deal with it? I simply did not have anything in common with my new neighbours, so the second emotion to affect me after the terror was absolute loneliness. The first time I was called a 'nonce' was during our daily hour of exercise within the secured yard. Whilst [we were] protected from the other prison population, the other wings looked onto this yard, and the abuse and threats from the cell windows were and are relentless. Little did I know that this pain and anguish was to be perpetuated a million times worse upon my release.

For some fortunate reason, my initial trial and conviction was not made public within the press. I remember thinking—naively, at the time—that perhaps this was because they knew I was innocent. My first appeal application, however, was reported in the local press by some crass journalist leading with headlines such as 'Local pervert loses appeal' and went viral within hours of publication. I have never wanted to hurt anyone in my life before now, but I admit I did on that occasion. Since my release, I [have] hardly dared to look up my name on the internet, but I now know of at least seven websites whereby my name has been linked, as a sex offender, and [I am] now on the sex offender register. It makes you paranoid, even walking down the street, worrying about what people may be thinking, especially as they do not know the facts. As for going out and socializing—forget it. How do you meet someone and say, 'Hello my name is ___ and, by the way, in the eyes of the law I am a sex offender'? I've become a recluse.

I really cannot explain the anguish and pain of being treated as a nonce. I'm not allowed to have contact with my children, which breaks my heart. I imagine [that] when you're guilty, it's tough enough, but when you are not guilty, it is like suffocating under a cloud without any precipitation; it's a living nightmare that won't end. It shames me to admit that, hitherto, I had always had little patience with people who complained of depression, holding a 'pull yourself together' attitude. Not only did I become diagnosed with severe depression, [but] I also developed chronic insomnia, as I was simply unable to switch off from my plight. My feelings of initial fear were followed by anger, despair and frustration, and hatred. I'd never thought beforehand about the origins of that line 'The law is an ass' and had always believed that the British legal system was the best in the world. I have now learned first-hand the truth behind the first statement and know that, like others, I had been conditioned into believing the second thought. I was brought up as a Catholic and didn't question my faith. Another consequence of what has happened is that I now no longer believe in God. How can there be a God who could allow this to happen?

ACCOUNT FIVE: BEARING AN UNDESERVED 'MARK OF CAIN'

A false allegation of sexual abuse penetrates every corner of the mind and every relationship in the falsely accused person's (FAP) milieu. Even before a jury transfers falsehood into 'legal fact', those closest to the FAP are wounded by the vicious abuse that, typically, follows publicity. Contamination by association is added to grief and loss when the FAP is imprisoned. If these loved ones are children, they, as a condition of contact, will have to be asked whether they have been abused by the FAP. Forced thus to contemplate such violation of the relationship, their innocence is, perversely, violated by agents of supposed protection.

A spouse is likely to be treated as a fool or a liar. Professional colleagues, even if not forbidden to contact the FAP, might be unwise to do so.

For me, the harm to my loved ones is worse, by far, than the experience of prison. I feel toxic to them and desperate, yet powerless, to protect them, especially in an age when the electronic 'poison pen' gives such impunity to those who take pleasure in the pain and distress of others.

During wakefulness, anxiety pulses constantly at the edge of awareness. In sleep, it migrates to centre stage, waking me early each morning with obsessive fear for the safety of my loved ones. I want to call and say, 'Take care...Drive carefully...Look both ways when crossing...Please, please don't die.'

What we FAPS have lost, over and above precious years, can never be fully regained. We shall, whatever happens, bear an undeserved 'mark of Cain'. Even if, in the manner of George Anderson and Margaret Hewitt,[6] I were to be miraculously acquitted by my remorseful or boastful accusers, I feel I should never again be the subject of lighthearted conversation.

I ought, some say, to feel angry, but I know that, when sustained, it is a self-destructive emotion, so I do work at not being its captive. My false accusers probably thought no further than the 'friendships' or forgiveness they might buy with their fraudulent gains. We—my former colleagues and I—had a pretty good idea of what they had suffered before their receptions into local authority care. The fragmented 'archipelagos'[7] of their moral characters protect them from feelings of guilt. Several of them, for sure, suffered sustained, secret, self-implicating abuse within or close to their unprotecting families. This, it is known, often includes a thorough and detailed training in the skills of deception. Accomplished liars from an early age, they cannot be held entirely culpable for being careless of the harm they cause. When I think about the suffering of my loved ones, it is hard to remain objective. Even so, I should not want these false witnesses punished for their perjury or their children to suffer as mine have.

---

[6] George Anderson and Margaret Hewitt were released in 2006, a few months into sentences of, respectively, 18 years and 15 years, when one of their false accusers volunteered a remorseful confession and another boasted to his probation officer about their profitable scam.

[7] Following Winnicott (1964), Barbara Dockar-Drysdale (1969) described the 'archipelago child' as one who has experienced a disrupted childhood during which islands of 'good-enough caring' have been broken up by periods of neglect and abuse.

I shall say a few words about people employed in prisons and probation. For any of them, it would be career suicide to admit the possibility that any prisoner might be wrongly convicted. They have to play their parts in the perversely utilitarian fiction that the justice system is so rarely wrong that owning up to the likely innocence of some prisoners is less important than 'public confidence' in the system.[8] Consequently, the wrongly convicted prisoner is under constant pressure to change what is called his or her 'stance'. About this, I will say only that if a FAP capitulates to pressure to make a tactical false admission of guilt, [he or she] too becomes a liar and throws further doubts on those of us who uphold the truth.

ACCOUNT SIX: MY INNOCENT HEAD ON THE POLE OF CHILD PROTECTION

It is only those who have been falsely accused of child abuse who can truly understand the way it invades every last cell of their body like a cancer that can never be purged. You feel abandoned and betrayed by justice—and incredulous that someone who has always been law-abiding and protective of others could suddenly be perceived and condemned as a child molester. Your own implicit faith in natural justice is thrown on its head.

I had been running an organization in Asia when I was subjected to false allegations of child abuse by a small, unregulated, 'child protection' organization, [which had] big contacts in the government and justice system of that country, and [was] able to raise considerable investments by promoting concerns about widespread child abuse. Despite there being not one actual allegation from within my organization nor any forensic evidence against me, nor any witnesses called, I was subjected to a two-hour 'trial' in a language I do not speak, without the opportunity to be legally represented and without being given the opportunity to enter my plea of 'not guilty'. I was even told the verdict and sentence before I got to the court house!

This resulted in me spending one year in a prison, sleeping on the floor in a cell shared with between twelve and nineteen other prisoners. I cannot convey the awfulness of what I went through emotionally and physically, and how much my life was changed by this. One morning, the police turned up, and I never saw my home again, or many of my friends, or the children and staff I so cared about. Overnight, I had to come to terms with, for the first time in my adult life, having no say or control over my daily life or what would happen to me. I felt totally vulnerable: I was in a foreign country and didn't speak the language, and there was no one in authority prepared to stand by me. I had become a leper—labelled a child abuser with my head held high on a pole by the child protection industry as a trophy. This label removed any hope of help, as the British Embassy and human rights organizations didn't help me fight my case. It

---

[8] Lord Denning, alone, has said publicly, 'It is better that a few innocent men remain in prison than that the English legal system be impugned' (cited in Mansfield and Wardle, 1993: 261). I believe this represents the attitude of the judiciary as a whole.

appears that, when you are labelled a child abuser, none of the organizations choose to help you because they are afraid of losing donors. It made me feel worthless.

In my case, what made it even more outrageous was discovering that this was no error or honest mistake, but something that had been brought upon me deliberately by someone with a grudge after we had argued. The accuser went about framing me with the enthusiasm and evil of Dr Mengele carrying out one of his experiments at Auschwitz, injecting... a poison that seeps into every aspect of your life and [which] will be with you forever. It is only when you are in the invidious position of being wrongly criminalized, as I was, that you come to appreciate how readily that accusation is believed and how rapidly the machinery goes into action to keep others away from this presumed guilty person.

The organization I had spent years building up from nothing was destroyed and around forty staff lost their jobs. I think about it every day; it seems so unfair so wrong. We have all been left without closure. In 2007, I had visited the Andaman coast in Thailand on business, where the tsunami had struck, killing so many innocent people. I met people who had, in an instant, lost their loved ones and everything they owned, and I saw how they were rebuilding their lives. While I was in the prison, I tried to draw upon their example of strength to see me through. However, I kept returning to the same thought that the tsunami was a natural disaster; what I had suffered was man-made: it was planned and executed like a military operation. It was a deliberate act, driven by hate and greed hiding behind the banner of 'child protection'. Child protection is a good thing, right? The injustice to me and my suffering therefore seem to be permitted and sustained, by default of action, with society's approval.

Eventually, I was released, and I chose to return to the UK, believing that, once there, I would be able to get proper justice. But, no, this was not to be the case. Once again, I had underestimated the power of 'child protection' mania. Regardless of the fact that I had been denied the human right to a fair trial according to due process and with a defence, and despite there being no evidence against me, I was given a criminal record, placed on the sex offenders register, and banned from leaving the country. Effectively, I was under country arrest. As if I hadn't already been to the fires of hell, they were now pouring petrol on the fire. With restriction on what work I could do, three-monthly home visits from the police (to make sure I haven't run away), and an annual visit to my local police station, I am receiving constant punishment and reminders for something I haven't done.

EDITOR'S CONCLUDING OBSERVATIONS

Among the recurring themes in the preceding accounts, two that stand out are the abiding sense of injustice and the inability of the accused to get 'closure' (to use a concept regularly applied to victims of sexual abuse), even if cleared or never charged.

In the blundering exchanges that take place in families, in workplaces, and in other social interactions, being wrongly accused of some transgression is a common experience in life, yet the 'level of indignation we feel at being falsely accused of even a petty matter *strikes at our moral being*' (Brand, 2007: 19, emphasis added). How much more objectionable, therefore, and how much greater the sense of injustice to be wrongly accused of child abuse or sexual offences—and then not only to have one's claims of innocence disbelieved, but also to be accused of being 'in denial'. Finding a way out of this trap is likely to be unattainable in jurisdictions that accept uncorroborated accusations as evidence of guilt.

The third contributor in this chapter referred to the 'uphill battle of trying to prove a negative—that something had not happened'—a conundrum that must add to the oft-cited surreal or Kafkaesque quality of charges for these offences, especially when they refer to alleged incidents many years ago. This inability, in many such cases, to produce physical proof of innocence when there is no physical proof that a crime occurred ensures that the individual will never receive the public exoneration and apologetic sympathy that, for example, was granted to Christopher Jefferies, who was arrested and charged with sexual assault and murder until DNA provided evidence of the real perpetrator (O'Donovan, 2014). Without such exculpatory evidence, even when acquitted, the accused person is punished by the continuing stigma and has 'his or her good name sullied forever just because of some unfounded allegations... cleared, yes, but there's still that smell of it' (Warr, 2015: 8–9). Being accused is a punishment all by itself. The home page of a US Internet blog entitled *Community of the Wrongly Accused* (COTWA)[9] puts this well: 'Accusations of serious criminality, especially alleged sexual wrongdoing, are often their own convictions in the high court of public opinion because the stigma is so severe, and because definitively proving innocence in a disputed sex case often is impossible.'

REFERENCES

BRAND, N. (2007) *Fractured Families: The Untold Anguish of the Falsely Accused*, Bradford-on-Avon: British False Memory Society.
DOCKAR-DRYSDALE, B. (1969) *Consultation in Child Care*, London: Free Association Books.
GRAY, D., and WATT, P. (2013) *Giving Victims a Voice: A Joint MPS and NSPCC Report into Allegations of Sexual Abuse Made against Jimmy Savile under Operation Yewtree*, London: Metropolitan Police Service/NSPCC.
HOYLE, C., SPEECHLEY, N.-E., and BURNETT, R. (2016) *The Impact of Being Wrongly Accused of Abuse in Occupations of Trust: Victims' Voices*, Oxford: Centre for Criminology, University of Oxford.
KÜBLER-ROSS, E. (1969) *On Death and Dying*, New York: Macmillan.
LANCASTER, R. N. (2011) *Sex Panic and the Punitive State*, Berkeley, CA: University of California Press.
MANSFIELD, M., and WARDLE, T. (1993) *Presumed Guilty: The British Legal System Exposed*, London: Heinemann.

---

[9] See <http://www.cotwa.info/>

O'Donovan, G. (2014) 'We All Screwed up on Christopher Jefferies', *The Telegraph*, 9 December. Available online at <http://www.telegraph.co.uk/culture/tvandradio/11274171/Screenwriter-Peter-Morgan-The-Lost-Honour-of-Christopher-Jefferies.html> [accessed May 2016].

Warr, S. (2015) 'Something Good Has to Come from This', Paper presented to FACT Conference, Cardiff Law School, 30 May, reproduced in *FACTion*, 6(1): 7–10.

Winnicott, D. W. (1964) *The Child, the Family and the Outside World*, London: Penguin.

PART II

CULTURE; IDEOLOGY; POLITICS

WHAT IS THE TERRAIN THAT GIVES RISE TO FALSE ALLEGATIONS?

3

DEMONS, DEVILS, AND RITUAL ABUSE

INTERDISCIPLINARY PERSPECTIVES

Mary deYoung

Over the decades of the 1980s and beyond, more than 100 day care centres in large cities and small towns across the vast expanse of the United States were investigated. Scores of providers, most of them middle-aged women, were arrested and subjected to public opprobrium, merciless media scrutiny, and, in many cases, criminal prosecution. Those convicted more often than not received draconian prison sentences. It was alleged in these investigations that the providers had sexually abused their young charges in satanic rituals that involved such ghastly acts as infant sacrifice, blood-drinking, and cannibalism. Narratives of such horrific acts were at the extreme end of a more generalized moral panic about child abuse that was spread to other parts of the world and different institutions involved in child care.

Satanic ritual abuse, as the parlance of that era would term it, was considered by many to constitute the 'most serious threat to children and to society that we must face in our lifetime' (Summit, 1990: 39). In the frantic rush to uncover victimized children and punish their perpetrators, the cultural landscape was littered with bizarre ideas, fear and anxiety, newly minted experts, rushes to judgement, and egregious miscarriages of justice.

My brief in this chapter is to examine the historical, religious, and cultural roots of the fantastical idea that a satanic conspiracy posed a real and exigent threat to children, and to demonstrate and illustrate how this idea led to both wrongful allegations and miscarriages of justice. As David Frankfurter (2006) points out, myths about evil conspiracies have not only occurred throughout history and across cultures—witch cults, Jewish ritual murder cults, subversive cults, black magic cults, and antinomian and libertine cults are just some examples—but also form in almost any ideological scheme, where they remain latent until activated.

The 'decade of nightmares', as Philip Jenkins (2006) refers to the 1980s, provided the perfect context for their activation. During that decade, the United States was prickling with anxiety about threats to its security by enemies outside and bristling with fear about threats to its stability by enemies inside. Dark pessimism was eclipsing the starry-eyed optimism of the previous generation and hard-headed conservatism was replacing its raucous radicalism. As American society slouched towards the new millennium, it was expressing its millenarian anxiety in Manichaean thinking, nostalgic desires, crippling fears, and volatile moral panics. And one of those moral panics was about the satanic ritual abuse of young children in day care (deYoung, 2004).

In his ground-breaking work, Stanley Cohen (1972/2002) defines a moral panic in terms of a volatile and repressive reaction, incited and spread by interest groups and claims-makers, and often reinforced by knee-jerk laws and policies, towards what he terms 'folk devils'—that is, people who stand in proxy for unsettling social and moral strains. One of those social strains in 1980s America had to do with children—or at least with their welfare and protection in light of the discomfiting changes that were occurring in that era in the traditional family, as well as in the conventional gender roles that supported and maintained it. Increasing rates of cohabitation, out-of-wedlock births, dual-income marriages, and divorce were not only changing the traditional family and undermining the hegemony of its familiar patriarchal authority, but also often cast in terms of an evil that was insidiously undermining the moral foundation of society. In that zeitgeist, the daily care of children was both problematized and moralized. Parents scrambled to find accessible and affordable day care, and often settled for, rather than chose, such facilities, thus reluctantly and anxiously transforming the sacralized duty of caring for their own children into secularized contractual relations with day care providers (Bromley and Busching, 1989).

THE DEVIL GOES TO DAY CARE: THE MCMARTIN PRESCHOOL CASE

The McMartin Preschool was unsteadily situated on that strain. It was there that the satanic ritual moral panic began. Not at all the dark satanic mill of cultural imagination, the preschool was a rambling building on the main boulevard of the southern California city of Manhattan Beach. The family-owned and -run preschool enjoyed an enviable reputation and a long waiting list. On that list was a 2-year-old boy who, one day in 1983, was unceremoniously dropped off at the playground by his mother. The providers took him in and, over the next several months and without incident, allowed the boy to attend the centre occasionally, knowing that his mother was burdened with the care of an older, terminally ill child.

After one stay at the centre, the boy returned home with a reddened anus, telling his mother upon questioning that Raymond Buckey, the sole male provider and grandson of the centre's founder, had taken his temperature rectally. Fearing that he had actually been sexually abused by Buckey, the mother contacted the police. In subsequent interviews with a detective, the boy disclosed nothing—although his mother insisted that, in the privacy of their own home, he had confirmed that Buckey had sexually abused him. The local police department then sent letters to 200 parents of current or recent enrollees at the preschool, asking them to question their children about experiencing or witnessing sexual abuse, and naming Buckey as the prime suspect. Over the next several weeks, as terrified and outraged parents interrogated their children and met with each other to exchange facts and rumours, more children began disclosing sexual abuse—so many, in fact, that the county prosecuting attorney called a community meeting and encouraged parents to take their children to a local child abuse treatment centre for evaluation.

Over the next year, social workers at the centre interviewed more than 400 children. While doing so, however, they were privy to a fact that the parents, if they had heard it all, most likely had initially dismissed as nonsense: that, according to the mother of the initial complainant, her son was also describing infant and animal sacrifices, blood-drinking, cannibalism, live burials, and photographed orgies with his robed and hooded providers in the classrooms, in tunnels under the centre, and in cemeteries and churches.

Such Grand Guignol trappings, however, resonated with the social workers, who, for some time, had been discussing the bestseller, *Michelle Remembers* (Smith and Pazder, 1980)—the 'shockingly true story of the ultimate evil, a child's possession by the Devil', as the book cover proclaimed—and had heard the Canadian authors speak at conferences where the term 'satanic ritual abuse' was coined and bandied about. It would be years before Smith, the eponymous 'Michelle', and Pazder, her psychiatrist and later husband, would be thoroughly discredited. At the start of the 1980s, though, their claims not only made sense in a society that was increasingly framing its strains and stresses in terms of 'moral absolutes, of dangerous, evil outsiders who can be identified and combated' (Jenkins, 2006: 3), but also added a tantalizing frisson that transformed the daily drudge of assessing and treating children into the morally vaunted activity of rescuing them from evil.

Certain that the McMartin Preschool was the first case of a vast satanic conspiracy yet to be discovered, the social workers relentlessly grilled the children, many of whom soon figured out that 'round, unvarnish'd tales' were not what their interrogators wanted to hear. So they said what was expected: they told tales about the disinterment and mutilation of corpses, about ceremonial ingestions of faeces, urine, semen, and menstrual blood, about secret rooms and trap doors, and about devils and witches. In the end, more than 350 children were identified as victims and all seven of the McMartin providers as their satanic ritual abusers (Nathan and Snedeker, 1995).

In 1984, the providers were arrested. Six years later, after the charges had been dropped against five of them for lack of evidence, the jury in the longest and most expensive criminal trial in US history returned its verdict: Raymond Buckey was acquitted of most of the charges against him; his mother, Peggy McMartin Buckey, was acquitted of all charges. Buckey was retried on eight of the strongest remaining charges. The jury deadlocked on all of them. The charges were then dismissed.

Between the accusation and the verdict, and for a few years beyond, not only were more than 100 day care centres investigated in the United States, but also allegations of the satanic ritual abuse of children surfaced in the UK, in some countries in Europe, and in Australasia (LaFontaine, 1998; Hill, 2005; Hjelm et al., 2009; Tartari, 2013). In reality, those cases were nothing more than an indication that the satanic ritual abuse moral panic had spread abroad, as visiting American claims-makers 'hailed' their international colleagues in invited lectures and case consultations (Althusser, 1971). In imagination, though, they were evidence of an evil satanic conspiracy of global proportions.

Now activated, the once-latent myth of a satanic conspiracy was spread by the social workers involved in the McMartin Preschool case and by their 'hailed' colleagues, as well as by the popular media, a colourful assortment of self-identified satanism experts, and proselytizers from the politically and socially powerful New Christian Right, who used their vast technological infrastructure to spread the myth. That myth guided intervention, investigation, public reaction, and the criminal prosecution of subsequent cases. It also rationalized the moral panic, providing a new worldview for interpreting that decade's anxieties about vulnerable children, a new and portable language for interpreting their alleged abuse in the 'radically polarized terms of Satanic evil' (Frankfurter, 2006: 8), and a new urgency to battle that evil.

MYTH, METANARRATIVE, AND THE MAKING OF MONSTERS

A satanic conspiracy myth is a metanarrative—that is, a story about a story. Like most stories, it adheres to the most basic of literary conventions: it has a beginning, middle, and end. Seeking the familiarity of that convention, one of the first tasks of interest groups and claims-makers was to historicize the satanic ritual abuse of children. They searched for its beginning in order to explain it as part of a historically recurring evil. To that end, the apocalyptic teachings of the New Christian Right, folklore and urban legends, decontextualized historical accounts of satanic conspiracies, cross-cultural case studies, and popular culture representations of Satan and evil became invaluable, albeit eclectic, sources of information (Hicks, 1991; Mulhern, 1992; Ellis, 2000; Medway, 2001). They were mined with enthusiasm, although not with much consistency.

A few examples will suffice. Sally Hill and Jean Goodwin, social worker and psychiatrist, respectively, traced eleven practices of an alleged fourth-century satanic cult that were consistent with some of the allegations being made in the day care cases (Hill and Goodwin, 1989). Although dismissed as a naive reading of history (Noll, 1989), their historiography was stamped with the imprimatur of the editors of the journal *Dissociation*, repeated as fact in conferences and trainings, and cited uncritically in published articles and books. Not to be outdone in spelunking history, psycho-historian Lloyd DeMause (1994) claimed that the satanic ritual abuse of children could be traced to the Paleolithic era and is depicted in cave drawings. An alternative history was postulated by J. Randy Noblitt, a psychologist whose expert testimony featured prominently in the Fran's Day Care case: he claimed that the providers in that case were engaging in satanic rituals that had their cultural origins in African voodoo (Noblitt and Perskin, 1995).

Such historicizing created a beginning of the metanarrative of a satanic conspiracy to harm children and rationalized its recurrence. All questions of the historical truth of any or all of these assertions aside, historicizing in general set out the claim that satanic ritual abuse was being *discovered* in day care, not constructed out of the remnants of millenarian anxiety, therapeutic pseudoscience, and religious apocalyptic discourse.

The metanarrative also had a middle—a space or a realm both separate from, and yet inextricably entwined with, daily life (Bromley, 1991). That otherwise ordinary, socially conforming day care providers, at their own initiative, had started ritually abusing their young charges in the 1980s strained credulity throughout that decade. To render their alleged evil agency understandable required that they be imaginatively positioned within a highly organized conspiratorial network.

One of the most prolix of the claims-makers, psychiatrist Bennett Braun, whose eagerly anticipated conference and workshop presentations around the United States were always well attended, asserted that day care providers took their orders 'from above' (Braun, 1988). That handy colloquialism simultaneously conjured up a separate realm of powerful and unknown satanists, and a discoverable presence of 'everyday' satanists who were wreaking havoc in daily life. Dark and mysterious, the former was quickly filled with the political, social, and moral enemies of the 1980s: communists, cloak-and-dagger organizations such as the Central Intelligence Agency (CIA), drugs and weapons cartels, child prostitution and pornography rings, and cabals of politicians, social dissidents, and capitalists. Historically, that realm has always served as a repository for moral enemies—Christians in the Roman era, witches in the medieval era, Jews in the early modern era—who then were imagined to be the titular masterminds of that era's satanic conspiracy.

Day care providers, interest groups and claims-makers agreed, were the actual ritual abusers in the 1980s. But they were said to be aided and abetted by other satanists, who, like themselves, were hiding behind the facade of respectability. These included physicians, police officers, news reporters, morticians, educators, judges, and public workers, who, as part of their everyday roles, 'influenced media accounts, derailed investigations... and hired officials to make public statements on behalf of a national law enforcement bureau to the effect that no substantial evidence of ritual abuse exists' (Gould, 1995: 336).

It was the lack of substantial evidence—indeed, of any evidence at all—that made the psychological profiling of the accused day care providers a necessity. In a rush to address why it was providers, most of them women, who had been recruited into satanism and who had then demonstrated their fidelity, or perhaps obedience, by ritually abusing their enrollees, the National Center on Child Abuse and Neglect, in partnership with the National Institute of Mental Health, funded a research project. Its findings were published as a widely read and oft-cited book entitled *Nursery Crimes: Sexual Abuse in Day Care* (Finkelhor and Williams, 1988).

Thirty-six of the 270 day care sexual abuse cases that comprise the sample of this study were substantiated cases of satanic ritual abuse. While the word 'substantiated' implies that the bizarre allegations in these cases are veridical, a close reading of the text reveals just how slipshod its definition really is. A day care satanic ritual abuse case was considered substantiated if at least one of the local investigating agencies had decided that the abuse had occurred, even if that decision did not result in formal action, such as the suspension of the day care licence, let alone an arrest. This standard elides a couple of important facts. First, each of the alleged day care ritual abuse cases was investigated by a variety of local, state, and federal agencies, each of which had its own threshold of suspicion that had to be met before it could decide whether satanic ritual abuse had occurred. Second, representatives of the same agency, and of different agencies, often rancorously disagreed whether a given case could be substantiated as one of satanic ritual abuse; in fact, they often disagreed whether abuse of any kind had occurred at all (deYoung, 2008).

Despite these caveats to a strict interpretation of the word 'substantiated,' thirty-six cases of day care ritual abuse were examined in the study. In each, the accused was a woman provider who was alleged to have acted alone, in consort with other women providers, and/or with men who were affiliated in some way with the day care centre in question. The authors acknowledged that the familiar concepts of 'pedophilia, regressed type sexual acting out, and many other ideas' (Finkelhor and Williams, 1988: 63) that explained incest and molestation perpetrated by men were inadequate to the task of explaining satanic ritual abuse by women providers. Thus they went to great lengths to make the latter culturally intelligible by cobbling together scraps of information, speculation, and rumour with remnants of historiographies, folklore, popular culture, and the apocalyptic exhortations of the New Christian Right to construct two psychological profiles of satanic ritually abusive women providers.

The first such profile describes a woman provider whose festering anger and resentment over her own early experiences of childhood sexual abuse, sexual repression, or some other humiliation create an insidious envy of the children in her care. By ritually abusing them, she 'mortifies' their sexuality (Finkelhor and Williams, 1988: 63), corrupting their innocence and happiness just as her own had been corrupted when she was a child.

The second profile describes a woman provider whose self-concept was so damaged after failing time and again to live up to the expectations of her rigidly moralistic parents that she 'falls prey to a reversal of [their] whole value system' (Finkelhor and Williams, 1988: 64). As a result, she 'discover(s) a sense of power and spiritual fulfilment in a doctrine that celebrates participating in intentionally evil acts' (Finkelhor and Williams, 1988: 64). Her ritual abuse of the young children in her care, then, is an expression of her 'identification with evil' (Finkelhor and Williams, 1988: 64).

Neither profile is supported by data of any kind, yet each is briefly illustrated with snippets from some of the 'substantiated' day care ritual abuse cases in the study. Because all identifying case details are altered, however, including the names of the providers and the names and locations of the day care centres, neither the illustrations nor the profiles are easily checked for validity or veracity. As a result, the two profiles of ritually abusive women providers, which do little more than replicate the familiar cultural stereotypes of the 'woman scorned' and the 'evil woman' that have been the targets of witch hunts around the world for millennia, stood unchallenged (deYoung, 2008).

That these profiles were taken for granted by child abuse professionals is reflected in the fact that both during and after the day care ritual abuse moral panic, no in-depth case studies or empirical studies were conducted using the accused women providers as subjects; rather, the profiles were repeated as fact in one professional conference and workshop after another, thus priming conferees for the kind of case finding and case interpretation that fuelled and spread the moral panic (Hicks, 1991; Mulhern, 1992). The profiles also were used by prosecutors to discursively frame the women providers in their criminal trials, thus convincing jurors that these women who were engaged in the most gendered and trusted of roles were capable of such unspeakable evil.

The mass media also stepped in as profilers of both the accused women and men. Through the unrestrained use of such words as 'monstrous', 'grotesque', and 'evil', and the untutored use of such diagnostic terms as 'psychopath', 'pathological liar', and 'sexual pervert', the media vested the accused providers with evil agency. Hence the day care providers, the folk devils of the satanic ritual abuse moral panic, were seen more as 'devils' than 'folk'. They were discursively transformed into evil agents, then retrospectively understood as such. In their criminal trials, there was little by way of character defence. Raymond Buckey's diffident demeanour was ridiculed by the prosecuting attorney as nothing more than a facade that hid his satanic perversity. The pious religiosity of Frances Ballard, who was convicted of one count of sexual abuse in the Georgian Hills day care case and sentenced to between five and thirty-five years in prison, was presented to the jury as a ruse to hide her satanism. And Kelly Michaels, who was convicted of 115 counts of sexual abuse in the Wee Care case and sentenced to prison for forty-seven years, was not only profiled in *Nursery Crimes* as driven by psychological illness to mortify the sexuality of her young enrolees and labelled in the press as the 'Demon Seed', but also cross-examined on the witness stand about rumours that her own father had kissed and sexually groped her during a visit to her jail cell (Nathan and Snedeker, 1995).

The verdicts in Buckey's cases have already been discussed. Ballard's conviction was overturned on grounds of a violation of the discovery statute, in that investigators had destroyed audiotapes of their early interviews with the day care centre enrollees, most of whom initially denied having been satanic ritually abused, thus depriving the defence of evidence it could have used to cross-examine them at trial. All charges were then dismissed and Ballard's criminal record expunged. After years of appeals, Michaels' conviction was overturned on the grounds that the trial judge had erred by allowing the accusing children to testify via closed-circuit television (CCTV) without having first determined, as per state statute, whether each child's fear of testifying in open court was likely to compromise his or her competence and truthfulness as a witness. The appellate court also cited the admission of unfounded, unreliable, and unaccepted psychological expert testimony as grounds for a reversible error. Rather than order a retrial, the court dismissed all charges against Michaels (deYoung, 2007).

The wheels of justice turn slowly in the United States. By the time appeals had reversed the convictions of so many of the day care providers and the lower courts had then dismissed all charges, much of the emotive steam of the satanic ritual abuse moral panic had already dissipated. But when the cases had first come to public attention, and during the long trials, the public reacted against the demonized providers. As David Frankfurter (2006: 212) reminds us:

> [T]he scope of a people's response to the perceived threat of organized evil—that is, whether panic, inquisition, or pogrom—depends on the means available to mobilize, the nature of the institutions behind the dissemination of that threat, and, in recent times, legal or political barriers.

Indeed, in the United States in the late modernity of the 1980s, there was neither inquisition nor pogrom, but there were more than a few incidents of 'panic', in the form of vigilantism directed against the property and person of the accused day care providers who had been discursively transformed into 'the Other' (Frankfurter, 2006), 'the stranger' (Bauman, 1997), and 'the monster' (Foucault, 2003), and whose evil, it was feared, could not be checked by the law and the courts alone.

Perhaps there is no better example of the civic rubric of monster-making and monster-staking than that of Dawn Reed and Christopher Lillie.[1] The two nursery nurses had been acquitted on the basis of unreliable evidence of sexually abusing children at the Shieldfield Nursery in Newcastle, in the UK, in 1994. Infuriated parents stormed the court's dock, and then took to the streets with other citizens in a ceremony of fear that shaped private emotions into a socially acceptable and publicly expressible form. An official inquiry into the case was demanded and delivered. It, however, declared the two providers guilty of the original charges—and more, including sexually abusing more than sixty of their young charges, and supplying many of them to paedophile and pornography rings. Having already fled the city after being hounded by angry parents and pilloried by the press, Reed and Lillie then became the subjects of a modern-day persecution, fuelled by a grammar of monstrosity that proclaimed each of them to be 'categorically different from any actual person by virtue of failing even the category of person' (Ingebretsen, 2001: 44). An advert run in one newspaper asked readers to call if they knew where 'perverts Lillie and Reed are now'. And after years of living under assumed names, moving from one place to another, losing contact with family and friends, and considering suicide, each was tracked down.

One of the conceits of this kind of discursive transformation is that it deprives those portrayed as civic monsters of voice; their responses to their characterizations are interpreted as evidence of their monstrosity. Reed and Lillie, though, rejected their demonization and filed a libel suit against the press, the local council, and the authors of the report—and they prevailed. Nearly a decade after they were pronounced factually innocent of the charges against them, they were proclaimed actually innocent: 'They are to be vindicated and recognized as innocent citizens who should, in my judgment,' the presiding judge ruled, 'be free to exist for what remains of their lives untouched by the stigma of child abuse.'[2]

A metanarrative is a story about a story—or, perhaps better stated, a grand story about 'little' stories, in the plural—and its ending has to do with the imaginative recreation of the familiar core account of satanic evil: the account that has to do with the inverse of what is normative and valued (Bromley, 1991). That core account depicted not only the evil lurking behind ordinary facades and the innocence of children brutalized by sexual assault, but also a set of rituals, ceremonies, and practices that trans-historically and cross-culturally have been associated with evil conspiracies. The sacrifice of infants and animals, the eating of human flesh and faeces, and the drinking of blood, urine, menstrual blood, and semen have served simultaneously as

---

[1] *Lillie & anor v Newcastle City Council & ors* [2002] EWHC 1600 (QB).   [2] ibid [1551].

powerful metaphors for evil and as heuristics, of a sort, that render the unimaginable as imaginable and even coherent.

To coax that core account of children in the day care cases, social workers, law enforcement officers, and other interrogators resorted to suggestive, leading, and sometimes even coercive interviewing techniques (Ceci and Bruck, 1995). But along with the core account came 'little stories' that differed considerably within a single day care case. A few of the children in the Fran's Day Care case, for example, alleged that they had been thrown into a blood-filled swimming pool filled with sharks. Even their interrogators were sceptical at first, until they appealed to the totalizing discourse of the metanarrative's grand story for explanation: the satanic providers, like all satanists before them, must have used dark magic to trick these children into believing that it had happened, they decided, and had done so for the diabolic purpose of undermining their credibility as victims. The jury agreed. Fran and Dan Keller were sentenced to forty-eight years in prison in 1992 in the last (at time of writing) of the day care satanic ritual abuse cases in the United States. When the prosecuting attorney agreed that their trial had been tainted by false medical evidence that the accusing child had been sexually abused, the Kellers were released. That was in 2013. They had been in prison twenty-one years.

The grand story of the metanarrative also absorbed differences between cases into its totalizing discourse. This was especially noticeable when the satanic ritual abuse moral panic spread abroad. In some international cases, such as the Civic Creche case in Christchurch, New Zealand, day care centres and their environs were the site of the alleged satanic ritual abuse; in others, such as the Langley Estate case in Rochdale, England, lower class housing estates were the locus. There was even more divergence. In the Oude Pekela case in the Netherlands, the accusations came from neighbourhood playmates who described their alleged satanic ritual abusers as strangers with a foreign accent; in Pescara, Italy, the alleged abusers were family members and friends, who were said to be involved in a child prostitution and pornography ring. It mattered not at all to interest groups and claims-makers that the sites and alleged perpetrators in these cases were not day care centres and their providers. The grand story of a satanic conspiracy linked day care providers with parents, friends, neighbours, and strangers anywhere in the world, and they in turn were linked through the same conspiratorial imagination with all of the other alleged perpetrators the children mentioned—from celebrities, athletes, politicians, the captains of industry, and members of royal families, to strangers in masks or hooded robes.

CONCLUSION

By way of a conclusion, I will emphasize two points. First, the notion of an evil conspiracy has always been easily conjured, rationalized, and legitimated in times of social stress and strain. Historical accounts give plenty of evidence of that. Once made real, if only by imagination, the evil must be purged. Historical accounts give plenty of evidence of that, too. The satanic ritual abuse moral panic, then, was a successor of these historical waves of moral panics. But—and this my second point—it is also the predecessor of even more contemporary waves of moral panics about predatory paedophiles, cyber-predators, and sex traffickers, as examples.

As Richard Webster (2005) reminds us, our fear of sexual threats to children is made all the more powerful by the fact that sexual abuse *does* exist. Onto this unsettling fact we project time-tested narratives of evil, stoking our fear and morally justifying our reactions to it. '[S]o urgent is our need to rid the world of anyone who might conceivably be a paedophile, that the requirement of evidence has all but disappeared', writes Webster (2005: 538). 'It is for this reason that the innocent are almost as likely to be arraigned as the guilty.' That, in the end, was so in the case of the satanic ritual abuse moral panic.

REFERENCES

ALTHUSSER, L. (1971) *Lenin and Philosophy and Other Essays*, London: New Left Books.
BAUMAN, Z. (1997) *Postmodernity and Its Discontents*, New York: New York University Press.
BRAUN, B. (1988) 'Recognition of Possible Cult Involvement in MPD Patients', Paper presented to the Fourth Annual Conference on Multiple Personality/Dissociative States, Chicago, IL, November.
BROMLEY, D. G. (1991) 'Satanism: The New Cult Scare', in J. T. Richardson, J. Best, and D. G. Bromley (eds) *The Satanism Scare*, New York: Aldine deGruyter.
BROMLEY, D. G., and BUSCHING, B. C. (1989) 'Understanding the Structure of Contractual and Covenantal Social Relations', *Sociological Analysis*, 49(5): 15–32.
CECI, S. J., and BRUCK, M. (1995) *Jeopardy in the Courtroom*, Washington, DC: American Psychological Association Press.
COHEN, S. (1972/2002) *Folk Devils and Moral Panics*, London: MacGibbon & Kee.
DEMAUSE, L. (1994) 'Why Cults Terrorize and Kill Children', *Journal of Psychohistory*, 21(4): 505–18.
DEYOUNG, M. (2004) *The Day Care Ritual Abuse Moral Panic*, Jefferson, NC: McFarland.
DEYOUNG, M. (2007) 'Two Decades after McMartin: A Follow-up of 22 Convicted Day Care Employees', *Journal of Sociology and Social Welfare*, 34(4): 9–33.
DEYOUNG, M. (2008) 'The Devil's Walking Parody', *Contemporary Issues in Criminology and the Social Sciences*, 2(1): 33–59.
ELLIS, B. (2000) *Raising the Devil*, Lexington, KY: University Press of Kentucky.
FINKELHOR, D., and WILLIAMS, L. (1988) *Nursery Crimes*, Newbury Park, CA: Sage.
FOUCAULT, M. (2003) *Abnormal: Lectures at the College de France, 1974–1975*, London: Verso.
FRANKFURTER, D. (2006) *Evil Incarnate: Rumors of Demonic Conspiracy and Ritual Abuse in History*, Princeton, NJ: Princeton University Press.
GOULD, C. (1995) 'Denying the Ritual Abuse of Children', *Journal of Psychohistory*, 22(3): 329–39.
HICKS, R. (1991) *The Pursuit of Satan*, Buffalo, NY: Prometheus Books.
HILL, M. (2005) 'The Satanism Scare in New Zealand', in A. Kirkman and P. Maloney (eds) *Sexualities in Aotearoa, New Zealand*, Dunedin: Otago University Press.
HILL, S., and GOODWIN, J. (1989) 'Satanism: Similarities between Patient Accounts and Pre-inquisition Historical Sources', *Dissociation*, 2(1): 39–44.

HJELM, T., BOGDAN, H., DYRENDAL, A., and PETERSEN, J. (2009) 'Nordic Satanism and Satanism Scares', *Sociological Compass*, 56(4): 515–29.
INGEBRETSEN, E. H. (2001) *At Stake*, Chicago, IL: University of Chicago Press.
JENKINS, P. (2006) *Decade of Nightmares*, New York: Oxford University Press.
LAFONTAINE, J. S. (1998) *Speak of the Devil*, Cambridge: Cambridge University Press.
MEDWAY, G. J. (2001) *Lure of the Sinister*, New York: New York University Press.
MULHERN, S. A. (1992) 'Ritual Abuse: Defining a Syndrome versus Defending a Belief', *Journal of Psychology and Theology*, 20(3): 230–2.
NATHAN, D., and SNEDEKER, M. (1995) *Satan's Silence*, New York: Basic Books.
NOBLITT, J. R., and PERSKIN, P.S. (1995) *Cult and Ritual Abuse*, Westport, CT: Praeger.
NOLL, R. (1989) 'Satanism, UFO Abductions, Historians and Clinicians: Those Who Do not Remember the Past', *Dissociation*, 2(1): 251–3.
SMITH, M., and PAZDER, L. (1980) *Michelle Remembers*, New York: Congdon & Lattes.
SUMMIT, R. C. (1990) 'Satanic Ritual Abuse', in Office of Criminal Justice Planning (ed.) *Occult Crime: A Law Enforcement Primer*, Sacramento, CA: Office of Criminal Justice Planning.
TARTARI, M. (2013) 'Moral Panic and Ritual Abuse', in C. Critcher, J. Hughes, J. Petley, and A. Rohloff (eds) *Moral Panics in the Contemporary World*, London: Bloomsbury Academic.
WEBSTER, R. (2005) *The Secret of Bryn Estyn: The Making of a Modern Witch Hunt*, Oxford: The Orwell Press.

4

MORAL CRUSADES, CHILD PROTECTION, CELEBRITIES, AND THE DUTY TO BELIEVE

Frank Furedi

Debates surrounding accusations of victimization and abuse often focus on the question of 'whom do you believe'. At the time of writing, a heated controversy had broken out over Dylan Farrow's allegation that film director Woody Allen had abused her when she was a child. 'Between labelling Woody Allen a child molester or his daughter a liar, I feel utterly stuck,' stated one columnist for *The Guardian* (Coren Mitchell, 2014). Many other commentators felt that they had an obligation to demonstrate solidarity and a duty to believe the accuser. 'If we don't at least give child accusers the benefit of the doubt, then what message are we sending?' asked a columnist in *The Telegraph* (Magnanti, 2014). In this controversy, as in numerous related cases, it often appears as though the distinction between truth and falsehood is based on moral positioning, rather than on empirical reality. Regardless of the evidence or of its absence, an accusation of abuse carries serious moral weight.

According to the dominant narrative of 'believe the victim', an accusation of abuse contains an important truth, because it is claimed that this experience is painful to acknowledge publicly. 'One reason to believe Dylan Farrow: Talking about it hurts more than silence' is one key argument that has been advanced to condemn Woody Allen (Todd, 2014). The assertion that an accusation of abuse conveys an intrinsic truth is frequently voiced by victim advocacy professionals and by leading figures associated with the criminal justice system. The moral doctrine that underpins this worldview is the conviction that allegations of victimization always contain an existential truth and that therefore society has a duty to affirm them.

The cultural narrative through which allegations of abuse are conveyed presumes that there is no such thing as a false accusation. Accordingly, even an accusation that is made up can still convey an intrinsic truth. This doctrine is sometimes expressed in the maxim 'children never lie'. According to one account, false accusations in child sexual abuse are rare, but 'when they occur it is nearly always a cry for help'; it is 'clear that the children who make false allegations require help and support and as such these allegations should not be ignored' (Anthony and Watkeys, 1991: 120). Such empathy is rarely extended to the accused, and since allegations, even when they are false, 'should not be ignored', those at the receiving end cannot be entirely absolved of suspicion. Thus the homily 'there is no smoke without fire' is transformed into a moral imperative.

The quasi-sacred status assigned to the moral authority of the victim—and particularly that of the child—was dramatically conveyed in England in the context of Operation Yewtree, the Metropolitan Police investigation into allegations of criminal behaviour by the deceased celebrity Jimmy Savile. Although Yewtree assumed the form of a police inquiry, this operation swiftly mutated into a crusade focused on dramatizing the scale of crimes allegedly committed by celebrity abusers. The inquiry itself explicitly acknowledged that its investigation of historic allegations was not so much about fighting or solving crime as it was about giving a 'voice to victims'.

The main accomplishment of the first Operation Yewtree Report, published in January 2013, was to elevate the moral authority of an allegation of abuse (Gray and Watt, 2013). In effect, the authors of the report called for allegations of abuse to be regarded as *de facto* truths. The report justified this casual attitude towards eliminating the burden of proof on the ground that it had received a 'volume of allegations' that painted a 'compelling picture of widespread sexual abuse by a predatory sex offender' (Gray and Watt, 2013: 5). The vast quantity of allegations funnelled through a highly visible public relations (PR) operation served as justification for a fundamental revision of the language of due process. The authors of the report took it upon themselves to define accusers as 'victims' rather than 'complainants'; moreover, they decided not to regard 'the evidence they have provided as unproven allegations' (Gray and Watt, 2013: 5). The displacement of the phrase 'unproven allegation' with the term 'evidence' represents a remarkable revision of the carefully calibrated vocabulary associated with the due process of the law: the mere allegation of victimization is all that is required to gain the designation of a victim. This implicit rebranding of an unproven allegation into evidence all but relieves the accuser of the burden of proof.

A MORAL CRUSADE AND THE DUTY TO BELIEVE

Yewtree's equation of an allegation of abuse with the status of evidence is an outcome of decades of crusading by moral entrepreneurs, who argue that society has a duty to believe the victim. The moral imperative to *believe* is conveyed through a narrative that condemns the unbeliever for raising questions about an allegation of abuse. Those who dare question such an allegation are deemed complicit in 'victim-blaming', or 'secondary victimization', or 're-traumatization'. The moral prohibition against the contestation of a victim's allegation acquires its most virulent form in relation to those made by children. In such cases, the sceptic is condemned for contributing to the further victimization of the child.

From the standpoint of cultural sociology, what is particularly interesting is the relative ease with which duty to believe has become a master-narrative through which allegations of victimization are interpreted. The ascendancy of this narrative is testimony to the effectiveness of a moral crusade that has succeeded in turning victimization—particularly that of children by paedophiles—into a constant focus of public anxiety. According to sociologist Howard Becker (1963: 153), a moral crusade is oriented towards altering people's behaviour through the promotion of an ideology of evil. Such movements possess little capacity for tolerating dissident views and behaviours, and are therefore continually in the business of rule-making and policing people's lives.

Moral crusades are convinced that they possess a profound truth that need not be tested according to the normal standards of evidence. On the contrary, they contend that the idea that the guilt of an abuser requires proof in accordance with the standard of 'beyond a reasonable doubt' represents a violation of the victim. Such sentiments were vigorously advocated in response to the allegations made against Woody Allen. According to one account, the demand for proof that is beyond reasonable doubt leads to 'sacrificing the well-being of most abuse victims in order to protect the very rare man who has a cleverly manipulative ex-girlfriend who does manage to convince people he's guilty when he's innocent without actually offering proof' (Marcotte, 2014). Accordingly, what is needed is a different standard of proof:

> I look at the Woody Allen situation and feel that it really shows that preponderance of evidence standard really is a better one for the social situation than the beyond a reasonable doubt standard. Can you prove it in court that he molested Dylan Farrow? No. But you can build a case, brick by brick, that he's probably guilty due to his creepy behavior.
>
> (Marcotte, 2014)

The casual manner with which conventional standards of evidence are held responsible for 'sacrificing' victims of abuse is matched by the ease with which an individual is demonized on the basis of his or her 'creepy behaviour'.

The success of the moral crusade promoting the victim's truth is shown by the significant influence over popular and public culture. Politicians on both sides of the Atlantic are loath to risk their careers by challenging the ever-expanding demand for victims' rights. According to one study of this phenomenon, 'such is the moral sanctity of the victims' rights lobby, and so fearsome its political clout, that few are willing to express their unease publicly' (Shapiro, 1997: 19).

The demand that the victim must be believed—especially in the domain of sex crimes—is vigorously promoted by campaigners. They take particular exception to the right of a defendant's lawyers to challenge a victim's version of events. The robust questioning of an accuser is frequently characterized as a form of harassment. Campaigners assert that victims require special protection from aggressive questioning. And, as we noted, they contend that the usual standards of evidence should not apply in such cases. One American prosecutor, Steve Chaney, informed a national symposium on child molestation that he was not asking the question, 'Was the child abused?'; rather, he was asking, 'Can the child perform for us in the courtroom?' Chaney claimed that whereas adult witnesses constantly lied, children tended to tell the truth, and therefore his task was to create an environment in which their story could be told (Nathan and Snedeker, 1995: 200–1). During the past twenty years, this sentiment has been widely supported by advocates on both sides of the Atlantic.

The proposition that children's evidence is *ipso facto* the truth has been widely promoted by child protection advocates. This cavalier approach to evidence is well illustrated by Lucy Berliner, an American feminist social worker, in her comments on child abuse:

> A legal decision should never be confused with the truth. If we believe what children say we will be right 95–99 per cent of the time. If we want signs and symptoms as proof we will be right 70–80 per cent of the time. If we require medical evidence we will be right 20 per cent of the time and if we have to wait for a witness we will be right 1 per cent of the time.
>
> (Quoted in Taylor, 1993: 132).

From this perspective, the demand for proof simply detracts from the transcendental truth of abuse. Even the manifest examples of false accusation are seen as containing some intrinsic truths.

For victim activists, the obligation to believe the victim has the character of a moral imperative. The now-discredited campaign against satanic ritual abuse attempted to disarm sceptics by insisting that probably the worst thing that can happen to the victim of sadistic ritual abuse is not to be believed. One campaigner sought to morally blackmail sceptics along the following lines:

> It may be that some accounts which are reputed to be of 'satanic' abuse are delusional, and the narrators may indeed be psychotic in some cases. But we must still face the awful fact that if some of these accounts are true, if we do not have the courage to see the truth that may be there ... we may tacitly be allowing these practices to continue under the cover of secrecy, supported also by the almost universal refusal to believe that they could exist.
>
> (Casement, 1994: 24).

From this standpoint, those who refuse to believe accusations of satanic abuse are themselves complicit in the act of victimization.

For a moral crusade, the duty to believe is non-negotiable. That is why supporters of a cause reserve their most venomous rhetoric for their critics. Intolerance of sceptics has been a historical constant of moral crusades. The medieval witch hunt offers the classic paradigm of a moral crusade. The so-called witch-hunter's bible, the *Malleus Malleficarum* ('The Hammer of Witches'), published in 1486 in Germany, explicitly targeted those who were sceptical of the existence of witchcraft. The expertise of professional demonologists could be affirmed only by means of discrediting and silencing those who questioned the existence of witchcraft. When this manual was published, it declared on its title page the epigraph *Haersis est maxima opera maleficarum non credere* ('To not believe in witchcraft is the greatest of heresies'). This point was echoed by Jean Bodin, the famous sixteenth-century political theorist and jurist, whose text *On the Demonic Madness of Witches*, published in 1580, played a crucial role in the promotion of the witch scare. Bodin asserted that those who denied the existence of witches were themselves witches. Because of the gravity of the offence, normal legal procedures and rules of evidence were suspended in witch trials—for, as Jean Bodin asked rhetorically, how could ordinary procedures help to prove such extraordinary crimes? Bodin took the view that not one in a million would be punished if the procedure were to be subject to ordinary laws. From his standpoint, the allegation of practising witchcraft conveyed the automatic presumption of guilt.

As in the past, so today, moral crusaders are uniquely intolerant of the sceptic. Anyone who dares question their message faces their censure and their wrath. In the fifteenth and sixteenth centuries, they also faced torture and death. During the era of the witch hunt, anyone who questioned the existence of demonic forces could be denounced as an associate of Satan. Such was the power and influence of the mentality of the Inquisition that few were prepared to question the existence of witchcraft. As a recently published study remarked, the 'threat to execute anyone who objected to the execution of a witch' had the effect of suppressing 'any kind of discussion or of objection to witch persecution for centuries' (Kord, 2008: 67).

The powerful influence of the doctrine of the duty to believe the victim has been demonstrated by in post-Savile-scandal Britain. During the weeks following the outbreak of the scandal, rumour-mongering acquired a powerful momentum as different groups of moral entrepreneurs harnessed the fears fuelled by press speculation to promote their cause.[1] The mere hint by Tom Watson, Labour MP for West Bromwich East, that there was a Tory paedophile ring lurking in the shadowy wings of Westminster helped to unleash a frenetic Twitter campaign designed to unmask the culprits. The suggestion of a conspiracy involving a shadowy network of powerful individuals signalled fears of a massive establishment cover-up. Conspiracy theories were in circulation within a few days of the story breaking. Some of these conspiracy stories implicated Downing Street, while others suggested that the British royal family had close connections with powerful paedophile rings.[2] These storylines would not have been out of place in the narratives of medieval demonologists.

One target of this campaign, senior Conservative Party figure Lord McAlpine, was falsely accused of being an arch-paedophile. From a sociological standpoint, what was remarkable about this campaign of vilification was the manner with which reputable public figures and journalists justified their complicity in the circulation of false accusations. When some of them were eventually forced to apologize for their false allegation of paedophilia, they justified their behaviour on the grounds that they got caught up in the heady atmosphere of frenzy. Many of them sought to minimize their responsibility for their false allegation by blaming the febrile atmosphere. The sentiment they seemed to convey was that, in circumstances in which evil threatened the natural order, something had to be done. 'I felt a powerful compulsion to do what I have done throughout my career: to help the voiceless be heard', wrote one journalist in his letter of apology (Monbiot, 2012).

It appeared that, for far too many figures in the media, the imperative of helping the 'voiceless be heard' served as a warrant for the irresponsible demonization of the targets of malicious rumours. The readiness with which an unsubstantiated allegation of abuse against Lord McAlpine was interpreted as fact by leading journalists and commentators, and even a major national institution such as the British Broadcasting

---

[1] The role of a 'trial by media' is discussed in Greer and McLaughlin (2013: 249).
[2] See, e.g., Frith (2012).

Corporation (BBC), indicates that the usual standards of proof have, in practice, been dispensed with. Indeed, as Greer and McLaughlin (2013: 260) noted, the very denial of an allegation of sexual abuse 'triggers trial by media'.

With so much at stake, moral crusaders are often indifferent to the destructive consequences of a false allegation of child abuse. From their standpoint, a mistaken allegation is a small price to pay for the higher truth. When the allegation against Lord McAlpine was exposed as false, numerous advocates of the 'victim's voice' decried the fact that the outcome of this incident would be to question such accusations in the future (Halliday, 2012). Their concern was not the falsely accused, but the negative consequences of this embarrassing episode for their cause. One leading moral crusader complained that such exposures strengthened the hand of their foes, and lamented that 'no sooner is child abuse aired than we are warned against witch hunts, obsession and hysteria' (Campbell, 2012). Such statements indicate that, for a moral crusade, the necessity for defeating evil means that the collateral damage caused by false allegations is an acceptable price to pay. The duty to believe trumps other considerations.

INCONTROVERTIBLE TRUTHS

The intensely moralized language surrounding allegations of victimization is underwritten by the conviction that what is at stake is not simply a number of individual criminal acts, but a conspiracy of evil. Victimization is frequently represented as a ubiquitous threat. Moral entrepreneurs use the rhetoric of big numbers to suggests that 'we are all at risk' of abuse. A few months before the revelation of Savile's crimes, England's Deputy Children's Commissioner, Sue Berelowitz, declared that 'there isn't a town, village or hamlet in which children are not being sexually exploited' (Wilson, 2012). The moral weight of such dramatic claims are rarely contested, since anyone who questions the doctrine of the omnipresence of abuse is likely to be denounced as an appeaser of the child predator.[3]

Historically, moral crusaders tended to draw on the cultural resources provided by the authority of religion. Although moral crusades continue to communicate their cause in a moralized and quasi-religious form, in the twentieth and twenty-first centuries they often draw on culturally secular resources, and even on claims legitimated by professional expertise and academic knowledge. In effect, the religious condemnation of immorality has given way to the secular pathologization of sexual behaviour. In its most dramatic form, victimization is associated with destructive sexual behaviour. One of the paradoxes of our times is that a highly sexualized Western culture coexists with a belief that regards sexual relations—particularly heterosexual ones—as intrinsically risky, if not violent or destructive.

Since the 1980s, sex has frequently been represented as a fundamentally victimizing experience, with potentially traumatic consequences. American psychologist Paul

---

[3] That there is no need for evidence for a crime to cause moral outrage is discussed in Victor (1998: 560).

Okami (1992: 116) persuasively argues that, during the late 1970s and the 1980s, there was a noticeable shift from the previous, relatively benign, representation of sex: 'Sexual aggression, abuse, and harassment became topics of concern for a great many professional and popular writers, as did the medical and social consequences of sexually transmitted diseases.' Okami (1992: 116) further observes that 'high levels of sexual activity and unusual sexual practices became pathologised in diagnoses such as "sex addiction" and "sexual compulsivity"'. To substantiate this thesis, Okami points to the ever-growing interest in the negative dimensions of human sexuality, which is confirmed in his review of listings in *Psychological Abstracts*.[4] In 1969, there were no index categories for 'sexual abuse', 'sex offenders', 'sexual harassment', 'rape incest', 'sexual sadism', or 'paedophilia'. All of these acts were subsumed under the category 'sexual deviations', which contained sixty-five entries. However, by 1989, all of these index categories had been added to *Psychological Abstracts*, and in that edition there were more than 400 articles dealing with sexual aggression, crime, and intergenerational sex. This constituted a twenty-fold increase between 1969 and 1989 in the listings of such sex-related pathologies, according to Okami (1992: 117). These trends are clearly reflected in popular culture, where the themes of abuse, sexual violence, stalking, and serial sex crime constitute the staple diet of contemporary fiction and television.

The main protagonist in the current ideology of evil is the child predator: the paedophile. The paedophile possesses the stand-alone status of the embodiment of malevolence. At the same time, the cultural narrative regarding paedophilia invites us to regard all strangers—particularly men—as potential child molesters. The concept of 'stranger danger' and the campaigns that promote it have as their goal the educating of children to mistrust people whom they do not know. Stranger danger helps to turn the unthinkable into a constant threat. In effect, it turns paedophilia into a normal, everyday feature of life. That is why physical contact between adults and children has become so intensely scrutinized and policed.

A key contribution to construction of the narrative fear towards paedophilia was made by cultural feminism from the 1970s onwards. Some of its proponents argued that the sexual abuse of children was an open secret among men, who regarded it as an essential component of socializing their daughters into a life of submission to males. Advocates of this thesis contend that the majority of young girls are subjected to some form of sex abuse by family members.[5] While demonizing men as sexual predators may not quite have added up to an old-fashioned witch hunt, it has contributed to a climate of permanent obsessive paranoia about male paedophiles. Garland (2008: 15) suggests that this 'recurring contemporary panic' may be linked to 'unconscious guilt about negligent parenting'.

Cultural feminists have also been instrumental in popularizing the view that heterosexual relationships are based on the projection of male violence against the female victim. They contend that, in practice, it is difficult to draw a dividing line between normal male sexual acts and the application of violence. One leading advocate of this

---

[4] *Psychological Abstracts*, published by the American Psychological Association (APA) between 1927 and 2006, contained non-evaluative summary abstracts of literature in the field of psychology and related disciplines.

[5] See discussion in Webster (2005: 570).

thesis, Catherine MacKinnon (1989: 146), was anxious to point out the similarity between 'the patterns, rhythms, roles and emotions, not to mention acts, which make up rape (and battery) on the one hand and intercourse on the other'. Mackinnon (1989: 146) finds it hard to distinguish 'pathology and normalcy' and 'violence and sex'. From her perspective, heterosexual penetrative sex is rendered pathological and the male lover is a potential rapist. This view is rooted in the premise that women are the universal victims of male sexual passion—a claim that was robustly advanced by feminist philosopher Marilyn Frye (1992: 130):

> For females to be subordinated and subjugated to males on a global scale, and for males to organize themselves and each other as they do, billions of female individuals, virtually all who see life on the planet, must be reduced to a more-or-less willing toleration of subordination and servitude to men. The primary sites of this reduction are the sites of heterosexual relation and encounter—courtship and marriage-arrangement, romance, sexual liaisons, fucking, marriage, prostitution, the normative family, incest and child abuse.

Heterosexuality is recast as, by definition, an essentially victimizing experience responsible for the systematic violation of billions of people.

Theories promoting the demonization of male sexuality, which first emerged on the margins of the academic community in the 1970s, had, by the 1980s, gained significant influence in the media and popular culture. As a result, a permanent sense of alarmism surrounds childhood, and its protection from sexual predators has emerged as one of the moral imperatives of our time (Pratt, 2005).

THE CHILD AS A MORAL SHIELD

The moral foundations of Western societies have lost much of their cohesion. Very few norms and values are beyond question. Ideas about what constitutes an appropriate form of family life, or what is acceptable as opposed to unacceptable behaviour, are continually contested. Disagreement about fundamental questions of value is refracted through debates on issues such as family life, abortion, gay marriage, and assisted suicide. Such disagreements have tended to weaken clarity about the line that separates the moral from the immoral and right from wrong (Garland, 2008: 17).

But, in contrast to the disputes fought on a wide range of controversial issues, there is a rare example of moral consensus in the affirmation of the moral status of the child. This consensus is best exemplified through the veneration of the innocence of childhood and a universal loathing for the child abuser. As Ian Hacking (2003: 40) noted, the innocence of children has become the symbol of purity. This symbol of purity offers an important moral focus through which society's ideas about right and wrong gain meaning and definition. French psychoanalyst Gerard Wajcman (2008: 68) contends that the 'sole remaining prohibition, the one sacred value in our society to remain has to do with children'. While many of the moral transgressions of the past have lost significance, those directed at children are policed more intensively that at any time in human history.

'In an age when sexuality is exhibited on every street corner, the image of the innocent child has, strangely, returned with a vengeance', observes Wajcman (2008: 68).

According to some accounts, the intense moralization of childhood is fuelled by the imperative of fulfilling society's need for clarity about the constitution of good and evil (Webster, 2005: 567–73). With such intense moral sentiments attached to this symbol of innocence and purity, it is not surprising that the vulnerable child serves as a catalyst for the mobilization of so much fear and anxiety. There is a 'particularly close fit between innocence and vulnerability', which endows childhood with a singular moral intensity (Meyer, 2007: 102).

The unique moral status of the sacred child is literally beyond discussion. As Meyer (2007: 99) observes, '"the child" becomes a shorthand for sacralisation and moral status; its meaning no longer has to be made explicit', concluding that this narrative is 'so powerful that in fact any opinion can be justified by simply referring to children, and without having to explain why and how children justify it'. The very mention of the word 'children' closes down discussion; the discourse on the perils of childhood provides an uncontested validation for claims-making and 'anything can be justified via children as children make the case good and right' (Meyer, 2007: 100).

Childhood also provides the moral resources for claims-making. Claims-making involves making statements about problems that deserve, or ought to deserve, the attention of society. A claim constitutes a warrant for recognition or some form of entitlement; thus claims demanding that a newly discovered risk to children be recognized draw on prevailing assumptions about the vulnerable child. As Joel Best (1999: 164) reports, in his important analysis of claims-making, 'how advocates describe a new social problem very much depends on how (they and their audiences—the public, the press, and policy-makers) are used to talking about, already familiar problems'. Claims-makers who draw on a widely familiar moral discourse on childhood often gain status and respectability for their stance. As Meyer (2007: 102) notes, 'justifying attitudes and practices in the name of the child can serve to represent yourself as a moral person'. Mention the word 'child' and people will listen. Raise the moral stakes by claiming that a 'child is at risk' and people will not only listen, but also endorse your demand that 'something must be done'.

Social constructionist sociology interprets the framing of threats in terms of their effects on children as a form of symbolic politics. An example of this trend has been the rebranding of the problem of poverty as that of '*child* poverty'. Such emphasis is motivated by the belief that the poverty faced by children is likely to provoke far greater sympathy than a more general appeal to alleviate the plight faced by their families. In this way, campaigners against the reduction of state housing benefits have argued that this policy 'leaves young at risk of abuse' (Sherman, 2012). Almost every social problem—homelessness, drug addiction, obesity, prostitution—becomes amplified through its association with children or young people. The framing of a problem as one that threatens the vulnerable child is likely to gain attention for the message of moral entrepreneurs: 'Because the child-victim menaced by the adult deviant is a particularly dramatic, emotionally powerful image, claims-makers sometimes adopt the language and imagery of child-victims when describing children threatened by poverty or other impersonal conditions', writes Joel Best (1994: 11).

Although there is sometimes an element of opportunism in the way in which general problems are rebranded as threats directed specifically at children, such sentiments are usually sincerely held. Childhood is not simply the symbol of innocence; it also provides the moral resources necessary for giving meaning to experience. For crusades, anxiety about childhood serves as a vehicle for transforming the threat of victimization into a moral hazard. It is important to understand that it is not cynicism or opportunism that motivates moral crusaders: while they are often 'fervent' and 'self-righteous', they are motivated by the impulse of helping others (Becker, 1963: 148). However, zealous crusades often have a habit of interpreting the ambiguities of everyday life through the prism of a doctrine of evil.

The moral entrepreneur is a rule creator. Such a person 'feels that nothing can be right in the world until rules are made to correct it' (Becker, 1963: 147). However, since evil is omnipresent, every new rule serves only as a prelude to the next. A moral crusader is a 'professional discoverer of wrongs to be righted, of situations requiring new rules' (Becker, 1963: 147–8, 153). Becker (1963: 156) concludes that the 'final outcome of the moral crusade is a police force'. What begins as singular accusation of victimization is, by means of the activity of the moral crusader, transformed into evidence of a conspiracy against childhood. In a crusade against evil, the usual rules of tolerant and civilized conduct are regarded as inappropriate. Those who stand on the side of the child have the duty simply to believe and to close ranks against the predators lurking in the dark corners of our communities—and that is why the term 'false accusation' has lost so much of its cultural meaning.

REFERENCES

Anthony, G., and Watkeys, J. (1991) 'False Allegations in Child Sexual Abuse: The Pattern of Referral in an Area Where Reporting is Not Mandatory', *Children and Society*, 5(2): 111–22.

Becker, H. S. (1963) *Outsiders: Studies in the Sociology of Deviance*, New York: The Free Press.

Best, J. (1994) 'Troubling Children: Children and Social Problems', in J. Best (ed.) *Troubling Children: Studies of Children and Social Problems*, New York: Aldine de Gruyter.

Best, J. (1999) *Random Violence: How We Talk about New Crimes and New Victims*, Berkeley, CA: University of California Press.

Campbell, B. (2012) 'Our Paedophile Culture', *London Review of Books*, 34(23). Available online at <http://www.lrb.co.uk/v34/n23/letters> [accessed May 2016].

Casement, P. (1994) 'The Wish not to Know', in V. Sinason (ed.) *Treating Survivors of Satanist Abuse*, London: Routledge.

Coren Mitchell, V. (2014) 'Between Labelling Woody Allen a Child Molestor or His Daughter a Liar, I Feel Utterly Stuck', *The Guardian*, 9 February. Available online at <http://www.theguardian.com/commentisfree/2014/feb/09/woody-allen-dylan-farrow-alleged-sexual-abuse> [accessed May 2016].

Frith, C. (2012) 'David Icke Identified Savile as a Procurer of Children for the Royal Family Years Ago', 14 October. Available online at <http://beforeitsnews.com/eu/2012/10/david-icke-identified-savile-as-a-procurer-of-children-for-the-royal-family-years-ago-2455358.html> [accessed May 2016].

FRYE, M. (1992) *Willful Virgin: Essays in Feminism, 1976–1992*, Freedom, CA: Crossing Press.

GARLAND, D. (2008) 'On the Concept of Moral Panic', *Crime Media Culture*, 4(1): 9–30.

GRAY, D., and WATT, P. (2013) *Giving Victims a Voice: A Joint MPS and NSPCC Report into Allegations of Sexual Abuse Made against Jimmy Savile under Operation Yewtree*, London: Metropolitan Police Service/NSPCC.

GREER, C., and MCLAUGHLIN, E. (2013) 'The Sir Jimmy Savile Scandal: Child Sexual Abuse and Institutional Denial at the BBC', *Crime Media Culture*, 9(3): 243–63.

HACKING, I. (2003) 'Risk and Dirt', in R. Ericson and A. Doyle (eds) *Risk and Morality*, Toronto, ON: University of Toronto Press.

HALLIDAY, J. (2012) 'Newsnight Furore "May Dissuade Abuse Victims from Speaking out"', *The Guardian*, 11 November. Available online at <http://www.theguardian.com/society/2012/nov/11/child-abuse-victims-witch-hunt?CMP=twt_fd> [accessed May 2016].

KORD, S. (2008) 'Ancient Fears and the New Order: Witch Beliefs and Physiognomy in the New Age of Reason', *German Life and Letters*, 61(1): 61–78.

MACKINNON, C. A. (1989) *Toward a Feminist Theory of the State*, Cambridge, MA: Harvard University Press.

MAGNANTI, B. (2014) 'Woody Allen Sex Abuse Allegations: Why I Want to Believe Dylan Farrow', *The Telegraph*, 3 February. Available online at <http://www.telegraph.co.uk/women/womens-life/10614585/Woody-Allen-sex-abuse-Why-I-want-to-believe-Dylan-Farrow.html> [accessed May 2016].

MARCOTTE, A. (2014) 'In the Court of Public Opinion, Let's Try Preponderance of Evidence as Standard', *Pandagon*, 4 February. Available online at <http://www.rawstory.com/rs/2014/02/04/in-the-court-of-public-opinion-lets-try-preponderance-of-evidence-as-the-standard/> [accessed May 2016].

MEYER, A. (2007) 'The Moral Rhetoric of Childhood', *Childhood*, 14(1): 85–104.

MONBIOT, G. (2012) 'Lord McAlpine: An Abject Apology', 10 November. Available online at <http://www.monbiot.com/2012/11/10/lord-mcalpine-an-abject-apology/> [accessed May 2016].

NATHAN, D., and SNEDEKER, M. (1995) *Satan's Silence: Ritual Abuse and the Making of a Modern American Witch Hunt*, New York: Basic Books,

OKAMI, P. (1992) '"Child Perpetrators of Sexual Abuse": The Emergence of a Problematic Deviant Category', *The Journal of Sex Research*, 29(1): 109–30.

PRATT, J. (2005) 'Child Sexual Abuse: Purity and Danger in an Age of Anxiety', *Crime, Law & Social Change*, 43(4–5): 263–87.

SHAPIRO, B. (1997) 'Victims and Vengeance', *The Nation*, 10 February. Available online at <http://www.sweetcommunication.com.au/files/dart/BruceShapiro_article1.pdf> [accessed August 2014].

SHERMAN, J. (2012) 'Axing Housing Benefit Leaves Young at Risk of Abuse', *The Times*, 22 November. Available online at <http://www.thetimes.co.uk/tto/news/politics/article3607784.ece> [accessed May 2016].

TAYLOR, G. (1993) 'Challenges from the Margin', in J. Clarke (ed.) *A Crisis in Care? Challenges to Social Work?* London: Sage.

TODD, G. (2014) 'One Reason to Believe Dylan Farrow: Talking about It Hurts More than Silence', *The Chronical of Social Change*, 10 February. Available online at <https://chronicleofsocialchange.org/opinion/one-reason-to-believe-dylan-farrow-talking-about-it-hurts-more-than-silence/5140> [accessed May 2016].

VICTOR, J. S. (1998) 'Moral Panics and the Social Construction of Deviant Behavior: A Theory and Application to the Case of Ritual Child Abuse', *Sociological Perspectives*, 41(3): 541–65.

WAJCMAN, G. (2008) 'The Intimate Extorted, the Intimate Exposed', *Journal of the Jan van Eyck Circle for Lacanian Ideology Critique*, 1(1): 58–77.
WEBSTER, R. (2005) *The Secret of Bryn Estyn: The Making of a Modern Witch Hunt*, Oxford: The Orwell Press.
WILSON, G. (2012) 'Shocking Scale of Abuse', *The Sun*, 13 June.

5

TELLING STORIES?
ADULTS' RETROSPECTIVE NARRATIVES OF ABUSE IN RESIDENTIAL CHILD CARE

Mark Smith

RECEIVED WISDOM ON HISTORICAL INSTITUTIONAL ABUSE

A belief that physical and sexual abuse took place on a massive scale in children's homes and residential schools has become what Webster (2005: 10) terms 'an unquestioned orthodoxy'. In 1996, Rhodri Morgan, then the UK Labour Party's Welsh Affairs spokesman, described children's homes and schools as dishing out 'a diet of sadism by day and sodomy by night' (quoted in Webster, 2005: 3). This has become received popular wisdom. While my focus in this chapter is primarily on the UK, jurisdictions across the world face the reverberations of allegations of historical abuse from adults brought up 'in care'.

Until the early 1990s, however, there was no sense of there being any systemic problem in residential care. Indeed, most of the evidence was of a reasonably well-functioning system (Corby, Doig, and Roberts, 2001). Of course, proponents of an abuse discourse might attribute this absence of concern to the complicity or ignorance of those working in the sector; this chapter proffers an alternative view, arguing that the reason for the absence of concern was that there was little to be concerned about. That there were instances of abuse in residential child care broaches no dissent: some individuals admitted offences and others were correctly found guilty in courts of law; any scare or panic generally has some legitimate concern at its heart (Cree, Clapton, and Smith, 2015). However, panics are also characterized by disproportionate responses. In the case of residential child care, the lack of proportion in responses is such that, as a wider social phenomenon, the assumption of *endemic* abuse is described by Webster (2005) as a collective fantasy. Webster (2005: 10) goes on to note that 'when fantasy is mixed with fact in unequal proportion, fantasy can overtake fact', with hugely destructive consequences. In this case, this unequal mix established the conditions for a witch hunt of residential care workers.

The use of terms such as 'fantasy' around such moralized subject matter as the abuse of children in care is guaranteed to see a charge of 'denial' levelled at anyone so daring.

Denial is increasingly used as 'a synonym for refusing to acknowledge the truth' and a device to impute the motives of those identified as 'deniers' (Furedi, 2007). Sen and colleagues (2008: 418), writing about abuse in residential child care, claim that 'denial of abuse has been noted as a key impediment to preventing abuse'. A similar warning shot is sounded in *Time to Be Heard* (TTBH), a Scottish government initiative in response to allegations of abuse in care, which claims that '[w]here the disclosure of abuse is met with scepticism and doubt, survivors have reported, both in research and clinical settings, feeling traumatized and having adverse effects' (Shaw, 2011: para. 3.3.3). Dissenting voices thus stand accused of both impeding the prevention of abuse and re-traumatizing victims. For some of these reasons, academics have failed to ask pertinent, or indeed any, questions of what has become the received historical abuse discourse. Abrogation of academic responsibility to properly interrogate knowledge of this subject, however, opens up the possibility of a whole series of further abuses in respect of false allegations (and convictions) made against care workers.

Hiding behind charges of denial actually masks the intellectual shallowness of most current discourse on this issue, which is based around a dogmatic and one-dimensional mantra of listening to victims. This may or may not be acceptable were the intentions and consequences of such listening merely of therapeutic benefit to victims of abuse. Victim stories, however, inevitably implicate, and have devastating consequences on the lives of, others. In such cases, it is not disrespectful to probe and question accounts of abuse in a sensitive and respectful manner; rather, it is naive and hubristic *not to* (Smith, 2010). I will be accused, in taking the stance that I do in this chapter, of belittling the experiences of victims of abuse. However, it is not they, but those moral entrepreneurs whom Webster (2005: 64–70) accuses of exhibiting a 'psychology of righteousness' in their readiness to use narratives of abuse for their own ends who are the focus of my critique.

BELIEVING IN DARK FORCES AT WORK

The issue of abuse in residential child care needs to be understood as only one, albeit one enduring, episode in what Furedi (2013) identifies as a moral crusade against child abuse. The beginnings of this crusade might be traced back to the McMartin trial into allegations of satanic ritual abuse in a Californian preschool in 1983. Although there were, ultimately, no convictions in the McMartin case, an ideology took hold, speaking of dark forces at work and of a need to believe children when they told of such, no matter how seemingly bizarre their allegations might be (see Chapter 3 in this volume). This ideology, in the form of satanic ritual abuse indicators, was imported to the UK by Christian fundamentalist Ray Wyre. Satanic ritual abuse (SRA) scares erupted across England during the late 1980s and in the Orkney Isles in Scotland in 1991. Individual episodes were investigated and found wanting. Then, in 1994, the Department of Health commissioned anthropologist Jean La Fontaine to investigate the phenomenon. Her report provided an authoritative rebuttal to a movement supporting claims of SRA and stalled the momentum that had built up (La Fontaine, 1994).

Among the eighty-four cases that she investigated, she found no evidence of alleged ritualized, devil-worshipping abuse, while three cases of sexual abuse within the family were substantiated and found to be the crucible for talk about the devil and stories of organized child abuse.

Rather than putting the subject to rest, however, Corby and colleagues (2001) suggest that disquiet over the way in which child protection panics in community and family settings were managed had the effect of redirecting efforts to find abuse onto residential child care. The same cast of moral entrepreneurs who had been behind the satanic abuse scares merely refocused their attentions. Residential care was—rightly, in most cases—considered a poor second to the family. It had a particularly ambivalent relationship with a social work profession that had set out its stall against 'institutional' care. As an option for bringing up children, it could count many detractors and only lukewarm defenders. It consequently struggled to defend itself when allegations of historical abuse started to emerge and has limped from one episode to the next, in a continuing process.

Throughout the 1990s, a rising tide of allegations of historical child abuse emerged in relation to residential care establishments across England and Wales. Claims around establishments in North Wales, in particular, refused to go away. Police inquiries, however, found no evidence of systematic or widespread abuse. Suddenly, though, all of this changed when California came to Clywd: orthodoxies that had emerged in the McMartin case around believing children—and, by extension, adults who had once been children in care—took hold. A new cadre of 'experts' emerged as masters (or mistresses) in the detection of evil. This 'field of experts grew and diversified: a new professional corps of social workers and police, claiming unique abilities to discern (abuse)... and to extract evidence for it from ostensibly afflicted children and adults' (Frankfurter, 2006: 56).

Up until that point, the North Wales constabulary would have been unlikely to be taken in by psychobabble from the West Coast of the United States, being used to old-fashioned evidence-gathering. However, in coming out as 'unbelievers' by failing to find evidence of abuse in earlier investigations, the police themselves were accused of complicity in an elaborate cover-up. In a febrile and increasingly politicized atmosphere, they, institutionally, were thus co-opted to the child protection movement, swallowing orthodoxies about widespread organized abuse and affording 'victims' the opportunity to disclose. All of this created a powerful upwelling of belief in widescale abuse. The ability claimed by 'experts' to 'discern' evil dispensed with the need for more traditional means of evidence-gathering. Ideology supplanted evidence, and the conditions for a collective fantasy and subsequent witch hunt of residential workers took root.

The prospect of thousands of 'victims' of institutional abuse just waiting to 'disclose' led investigators across the Welsh–English border into Cheshire and Merseyside—and indeed to almost every police authority in the British mainland. The result of this is that, over the course of the 1990s, some 8,000 care workers were caught up in police 'trawling' operations, whereby the police, rather than investigating reports of abuse, set about uncovering such accounts through largely unsolicited interviews with former residents of care homes. Their methods and their persistence is evident from the account of an ex-prisoner-turned-penal-reformer's account of his own experience of the process (Gunn, 2013). These trawling expeditions, hardly surprisingly, unleashed waves of fabrication and fantasy, engulfing thousands of innocent care workers.

The difficulties inherent in the practice are acknowledged in a parliamentary Home Affairs Select Committee report from 2002, which describes it as an:

> …absolutely unregulated process tailor-made to generate false allegations. There is deep concern over the conduct of police interviews and the integrity of witness testimony. Set in the context of a growing compensation culture…the risks of effecting a miscarriage of justice are unusually high.
> (Home Affairs Select Committee, 2002: para. 1)

'It has been suggested,' it goes on to claim, 'and we believe it to be so, that a new genre of miscarriages of justice has arisen.'

The practice of 'trawling' was compounded by a legal system increasingly inclined to accept cases built around evidence of 'similar fact'. Thus if two complainants told similar stories of having been abused by the same person, then conviction became a distinct possibility. The prosecution services might respond that it is only in certain circumstances that this could happen and, specifically, where the accounts were independently generated. This, however, places the onus of proof on the defence to show that individuals' paths had crossed and that a story might have been concocted—and the possibility of stories being generated in a social space, either through dubious policing methods or the collective construction of memories, has now become even more likely with the advent of the Internet and social networking sites.

Despite these ethical, if not strictly legal, impediments to a fair trial, hundreds are believed to have been jailed on the basis of convictions secured by such methods (Webster, 2005; Grometstein, 2008; Barlow and Newby, 2009; Naughton, 2013).

THE WATERHOUSE INQUIRY: MAKING IT OFFICIAL

As the panic over institutional abuse began to generate some political heat, the then Conservative government set up a tribunal of inquiry, led by Sir Ronald Waterhouse, to investigate events in North Wales. The Inquiry's report, *Lost in Care*, was published in 2000 (Waterhouse, 2000). Waterhouse found no evidence of the *organized* abuse that had been widely claimed, but did confirm widespread physical and sexual abuse in homes and schools across North Wales. The Waterhouse Report quickly took its place at the heart of a self-referential literature on this subject, creating a 'powerful version of social reality' (Prior, 2004: 74) that spoke of endemic, systemic abuse. Following its publication, still more residential workers were prosecuted—a task made easier as a result of Waterhouse's apparent confirmation of the scale of institutional abuse. In that sense, Waterhouse fulfilled its political purpose: to establish a particular 'master narrative' (Butler and Drakeford, 2005).

Any inquiry, however, for all that it might claim objectivity and veracity, 'is only one partisan version of many possible accounts' (Butler and Drakeford, 2005: 235). Beneath this master narrative, 'dissenting and questioning voices are to be discovered'

(Butler and Drakeford, 2005: 137). Despite its elaborate and theatrical constitution, and its massive cost (£12.8 million baseline), Waterhouse is a deeply flawed document.

The major dissenting voice raised against it is that of cultural historian Richard Webster (1950–2011), whose book *The Secret of Bryn Estyn* (2005) systematically deconstructs the Waterhouse Report, providing compelling evidence to dispute the scale of the abuse claimed and casting serious doubt upon the efficacy of several prosecutions. We cannot do justice to Webster's book, the fruit of nine years of work and running to more than 700 pages, in this chapter. The forensic nature and academic rigour of his research, though, ensures that while his findings may have been ignored, they have not been rebutted. His work casts a shadow over this entire issue, which at some point is going to have to be confronted by those who wish to perpetuate claims of widespread institutional abuse. On reading Webster (2005), Christian Wolmar (2005), a journalist who had previously written a book highlighting the problem of abuse in care, concluded that the Waterhouse Report 'was a shoddy piece of work… which started from the wrong premise because it was based on the assumption that the allegations were true, rather than making any attempt to assess their worth'. This assessment, with which is hard to disagree, renders any subsequent attempts to support an abuse discourse based around Waterhouse shaky indeed—an argument built on sand.

Webster's forensic mind was required once again on the Channel Island of Jersey, where, in 2008, a team of police officers and forensic experts, aided by a trusted sniffer dog, announced to the world's media that they had found children's remains at the site of a former children's home, Haut De La Garenne. The story unfolded to include lurid tales of a paedophile ring, up to half a dozen bodies, dozens of milk teeth, sex abuse bunkers, and mass graves. One of the finds was said to be a skull fragment. With a little basic investigative work, however, Webster was able to confirm that the skull fragment was a piece of wood or coconut shell. On the strength of Webster's interventions, the Jersey episode fizzled out almost as quickly as it had erupted. No evidence was found for any of the more lurid claims made and the police officers leading the investigation were removed from their duties. Nevertheless, the case was not without its casualties, stuttering to an ignominious conclusion with the sacrificial conviction of an elderly couple on what, in the great scheme of claims made, were trivial offences. The wider problem in this respect is that, having set out down a particular trail, the police and prosecutors have to show *something* for their efforts.

The most recent and prominent eruption of concern over allegations of historical sexual abuse are those concerning former disc jockey and television celebrity Jimmy Savile. It should come as no surprise that the initial allegations made against Savile emanated from a residential care establishment, Duncroft, a residential school in the south of England for 'wayward, but intelligent young ladies'. Early allegations appeared on Friends Reunited, a social networking site, and spoke of Savile using his fame to groom and abuse girls. The case generated massive media attention and has spawned several public reports. It has also provoked the reopening of inquiries into previous cases of historical abuse in care settings in North Wales, in the form of the Macur Review and the police's Operation Pallial. At a wider cultural level, the case has shaken the legitimacy of institutions such as the British Broadcasting Corporation (BBC). The subject of abuse in care has thus become a totemic cultural phenomenon despite its decidedly shaky foundations.

THE DYNAMICS OF TELLING STORIES

A number of factors come together to create the conditions through which the ongoing moral crusade against historical abuse could take root and assume a significance way beyond any empirical or rational evidence for its scale or nature. The simplest explanation is that those who falsely claim to have been abused are motivated by the lure of financial compensation. The role of personal injury lawyers and the police has been central to generating claims of abuse (Home Affairs Select Committee, 2002; Kaufman, 2002; Webster, 2005; Rose, Chapter 12 in this volume). Those who support an abuse discourse are uncomfortable with the use of the term 'false' allegations, because it requires that they disbelieve 'victims'. I use the term here, following Sikes and Piper (2010), in such a way that 'false' does not necessarily imply malicious. False allegations may, indeed, be malicious, but they may also be unfounded or unsubstantiated. Having said that, there is no doubt that, in this matter, some allegations are deliberately constructed for financial gain (Gunn, 2013). To fail to acknowledge that former residents of care homes, perhaps down on their luck, might succumb to the temptation of posters on prison walls asking if they have been abused in care and advertising the wares of compensation lawyers (for example in the prisoners' newspaper *Inside Time*), or that they might eventually agree with the persistent suggestions of police officers that they were indeed victims of abuse, would be naive in the extreme.

But other dynamics feed into the explosion of claims of historical abuse. Hacking (1995: 284) notes that, 'when vile stories are rampant, minds that are sufficiently confused, angry and cruel will turn fiction into fact'. Media reporting and the incessantly stated mantra from prosecutors that they will take action on behalf of 'victims' of historical abuse does not merely provide an opportunity for those genuinely abused to come forward, as is the stated intention; it also opens the floodgates for anyone with an axe to grind, or any poor soul trying to make some sense of confusing life experiences, to report himself or herself as a victim. Thus the victim story takes on a life of its own, independent of the truth of its content (Radstone, 2005).

This dynamic feeds a paradigm shift in criminal justice policy whereby the focus is moved away from ensuring safeguards against wrongful conviction towards a 'clamour to ensure that no guilty offenders escape their just deserts' (Naughton, 2005: 65). Ironically, the role of a seemingly liberal intelligentsia in advancing the rights of victims is actually complicit in trends that erode long-established safeguards against wrongful convictions. A noteworthy feature of the Savile case is that it reifies erstwhile concerns that sex crimes are used not only to erode, but also to entirely dismantle a presumption of innocence in English law. For example, in her report regarding Savile, Alison Levitt QC, principal advisor to the Director of Public Prosecutions (DPP), notes that the term 'complainant' is inappropriate and substitutes the term 'victim' throughout the report (Levitt, 2013: 1). Thus Savile is effectively pronounced guilty of serial sexual abuse with no due process of law.

A particular problem with accusations of historical abuse is that past behaviours come to be judged by the standards and laws of the present. This itself assumes that the concept of child abuse is static and well understood. It is not. It is a social construct, if ever there was one. Hacking (1992: 257) identifies child abuse as a diffuse and burgeoning category, which has come to include 'some things that were not even counted as especially bad three decades ago'. He goes on to say that 'no one had any glimmering, in 1960, of what was going to count as child abuse in 1990'. Now, in 2014, a so-called Cinderella Law, promoted by a children's charity and politicians, threatens to subject parents who deny their children love and affection—however that may be defined—to prosecution in the criminal courts.

While most social scientific thought would recognize the social construction of abuse, official and legal responses proceed as though it were a discrete and unproblematic concept. According to TTBH (Shaw, 2011: 85): '[d]efining abuse was straightforward'; the initiative had merely adopted the definitions established by the Scottish Office (1998), which refer to physical injury, physical neglect, emotional abuse, sexual abuse, and non-organic failure to thrive. Yet defining abuse should never be considered 'straightforward'. Considering it so leads to situations in which former care workers are judged against a class of act—that is, child abuse—that did not exist in policy for most of the period being investigated. This raises the distinct possibility that former care workers may be convicted for practices of care considered commonplace in the 1960s and 1970s, but which, judged by the standards of another day, are cast in a sinister hue by those intent on proving abuse. This in turn raises questions of retrospective justice, contrary to principles of human rights.

I now turn to a basic epistemological problem at the root of responses to historical allegations of abuse: the fact that prosecutions are based upon a naive realist paradigm, whereby reported accounts of abuse are assumed to accurately mirror the way of things in real life. There is no blood on the floor in such cases, no forensic evidence, and generally no independent witness statements; there are only personal accounts. In fact, other sources of evidence often give a different picture of events. A Swedish study, for example, notes that documentary records reflect different perspectives on an individual's history to the story that he or she may tell (Sköld, Foberg, and Hedström, 2012). One is entitled to wonder whether writers of records across all state institutions could have the foresight to exclude references to abuse, lest it raise its head thirty or forty years down the line. It ought to be considered that perhaps there are no references to abuse not because there was some elaborate cover-up, but because there was no evidence of it being a major problem.

Yet 'victim' accounts trump any other source of evidence; they are afforded a privileged—almost a sacred—status, certainly not to be doubted. The Scottish TTBH initiative highlights this state of affairs, noting that it aimed to 'hear such accounts in an atmosphere of supportive non-judgemental acceptance.... Our intention was to hear their accounts and not interrogate or question in any way other than to obtain clarification where necessary' (Shaw, 2011: 83). Thus, when a former resident said that he or she had been abused, then he or she had been. Yet the literature from a whole range of disciplines cautions against such literal acceptance of people's stories. People tell stories for a whole range of reasons: '[G]enuine misunderstandings occur (not only on the part of young people) and displaced cries for help will sometimes be made. On occasion though, pupils can exact revenge, gain a sense of power and importance, or simply create some excitement' (Sikes and Piper, 2006). Recognising this multiplicity of reasons for telling stories, Riessman and Quinney (2005: 393) caution that situations in which 'a story seems to speak for itself, not requiring interpretation—[is] an indefensible position for serious scholarship'. Yet this is the situation that we have reached in relation to allegations of historical abuse. One might imagine that when some semblance of perspective returns to this issue, as surely it must, then this facile acceptance of people's stories as providing a mirror to reality will be the undoing of the entire edifice that has built up around it.

IMAGINING EVIL

The explanations for the scale and nature of what has happened to residential care workers proffered above remain in the realms of the rational; they are at least open to debate or falsification. But they come together to feed into wider social forces that are far from rational. To understand what has happened and is happening in such cases requires anyone engaging in serious analysis of this issue to look for explanations in the deeper reaches of the human psyche.

Some of what is going on has to do with our ambivalent relationships with children. The very idea of protecting children seems to appeal to a deep-seated human need to reclaim and safeguard a state of childhood innocence (Gittins, 1997). This need to protect is linked to an equally primitive tendency to perceive children as being prey to 'evil' threats (Frankfurter, 2006). And, of course, the prospect of brutes in the employ of the state exploiting vulnerable children constitutes an inversion of our very notion of what care should be like. As a result, it is a story that pushes our buttons. But it is a story—a story based around an idea of evil and the need to root it out. As a wider social phenomenon, historical abuse is a myth—less a crime than a state of mind (Frankfurter, 2006).

A search for evil leads to witch hunts. What has happened in respect of care homes in recent decades has roots in the same need within the human condition for demonological fantasy that fuelled the literal witch hunts of medieval times. Now, it is a secularized version driven not by the Church, but by the media, the political establishment its high priests and custodians of morality. As Webster (2005: 1) notes:

> The widespread belief that, belonging as we do to a rational, scientific age, we are no longer vulnerable to such fantasies is itself one of the most dangerous of all our delusions. For it is precisely because of our rationalism, and the difficulty we have in acknowledging our own violence and the full depth and complexity of our sexual imagination, that we are probably more susceptible to dangerous projections than we ever have been.

Features of historical witch hunts included a belief in the supernatural powers of witches and a tendency to readily accept bizarre accounts of events. This was used to justify dispensing with normal rules of prosecution (Beckett, 2002). Witchcraft was considered *crimen exceptum*—that is, an exceptional crime demanding that normal evidential safeguards against wrongful prosecutions be dispensed with. The witch-hunt metaphor, in the context of allegations of satanic ritual abuse, is captured by the Broxtowe Joint Enquiry Team (Nottinghamshire County Council, 1990: Conclusions), which investigated the management of such a case in Nottinghamshire: 'All the elements appear to us to be present; rigid pre-conceived ideas, dubious investigative techniques, the unwillingness to check basic facts, the readiness to believe anything however bizarre.' The same dynamic is all too evident in the way in which the persecution of care workers has proceeded. The readiness to believe or not to question allegations of abuse is manifest in some bizarre examples. The Bryn Estyn case evokes pictures of adolescent boys being launched over goalposts, of a boy having a boat hook inserted into his backside—a feat that Webster (2005) discounts as medically impossible—and of instances of buggery casually perpetrated as boys walked from one room to another.

Another case reportedly about an Irish-approved school and recounted in a press interview with Peter Mullan, director of the film *The Magdalene Sisters* (2002), tells of boys taken by minibus in the dead of night to a layby, where they were met by a vanload of trainee dentists who proceeded to perform extractions without the benefit of anaesthetic (Gibbons, 2003). In a recent Scottish case, one of the complainers alleged that, as a punishment for absconding, her wrists were tied together with kettle wire over a large pipe running along the ceiling and she was kept in that position, suspended, without her feet touching the ground from one day to the next. A cursory Internet search, however, would identify this description of events as tantamount to crucifixion, which would have killed the person so suspended within hours. All of this is apocalyptic stuff. Yet this latter case was prosecuted by the Scottish Crown Office, which overturned the local Sheriff's original decision to drop the case.

This last point takes me to what is a key feature in such cases: witch hunts, contrary to popular assumption, are not the preserve of the untutored mob, but are invariably fuelled by a cultural elite that 'causes, creates, engineers or orchestrates' moral panics (Goode and Ben-Yehuda, 2010: 62). Quoting de Montesquieu, Webster (2005: 537) notes: 'There is no crueller tyranny than that which is perpetrated under the shield of law and in the name of justice.' The persecution of care workers proceeds under the guise of just such a quest for justice and is often, ironically, based on claims of human rights.

Frankfurter (2006), again, is helpful in elucidating this dynamic. He cautions that 'the real atrocities of history seem to take place *not* in the perverse ceremonies of some evil cult but in the course of purging such cults from the world. Real evil happens when people speak of evil' (Frankfurter, 2006: 12). Kelly (2007: 200) speaks of those accused of child abuse as being 'regarded as the face of evil'. In its pursuit of evil, the state can behave more oppressively than any religious regime, its adherents sustained by what Webster (2005: 64–70) calls a 'psychology of righteousness' every bit as strident and dangerous as erstwhile religious zeal.

The real atrocity in the case of historical abuse in residential care is the overzealous persecution of residential care workers. Those prosecuted and convicted of abuse have their lives destroyed, are imprisoned, and are denied access to children and grandchildren, even on release. They are confronted with yet further hurdles on release in terms of things that one might not think of, such as being denied household insurance. Those against whom allegations are made, but not pursued through the courts, are not off the hook either. Even when cases against them lack any foundation, they too may find themselves caught up in child protection procedures, with implications for contact with children. The fact that they have been investigated at all will show up in police records and will impact on employment prospects. They may well find themselves on lists of those deemed unsuitable to work with children. As Webster (2005) asserts, we thus compound lack of gratitude to residential workers by demonizing them.

This is a story that cannot be left as a simple morality tale—of good rooting out evil. Such a one-dimensional understanding amounts to 'intellectual laziness, shutting off inquiry and the proper search for context' (Frankfurter, 2006: 11–12). This is a matter on which '[n]ew thinking is urgently required' (Keenan, 2009: 219). When this particular episode in our cultural history and when a more rounded story of residential care comes to be told, the work of Richard Webster (1950–2011) will be recognized as the tour de force that it is. This chapter owes a debt of gratitude to Richard and his work.

REFERENCES

Barlow, M., and Newby, M. (2009) 'The Challenges of Historic Allegations: The Way Ahead', Paper presented to the Conference on the Challenges of Historic Allegations, Garden Court North Chambers, Manchester, 16 February. Available online at <https://justicebox.files.wordpress.com/2011/01/mark-barlow-and-mark-newby-the-challenges-of-historic-allegations-of-past-sexual-abuse-16-02-2009.pdf> [accessed December 2015].

Beckett, C. (2002) 'The Witch-Hunt Metaphor (and Accusations against Residential Care Workers)', *British Journal of Social Work*, 32(5): 621–8.

Butler, I., and Drakeford, M. (2005) *Scandal, Social Policy and Social Welfare*, Bristol: Policy Press.

Corby, B., Doig, A., and Roberts, V. (2001) *Public Inquiries into the Abuse of Children in Residential Care*, London: Jessica Kingsley.

Cree, V., Clapton, G., and Smith, M. (eds) (2015) *Revisiting Moral Panics*, Bristol: Policy Press.

Frankfurter, D. (2006) *Evil Incarnate: Rumors of Demonic Conspiracy and Satanic Abuse in History*, Princeton, NJ: Princeton University Press.

Furedi, F. (2007) 'Bad Ideas: Denial', *Spiked Online*, 31 January. Available online at <http://www.spiked-online.com/newsite/article/2792#.UurFbnd_uaQ> [accessed May 2016].

Furedi, F. (2013) *Moral Crusades in an Age of Mistrust: The Jimmy Savile Scandal*, Basingstoke: Palgrave Macmillan.

Gibbons, F. (2003) 'In God's Name', *The Guardian*, 7 February. Available online at <http://www.theguardian.com/culture/2003/feb/07/artsfeatures> [accessed May 2016].

GITTINS, D. (1997) *The Child in Question*, Basingstoke: MacMillan.

GOODE, E., and BEN-YEHUDA, N. (2010) *Moral Panics: The Social Construction of Deviance*, 2nd edn, Chichester: John Wiley & Sons.

GROMETSTEIN, R. (2008) 'Wrongful Conviction and Moral Panic: National and International Perspectives on Organised Child Sexual Abuse', in C. R. Huff and M. Killias (eds) *Wrongful Conviction: International Perspectives on Miscarriages of Justice*, Philadelphia, PA: Temple University Press.

GUNN, B. (2013) 'The Compensation Carrot and False Allegations of Abuse', *FACTion*, 4(1): 10–12.

HACKING, I. (1992) 'World-making by Kind-making: Child Abuse for Example', in M. Douglas and D. Hull (eds) *How Classification Works: Nelson Goodman among the Social Sciences*, Edinburgh: Edinburgh University Press.

HACKING, I. (1995) *Rewriting the Soul: Multiple Personality and the Sciences of Memory*, Princeton, NJ: Princeton University Press.

Home Affairs Select Committee (2002) *The Conduct of Investigations into Past Cases of Abuse in Children's Homes: Fourth Report of Session 2001–02*, London: HMSO. Available online at <http://www.publications.parliament.uk/pa/cm200102/cmselect/cmhaff/836/83603.htm> [accessed November 2014].

KAUFMAN, F. (2002) *Searching for Justice: An Independent Review of Nova Scotia's Response to Reports of Institutional Abuse*, Halifax: Nova Scotia Department of Justice. Available online at <http://novascotia.ca/just/kaufmanreport/fullreport.pdf> [accessed November 2014].

KEENAN, M. (2009) '"Them and Us": The Clergy Child Sexual Abuser as "Other"', in T Flannery (ed.) *Responding to the Ryan Report*, Blackrock: Columba Press.

KELLY, H. (2007) *Kathy's Real Story: A Culture of False Allegations Exposed*, Dunleer: Prefect Press.

LA FONTAINE, J. (1994) *The Extent and Nature of Organised and Ritual Abuse*, London: HMSO.

LEVITT, A. (2013) *In the Matter of the Late Jimmy Savile: Report to the Director of Public Prosecutions*. Available online at <http://www.cps.gov.uk/news/assets/uploads/files/savile_report.pdf> [accessed May 2016].

NAUGHTON, M. (2005) '"Evidence-based Policy" and the Government of the Criminal Justice System: Only If the Evidence Fits!', *Critical Social Policy*, 25(1): 47–69.

NAUGHTON, M. (2013) *The Innocent and the Criminal Justice System*, Basingstoke: Palgrave Macmillan.

Nottinghamshire County Council (1990) *Report of the Joint Enquiry Team on the Broxtowe Case* (The 'Jet Report' and the 'Broxtowe Files'). Available online at <http://www.users.globalnet.co.uk/~dlheb/jetrepor.htm> [accessed November 2014].

PRIOR, L. (2004) 'Doing Things with Documents', in D. Silverman (ed.) *Qualitative Research: Theory, Method and Practice*, London: Sage.

RADSTONE, S. (2005) 'Reconceiving Binaries: The Limits of Memory', *History Workshop Journal*, 59(1): 134–50.

RIESSMAN, C. K., and QUINNEY, L. (2005) 'Narrative in Social Work: A Critical Review', *Qualitative Social Work*, 4(4): 391–411.

Scottish Office (1998).

SEN, R., KENDRICK, A., MILLIGAN, I., and HAWTHORN, M. (2008) 'Lessons learnt? Abuse in residential child care in Scotland', *Child & Family Social Work*, 13(4): 411–22.

SHAW, T. (2011) *Time to be Heard: A Pilot Forum*, Edinburgh: Scottish Government.

SIKES, P. and PIPER, H. (2006) 'True stories? Dilemmas in research into "false" allegations of sexual misconduct', Paper presented to British Educational Research Conference, University of Warwick.

SIKES, P., and PIPER, H. (2010) *Researching Sex and Lies in the Classroom: Allegations of Sexual Misconduct in Schools*, London, Routledge/Falmer.

SKÖLD, J., FOBERG, E., and HEDSTRÖM, J. (2012) 'Conflicting or Complementing Narratives? Interviewees' Stories Compared to Their Documentary Records in the Swedish Commission to Inquire into Child Abuse and Neglect in Institutions and Foster Homes', *Archives and Manuscripts*, 40(1): 15–28.

SMITH, M. (2010) 'Victim Narratives of Historical Abuse in Residential Child Care: Do We Really Know What We Think We Know?', *Qualitative Social Work*, 9(3): 303–20.

WATERHOUSE, R. (2000) *Lost in Care*, London: HMSO.

WEBSTER, R. (2005) *The Secret of Bryn Estyn,* Oxford: The Orwell Press.

WOLMAR, C. (2005) 'Review of *The Secret of Bryn Estyn*', *The Oldie*, 1 May. Available online at <http://www.christianwolmar.co.uk/2005/05/the-secret-of-bryn-estyn-the-making-of-a-modern-witch-hunt/> [accessed November 2014].

6

'RAPE CULTURE' NARRATIVE, STATE FEMINISM, AND THE PRESUMPTION OF GUILT

John Brigham

This chapter examines the background and influence of feminist conceptions of society as 'rape culture', and the extent to which this perspective has been taken up politically and has been the basis for civil and criminal justice responses to allegations of sexual assault. The focus is the United States, where, since the 1990s, 'rape culture' ideology has been incorporated into legislation and state policy. While concern about the extent of rape and violence against women has undoubtedly been reflected in criminal justice and policy developments in other countries, in prosecutors' offices in the United States and, very prominently, across college campuses, belief that male sexual aggression and rape of females is endemic has become legal orthodoxy. The following discusses the emergence of feminist arguments that rape and male sexual aggression are instrumental to male privilege and the subordination of females in patriarchal societies. It considers how this radical belief has become normalized and has transformed a feminism of equality, and has created the conditions in which allegations of sexual abuse can be presumed to be true and penalized without the safeguards of due process. The chapter draws on critiques of rape culture narrative, and argues that the conversion of rape culture ideology into state policy and legislation too readily criminalizes male heterosexuality and also undermines the pursuit of equality that was once a hallmark of feminism.[1]

The notion of rape culture was introduced by a faction of 1970s feminism that embraced Susan Brownmiller's 1975 volume, *Against Our Will: Men, Women, and Rape*, which held that the status of men derives from the power to rape. Developed by Andrea Dworkin (1981, 1987), Catharine MacKinnon (1987), and others, this conception of male–female relationships, and of female victimization and disempowerment, underlies broader conceptions of rape culture that have significantly influenced policy. The doctrine that

---

[1] This chapter builds on papers presented at the New England Political Science Conference, Hartford, CT, 30 April 2011, and the Conference on Feminism and the State, Ohio University, Athens, OH, 20–22 May 2011. Meg Mott, Charles DiMare, Howard Rubinstein, and Susan Ball offered critical commentary.

we live in a culture that excuses male sexual aggression while blaming victims was incorporated into law some twenty years later in the US Violence Against Women Act of 1994 (VAWA). This legislation is a version of 'state feminism' (MacKinnon, 1987) in that it operates through prosecutors' offices, victim advocates, and federally funded rape crisis centres. In the United States, the federal adoption of rape culture ideology into legislation, as well as zealous policies to deal with alleged rape in campus tribunals without due process of law, are part of an unusual propensity to criminalize social problems such as young people's substance abuse and antisocial behaviour.

Rape culture narrative has developed into a more politicized feminist critique of heterosexual relations in westernized societies in which the central tenets are that 'rape myths are pervasive, women are frequently sexually objectified, and sexual aggression and violence towards women is legitimized by the media' (Hildebrand and Najdowski, 2014: 1085). Sexual violence towards women, men, and children is abhorrent and needs to be countered by the full force of the law, but the concern of this chapter is that perceptions of men as rapists and women as their victims have led to civil procedures and legislation that promulgate inaccurate, scaremongering statistics (Sommers, 1995; Yoffe, 2014), and which err towards presuming all men are sexual predators and dangerous rapists, while removing responsibility and agency from women who engage in sexual interactions. This applies particularly to campus rape tribunals across the United States, but parallel developments have taken place in other English-speaking common law countries.

RAPE CULTURE AS NATIONAL POLICY

The elevation of the 'rape culture' meme from the fringes of feminism to a central premise for national policy is a remarkable story. It has three main elements: the idea itself, its institutionalization in VAWA, and the muted reaction. This story has qualities that are distinct dimensions of policy in the United States, but there are clear international implications—some connected to the United States and others part of larger cultural trends.

ORIGINS

Susan Brownmiller offered a feminist critique of rape in the 1970s. Her book *Against Our Will: Men, Women, and Rape* described 'woman's structural vulnerability to rape' (Brownmiller, 1975: 4). She argued that American culture and law condoned rape, which was a mechanism by which 'all men keep all women in a state of fear' (Brownmiller, 1975: 15).[2] The critique was provocative when it was first introduced, but it once represented only a fringe of second-wave feminism—albeit a fringe with a strong presence in the academy. The practical dimensions of economic equality and shared domestic responsibility made the idea of a rape culture seem peripheral to

---

[2] See also Mary Daly on rape (Hoagland and Frye, 2000: 215).

many feminists when it was proposed.[3] And, for some, the idea of a rape culture verged on racism, because of the ways in which racial stereotypes regarding rape have been used to buttress state power (Lee, 1960; Davis, 1981; Taylor and Johnson, 2007).

Male violence became more central to feminism in the United States in the late 1970s, with the critique of pornography and the successful interpretation of sexual harassment as sex discrimination. The work of Catharine MacKinnon (1979; Siegel and MacKinnon, 2004) linked male power to sexual harassment and the sex wars of the 1980s. Susan Estrich's 1986 book, *Real Rape*, refined the anti-rape position with regard to an important kind of sexual discord, particularly on college campuses—that is, 'date or acquaintance rape'—which she treated as 'real rape'.[4] Those who advance the idea of a rape culture hold that rape is an accepted reality and they deny meaningful distinctions between kinds of unwanted sexual contact. For MacKinnon (1987: 82), famously, 'rape is whenever a woman has sex and feels violated'. The extent to which this ideology has become law is dramatic in the United States.

NATIONAL LEGISLATION

Activists drove the rape culture paradigm, along with enthusiastic scholarly interest (Patai and Koertge, 1994; Merry, 2001), towards a culture of punishment and federal legislation such as VAWA. President Bill Clinton signed VAWA into law in 1994, following months of hearings and the sense that violence against women was a growing problem. The justification for the legislation was data reiterated at Congressional hearings, such as the often-repeated assertion that one in four women will be sexually assaulted during college. Among other things, VAWA provides US$1.6–1.8 billion annually for programmes supporting prosecution of sexual assault and domestic violence.[5] Senator Joe Biden supported the original legislation as chair of the Senate Judiciary Committee[6] and supported its 2013 reauthorization as vice president. Support for the legislation ranged from feminist groups such as the National Organization for Women (NOW) to the American Bar Association (ABA) and various law enforcement associations and institutes such as the National Institute of Justice (NIJ).

In the United States, the same statistics are often presented without analysis or critique. In 2010, a spokesperson stated on the White House blog that '[t]hree women still die every day at the hands of husbands and boyfriends' (Rosenthal, 2010), yet the National Crime Victimization Study shows that the incidence of rape has gone down in the last forty years (Pinker, 2011; Catalano, 2013). Although the rape culture idea

---

[3] The term 'rape culture' was also used as the title of a 1975 documentary by Margaret Lazarus and Renner Wunderlich, but the film's focus was much more limited.

[4] This chapter challenges the claim that men rely on rape for their power or that sexual assault in circumstances in which two people have been intimate (i.e. 'date rape' or 'acquaintance rape') is the same as sexual assault by a stranger.

[5] See the US Department of Justice Office on Violence against Women (OVW) Grant Awards Program, online at <http://www.ovw.usdoj.gov/fy2013-grant-program.htm>. The grants range from US$31 million for grants to encourage arrest to $200,000 for training court officers to process sexual assault and rape cases.

[6] Victoria Nourse, Senate Judiciary Committee counsel, and NOW Legal Defence and Education Fund (NOW LDEF) staff attorneys are described as 'lending lobbying expertise' (Shattered Men, undated, <http://www.shatterdmen.com/VAWA%20too.htm>, accessed May 2016).

stands on a weak empirical foundation, particularly in the United States, where the same statistics are often presented without analysis or critique, nevertheless the rape culture ideology in the United States is immune to the critique of its statistics and it has fuelled a 'moral panic' (Rubin, 1984; Goode and Ben-Yehuda, 1994) that finds expression in current crusades against rape in the military and on college campuses.

Under VAWA, the US government supports the rape culture paradigm with $2 billion a year in anti-rape and domestic violence funding.[7] Highly ideological data justified an alliance of radical feminism and state power, which defined male violence as a major social problem. The result is often a denial of due process for men and a lack of agency for women, particularly on college campuses where the culture of due process is weak and women are strong. Thus the rape culture ideology as government policy is evident in institutions, prosecutions, and the distribution of federal funds through grants to local agencies. Through these agencies, VAWA has legitimated positions once associated mainly with a radical fringe of a much more widespread and broad-based women's movement. These views now represent state policy.

In *United States v. Morrison* (2000),[8] the US Supreme Court held part of VAWA to be unconstitutional. The case stems from an incident at Virginia Tech. Freshman Christy Brzonkala charged two members of the football team with rape. Antonio J. Morrison (who is black[9]) admitted having sex with her, but contended that it was consensual.[10] Initially suspended, his punishment was rescinded by the administration. Brzonkala sued under VAWA's provisions for a private 'civil' remedy from the federal courts. The case went to the Supreme Court. Julie Goldscheid and Seth Waxman for the Attorney General's Office represented the United States; Michael Rosman of the Center for Individual Rights represented Antonio Morrison.

The justices decided in favour of Morrison, Chief Justice William Rehnquist writing the majority opinion and emphasizing the dual system of government in the United States where both national and local governments have made criminal law. Various newspapers and conservative pundits, including the *Washington Post* (2000), held that the Court 'got it right', and that federalizing rape and sexual assault would mean that anything could be subject to Congressional action. But, in the end, the rape culture paradigm flourished. As important as the Supreme Court's opinion was, the data it repeated established the presence of a rape culture as a fact of American life.

In 2013, VAWA was reauthorized after twenty years. It had strong institutional support, but had met with some conservative resistance when it was considered for reauthorization. Some of this resistance had been in response to extensions of protection to immigrants and Native Americans; some may have been a response to the Left's characterization of conservatives as conducting a 'war on women'. Under the influence of state feminism, VAWA was amended and reauthorized as the Violence against Women Reauthorization Act of 2013 (VAWA 2013).

---

[7] See the US Department of Justice Office on Violence against Women (OVW) Grant Awards Program, online at <http://www.ovw.usdoj.gov/fy2013-grant-program.htm>.

[8] *United States v. Morrison*, 529 U.S. 598 (2000).

[9] Noted because race is still a factor in rape prosecutions, although the doctrine of colour blindness works against acknowledging it.

[10] The Wiki and most VAWA commentary say that she was raped, although there was no criminal indictment.

INTERNATIONAL IMPLICATIONS

Significant comparative analysis is beyond the scope of this chapter,[11] but countries other than the United States are redefining the scope of what can be treated as sexual crimes. The rhetoric in Australia matches that of the United States: under former Prime Minister Julia Gillard, governments proposed a twelve-year plan to end sexual violence.[12] In Canada, anti-violence efforts, even among women's groups, show more concern about both sexes than is the case in the United States.[13] In the UK, work by groups such as End Violence Against Women incorporates an international focus more consistently than is the case in the United States today.[14] And in all common law countries, protection orders, victim advocates, specialized courts, special evidentiary rules, mandatory arrests, and 'no drop' policies have been introduced.

However, official support for the notion that we live in a rape culture seems to be a distinctively US propensity. The war has VAWA as its front line and primary source of funds. And when other countries are mentioned in the United States, as has been the case regarding sexual violence in India and in the combat zones of the Middle East, it is to shore up the argument of a rape culture where evidence is questioned in the United States.

The paradigm also has international implications, such as when sexual assault became the basis on which Sweden sought extradition of Julian Assange, founder of WikiLeaks, and Dominique Strauss-Kahn, former director of the International Monetary Fund (IMF), who was arrested and charged with rape in New York City. In both cases, the allegations of sexual assault or rape amplified the power wielded by the state.

RAPE ALLEGATIONS, TRIALS, AND DUE PROCESS

In the United States, the critique of how women were treated in rape prosecutions prior to the mid-twentieth century produced reforms such as rape shield laws, which protect against an alleged victim's sexual history or reputation being used as a defence against a rape charge.[15] Today, reports on crime regularly protect the anonymity of the person bringing a rape charge while identifying the accused. When rape was a capital crime, conviction was more difficult: corroboration was often required. Today, the definition of rape has been broadened: it is often used interchangeably with 'sexual assault' and legal definitions vary from state to state. Confusion over what is meant by 'rape' is confounded by changing notions of what is meant by 'consent' and how it is to be determined.[16] The impact of rape shield laws on the defence against a rape charge

---

[11] See the new UK guidelines for prosecuting and sentencing sexual offences.
[12] Gillard left office after three years.
[13] Act to End Violence Against Women, online at <http://www.acttoendvaw.org/>, is a group that spun off from the Jewish B'nai Brith in Canada in autumn 2011. See also Canadian Women's Foundation (undated).
[14] See <http://www.endviolenceagainstwomen.org.uk/campaigns>
[15] See article by Julie Stubbs (2007), which reiterates feminist criticism of legal policy.
[16] See RAINN (2009).

was raised in the Supreme Court of Canada, but was dismissed.[17] Today, sexual assault cases in the United States are pursued in the interest of combating a rape culture. Due process values such as the presumption of innocence, the opportunity to respond to witnesses, the notion of an impartial tribunal, and the conception of punishment are often sacrificed.

One of the challenges for due process is to ensure that verdicts are not influenced by gender (or race, or a function of wealth) and that guilt or innocence is determined on an individual basis. This position has foundations in the English common law and in the Fifth, Sixth, and Fourteenth Amendments to the US Constitution, which the Supreme Court discussed in *Coffin v. United States* (1895).[18] The arising legal principles place the burden of proof on the prosecution and include the defendant's right to question his or her accuser. In spite of the cries from some that providing due process amounts to 'victim bashing', essential protections of defendants' rights, such as the right to cross-examine a complainant, need to be affirmed and played out rather than sacrificed or compromised by assumptions about the victim status of accusers.

The confrontation clause in the Sixth Amendment to the US Constitution is one of the challenges for sexual assault prosecution. Chief Justice John Marshall proposed, regarding the confrontation clause, that he knew of no principle 'by undermining which, life, liberty and property, might be more endangered'.[19] In sexual cases, the ideal of confrontation is often challenged both in the United States[20] and in other jurisdictions. The justification is often that the accuser (who is generally referred to as the 'victim' here) has suffered enough or is too vulnerable to face the one whom she has accused.

Another due process provision is the idea that those sitting in judgment should be impartial and that institutions of the state need to be alert for bias or signs thereof.[21] However, the rape culture idea, given expression in the provisions of VAWA, challenges the institutional requirement for an impartial judge or jury. This is especially true on American college campuses where the standard for guilt in campus disciplinary hearings has become the 'preponderance of the evidence' or '50 per cent plus one'. The strong belief in male violence justifies this standard and compromises impartiality in exactly the places where it needs to be nurtured. In addition, the serious collateral consequences of rape charges can add potential bias to any prosecution. In a world that has become more partisan on sexual violence, the standard of impartiality is under pressure.

Enlightened punishment is also a casualty of rape culture. Moral panics put pressure on the fairness with which punishment is meted out. When crimes are considered monstrous, moderation and enlightened punishment may disappear. Rape was once a capital crime; the US Supreme Court declared execution for rape unconstitutional in 1977. Although it is rarely a capital crime anymore, it still carries special meaning. In the case of campus disciplinary proceedings for sexual misconduct, it is often argued that the sanctions faced by men are not of much consequence because

---

[17] *R v. Darrach* [2000] 2 SCR 443, 2000 SCC 46.
[18] *Coffin v. United States*, 156 U.S. 432 (1895).
[19] *United States v. Burr*, 25 F. Cas. 55, 000 (CCD Va 1807).
[20] *Bell v. Harrison*, 670 F.2d 656 (6th Cir. 1982).
[21] *Gonzales v. Beto*, 405 U.S. 1052 (1972).

they do not involve incarceration. However, the consequences of campus discipline, which may include suspension and being barred from campus, can have greater or equal consequences to some criminal sanctions on the lives of college men.

COLLEGE CAMPUSES: A SPECIAL CASE

Colleges are the epicentre of the rape culture ideology and have recently become a special focus of national policy in the United States. This was exemplified by President Barack Obama's January 2014 announcement of a presidential focus on the problem of sexual victimization in American colleges. Of course, colleges are a special place for examining the generation and reception of ideas about fairness and equality whether in matters of scholarship or sexuality. For the last twenty years, young men across campuses in the United States have been suspended or expelled for having sexual intercourse. Sometimes, it is forced, non-consensual sex. Sometimes, it is sex between students too drunk to consent. But, sometimes, it is a 'hook-up gone wrong', involving poor judgement or miscommunication, and at the opposite end of the spectrum of rape behaviours from what was traditionally called rape.

The statistic that one in four females experience rape or attempted rape from the age of 14 is repeated often in the context of policies to address the victimization of female students and to support polices that prioritize support for presumed victims over due process protections for accused male students, who can be expelled and denied the opportunity for legal representation. The figure is based on the 1987 study by Mary Koss and colleagues (Koss, Gidycz, and Wisniewski, 1987). On the website One in Four,[22] we find the statistic being used as part of recruitment to a 'men's group'. The 'one in four' claim was restated by Robin Warsaw (1994) in her book, *I Never Called It Rape*, together with the statistic that 84 per cent of all rapists know their victim. Koss and Warsaw's claims are part of a litany of statistics offered in support of rape culture claims. Another is that a third of high school relationships include battering or rape (Creighton and Kivel, 2011). More recently, a 'one in five' statistic has been substituted for the 'one in four', but this newer statistic is drawn from misleading headlines in media reports about a survey by the Association of American Universities (Cantor et al., 2015). The survey itself was more differentiated and complex, and did not make such a claim.

High-profile cases have fuelled the rape culture ideology. In 2003, a woman accused five lacrosse players at Duke University of rape. The public response supported the accuser. Commentators on campus and across the United States decried male violence, the violence of lacrosse players, and a culture of rape on campus. And while a defence costing millions of dollars showed that evidence had been manipulated by the prosecutor, leading to his disbarment and legal settlements for the Duke players (Taylor and Johnson, 2007), the rape culture ideology continued to thrive. In autumn 2010, Nancy Thompson, Dean of Students at Hamilton College, in rural New York State, mandated that male first-year students attend a lecture on the rape culture entitled

---

[22] Online at <http://www.oneinfourusa.org/>

'She Fears You', given by Keith Edwards, a leader in the 'pro-feminist men's movement' (Katz, 2006). Some feminists at Hamilton and around the country condemned the use of the college's authority to impose this point of view about men, and the talk was challenged by the Foundation for Individual Rights in Education (FIRE),[23] a group interested in First Amendment and due process issues on campus. Although the lecture was ultimately not mandatory, critical commentary remains minimal and Thompson is still dean at Hamilton.

Higher education institutions constitute a 'perfect storm' of forces fostering an uncritical and repressive approach to sexual misconduct. These include concern about lawsuits and publicity, the professionalization of student services, and a monoculture when it comes to certain public policy considerations. The online journal *Inside Higher Education* regularly reports on campus sexual violence prosecutions. Each story begins with the puzzling assertion that no one pays attention to sexual violence on campus. On 23 March 2011, the journal featured a sound clip on campus violence by Michele Paludi, one of the authors of the book *Sexual Harassment, Work and Education* (Paludi and Barickman, 1998).[24] Paludi argued that campuses had become more violent and that measures needed to be taken. In 2014, the same argument was made on the front page of *The New York Times* in an article about Hobart and William Smith College, which is in New York (Bogdanich, 2014).[25] In response, a number of groups advocating traditional civil rights are becoming more prominent, such as FIRE and Stop Abusive and Violent Environments (SAVE).[26]

Although *in loco parentis* was officially abandoned at American colleges in the 1960s, policing student conduct has brought university administration back into significant law enforcement roles. Recently, in the United States, the concern about student conduct has provided the basis for aggressive prosecution of sexual activity. There can be no doubt that some students do commit acts of sexual violence causing harm to victims and that this is a serious matter requiring the full weight of the law. For student affairs administrators and faculty members responding to an upset student claiming that she was raped, attention to due process issues may add to the confusion. In that environment, it is easy to see how a presumption of guilt may be made from the outset and how a victim-centred approach would then override the presumption of innocence and right to a fair trial that are the bedrock of due process.

Determining whether illegal and punishable acts have been committed, however, is not straightforward when the parties disagree about what occurred. Sex among young people may involve confusion and lack of clarity over consent, especially when alcohol or drugs have been imbibed. It may involve incivility, insensitivity, and offence. It quite often involves misunderstandings and less-than-ideal communication. In the intoxicating mix of romantic, sexual, and music- or alcohol-fuelled feelings, it is inevitable that people occasionally mistake the other's intentions and overstep the mark. It

---

[23] Online at <https://www.thefire.org>
[24] For the sound clip, see online at <https://www.insidehighered.com/audio/academic_pulse/campus_violence>
[25] See the response by Hobart and William Smith President, Mark Gearan (2014).
[26] Online at <http://www.saveservices.org>

is a moot point whether the party who took the initiative should then be treated as a rapist or sexual offender.

MEN, WOMEN, AND RAPE

Much of criminal law is about the violence that men do. Most of this violence is directed at other men, but a significant amount is directed at women. The violence of sexual assault and rape is being reinterpreted both as administrative and as criminal process. The current understanding that the violence of rape is about power changes the way in which that violence is understood. It takes the sex out of an equation that is all about sex even if it is about power. In the past, when rape was associated with sexual desire, it was regarded as an aberration.[27] Treating it as an essential feature of male power increases fear of rape and belief in its pervasiveness. Statutorily, VAWA made the claim for the pervasive threat of violence to women. The US Jeanne Clery Disclosure of Campus Security Policy and Campus Crime Statistics Act of 1990 (the Clery Act), named for a young woman who was raped and killed in her dorm room, chronicles that claim on campus.[28] Perception of rape as normal male behaviour changes the nature of male–female relationships.

THE CAMPAIGN AND MEN

The difference between the current rape culture idea and traditional conceptions of men who rape and how they should be tried in order to receive justice[29] is the conception of rape and rapists as unexceptional—even normal. This new perspective was codified in VAWA. The impact of this reconceptualization is that, for nearly a generation, men accused of sexual misconduct have been readily described as rapists, particularly on college campuses, without the opportunity to defend themselves according to the rule of law. In spring 2014, on national television, prominent US Senator Kristin Gillibrand described a male student at Brown University as a rapist when he had settled an accusation with the university by agreeing to a finding of sexual misconduct. Rape claims are also seen in divorce and child custody hearings. And there are charges in the context of college, in classes and in residence halls, as well as off campus.

The Violence Against Women Act supports those who accuse. These are the 'victims', as they are conventionally referred to in the United States. This designation has largely been without controversy. It is widely used in US newspapers with little comment. However, in the late spring of 2014, syndicated columnist George Will was dropped from some newspapers for suggesting that victims of rape have become

---

[27] In 1977, Bonnie Garland was killed with a hammer in her New York home by a former boyfriend and fellow student at Yale. The event was covered by psychiatrist Willard Gaylin, who explored campus sympathy for the killer who was released from prison after serving 17 years (Gaylin, 1982).

[28] A fellow student whom she did not know before he attacked her was convicted and faces the death penalty at time of writing.

[29] *Powell v. Alabama*, 287 U.S. 45 (1932).

heroic figures on American campuses and that the reported '20 per cent assault rate is preposterous' (Will, 2014). While Will is an establishment figure who has dismissed claims of there being an epidemic of sexual assault on campus, the significance of rape culture ideology in higher education and in law enforcement is enough for it to be considered authoritative (Friedersdorf, 2014). Its authority is in the criminal process and in the culture of the academy where it holds sway.[30]

At American colleges and in the criminal process, men's groups address the propensity of men for violence. In adopting the rape culture paradigm, they describe rape as detrimental to men as well as women and they often assert their superior sensitivity relative to other men. Writers such as Jackson Katz, Michael Kimmel, and Don McPherson have said that rape culture 'is intrinsically linked to gender roles that limit male self-expression and cause psychological harm to men' (Katz, 2002). The role of men as ideologues for the rape culture needs to be examined. This is especially true with regard to the appeal of male victims in justifying the rape culture framework.

One of the major instruments in the United States bearing on equality for women in American colleges is Title IX of the Education Amendments Act of 1972. This law is based on the old feminist standard that requires equal treatment of the sexes and is derivative of the equality language in the Civil Rights Act of 1964. In the United States, this has meant more opportunity for women, particularly in athletics. However, rape culture is not an equal opportunity framework: it is about bad men and vulnerable women. Rape culture disempowers women, making them into victims. Unlike the initial efforts of legislation such as Title IX, rape culture creates female victims rather than female athletes or students.

Attention to false rape accusations can sometimes result in charges of 'victim bashing.' Yet there are certainly vivid examples of accusations that turn out to be false. Some months after the Duke rape case was reported, the charges were determined to be groundless and the prosecutor—who, in his zeal to convict the male athletes, violated many laws—was himself ultimately prosecuted. Such men have their lives turned upside down. They are led off in handcuffs. They may be expelled from college, branded as sex offenders. Resistance to rape culture itself can lead to everything from mild hyperbole to vicious character assassination. 'Republicans for Rape', a site that operated in 2012 around the reauthorization of VAWA, was a handsomely produced fake website that depicted Republican senators as supporting rape because they voted against Senator Al Franken's proclaimed anti-rape amendment to the 2010 US Defence Appropriations Bill that would have prevented funds from going to the arms contractor Halliburton.

WOMEN IN LAW

Early critiques of rape prosecution often emphasized the difficulty of convicting the accused in a male-dominated justice system inhospitable to women bringing a charge of rape. These critiques were compelling. Women had to tell their stories of sexual

---

[30] Comparison with the UK in the extent to which it is possible to critique the rape culture paradigm suggests real limitations in the United States (Williams, 2014).

aggression to male police officers and district attorneys. A woman who accused a man of rape would also likely face a male defence attorney eager to place her in a bad light. That is no longer the case—at least to the same degree and particularly in the prosecution of sexual violence. Women now make up a significant part of the professional community prosecuting sex crimes.

Since 1970, the number of women attending law school in the United States grew from low single digits to 48.7 per cent in 2016, with the largest percentage gains coming by 1990 (ABA Commission on Women in the Profession, 2016). This is a significant aspect of how the legal process has changed and an element of feminist success with a bearing on how criminal justice in common law countries treats rape. While they are not equally represented as partners in large law firms, women now play significant roles as victim witness advocates, counsellors, defence attorneys, prosecutors, and judges. In the federal system, 34 per cent of the prosecutors are women (Lochner and Apollonio, 2012). Yet the influence of the increased role of women in criminal prosecution—particularly the prosecution of sexual violence—is rarely discussed in the context of how rape is handled today and neither has it been examined by social scientists.

It was in the period during which women were entering the legal profession in significant numbers that VAWA expanded the prosecution of sexual violence, including, in the United States, the infusion of billions of dollars a year to foster awareness and prosecution of sexual violence. While feminist doctrine regarding rape culture has influenced legal processes more generally and has been adopted by male lawyers to some extent, it would be interesting to discover whether male lawyers are as ready as female lawyers to dismiss some arguments as rape myths (such as that women sometimes lie about rape, that false allegations are common, that real rape involves force). In this author's view, the gender of prosecutors is as relevant to the current responses to rape allegations as was male dominance in the profession to the way in which rape was handled in the past. It seems inevitable that this influx of women into the profession and feminist ideology has impacted on the treatment of both complainants and suspects. As well as the desired objective of deterring sexual assaults and making perpetrators accountable, the extent to which social and sexual male behaviour has now been criminalized, and the impact more generally on heterosexual relationships between students, are among critical questions that merit investigation.

One of the elements described by Julie Stubbs (2007) as 'asymmetrical social relations' is offered as an absolute, rather than a condition, as in: 'Men have more power than women. Men can beat women up.' At the time that the rape culture critique was offered by radical feminists attacking the liberal paradigm, women were a small factor in the legal profession and in legal policymaking. While the demographics of faculties, student affairs administrators, and prosecutors' offices have changed, the critique of a gendered sexual assault has not evolved: 'asymmetrical' relations are posited and prosecutions incorporate that presumption at every level. The potential unfairness of the critique remaining the same, as more women enter prosecutorial positions, may be significant.

In its focus on men, sexual violence is similar to other crimes—particularly crimes of violence—but there is a difference. While the criminal process is meant to separate the (mostly male) guilty from the (mostly male) accused, the special case of sexual violence—especially of the acquaintance kind—is more often meant to distinguish a false from a true claim—that is, it must decide between a man and a woman. Just as there are horrendous crimes of violence against women, there are also false prosecutions.

WOMEN AS CRITICS

In the case of the rape culture posited in prosecutors' offices and on American college campuses from roughly 1990 to the present, a fringe position from second-wave feminism has come to characterize the structure of authority and the official teaching on sexuality. Some critical feminist positions express concern over the perceived vulnerability of women, while also commenting on the demonization of men. For example, Sharon Marcus (1992), in her book *Fighting Bodies, Fighting Words*, presents a feminist perspective of gender relations and sexuality that includes the emergence of women as victims. She argues that women need to be more aggressive in defending themselves against rape and in thinking about sexual violence. In the context of discussion about rape culture in which the penis is represented as a weapon, her analysis calls attention to the insignificance of the penis in a variety of dimensions, but particularly as an instrument of assault and a tool for maintaining gender dominance. This representation of power relations between males and females has implications for how we see rape culture and the state response.

Tracing the development of the feminist movement and its convergence with politics, Aya Gruber (2007) has shown how an assumption of male violence has become national policy in a 'feminist war on crime'. Gruber draws a connection between what she calls sex critical feminism and the police establishment. In her view of this movement, 'the victim is a foil, a tool of an even larger and more dangerous program of vigorous individuality and denial of social responsibility' (Gruber, 2007: 750). She also distinguishes between the liberal feminist movement for equality, which has minimal association with the criminal justice system, and the 'war on crime', which connects feminists to a criminal justice system that, in many respects, reifies patriarchy.

Under institutional mechanisms and criminal justice processes driven by the ideology of rape culture, there is little public support for those who are accused. While pro bono representation is available in criminal trials, a full-blown defence can cost up to $3 million.[31] And, as already mentioned, support for those who claim they are being falsely accused is seen in many circles as a further assault on the victim.

Yet there has been a rise in groups responding to accusations that they believe to be false. By no means confined to men's groups, many are made up of sisters, girlfriends, and mothers, as well as men. Groups such as The False Rape Society,[32] the Community of the Wrongly Accused (COTWA),[33] and SAVE support the accused through the legal process and via information on social media. The group Families Advocating for

---

[31] A conservative estimate of the *Duke Lacrosse* rape defence.
[32] Online at <http://falserapesociety.blogspot.com>   [33] Online at <http://www.cotwa.info>

Campus Equality (FACE),[34] focuses on campus discipline policies. Its founders have sons who were disciplined and then exonerated. The group is positioned to avoid being called reactionary, with pleas from mothers of falsely accused sons and a feminist message of equality and fair treatment at the forefront of its material.

Some say that wrongful prosecutions are the price a society has to pay to make women safe; others, that perhaps it is payback for a balance in rape prosecution that once tipped the other way. And it is common to hear that rape is a social problem and a policy challenge that deserves extraordinary measures. But, at present, there is too much of the view that men rape with impunity and benefit from a rape culture for this to be a sound foundation for sexual relations or equality between the sexes.

CONCLUSION

Concurrent with President Obama, who, in a White House memorandum, was still citing the discredited alarmist statistic that 'about one in five women is a survivor of attempted or completed sexual violence while in college' (Obama, 2014), outspoken senators, local prosecutors, and educational institutions adopting the rape culture idea have done little to enhance social and interpersonal relations between the sexes. The irony of state intervention to protect women is that it has detracted from the autonomy and freedoms of women. In cities across the country, women have lost a voice in their relations with men; in college, women are treated as hapless victims in an alcohol-fuelled subculture understood as a male creation. A culture of fear and loathing is not one that is conducive to healthy interpersonal and sexual relations. Such a climate in college will not foster the kind of exploration and experimentation that accompanied the sexual revolution or which might be considered part of growing up. Sex is an area in which there is not much history of successful state intervention, but in prosecutors' offices, whether local or on campus, legal bureaucrats profess to know 'what's best' for women.

The current campaign against sexual violence is doing very little to foster enlightened social and sexual relations. While lip service is paid to equality in federal legislation such as Title IX, the implementation of rape culture guidelines from the federal government puts men at a distinct disadvantage. And while the promise of due process was once a way in which to combat prejudice, racism, and inequality, it is now often ignored in instances in which men are charged with rape. This is not a good foundation for sexual equality or for justice. State feminism has inculcated a climate of suspicion and gendered righteousness that encourages women and girls to identify more and more of their experiences as rape or sexual assault, leaving widening scope for false allegations. State feminism has established conceptions of females as vulnerable victims and males as rapacious predators, based on statistics that do not stand up to scrutiny, yet it seems to be unable to see beyond its self-affirming belief that sexual violence is epidemic and receives insufficient attention.

---

[34] Online at <http://www.facecampusequality.org/>

REFERENCES

American Bar Association (ABA) Commission on Women in the Profession (2016) 'A Current Glance at Women in the Law (May 2016)'. Available online at <http://www.americanbar.org/content/dam/aba/marketing/women/current_glance_statistics_may2016.authcheckdam.pdf> [accessed May 2016].

BOGDANICH, W. (2014) 'Reporting Rape, and Wishing She Hadn't', *The New York Times*, 13 July. Available online at <http://www.nytimes.com/2014/07/13/us/how-one-college-handled-a-sexual-assault-complaint.html?smid=fb-nytimes&WT.z_sma=US_RRA_20140713&bicmp=AD&bicmlukp=WT.mc_id&bicmst=1388552400000&bicmet=1420088400000&_r=2> [accessed May 2016].

BROWNMILLER, S. (1975) *Against Our Will: Men, Women and Rape*, New York: Simon & Schuster.

Canadian Women's Foundation (undated) 'The Facts about Violence against Women'. Available online at <http://www.canadianwomen.org/facts-about-violence> [accessed May 2016].

CANTOR, D., FISHER, B., CHIBNALL, S. TOWNSEND, R., LEE, H., BRUCE, C., and THOMAS, G. (2015) *Report on the AAU Campus Climate Survey on Sexual Assault and Sexual Misconduct*, Rockville, MD: The Association of American Universities.

CATALANO, S. (2013) *Intimate Partner Violence: Attributes of Victimization, 1993–2011* (NCJ 243300), Washington, DC: Bureau of Justice Statistics. Available online at <http://www.bjs.gov/index.cfm?ty=pbdetail&iid=4801> [accessed May 2016].

CREIGHTON, A., and KIVEL, P. (2011) *Helping Teens Stop Violence, Build Community and Stand for Justice*, Nashville, TN: Hunter House.

DAVIS, A. Y. (1981) *Women, Race, and Class*, New York: Random House.

DWORKIN, A. (1981) *Pornography: Men Possessing Women*, London: Women's Press.

DWORKIN, A. (1987) *Intercourse*, New York: Free Press.

ESTRICH, S. (1986) *Real Rape*, Cambridge, MA: Harvard University Press.

FRIEDERSDORF, C. (2014) 'Sexual Assault and Rape Culture: Polarization is the Enemy of Progress', *The Atlantic*, 27 June. Available online at <http://www.theatlantic.com/politics/archive/2014/06/what-sort-of-public-discourse-will-reduce-rape-and-sexual-assault/373501> [accessed May 2016].

GAYLIN, W. (1982) *The Killing of Bonnie Garland*, New York: Simon & Schuster.

GEARAN, M. (2013) 'Message to the campus community', Hobart and William Smith Colleges and Smith Colleges, 13 July. Available online at <http://www.hws.edu/about/statements071314.aspx> [accessed May 2016].

GOODE, E., and BEN-YEHUDA, E. (1994) *Moral Panics: The Social Construction of Deviance*, Oxford: Blackwell.

GRUBER, A. (2007) 'The Feminist War on Crime', *Iowa Law Review*, 92(3): 741–833.

HILDEBRAND, M. M., and NAJDOWSKI, C. J. (2014) 'Potential Impact of Rape Culture on Juror Decision Making: Implications for Wrongful Acquittals in Sexual Assault Trials', *Albany Law Review*, 78(3): 1059–86.

HOAGLAND, S., and FRYE, M. (2000) *Feminist Interpretations of Mary Daly*, University Park, PA: Penn State University Press.

KATZ, J. (2002) *Tough Guise: Violence, Media, and the Crisis in Masculinity*, DVD, Northampton, MA: Media Education Foundation.

KATZ, J. (2006) *The Macho Paradox: Why Some Men Hurt Women and How All Men Can Help*, Naperville, IL: Sourcebooks.

Koss, M. P., Gidycz, C. A., and Wisniewski, N. (1987) 'The Scope of Rape: Incidence and Prevalence of Sexual Aggression and Victimization in a National Sample of Higher Education Students', *Journal of Consulting and Clinical Psychology*, 55(2): 162–70.

Lee, H. (1960) *To Kill a Mockingbird*, Philadelphia, PA: J. B. Lippincott.

Lochner, T., and Apollonio, D. E. (2012) 'The Effect of a Prosecutor's Gender on Federal Prosecutorial Decision Making', Paper presented at the Annual Meeting of the Western Political Science Association, Portland, OR, March. Available online at <http://wpsa.research.pdx.edu/meet/2012/lochnerandappollonio.pdf> [accessed October 2015].

MacKinnon, C. (1979) *Sexual Harassment of Working Women: A Case of Sex Discrimination*, New Haven, CT: Yale University Press.

MacKinnon, C. (1987) 'Rally against Rape', in *Feminism Unmodified: Discourses on Life and Law*, Cambridge, MA: Harvard University Press.

Marcus, S. (1992) 'Fighting Bodies, Fighting Words: A Theory and Politics of Rape Prevention', in J. Butler and J.W. Scott (eds) *Feminists Theorize the Political*, New York: Routledge.

Merry, S. E. (2001) 'Rights, Religion and Community: Approaches to Violence against Women in the Context of Globalization', *Law and Society Review*, 35(1): 39–88.

Obama, B. (2014) *Memorandum: Establishing a White House Task Force to Protect Students from Sexual Assault*, 22 January. Available online at <https://www.whitehouse.gov/the-press-office/2014/01/22/memorandum-establishing-white-house-task-force-protect-students-sexual-a> [accessed May 2016].

Paludi, M. A., and Barickman, R. B. (1998) *Sexual Harassment, Work, and Education*, 2nd Edition, Albany, NY: State University of New York Press.

Patai, D., and Koertge, N. (1994) *Professing Feminism: Cautionary Tales from the Strange World of Women's Studies*, New York: Basic Books.

Pinker, S. (2011) *The Better Angels of Our Nature: The Decline of Violence in History and Its Causes*, London: Penguin.

Rape, Abuse & Incest National Network (RAINN) (2009) 'Was I Raped?' Available online at <https://rainn.org/get-information/types-of-sexual-assault/was-it-rape> [accessed May 2016].

Rosenthal, L. (2010) 'Sixteen Years of the Violence Against Women Act,' *White House Blog*, 23 September. Available online at <https://www.whitehouse.gov/blog/2010/09/23/sixteen-years-violence-against-women-act> [accessed May 2016].

Rubin, G. (1984) 'Thinking Sex: Notes for a Radical Theory of the Politics of Sexuality', in C. Vance (ed.) *Pleasure and Danger: Exploring Female Sexuality*, Boston, MA: Routledge and Kegan Paul.

Siegel, R., and MacKinnon, C. A. (2004) *Directions in Sexual Harassment Law*, New Haven, CT: Yale University Press.

Sommers, C. H. (1995) 'Researching the "Rape Culture" of America', *The Real Issue*, 14(2): 1–13.

Stubbs, J. (2007) 'Beyond Apology? Domestic Violence and Critical Questions for Restorative Justice', *Criminology and Criminal Justice*, 7(2): 169–87.

Taylor, S., and Johnson, K. C. (2007) *Until Proven Innocent: Political Correctness and the Shameful Injustice of the Duke Lacrosse Rape Case*, New York: Thomas Dunne Books.

Warsaw, R. (1994) *I Never Called It Rape: The Ms Report on Recognizing, Fighting and Surviving Date and Acquaintance Rape*, New York: HarperCollins.

Washington Post (2000) 'States' Business', Editorial, 16 May.

WILL, G. (2014) 'Colleges Become the Victims of Progressivism', *The Washington Post*, 6 June. Available online at <https://www.washingtonpost.com/opinions/george-will-college-become-the-victims-of-progressivism/2014/06/06/e90e73b4-eb50-11e3-9f5c-9075d5508f0a_story.html> [accessed May 2016].

WILLIAMS, J. (2014) 'There Is No Rape Culture at British Universities', *Spiked*, 5 February. Available online at <http://www.spiked-online.com/newsite/article/there-is-no-rape-culture-at-British-universities/14612#.VCmy__ldXtI> [accessed May 2016].

YOFFE, E. (2014) 'The College Rape Overcorrection', *Slate*, 7 December. Available online at <http://www.slate.com/articles/double_x/doublex/2014/12/college_rape_campus_sexual_assault_is_a_serious_problem_but_the_efforts.html?wpsrc=sh_all_dt_tw_top> [accessed May 2016].

7

MAKING ACCUSATIONS
PRECAUTIONARY LOGIC AND EMBEDDED SUSPICION IN AN INSECURE AND UNCERTAIN WORLD

Bill Hebenton and Toby Seddon

> A democratic society, following popular views, will embody a form of risk aversion for low probability risks that might result in serious harm. The result will be in the direction of the Precautionary Principle.
>
> (Sunstein, 2005: 26)

> He who fights with monsters might take care lest he thereby become a monster.
>
> (Nietzsche, 1886: 146)

This chapter builds on previous work by the authors that characterized and analysed the significance of radical precaution in the processes of securing 'protection' for citizens against dangerous, violent and sexual offenders in countries such as the UK and United States. Precautionary logic, in particular, is transforming the meanings of, and relations between, allegations, truth-finding, and justice, badged under 'public protection'. Using this approach, our theme here is to contextualize the underpinnings of this broader cultural imperative through analysis of particular legal and policy developments, including development of 'counter-law' and surveillant assemblages against perceived dangers of sexual crime. We also illustrate how 'risk' itself is reconstituted in the politics of science and (un)certainty, with practical impacts on decision-making by professionals and apparent attempts at responsibilization of the wider public. The chapter thus presents an analysis of how the politics of risk and danger play out in identification, detection, and pre-emption of sexual crime.

The modern-day spectres of the sexual offender and his 'victim-in-waiting' could be said to haunt our modern 'social imaginary'—that arena of images, stories, and understandings shared by large groups of people, and which makes possible common practices and a widely shared sense of expectations (Taylor, 2004). In a 2009 article entitled 'From Dangerousness to Precaution', we made a foray into the dense undergrowth of the ways in which governments in both England and Wales and the United States had tried to protect society from the predations of the class defined as 'dangerous sexually violent offenders' (Hebenton and Seddon, 2009). Seeking to move beyond Robert Castel's landmark piece 'From Dangerousness to Risk' (Castel, 1991), to which our title alluded, we applied the framework of 'precautionary logic' to this specific problem field, to illustrate its significance as a key process in neoliberal cultures and to refine the theoretical contributions of key scholars on risk—notably, Francois Ewald (2000, 2002) and the late Richard Ericson (2007). Re-engaging with our previous work, our task in this chapter is to present an analysis of how the politics of allegation, truth-finding, risk, and danger play out in the interstices between the Scylla of 'failure to take all available precautions' and the Charybdis of a starkly foregrounded next 'victim-in-waiting'.

We articulate our theme as follows. First, we examine the cultural well-springs and political forms that underpin the nature of precautionary logic and sense of vulnerability to sexual violence. Second, we consider some specific legal and policy developments in the context of how the logic of precaution infuses attempts at reducing the riskiness of law itself (so called counter-law), and how it articulates with the other infrastructures of the management of risk. In conclusion, we consider the implications of the 'precautionary turn' for the politics of 'false allegations' of sex offending.

FEAR, RISK, AND THE LOGIC OF PRECAUTION

It is difficult to explain why Western societies should feel so overwhelmed by a sense of vulnerability (Furedi, 2009). In the comparative historical context, people living in Western societies have less familiarity with actual pain and suffering, hunger, debilitating disease, and death than ever before. Western societies enjoy what is, by historical standards, a good level of stability and prosperity. By any historical measure, we in the Western world are objectively less vulnerable. Steven Pinker (2012) argues that a range of data clearly demonstrates that violence has been in decline over millennia and that the present is probably the most peaceful time in the history of the human species. This decline, he argues, is enormous in magnitude, visible on both long and short time scales, and found in many domains, including military conflict, homicide, genocide, torture, criminal justice, and treatment of children, homosexuals, animals, and racial and ethnic minorities.

Yet despite this unprecedented level of stability and prosperity, contemporary culture continually communicates the idea that we are confronted by forces that threaten our everyday existence. Recognition of the inherent subjectivity of this is, of course, key. The cultural well-springs of this general sense of vulnerability have been diffusely articulated in the literature (Giddens, 1992; Garland, 2003; Bauman, 2006), much of it a variant on explanations that emphasize the experience of riding the 'juggernaut' of globalization and of making sense of change in a uncertain world (Furedi, 2009). But it is also clear from recent scholarship on England and Wales that the construction of a new subject, the 'vulnerable' subject, and the giving of institutional form and legitimacy to that subject draws explicitly from the politics and ideology of both New

Labour's Third Way and older Thatcherite neoliberal political forms (Ramsay, 2012). In short, and to summarize a complex trope, in Third Way thinking, the attempt to remoralize social life is based on the notion that the autonomy of each individual is dependent on the lifestyle choices of others, entailing a new 'life politics'. This idea is developed into a politics whereby the welfare state should be reconceived as a 'positive welfare society', in which welfare is understood as a psychological, rather than an economic, concept. A positive welfare society is concerned to ensure social cohesion—that is, cohesion between the different and diverse conditions of the psychological welfare of its self-fulfilling subjects. If their own psychological welfare is to be guaranteed, individuals acquire a duty to consider others' inner needs. The responsibility not to cause each other to fear crime is a key example of these responsibilities and, for that reason, freedom from fear of crime transforms into a basic citizenship right.

Neoliberal thought has also emphasized how societal cohesion under the 'free market' relies on traditional institutions and beliefs. Here, the individual turns out to be vulnerable to the vagaries of the market's impersonal forces. With the withering away of tradition, neoliberalism loses any distinctive moral grounds for the duties of citizenship and is left with only the unmediated experience of vulnerability in an insecure marketplace. As Ramsay (2012) suggests, neoliberalism without the traditional values is an apt description of the mainstream political experience in Britain in the 1980s and 1990s. In key respects, the two modes of political thought are quite different in their concerns, emphases, and priorities. These differences nuance the way in which each conceives of the vulnerability of the individual subject. Nevertheless, each of these dominant political forms of the last thirty years contains the assumption that the individual's autonomy is intrinsically vulnerable to the self-interested preferences of others. And it is this vulnerability that lays the normative basis for the liability to have behaviour—in our case, sexual behaviour that threatens personal safety—controlled.

If we now turn to consider the particular vulnerability at stake here, the 'victim-in-waiting' of sexual violence, then in the contemporary world sexual offences are considered—much more so than property offences or even physical assaults—to involve violations of the self that damage the very core of victims. Such damage can often involve a sense of moral pollution. Here, the Durkheimian distinction between the sacred and the profane is often invoked (Durkheim, 1964). The more sacred, pure, or innocent the victim, the more profane or unclean the assault and the person committing it are considered to be. There now appears to be no victim more sacred than a child victim and no offender more profane than one who spoils the innocence of children (Lynch, 2002; Leon, 2011; Douard and Schultz, 2013). The important cultural levers of modern sentiment are derived directly from contemporary conceptions of delineations between childhood and adulthood, and between sexuality and asexuality and innocence, as well as from a wider cultural context of developments in sexual morality (Boutellier, 2000; Kleinhans, 2002). Furthermore, in addition to their perceived sacredness, another important feature of children is their perceived vulnerability.

In US and British societies, fear and anxiety about threats to children's physical and psychological well-being are pervasive. While there is little statistical support for such fears, one can see that powerful emotions are at work: the fear of abduction and sexual assault out of all proportion to prevalence. Our response to the perceived 'dangerousness' of such 'predators'—indeed, our obsession with the protection of our children's moral and sexual innocence—has led us down a path strewn with inconsistencies (West, 2000). Arguably, it is only through a thorough review of these conceptual frameworks of 'childhood sexuality' that the target 'risk' of our collective fears can be begun to be understood. We need points of entry to more clearly understand why, more broadly, the trope of sexual violence occupies this prefigured space in public life now.

One point of entry into contemporary meanings of the sexual is via claims made by Anthony Giddens, in his 1993 book *The Transformation of Intimacy*, that in late modernity there is an experienced free-floating sexuality, removed from reproduction, becoming an expression of 'self' and personality. This liberation has resulted, according to Giddens, in a change of relations between the sexes—a striving for relationships no longer based on the gender hierarchy of the past. He argues that as 'plastic' sexuality is increasingly recognized, so a kind of violent reaction is provoked. Violent sex was the exception in an unequal, but highly regulated, status quo between the sexes. The equality of women in relations and sexual dealings offers an entirely different context for sexual violence. It no longer forms an exception in what are largely still unequal relationships. It is more easily understood as an encroachment upon sexual morality based on equality. Sexual violence is thus a ruthless rejection of female autonomy—an eruption of power in a context of equality. While Giddens (1993) focuses on the effects of plastic sexuality on intergender relations, his analysis also lends itself to a discussion of intergenerational sexuality and its 'ethical' context. We thus have a sexualized culture that is a vortex of seething, contradictory sexual structures.

Turning to available sociohistorical studies of sexual crime in England and Wales, this suggests that each post-war decade has seemed to take a particular focus:

- in the 1950s, it was concern about organized prostitution;
- the move towards partial decriminalization of homosexuality was the focus in the 1960s;
- the new wave of the women's movement took rape as a major concern in the 1970s (vying with child physical maltreatment);
- child sexual abuse was recognized in the 1980s; and
- in the 1990s, the apogee of concern fell on the more general figure of the predatory 'sexual offender' at large (Soothill and Francis, 2002).

Culturally, contemporary conceptions of the predatory sexual offender can be said to possess a durability that their predecessors lacked (Jenkins, 1998; West, 2000). As one commentator has noted, this comprises pathological sexual orientation, sexual specialization, fixed sexual proclivities, and a high level of future sexual dangerousness, all of which are largely unsupported by available research (Janus, 2007).

It is against this politico-cultural backcloth that precautionary approaches to public policy have spread out and expanded in recent years from their origins in German environmental politics in the 1970s. Precaution is now a key tool in diverse policy areas, including the specialist domain that we examine here. Precautionary logic constitutes a set of principles for addressing certain problems associated with governing the future. Vulnerability and uncertainty are 'absolute presuppositions of precautionary logic' (Arnoldussen, 2009: 260). The emphasis is on the ease with which things can go wrong. We are vulnerable because there is a great potential for catastrophe. There is an equal presumption that uncertainty is everywhere, related in part to the ambiguity of scientific explanation. Precautionary logic implores all to seek to pre-empt risk by heeding warnings, being suspicious, and embedding security measures in everyday life. The political culture of neoliberal societies is 'obsessed with uncertainty' and, increasingly, with a simple idea for its regulation: in case of doubt, follow the precautionary principle—that is, avoid steps that will create a risk of harm until safety (security) is established, be cautious (indeed, be cautious about being cautious), and do not require unambiguous evidence before acting.

Both Ewald (2000) and Ericson (2007) come to this through the prism of the 'insurance-based society' and point to the key matter as being that pre-emption entails *a responsibility for radical precaution in the face of uncertainty*. In many controversies about how to govern the future, the language of scientific risk has given way to that of scientific uncertainty. Precaution 'finds its condition of possibility in a sort of hiatus and time-shift between the requirements of action and the certainty of knowledge' (Ewald, 2000: 73). As an ethical (behavioural stance) in the face of uncertainty, precaution is the product of the 'necessity of decision' for the policymaker. Importantly, 'this does not mean that scientific expertise is useless, but that it will not release the politician from the sovereignty of his or her decision' (Ewald, 2000: 77). Under the logic of precaution, all are held responsible. Uncertainty is no longer an excuse for inaction and becomes the engine for ever-increased surveillance. Assessed against the 'worst-case possibilities', rather than risk 'probabilities', all are responsibilized in doing their part. The logic is a response to the realignment towards a 'zero-risk problematic' (Ewald, 2000: 378). Crucially, traditional criminal law models in which uncertainty may spell innocence are reconfigured. The priority is no longer to minimize false accusations ('false positives') in the manner of Blackstone's famous ratio; the imperative is now to minimize 'false negatives'—to eliminate their very possibility. In this sense, the logic of precaution drives an inversion of the traditional criminal justice paradigm.

COUNTER-LAW

Within precautionary logic, the institution of law is displaced, or at least 'relocated'. Indeed, law is seen in certain respects to impede attempts to pre-empt harms. Accordingly, precautionary logic leads to what Ericson (2007) calls criminalization through 'counter-law'—explicitly drawing from Foucault's use of this term in *Discipline and Punish* (1977). Counter-law refers to two strategies: first, the deployment of 'law against law' in order to erode, eliminate, or circumvent laws or legal procedures that are perceived to get in the way of the pre-emption of harms—for example lowering the bar on the seriousness of harm required for legal action, or lowering due process standards to facilitate investigations; and second, the creation of new surveillance assemblages to identify, monitor, and track potential sources of harm. Again, these assemblages may conflict with established legal norms, in terms of data protection or privacy. Fundamentally, counter-law is underpinned by the claim or assertion that the 'legal order must be broken to save the social order' (Ericson, 2007: 26). Arguably, under precautionary logic, law becomes ever more closely intertwined with a proliferating assemblage of expertise, risk consulting, administration, and discretion, inhabiting an inescapable paradox (Krasmann, 2012). Law as medium for challenging governmental encroachment and, notably, the 'rule of law' represent the very principles to be defended. Subsequently, however, law encounters its own legislation: the modes of risk management that it once itself authorized and which will now have to be amended in accordance not only with the principles of the rule of law, but also with the identified necessities of 'taking all available precautions' to protect the next 'victim-in-waiting'.

Elsewhere, under the banner of counter-law, we have illustrated how, in relation to those who have already offended and are deemed dangerous, the aim was to get around legal barriers to the use of coercive confinement (Hebenton and Seddon, 2009). In particular, we examined the US Sexual Violent Predator (SVP) legislation of the early 1990s (which provided a means of circumventing the 'problem' of release of such offenders from prison at the end of fixed-term sentences and allowed for their indefinite commitment), the Dangerous Prisoners (Sexual Offenders) Act 2003 of Queensland, Australia, and the UK's Dangerous and Severe Personality Disorder (DSPD) Programme, together with the sentencing powers brought in by the Criminal Justice Act 2003 covering extended and indeterminate confinement for public protection. As we pointed out, legal decision-making in US SVP cases is replete with uncertainty, because the legislation itself does not define all of the relevant terms of debate invoked; consequently, the legal system relies heavily on a competitive battleground of purveyors of 'expertise' (Hamilton, 2011). The courtroom and its 'battle of the experts' is where precaution confronts the limits of science, illustrated by the heated methodological debates in which the challenge posed by allegedly 'bad' science insinuates further doubt (Prentky et al., 2006).

These examples refer primarily to those previously convicted of an offence and in cases in which confinement was the goal. Yet counter-law works more broadly, for example through civil measures. Civil court orders in England and Wales are imposed on people to prohibit them from engaging in activities that *could* lead to a risk of sexual harm or to actual sexual offending (Ramsay, 2012), and such orders share a number of generic features, including that:

- they are granted in civil proceedings, or administratively with some judicial oversight;
- they are granted on some satisfaction of some undesirable conduct (often not criminal);
- the terms of the order may be prohibitive in nature, to prevent future instances of the behaviour; and
- their breach is a criminal offence of strict liability.

The procedures amount to a risk assessment of the clinical type (Ramsay, 2012). They seek to provide sufficient credibility to the judgment that the person presents a risk of sexual harm to children, so that a preventive order is necessary to protect against that risk.

A risk of sexual harm order, for example, can be granted by a magistrates' court where it is satisfied that the defendant has, on at least two occasions, engaged with a child in a very widely defined range of conduct that is related in some way to sexual activity or 'sexual communication' with a child, so that, as a result, 'there is reasonable cause to believe that it is necessary for such an order to be made'.[1] The behaviour that lays the ground for the order includes both conduct that would be a criminal offence and conduct that would not. What links these two different groups into a single set of grounds for action is that they all lend sufficient credibility to the judgment of risk requiring a prohibitory order for protection (Ramsay, 2012). The terms of the order itself may prohibit any conduct, prohibition of which is necessary to protecting children under the age of 16 generally or any particular child under the age of 16 from harm from the defendant. Many acts prohibited under the terms of the order will, in fact, create a risk of sexual harm, but since there need be only reasonable cause to believe that the order is necessary, there is no requirement that the prohibited acts in fact create any risk. By specifically prohibiting these acts, the terms of the order construct the person subject to them as a specific threat of sexual harm to children.

The reassurance aspect of these grounds for the order is reinforced when the precise definition of sexual activity and sexual communication for the purposes are taken into account. The order seeks to prevent adults from initiating contact with children to 'groom' them—that is, to build a relationship with a particular child or group of children in readiness for the initiation and perpetuation of their sexual abuse (Craven, Brown, and Gilchrist, 2006). The order was an attempt to prevent preparatory interactions between adult and child from taking place whether online or in person (Almandras, 2010). An activity or communication is sexual if a reasonable person would, in all of the circumstances, but regardless of any person's purpose, consider it to be sexual. This means that activity that is in fact sexually motivated, but which a reasonable observer would not perceive to be, does not create grounds for an order and vice versa. What is manifest to the reasonable observer, not actual sexual motive, is the substantive key to liability.

These orders give legal protection to any potential 'victim-in-waiting' by imposing a liability for a failure to reassure (Ramsay, 2012). The conduct concerned is defined as that which represents a risk of harm in the minds of the magistrates. In other words, the magistrates harbour a reasonable suspicion that the defendant will cause sexual harm to children in the future. The defendant is liable to the order and the order is necessary because the defendant's conduct fails to reassure the magistrates that he or she represents no threat to the next 'victim-in-waiting'.

An application for a risk of sexual harm order can be sought against anyone; there is no necessity that the person be already convicted for earlier sexual offences, as is the case with the other prevention orders under the 2003 Act. Applicants have to demon-

---

[1] Sexual Offences Act 2003, s. 123.

strate only the behaviour patterns listed above (Almandras, 2010). To now say that *anyone* could be a potential child sexual offender is recognition of the scope of who might be deemed a sex offender. Through this type of counter-law, embedded suspicion becomes the norm.

Following a review published by the Association of Chief Police Officers (ACPO) in May 2013 (Davies, 2013), the government has now repealed the old orders and introduced a sexual risk order (SRO), which may be made in relation to a person without a conviction for a sexual or violent offence (or any offence), but who poses a risk of sexual harm.[2] The threshold for risk will be lowered to cover *any* case of sexual harm, not only cases of serious sexual harm (Thomas and Thompson, 2013).

The second aspect of counter-law, surveillance assemblages, operates through spatial or behavioural exclusion. Here, we are witnessing, under precautionary logic, the rapid harnessing of electronic technologies and innovative controls that act as 'practical expressions of certainty' (Ericson, 2007: 156). This surveillance infrastructure is a parallel elaboration within society intended to pre-empt harm to the 'victim-in-waiting'. At the forefront are electronic databases, electronic monitoring and tracking, and residential restrictions. In our earlier article, we examined post-release controls on offenders in both the United States and England and Wales. In the US context, principally, we analysed the significance of the emergence of sexual offender registration and community notification policies, residential zoning, and electronic tracking. Whereas physical incapacitation of the offender has always invoked some measure of constitutional scrutiny in the United States, as Murphy (2008) has noted, virtually no legal constraints circumscribe the use of technological counterparts; the discipline of this form of counter-law operates beneath the law, 'on the underside of the law, a machinery that is both immense and minute, which supports, reinforces, multiplies the asymmetry of power and undermines the limits that are traced around the law' (Foucault, 1977: 222).

In England and Wales, agencies managing and monitoring child sex offenders in the community have long had the power to disclose information about those offenders to other agencies, and sometimes to individual members of the public. This process has variously been referred to as 'discretionary disclosure' or 'controlled disclosure'. In essence, 'discretionary disclosure' works by allowing those managing sex offenders in the community to disclose information to third parties otherwise not engaged in the management process. Information about a known offender and his or her offences could be made known to relevant individuals if a possible risk to children were to be identified (Thomas, 2010). While British politicians have resisted a US-style Megan's Law, the Child Sex Offender Review (CSOR) undertaken by the Home Office in 2006–07 recommended a limited scheme to allow members of the public to make applications for disclosure (Home Office, 2007). The Review cited the example of a single mother who might be unaware that she was sharing a home with a registered sex offender (Home Office, 2007). Subsequently, the Home Office carried out a pilot scheme to allow parents to register a child protection interest in a named individual with whom they have a personal relationship and who has regular unsupervised

---

[2] Anti-social Behaviour, Crime and Policing Act 2014, s. 113, amending the Sexual Offences Act 2003.

access to their child (Home Office, 2008). In 2008, new laws were passed to strengthen this process and to allow designated members of the public to request such information, imposing a new duty on agencies considering disclosure to conduct those considerations with a 'presumption to disclose' (Thomas, 2010). In those cases in which the offender has a conviction for child sexual offences and the risk justifies it, there is a presumption for disclosure to the applicant (Kemshall et al., 2010). The member of the public can request information from the police, who will check the named individual's criminal record (if any) and whether or not he or she poses a risk to children. Thus, through this type of counter-law, embedded suspicion becomes the norm, providing fertile ground for accusations to be made.

In terms of technological deployment, satellite 'tagging' is now established for those deemed the most serious offenders, who number around 1,000 annually. Compulsory polygraph testing has now been fully instituted, after several years of delay (Ministry of Justice, 2014). In the United States, for example, the polygraph has received wide acceptance in the treatment and supervision of offenders, where it is used for supervising and monitoring sexual offenders on parole or probation (Grubin, 2003). In many US states, the polygraph has become a routine tool in the management of sexual offenders, whose adherence to community restrictions and factors associated with relapse are closely monitored as part of their licence supervision. Just under 80 per cent of community programmes and more than half of residential treatment programmes in the United States used polygraph testing. Despite widespread usage, however, controversy has surrounded the polygraph, because the research used to assess its effectiveness has generally lacked scientific rigour (see McGrath et al., 2007, 2010). Compulsory lie detector testing started in England and Wales in October 2014. This testing is in addition to existing licence conditions, which can include signing the sex offenders register, exclusion zones, non-contact orders, curfews, Internet restrictions, and compliance with sex offender treatment programmes. Offenders are required to take the test every six months (Ministry of Justice, 2014). Whereas, in the past, suspicion underpinned law enforcement work,[3] this was largely subject to the individual discretion of the police officer on the street; now, precautionary and pre-emptive criminalization is embedded not only within legislation, policies, and institutions, but also within technologically based, automated surveillance practices.

FROM COUNTER-LAW STRATEGY TO DECISION-MAKING

Consider the following story, recounted by Minnesota law professor Eric Janus (2007: 8–9):

> In 1995, responding to the imminent release, after decades in prison, of an infamous rapist who had killed a fourteen year old, the governor of Minnesota called a special session of the legislature to pass a new predator commitment law. The media attention

[3] See, e.g., Vagrancy Act 1824, s. 4.

on the matter was persistent and intense. At a legislative hearing to consider the bill, critics pointed out the serious questions of constitutionality that such preventive detention raises. In response, one of the most thoughtful (and politically liberal) members of the state senate posed the question: 'How could any politician vote against this law? If we defeat this law what could I say to the family of the next victim, killed or raped by a person who would have been committed under this law?'

This powerful question has captured the American public's imagination, according to Janus (2007). It seems intuitively obvious that we ought to do all in our power to save the 'next victim' from harm. Our failure to take available precautions seems to implicate us in the tragedies that, in hindsight, seem so preventable. For the decision-maker, the option of acting in the present to manage the future rapidly mutates into an *obligation* (Rose, 2002: 212).

The decision-maker's epistemological world, under precautionary logic, appears to possess several characteristics. First, it is heavily situational, and thus there are serious questions about how to discern the 'facts of the matter' in terms of whether a particular strategy will serve to protect or not. A key part of such a situational rationality lies in the underpinnings of individual and social judgement (as explored at length by both psychologists and behavioural economists—see Sunstein, 2005). A body of social psychological research on our use of heuristics or rules of thumb suggests ways in which we simplify our judgement of actual levels of risk. Systemic neglect of precautionary action itself is also important. By this, we mean instances in which effects across an intervention strategy are not fully considered, with the focus instead being on the target risk of sexual violence. Arguably, this is one way in which to view the North American approach, whereby a part of the problem substitutes for the whole. Dangerous sexual offenders are rare, but appear to have become archetypical for the purposes of policymaking. The problem of sexual violence in society has become the 'problem of the worst of the worst'. Putting resources behind sexual predator laws inevitably means having fewer for alternative purposes, including other efforts to combat sexual violence. The decision-making dynamics of this 'risk–risk' problem need greater scrutiny.

Second, and relatedly, decision-making within precautionary logic deals with worst-case scenarios. Precaution 'invites one to anticipate what one does not yet know, to take into account doubtful hypotheses and simple suspicions' (Ewald, 2002: 288). Precautionary actions are taken to avoid the worst eventuality that can be imagined, rather than to reduce the likelihood that a probable event will occur. As such, the logic of precaution is concerned with avoiding the subjectively defined personal catastrophe of the 'victim-in-waiting'. Fear and anxiety are the catalysts for action, and we therefore need to know more about how individual and social decision-making operates in this context (Loewenstein et al., 2001).

Third, the precautionary world is a mediated world. It is clear that mass-media fact and fiction messages often result in the valorization of fear, simply by offering crime examples in which the 'worst case' has indeed happened (Best, 2001). Our live, 24/7 television news continually engages in relaying future outcomes, for example of child kidnappings, into our present—a form of 'premediation' or 'what might happen next' scenario-based thinking that further stokes our fears (Grusin, 2004). It is a pervasive cultural trope in the crime prevention literature: '[F]ear is now held out as an important emotion that can help keep you alive or at least reduce your chances of criminal victimisation' (Haggerty, 2003: 205–6). This appeal to 'eternal vigilance' is evident in the websites of our key child protection organizations, such as the Child Exploitation and Online Protection (CEOP) Centre of the National Crime Agency, the National Society for the Prevention of Cruelty to Children (NSPCC), and other charities.[4]

CONCLUSIONS: WHO SETS THE SUSPICION CLOCK?

What is revealing about our excursion into precautionary logic is the extent to which it is dependent on both future predictions based on risk assessment procedures and 'worst-case scenarios'. In terms of the former, and in spite of statistical developments, the inescapable uncertainties and dilemmas of prediction remain (Berk, 2008). One key dimension of uncertainty is whether the risk distribution curve will, in fact, have the same shape as that indicated by the historical data on which prediction tools are based. This type of uncertainty can be improved by detecting and eliminating sources of bias in samples, by increasing sample sizes, and so on, but it can never be excluded. And, fundamentally, attempting to predict the future in this way involves determining in advance an acceptable error rate, with prespecified levels of 'false positives' to 'false negatives'. This is referred to as the 'cost ratio'—essentially, a key setting of our suspicion clock. Before any prediction tool can be built, the ratio of these costs must be approximated. It is not enough to simply say that false negatives are generally more costly than false positives; rather, an actual *value* must be provided. This 'technical' process is, of course, a political process and outcome, but rarely acknowledged as such (Harcourt, 2007). It is a form of *displaced* politics, whereby we establish the (re)distribution of certain risks of harm between potential offenders and potential victims.

Of course, morally grounded rejections of this speculative approach have a long pedigree: writing some thirty years ago, in his critique of the Floud Committee's core idea that preventive action against an individual should be justified by virtue of the risk that he (or she) represented, doyen of British criminology Sir Leon Radzinowicz argued:

> We reject this speculative approach[, which] amounts to asserting that it is an offence to present oneself as a risk, even though it has to be admitted, on the empirical evidence, that the risk may not be high and in more cases than not will fail to materialise.
>
> (Radzinowicz and Hood, 1981: 758)

Thirty years on, we too, as a society, need to confront the reality of the reshaping of justice that is the corollary of contemporary precautionary logic. From the more classic or formalist legal tradition, the finding of guilt for a criminal act conventionally served to justify punishment, and to assuage our moral and political conscience; in

---

[4] See the web directory available online at <http://www.charitychoice.co.uk/charities/children-and-youth/child-protection>

the absence of a criminal act as predicate, it has generally been scientific expertise (now rather increasingly seen as 'insinuating' doubt) or procedural protections that have satisfied our sense of justice. But where the predicate criminal act is actually absent and the claim of expertise becomes more attenuated, our concerns are heightened. A political culture of embedded suspicion, coupled with the prioritization of minimizing 'false negatives' rather than 'false positives', will inevitably increase the level of false accusations of sexual offending. The challenging question for society as a whole is therefore whether this is a price worth paying.

REFERENCES

ALMANDRAS, S. (2010) *Registration and Management of Sex Offenders under the Sexual Offences Act 2003*, London: House of Commons Library.

ARNOLDUSSEN, T. (2009) 'Precautionary Logic and a Policy of Moderation', *Erasmus Law Review*, 2(2): 259–85.

BAUMAN, Z. (2006) *Liquid Fear*, Cambridge: Polity Press.

BERK, R. A. (2008) 'Forecasting Methods in Crime and Justice', *Annual Review of Law and Social Science*, 4: 219–38.

BEST, J. (2001) *Random Violence: How We Talk about New Crimes and New Victims*, Berkeley, CA: University of California Press.

BOUTELLIER, H. (2000) 'The Pornographic Context of Sexual Offences: Reflections on the Contemporary Sexual Morality', *European Journal on Criminal Policy and Research*, 8(4): 441–57.

CASTEL, R. (1991) 'From Dangerousness to Risk', in G. Burchell, C. Gordon, and P. Miller (eds) *The Foucault Effect: Studies in Governmentality*, Chicago, IL: University of Chicago Press.

CRAVEN, S., BROWN, S., and GILCHRIST, E. (2006) 'Sexual Grooming of Children: Review of Literature and Theoretical Considerations', *Journal of Sexual Aggression: An International, Interdisciplinary Forum for Research, Theory and Practice*, 12(3): 287–99.

DAVIES, H. (2013) *Civil Prevention Orders: Sexual Offences Act 2003—ACPO Commissioned Review of the Existing Statutory Scheme and Recommendations for Reform*. Available online at <http://www.ecpat.org.uk/sites/default/files/the_davies_review.pdf> [accessed May 2016].

DOUARD, J., and SCHULTZ, P. D. (2013) *Monstrous Crimes and the Failure of Forensic Psychiatry*, New York: Springer.

DURKHEIM, E. (1964) *The Elementary Forms of Religious Life*, London: Allen & Unwin.

ERICSON, R. V. (2007) *Crime in an Insecure World*, Cambridge: Polity Press.

EWALD, F. (2000) 'Risk in Contemporary Society', *Connecticut Insurance Law Journal*, 6(2): 365–79.

EWALD, F. (2002) 'The Return of Descartes' Malicious Demon: An Outline of a Philosophy of Precaution', in T. Baker and J. Simon (eds) *Embracing Risk: The Changing Culture of Insurance and Responsibility*, Chicago, IL: University of Chicago Press.

FOUCAULT, M. (1977) *Discipline and Punish: The Birth of the Prison,* Harmondsworth: Penguin.

FUREDI, F. (2009) 'Precautionary Culture and the Rise of Possibilistic Risk Assessment', *Erasmus Law Review*, 2(2): 197–220.

GARLAND, D. (2003) 'The Rise of Risk', in R. Ericson and A. Doyle (eds) *Risk and Morality*, Toronto, ON: University of Toronto Press.
GIDDENS, A. (1992) 'Risk, Trust, Reflexivity', in U. Beck, A. Giddens, and S. Lash (eds) *Reflexive Modernization*, Cambridge: Polity Press.
GIDDENS, A. (1993) *The Transformation of Intimacy: Sexuality, Love and Eroticism in Modern Societies*, Stanford, CA: Stanford University Press.
GRUBIN, D. (2003) 'The Role of the Polygraph', in A. Matravers (ed.) *Sex Offenders in the Community: Managing and Reducing the Risks*, Cullompton: Willan.
GRUSIN, R. (2004) 'Premediation', *Criticism*, 46(1): 17–49.
HAGGERTY, K. D. (2003) 'From Risk to Precaution', in R. Ericson and A. Doyle (eds) *Risk and Morality*, Toronto, ON: University of Toronto Press.
HAMILTON, M. (2011) 'Public Safety, Individual Liberty, and Suspect Science: Future Dangerousness Assessments and Sex Offender Laws', *Temple Law Review*, 83: 698–755.
HARCOURT, B. (2007) *Against Prediction: Profiling, Policing and Punishing in an Actuarial Age*, Chicago, IL: University of Chicago Press.
HEBENTON, B., and SEDDON, T. (2009) 'From Dangerousness to Precaution', *British Journal of Criminology*, 49(3): 343–62.
Home Office (2007) *Review of the Protection of Children from Sex Offenders*, London: HMSO.
Home Office (2008) *Keeping Our Communities Safe: Managing Risk through MAPPA*, London: HMSO.
JANUS, E. (2007) *Failure to Protect: America's Sexual Predator Laws and the Rise of the Preventive State*, Ithaca, NY/London: Cornell University Press.
JENKINS, P. (1998) *Moral Panic: Changing Conceptions of the Child Molester in Modern America*, New Haven, CT: Yale University Press.
KEMSHALL, H., and WOOD, J., with WESTWOOD, S., STOUT, B., WILKINSON, B., KELLY, G. N., and MACKENZIE, G. (2010) *Child Sex Offender Review (CSOR): Public Disclosure Pilots—A Process Evaluation*, London: HMSO.
KLEINHANS, M.-M. (2002) 'Criminal Justice Approaches to Paedophilic Sex Offenders', *Social & Legal Studies*, 11(2): 233–55.
KRASMANN, S. (2012) 'Law's Knowledge: On the Susceptibility and Resistance of Legal Practices to Security Matters', *Theoretical Criminology*, 16(4): 379–94.
LEON, C. (2011) *Sex Fiends, Perverts, and Paedophiles: Understanding Sex Crime Policy in America*, New York: New York University Press.
LOEWENSTEIN, G., WEBER, E., HSEE, C., and WELCH, N. (2001) 'Risk as Feelings', *Psychological Bulletin*, 127(2): 267–86.
LYNCH, M. (2002) 'Pedophiles and cyber-predators as contaminating forces', *Law and Social Inquiry*, 27(3): 529–66.
MCGRATH, R. J., CUMMING, G. F., BURCHARD, B., ZEOLI, S., and ELLERBY, L. (2010) *Current Practices and Emerging Trends in Sexual Abuser Management: The Safer Society 2009 North American Survey*, Brandon, VT: Safer Society Press.
MCGRATH, R. J., CUMMING, G. F., HOKE, S. E., and BONN-MILLER, M. O. (2007) 'Outcomes in a Community Sex Offender Treatment Program: A Comparison between Polygraphed and Matched Non-polygraphed Offenders', *Sexual Abuse: A Journal of Research and Treatment*, 19(4): 381–93.
Ministry of Justice (2014) 'Compulsory lie detector tests for serious sex offenders', Press release, 27 May. Available online at <https://www.gov.uk/government/news/compulsary-lie-detector-tests-for-serious-sex-offenders> [accessed December 2015].

Murphy, E. (2008) 'Paradigms of Restraint', *Duke Law Journal*, 57: 1321–42.
Nietzsche, F. (1886) *Beyond Good and Evil*. Available online at <https://www.gutenberg.org/ebooks/4363> [accessed November 2014].
Pinker, S. (2012) *The Better Angels of Our Nature: A History of Violence and Humanity*, London: Penguin Books.
Prentky, R., Janus, E., Barbaree, H., Schwartz, B., and Kafka, M. (2006) 'Sexually Violent Predators in the Courtroom: Science on Trial', *Psychology, Public Policy and Law*, 12(4): 357–93.
Radzinowicz, L., and Hood, R. (1981) 'Dangerousness and Criminal Justice: A Few Reflections', *Criminal Law Review*, 3: 756–61.
Ramsay, P. (2012) *The Insecurity State: Vulnerable Autonomy and the Right to Security in the Criminal Law*, Oxford: Oxford University Press.
Rose, N. (2002) 'At Risk of Madness', in T. Baker and J. Simon (eds) *Embracing Risk: The Changing Culture of Insurance and Responsibility*, Chicago, IL: The University of Chicago Press.
Soothill, K., and Francis, B. (2002) 'Moral Panics and the Aftermath: A Study of Incest', *Journal of Social Welfare and Family Law*, 24(1): 1–17.
Sunstein, C. (2005) *Laws of Fear: Beyond the Precautionary Principle*, Cambridge: Cambridge University Press.
Taylor, C. (2004) *Modern Social Imaginaries*, Durham, NC: Duke University Press.
Thomas, T. (2010) 'A Presumption to Disclose', *Child Abuse Review*, 19(2): 97–106.
Thomas, T., and Thompson, D. (2013) 'New Civil Orders to Contain Sexual Offending: A Matter of "Purposive" Logic', *Criminal Law and Justice Weekly*, 26 October. Available online at <http://www.criminallawandjustice.co.uk/features/New-Civil-Orders-Contain-Sexual-Offending-%E2%80%93-Matter-%E2%80%9CPurposive-Logic%E2%80%9D> [accessed May 2016].
West, D. J. (2000) 'The Sex Crime Situation: Deterioration More Apparent than Real?' *European Journal on Criminal Policy and Research*, 8(4): 399–422.

PART III

THE ALLEGATION: CAUSES; MOTIVATIONS; CASE STUDIES

WHY WOULD ANYONE MAKE A FALSE ACCUSATION?

8

WHY AND HOW FALSE ALLEGATIONS OF ABUSE OCCUR

AN OVERVIEW

Felicity Goodyear-Smith

This chapter provides a broad overview of the various causes, motivations, and cognitive biases that can lead to erroneous allegations and prosecution. Abuse and false accusations of abuse both happen, and both can do considerable harm. An allegation may be true, partly true, or false. 'Partly true' includes an embellished or distorted recollection, or a misinterpretation that the action of another involved sexual intent. A false allegation may be made knowingly and deliberately, or it may be the result of a belief that something happened that never took place. True and untrue allegations may be hard to distinguish: typically, there is no physical means of verifying or disproving the allegation. Sometimes, there is corroborative evidence that an event either did or did not occur. But most sexual abuse has happened in secret: there are no witnesses and, frequently, we cannot know for sure whether something actually happened or not, especially when allegations may refer to events claimed to have occurred decades in the past.

From the standpoint of victims of sexual abuse, who believe that others like them are telling the truth, any questioning of the veracity of abuse allegations is adding insult to injury, and any inquiry into the motivations and causes of false allegations may seem morally repugnant and unethical—especially when 'false' is taken in its narrower sense to mean deliberately untrue. It is held that children and women rarely lie about such matters, and that therefore false reports are a myth. This may partly explain the scarcity of studies that have focused on examining the causes and reasons for untrue claims of abuse (exceptions including Kanin, 1994; O'Donohue and Bowers, 2006; Engle and O'Donohue, 2012). Increasingly, however, allegations of child abuse are made retrospectively by *adults* referring back to their childhood— and, often, the initial suspicion or reporting of abuse is by someone other than the identified victim. More pertinently, *deliberate* falsehoods are only one category among several others whereby false claims are *made in good faith*. Looked at more broadly, as in the present volume, a wide range of variables, singly or in combination, can be drawn on to account for the incidence of wrongful allegations. Another barrier to inquiry about causation is the stark division between true and false allegations (echoing the bifurcation between guilty and not guilty pleas), not allowing for allegations that may be partly false and partly true. Once we move away from narrowly defining false allegations as intentions to deceive made for ulterior motives and from a simple 'true' or 'false' dichotomy, however, then the value of differentiating causal patterns becomes more evident.

In understanding how false allegations can be made, and then come to be accepted as true, it is important to distinguish between individual motivations and external influences that contribute to their construction. Blame or responsibility for untrue allegations cannot simply be attributed to those who make them; rather, they may be, on some level, jointly constructed—by psychologists, police, victim support workers who are on the lookout for signs of abuse, who recognize symptoms and jump to conclusions—in the context of vigilance and awareness of widespread incidence of child abuse and sexual exploitation, and belief that many behavioural problems and mental illness are attributable to abuse in the person's childhood. External factors include changes in cultural beliefs and investigative procedures and policies that influence decisions, while individual factors include characteristics of accusers and objectives of investigators. Cutting across these dimensions, and drawing on known cases of false allegations of child abuse and sexual assault, a number of causal and motivational patterns can be discerned.

While this chapter outlines the various causes and motivations of false allegations under the broad categories of external and individual factors, in many cases there is considerable overlap and interplay of influences. This typology should thus be seen as illustrative, but not prescriptive.

CULTURAL BELIEFS AND INVESTIGATIVE BIASES

Cultural values and external factors contribute to erroneous allegations of sexual abuse. 'Child abuse' is a modern social construct (Robin, 1991; Lancaster, 2011) and became a serious public concern after the publication of a seminal paper on the 'battered child syndrome' in 1962 (Kempe et al., 1962). Once child abuse was 'discovered', it was defined and brought to public attention, and became the subject of state intervention (Parton, 1985). There was a shift from seeing childrearing as an individual moral duty to seeing it as a national responsibility (Weeks, 1989). Social services and legislative changes were instigated in the 1970s to address the problem, which was soon recognized as reaching 'epidemic' proportions, with identified cases considered only 'the tip of the iceberg' (Robin, 1991).

The incidence of both physical and sexual reported abuse escalated. The more widespread a problem, the more it attracts attention and resources, and the rhetoric in making these claims helped to shape policy (Best, 1987). By the 1980s, the claim that at least one in four girls is sexually abused became accepted fact (Peters, Wyatt, and Finkelhor, 1986). There was an increasing dichotomization of sexual assault victims (usually women and children) and offenders (usually men), with a 'punish the offender, treat the victim' paradigm, along with a movement to demonize all perpetrators as equally evil and incorrigible (Leon, 2011).

The belief that sexual abuse of children and women is extremely prevalent, whereas false allegations rarely, if ever, occur, provides the context for increased suspicion that sexual assault is taking place in a wide variety of contexts. False allegations will occur more often when abuse is believed to be endemic and where psychological distress or dysfunctional behaviour is assumed to have resulted from past undisclosed sexual assault.

IDEOLOGICAL AGENDAS

The women's liberation movement of the 1960s focused on equal opportunities and political, social, economic, and other rights of women to those of men. These ideals were replaced in the feminism of the 1980s and 1990s by the aim to disempower men rather than to stand alongside them. Women were seen as superior to men. The thesis that all sex is rape and all men are potential rapists, spearheaded by anti-pornography activist Andrea Dworkin (1987), was frequently cited in papers, books, and women's studies in the 1990s as mainstream feminism. Male oppression was seen to be the cause of all social woes and women were considered to be powerless victims of the patriarchy (Denfeld, 1995). Rape definition expanded to include wolf whistles, while women and children were said to rarely, if ever, lie and therefore to be believed when alleging sexual assault (Bass and Davis, 1988). All blame was attributed to men. This victim or gender feminism has had a profound effect on the generation of false allegations. It has also become a powerful political force in which legal principles to protect the innocent have been undermined, as discussed by John Brigham in Chapter 6 in this volume.

JUDICIAL AND LEGISLATIVE CHANGES

Other chapters in this book refer to relevant legislative developments in the UK and the United States, but similar developments have occurred globally. New Zealand provides an early example of a victim-centred approach to child abuse and interpersonal violence that has, arguably, undermined protections for defendants who may be innocent. By the 1990s in New Zealand, the police, prosecutors, judges, and others dealing with alleged victims were instructed that every sexual allegation must be treated as genuine. New Zealand police have been trained in the importance of believing the victim, to avoid revictimization should they approach a case with scepticism and critically examine any of the victim's testimony (Goodyear-Smith, 1996). From the outset, complainants are called 'victims', and provided with victim advocates to prepare them for court and support them at hearings, while the accused are labelled 'perpetrators'. This undermines the hallmark standard of justice in Western society, 'innocent until proven guilty'. Validating and supporting complainants at the expense of defendants compromises the impartiality of a system in which the principle of neutrality requires that a complainant is neither disbelieved nor uncritically believed, that a fair and objective investigation into the facts is conducted, and that both accuser and accused be afforded equal consideration and respect in accordance with the law of natural justice.

In 1986, the New Zealand Evidence Act 1908 was amended so that corroboration in cases involving allegations of sexual offences was no longer required.[1] Removal of the legal safeguard of corroborative evidence means that conviction now may be based solely on the testimony of one person's word against another (Goodyear-Smith, Laidlaw, and Large, 1997). Similarly, in England and Wales, the requirement for corroboration in order to convict was removed by section 33 of the Criminal Justice and Public Order Act 1994, section 32 of which abrogated the requirement for the judge to give the jury a warning about convicting the accused on the uncorroborated evidence in cases in which the offence charged is sexual and the evidence is given by the alleged victim.

A raft of other legislative changes have been introduced to support complainants in New Zealand. There is provision for witnesses to give evidence by closed-circuit television (CCTV) or by video link, or to be screened from the defendant, in which instances the latter loses the right to confront face to face a witness offering testimony against him or her. It is not permitted to question complainants about sexual experience with anyone other than the defendant. In the case of a serial accuser, this precludes juries learning that a complainant has made similar claims against others, who have been found not guilty (McLeod, 1997). Moreover, anonymity of complainants is frequently maintained after an acquittal, while the accused may have been named publicly.

The justice system in England and Wales has followed a similar path. For example, the *Report on Review of Ways to Reduce Distress of Victims in Trials of Sexual Violence* (Ministry of Justice, 2014) aims to reduce distress to victims during cross-examination. What is most notable about this document is the presumption of guilt: the word 'victim' not 'complainant' is used throughout. While all would agree that aggressive and other forms of brutal and traumatic questioning should be avoided where possible, the same courtesies should be extended to the defendant. At the outset of a trial, he (or she) is presumed innocent until proven guilty, and, should he (or she) take the stand, as a fellow human being he (or she) is entitled to the same care and respect afforded to his (or her) accuser.

MORAL CRUSADES

The collective belief in the innocence of childhood renders it beyond debate, and any suggestion of child molestation engenders horror and panic. The moral crusades that can occur to root out cases of sexual abuse and the '*duty to believe*' a complainant carry a presumption of guilt, and mean that the accused can never be absolved from suspicion even when shown to be innocent (Furedi, 2013). In the 1980s, moral panic about paedophile rings and satanic cults, believed to be responsible for intergenerational ritual abuse, led to a wave of false allegations in North America, the UK, and Europe,

---

[1] The 1908 Act was repealed by the New Zealand Evidence Act 2006.

especially against preschool workers, of which the McMartin case is one of hundreds (Finkelhor et al., 1988; deYoung, Chapter 3 in this volume). A US investigation of more than 12,000 accusations of satanic ritual abuse reported by psychologists and psychotherapists concluded that not one case was substantiated (Lanning, 1991). A study of cases involving allegations of ritual or satanic abuse in England and Wales were similarly shown to be unfounded (La Fontaine, 1994).

However, the belief in organized paedophile rings has persisted, and is now an article of faith for campaigners, and commissions of inquiry into historical sexual abuse persist. In the 1990s, belief that widespread child abuse had occurred in residential care homes in Wales and England resulted in massive police trawling investigations. Police sought out former residents and conducted unsolicited interviews. Accusations were mounted against hundreds of innocent care workers. The subsequent Waterhouse Tribunal did find evidence of abuse by some former staff, but did not find evidence of organized paedophile rings (Waterhouse, 2000). The background and unfolding of this prolonged moral panic is exhaustively researched in Webster's 2005 book *The Secret of Bryn Estyn*, and aspects are covered by Mark Smith (Chapter 5) and by David Rose (Chapter 12) in this volume.

SUGGESTIVE INTERVIEWING

Children, especially preschoolers, are prone to developing false memories from suggestive influences (Bruck, Ceci, and Melnyk, 1997). This may result from interviewer bias when an investigator or counsellor who believes abuse has occurred uses suggestive, forced choice or repeated questioning. Reinforcing the expected response (such as saying 'You are really brave for telling'), inviting children to first pretend or imagine a certain event and then visualize it, and use of aids such as 'anatomically correct dolls' can all generate false claims. Once such false recollections have been created and reinforced by repeated telling, they can become ingrained as enduring false memories. One of the most dramatic cases is that of the Virginia McMartin Preschool in California, where seven teachers were erroneously accused of abusing several hundred children. This case is covered in depth by deYoung in Chapter 3 in this volume. The allegations resulted from problematic questioning by interviewers who were convinced that the children had been abused.

MISINTERPRETATION OF REAL EVENTS

An overzealous sense of certainty that abuse has occurred or that a particular individual is guilty may result in the evidence presented being selectively withheld or distorted. At the time of writing, there have been 325 exonerations of wrongfully convicted individuals in the United States, including twenty inmates who were on death row awaiting execution. All of these exonerations were brought about by DNA testing (Innocence Project, 2016). While many of these cases involved violence additional to, rather than only, the sexual element and were replete with physical evidence of a crime—thus unlike many cases covered in the present volume in which the only evidence that abuse had occurred is verbal testimony—these cases exonerated by DNA evidence are valuable in indicating likely mistakes that occur more widely in prosecutions and convictions for sexual and child abuse, *but where there is no DNA to bring them to light.*

The causes of these false convictions were eyewitness misidentification, a known relationship or acquaintanceship between the victim and the defendant, invalid or improper forensic science, misconduct by police and prosecutors, and false confessions. In most of these exonerations, a crime was committed, but the wrong person was convicted for that crime. However, situations also arise in which individuals are accused, but no sexual assault ever actually occurred. Cases may arise in which a caregiver or professional decides that a child or vulnerable adult has been abused in the absence of complaint from the alleged victim, for example where the perceived victim is an infant, has a disability that prevents communication, or even is deceased. Professionals' acceptance, rejection, and interpretation of objective scientific and medical data may be coloured by this belief.

In one such instance, health professionals treating a 10-year-old girl with congenital HIV, who died from acute sepsis, misinterpreted anal tissue breakdown resulting from advanced HIV destructive disease as anal assault, then hypothesized that her hypoxia and organ failure was caused by suffocation (Goodyear-Smith, Sharland, and Nadel, 2014). The doctors and nurses involved in her care held a shared fixed and false belief (*idée fixe*) that what they saw was a 'great gaping wound', rather than tissues that were abnormal through natural causes. Confirmatory bias meant that the most likely clinical diagnosis—advanced HIV infection with subsequent overwhelming sepsis—was discarded, with ensuing criminal proceedings continuing for five years at huge legal and social cost (Goodyear-Smith, 2015).

MISCOMMUNICATIONS REGARDING SEXUAL CONSENT

There is also the vexed issue of what constitutes consent. Legally consent can be given only by those deemed capable of doing so. For example, in New Zealand[2] and Canada,[3] being under the legal age of consent, affected by alcohol or other drugs, asleep or unconscious, or affected by an intellectual, mental, or physical impairment renders a person unable to give consent. Consent can be granted only in the absence of threat or force. A report by the Office of the Children's Commissioner for England identifies that young people 'understand what is meant by *giving* consent to sex, but have a very limited sense of what *getting* consent might involve' (Coy et al., 2013: 10). Beres (2014: 385) writes that 'communicating a willingness to participate in sex is not the same thing as consenting to sex' and argues that consent is not for an event, but is 'a process that begins with sexual initiation and is ongoing throughout the sexual activity'. However, in most sexual encounters, verbal consent is not explicit, and nuances of both verbal and non-verbal behaviour, in the absence of active resistance, are generally perceived as willingness to proceed. In most circumstances, when there has been an initial enthusiastic 'yes', it is unlikely that consent is repeatedly sought and given throughout sexual activity.

---

[2] New Zealand Crimes Act 1961, s. 128A.   [3] Criminal Code of Canada, s. 273.

Even if, legally, consent may not be given when someone is intoxicated, in reality sexual activity, especially between young people, often takes place after both parties have been drinking. Alcohol can further cloud a situation both by lowering sexual inhibitions and by causing some memory impairment. Subsequent recall may lead to an honest distortion of memory or misperception of the other's intent. In one such incident at Occidental College, Los Angeles, CA, two young students became drunk and amorous. They subsequently had sex that neither could completely remember and which both later regretted (Banks, 2014). The young woman then filed a sexual misconduct complaint. The LA County District Attorney's office did not lay charges, concluding that both were 'willing participants exercising bad judgment'. The College decided that the young man was 'too drunk to recognize that [the young woman] was too drunk to consent', but expelled him. Thus while he was held accountable for his actions when drunk, she was not.

It may not be a case of one person telling the truth and the other lying; rather, both parties may give honest, but false, testimony. The indirect means by which consent often takes place, the potential for ambiguity of the interpretation of intent, and the vagaries of later recollection are further addressed by Villalobos, Davis, and Leo in Chapter 10 in the present volume.

COGNITIVE BIASES

Many cases of false allegations arise from the cognitive biases of the investigators. Once the decision has been made that abuse of a child or an adult has occurred, the professional may have tunnel vision (Findley and Scott, 2006). Confirmatory biases may operate whereby only evidence supporting the allegation is sought and contradictory evidence is supressed or misinterpreted (O'Brien, 2009). Sometimes, this will occur in the absence of any claim by the alleged victim. Once a stand has been made, beliefs become entrenched. It becomes increasingly difficult for people to see that they are mistaken. Being confronted by conflicting information may cause mental distress and cognitive dissonance, leading to self-justification and increasing conviction of being 'right' (Festinger, 1962). In the 1980s and 1990s, thousands of women 'recovered' false memories of incest and rape through misguided psychotherapy, which caused irreparable harm to them and to their families. Almost no psychotherapists have ever admitted that they were wrong in this belief and practice (Tavris and Aronson, 2007). Cognitive dissonance also makes it difficult for a complainant to retract an initial lie or mistake.

In 1987, in Cleveland in the UK, more than 100 children were diagnosed as having been sexually abused, based on the misinterpretation of reflex anal dilatation (RAD) when the children were medically examined by two paediatricians. Children with this sign were presumed to have been abused, removed from their families by social services, and placed into care. Eventually, most cases were shown to be unfounded in an inquiry led by Lord Justice Butler-Sloss and the children were returned to their parents (Butler-Sloss, 1988). Subsequent research has found that RAD is a commonly occurring sign in non-abused children (McCann et al., 1989).

In 1991, social workers decided that nine children on the South Ronaldsay Island, Orkney, Scotland, were victims of satanic ritual abuse and placed them in foster homes on the mainland (Goodyear-Smith, 1993). The stories were shown to be without foundation, fuelled by lengthy interviews and repeated coaching of the children by workers who believed that the abuse had occurred. The judicial inquiry by Lord Clyde determined that their handling of the case was fatally flawed (Clyde, 1992).

A similar case occurred in Oude Pekela, a small village in the Netherlands, in 1988. Initial belief that there was a dangerous child molester in the area led to widespread interrogations of children by police, social workers, psychotherapists, school teachers, and parents, with hundreds of children ultimately reporting incidents of satanic ritual abuse (Goodyear-Smith, 1993). Eventually, the contradictory testimonies and lack of corroborative evidence led to the conclusion that the allegations were not factually true, but created by overzealous questioning (Ministry of Justice, The Netherlands, 1994).

International guidelines claim that prepubertal children infected with gonorrhoea must have been sexually abused (American Academy of Pediatrics, 1998). This ignores the overwhelming evidence that children can contract this disease from both sexual and non-sexual means: for example, babies may become infected from the contaminated hands of their caregivers (Goodyear-Smith, 2007). While all cases must be considered seriously, ignoring the possibility that abuse may not have occurred may cause permanent harm, with children removed into foster care and parents criminally charged.

In 1995, Carol Hopkins testified before the US Senate, outlining a long list of child abuse cases between 1983 and 1995 for which there was compelling evidence of false charges and convictions based on 'a significant combination of investigative error, therapeutic malpractice, prosecutorial misconduct or malfeasance, and a climate of community hysteria regarding sex abuse charges' (Hopkins, 1995). The 'noble cause' of catching and convicting sex offenders can corrupt both police and prosecutors, who then justify pressurizing suspects, lying, disregarding or supressing evidence, and even planting evidence on the grounds that these means justify the end of successfully prosecuting the person believed to be guilty (Grometstein, 2007).

INDIVIDUAL MOTIVES AND DRIVERS

SELF-SERVING FALSE NARRATIVES OF ABUSE

Many people give truthful and accurate accounts of being sexually assaulted. However, all people—adults, adolescents, and children—may lie on occasion. Some allegations are deliberate fabrication; others may include deliberate exaggerations or distortions of what occurred that criminalize otherwise legitimate interactions or improprieties. This is usually motivated by some form of personal gain. The potential benefit varies.

Providing an alibi A false allegation might be made to account for an unexplained absence (BBC News, 2010) or to explain infidelity to a partner (DiSanto, 2013), including an unexpected pregnancy (Govan, 2009) or a sexually transmitted infection. Heather Atkins, a 26-year-old Columbian woman, claimed violent rape by two unknown men to explain a black eye actually inflicted by a woman who came home to find Heather in the shower with her boyfriend (Kuenzie, 2012). Sometimes, the potential gain might seem trivial in comparison to the damage to the accused that a false allegation may cause: for example, trainee barrister Rhiannon Brooker fabricated rape claims against her boyfriend to justify delay in sitting her legal examinations (Morris, 2014).

Seeking revenge or retribution False rape claims may be made as retribution against a boyfriend, ex-spouse, teacher, or employer, or to get rid of a current partner. It may be a situation of unrequited romantic interest. Tina Greenland, a nanny, falsely accused her boss Nicholas Mouna of rape after he made it clear that he did not want a relationship with her (Telegraph Reporters, 2012), while Welsh woman Leanne Black was jailed for multiple false rape allegations made over an eight-year period against five ex-partners (Duffin, 2013).

Teachers are particularly vulnerable to false abuse claims made by disturbed students. UK teacher unions are recognizing false physical and sexual abuse allegations as a growing problem, resulting from students with unrequited 'crushes', wanting reprisal when a teacher has reprimanded them or given them poor grades, or seeking attention because of problems at school or at home. In 2011, the largest teachers' union (NASUWT) found over 97 per cent of the 2,210 allegations of unlawful behaviour made against their members to be unsubstantiated (NASUWT, 2012). Daren Gee was a Yorkshire music teacher wrongly convicted of raping a pupil, who had made identical claims against another teacher (Herbert, 2006). Gee's conviction was posthumously overturned, four years after he had died in prison.

Obtaining sympathy and attention The attention and sympathy afforded to a rape complainant may fuel false allegations, with secondary gain from victim status (Engle and O'Donohue, 2012). Police investigated a 'very convincing' claim by a 15-year-old girl that a man had entered her home, hit her with a piece of timber, and sexually assaulted her. She gave a detailed description, including a dog-collar tattoo around his neck, and police issued an identikit picture. After two weeks and 235 investigating hours, it was established that the story was fabricated and the alleged offender did not exist (McGehan, 1999).

People knowingly making deliberate false complaints have an increased likelihood of having an antisocial, histrionic, or borderline personality disorder (Engle and O'Donohue, 2012). In Liverpool, a mother of four made thousands of hoax calls to police, claiming that she was a 14-year-old girl raped by her stepfather. Hundreds of police hours were wasted investigating her story. She received a suspended sentence after pleading guilty (Butler, 2008).

Law student Nick Wills was falsely accused of brutally raping a young woman who lived in his halls of residence (McGehan, 1996). He was imprisoned, lost his job, was named in the media, and was subjected to harassment. Fortunately, he had family support and resources enabling him to hire a private investigator. Watertight alibis were established. Evidence was also produced that his accuser had a history of telling untrue stories, such as her father owning his own plane, to gain attention and make her seem important to others. She admitted lying when confronted, was convicted of making a false statement, received a community sentence, and yet benefited from name suppression. Wills had faced the loss of his career and nine years in prison.

Celebrities may also be targeted for false allegations. Reg Traviss, ex-boyfriend of Amy Winehouse, was falsely accused of raping a 27-year-old woman and was acquitted in court only after CCTV footage confirmed his version of events (Duell, 2012). Seeking fame and fortune from media publicity, Nadine Milroy-Sloan falsely accused Tory MP Neil Hamilton and his wife Christine Hamilton of rape in 2001 (Crossley, 2014). And in 2012 there was a media frenzy of the British press, falsely accusing Tory peer Lord McAlpine and implicating Downing Street in a paedophile ring.

When an authority figure or celebrity is accused, the resulting official support, concern, and consideration may engender a sense of power and importance, leading to more and more stories of past abuse being fabricated. In the case of people previously disenfranchised from society—such as the past residents of care homes, who may feel insignificant and powerless, and who may have ended up on the wrong side of the law—making an allegation, supported and encouraged by police and social workers, can give great psychological satisfaction. This 'lying for love' may provide the emotional attention that they crave (Webster, 2005). The gains may be many: as well as getting attention from the authorities, the media, and their peers, the individual may be admired for his or her courage, befriended by other 'survivors', and gain status and recognition from belonging to a victim advocacy group.

Financial gain Money may also be a powerful motivator. In the 1990s, the New Zealand Accident Compensation Corporation awarded lump-sum payments in the order of NZ$10,000 per alleged past sexual abuse incident (Goodyear-Smith et al., 1997). Claimants required neither corroboration nor concomitant report to police. Payments escalated to hundreds of millions per annum until abolished by an Act of Parliament. Similar situations may arise when substantial financial compensation is offered to victims of abuse in residential care cases and other contexts fuelled by police trawling operations and litigation lawyers (Webster, 2005; Rose, Chapter 12 in this volume).

Brian Banks, a US college football star, was imprisoned for six years after fellow student Wanetta Gibson wrongfully accused him of rape. Following his release, she admitted that she had made the story up, but was reluctant to come forward because she did not want to pay back the US$1.5 million compensation payment she had received from the school (Powers, 2012).

Music manager Louis Walsh, formerly one of the judges on British TV show *The X Factor*, was falsely accused by Leonard Watters of sexual molestation in a nightclub toilet. Watters, who was subsequently imprisoned for making the false allegation, alleged that a reporter from *The Sun* had bought him dinner and paid him money to make the false complaint. After a High Court judge ruled that Walsh was entitled to discovery of documents relating to the story *The Sun* had published, the newspaper paid an out-of-court settlement of £403,500 in libel damages (Williams, 2012).

Victimhood may provide considerable financial and other payoffs, including being absolved of any responsibility for one's actions. Compensation for becoming a victim is further addressed by Hewson in Chapter 9 in this volume.

SINCERELY BELIEVED FALSE ALLEGATIONS

There are numerous ways in which allegations may arise that claimants sincerely, but falsely, believe are true. New information from any source can become incorporated into memory. People may persuade themselves that an incident they have imagined, heard, read about, or seen on video or film actually happened to them (Laney and Loftus, 2013). Introduction of post-event misinformation can cause people to create false memories (Loftus, 1997a; also French and Ost, Chapter 11, and Belli, Chapter 19, in this volume.)

In the late 1980s and 1990s, fed by the erroneous belief that one in three girls are sexually abused, mostly by their fathers (Bass and Davis, 1988), it was thought that many women had 'repressed' memories of childhood sexual abuse, leading to myriad adult problems including eating disorders, depression, relationship difficulties, and psychosis. There was widespread use of 'memory recovery techniques' by counsellors and psychotherapists. Such approaches included guided imagery, age regression or outright hypnosis, dream analysis, 'journal-keeping' exercises, use of self-help workshop books, and group sharing (Goodyear-Smith et al., 1997). The common features of these techniques are the use of relaxation, dissociation, suggestion, and absorption. These mesmeric methods create an uncritical, explorative state of mind, which can lead to the generation of false memories, along with an increased confidence that these were real events (Lindsay and Read, 1994).

Allegations made on the basis of memories recovered during therapy include recall of highly improbable events such as of abuse as an infant, of full penetrative intercourse and sodomy as a preschooler that went undetected by caregivers, and of abuse within satanic cults, including ritualized murders, cannibalism, and abortions (Spanos, Burgess, and Burgess, 1994). There is substantial and robust research on the propensity of memory recovery to create sincerely believed pseudo-memories (Laney and Loftus, 2013).

The veracity of a memory cannot be determined by the amount of visual, auditory, tactile, or olfactory details described (Principe and Schindewolf, 2012). There is no correlation between the emotional intensity (Laney and Loftus, 2008) or the confidence (Loftus, 1997b) with which an alleged event is recalled and its reliability; neither is the apparent sincerity of a witness a means by which to judge the accuracy of his or her claim. Similarly, the time between an alleged event and an allegation is neutral with respect to whether or not the event genuinely occurred: both immediate and delayed disclosures may be either true or false. However, the more historical the allegation, the less likely it is that there will be corroborative evidence and the greater the likelihood that people's recollections will have faded or become contaminated by other sources of information and by their imagination.

PARTLY TRUE ALLEGATIONS

Some elements of an allegation may be true, while others may be deliberately embellished, or incorrect aspects may result from honest mistakes. Eyewitness testimony can be persuasive, but there is a solid body of evidence that demonstrates that it is often unreliable (Sharps et al., 2007; Weiss and Alexander, 2013). In 1992, an 11-year-old girl raped at knifepoint by an intruder was convinced that the offender was her neighbour David Dougherty. He was convicted on her testimony. Subsequently, unequivocal DNA evidence found that the semen on her underpants could not have come from Dougherty—and yet the prosecution continued to believe the testimony of the girl rather than the DNA evidence. Eventually, in 1997, after five years in prison, Dougherty was acquitted on retrial. Despite the DNA clearly belonging to another man, the Justice Minister continued to claim that Dougherty had not been proven innocent, hypothesizing that he must have been present during the rape, although the girl had been clear there was only one assailant. In 2003, DNA matching proved that Nicholas Reekie, a known offender, was the real rapist (Cleave and Gower, 2003). On learning that it was Reekie who had raped her, the victim said of Dougherty: 'If I was wrong, then I feel really bad for him. For me, he's still the scary man. It's hard to get that out of your mind.'

The North Wales children's residential care cases demonstrate how some element of truth, such as boys visiting a care worker's room to watch television, can become incorporated into an elaborate web of false allegations (Webster, 2005). Convictions in these cases often depend on the volume of allegations from multiple complainants, despite contradictions between them and evidence that some of the events could not have occurred. The fact that a few of the many people accused are actually guilty can wrongly lend credence to the belief that all allegations resulting from police trawling exercises, fuelled by compensation payments, must be true.

What may start as a deliberate exaggeration or distortion of an event into an allegation of abuse may become incorporated into memory over time, with the complainant coming to sincerely believe in his or her own fabrication. As complainants retell their stories to their peers, counsellors, the media, police, prosecutors, and litigation lawyers, their reconstructed 'memories' may become their reality. As Carol Tavris writes: 'Memories create our stories, but our stories also create our memories. Once we have a narrative, we shape our memories to fit into it' (Tavris and Aronson, 2007: 77).

PARENTAL ALIENATION SYNDROME AND CUSTODY DISPUTES

Professor of child psychiatry Richard Gardner (1992) coined the term 'parental alienation syndrome' to describe a condition arising in the context of child custody disputes. A sexual abuse allegation is a powerful weapon that may facilitate a woman and her children to have no further contact with a hated spouse. The Spanish Supreme Court overthrew the conviction of a father jailed for sexually abusing his 12-year-old daughter. Statements from her brother—and from the defendant's girlfriend—that the girl admitted that her mother had told her to make a false accusation were ignored in the original trial (Fabra, 2014). Children may also play a part in this, wishing to hurt the parent who has abandoned them (Blush and Ross, 1987).

Allegations arising in the context of acrimonious custody disputes may have been contaminated by suggestive interviewing (Mikkelsen, Gutheil, and Emens, 1992; Webster, 2005). Misinformation that taints children's testimony may result from informal questioning by a parent, social worker, or teacher, or rumours and overheard conversations, prior to any formal interviewing, while erroneous reporting can appear as credible as a true disclosure (Ceci et al., 2007).

Normal child care practices of bathing, toileting, or dressing occurring during visitation, or affectionate contact between a parent and a child, such as kissing and hugging, may be misinterpreted as abuse (Green, 1991). Seven cases of abuse alleged in the context of a divorce dispute were all found to be invalid, and children's statements were seen as overinterpreted by anxious parents and projected back on the child in a 'positive feedback loop' (Schuman, 1986).

FACTITIOUS DISORDER AND MÜNCHAUSEN SYNDROME BY PROXY

Uncommonly, a false allegation may arise in the context of a factitious disorder in which signs or symptoms of illness are deliberately falsified by a patient. In Münchausen syndrome, a disease, illness, or psychological trauma is feigned to win attention and sympathy. British woman Gail Sherwood, for example, claimed to have been stalked and raped by an unknown male (Daily Mail Reporter, 2010). At one time, she was found naked below the waist, wearing rubber gloves, with her hands tied behind her back and her mouth covered by tape; on another occasion, police found her behind a fence with a white bandage stuffed in her mouth. Doctors examining her wounds concluded that they were self-inflicted and video evidence disproved her claim that she was kidnapped from her home. She admitted she had lied because she wanted attention.

However, factitious sexual allegations are more likely to be Münchausen syndrome by proxy, whereby a caregiver (usually a mother) invents a story of abuse that she reports to authorities such as police, social services, doctors, and teachers. Thirteen such cases have been reported, in which the mother also often fabricated physical disorders such as blood in the urine or faecal incontinence (Meadow, 1993; Schreier, 2004). None of these occurred in the context of parental separation, divorce, or custody disputes. The mothers of six children had trained them to disclose realistic accounts, in two instances using a tape-recording to help the children to rehearse the story.

FALSE CONFESSIONS

In cases of false confession of guilt, a conviction becomes likely even when contradictory evidence is available that supports the person's innocence. Most false confessions are police-induced (Leo, 2009). Such compliant false confessions may arise under circumstances in which confessing appears more beneficial to the accused than continuing to maintain his or her innocence. Influencing factors may include an overly long interrogation, exhaustion, or a belief that confession will lead to release. There may be coercive components, such as threats of physical harm, or promises that though the accused will be convicted, he or she will receive a more lenient sentence if he or she confesses. The suspect knowingly admits guilt and typically recants soon after the interview is over.[4]

---

[4] For a detailed analysis of vulnerability of sexual abuse suspects to false confession, see Villalobos, Davis, and Leo, Chapter 10 in this volume.

False confessions may also be voluntary, occurring without police questioning (Kassin, 2005). The person may be suffering from a psychological disorder, with the confession motivated by a desire for fame, a sense of guilt about real or imagined events, or a need for self-punishment, or because he or she may wish to protect the real perpetrator. Police tend to be more sceptical about voluntary than compliant confessions and more likely to discount them.

Less frequently, a persuaded false confession may occur, whereby someone becomes influenced by police interrogation to believe that he or she is guilty even though he or she has no memory of committing the crime (Leo, 2009). A well-known case is that of Paul Ingram, deputy sheriff in Olympia, WA. His daughter recovered memories of satanic abuse and rape by her father. After several months of interrogation, Ingram confessed, saying that even though he had no memory, it must be true, because his daughter would not lie. Using hypnotic techniques, police officers and a psychologist extracted from Ingram increasingly elaborate images of supposed abuse. Suspecting that Ingram was confessing to crimes imagined in a trance, sociologist Richard Ofshe invented an allegation. Initially, Ingram could not remember this, but following self-hypnosis wrote a detailed pseudo-memory of the alleged event (Ofshe and Watters, 1995). Yet despite this evidence and his subsequent recantation, Ingram was convicted and served twenty years in prison. He was released in 2003.

CONCLUSION

This chapter has ranged across the societal and the individual motivational factors that, singly or in combination, contribute to allegations of abuse being made or abuse being perceived, reported, and sometimes prosecuted when no crime has been committed, or where small transgressions and ambiguous actions are interpreted as heinous crimes. The belief that sexual abuse is extremely prevalent and that most goes undetected (Bass and Davis, 1988; McGregor, 2014) contributes to the cognitive bias. This bias is confounded by beliefs that both denial and retraction that abuse has occurred are a normal part of the investigation process, that women and children almost never fabricate stories of sexual assault, and that challenging their accounts will revictimize them (McGregor, 2014).

Policy shifts and legislation have made it too easy for untrue allegations to be taken as evidence or as self-verifying. Legislation in some countries has enabled juries to find defendants guilty without the need for corroboration. Given the various mechanisms and motivations outlined that may contribute to the generation of false allegations, the door is wide open for serious miscarriages of justice to occur. While requiring corroboration may allow some guilty to go free, the burden of proof should rest on the prosecution. Presumption of innocence is a basic tenet of justice.

REFERENCES

American Academy of Pediatrics (1998) 'American Academy of Pediatrics Committee on Child Abuse and Neglect: Gonorrhea in Prepubertal Children', *Pediatrics*, 101(1): 134–5.

Banks, S. (2014) 'Campuses Must Distinguish between Assault and Youthful Bad Judgment', *Los Angeles Times*, 9 June. Available online at <http://www.latimes.com/local/la-me-0610-banks-campus-assaults-20140610-column.html> [accessed May 2016].

Bass, E., and Davis, L. (1988) *The Courage to Heal*, New York: Harper Collins Publishers.

BBC News (2010) 'False Rape Claim Mother from Norfolk is Jailed', 24 June. Available online at <http://www.bbc.co.uk/news/10408102> [accessed May 2016].

Beres, M. A. (2014) 'Rethinking the Concept of Consent for Anti-sexual Violence Activism and Education', *Feminism & Psychology*, 24(3): 373–89.

Best, J. (1987) 'Rhetoric in Claims-making: Constructing the Missing Children Problem', *Social Problems*, 34(2): 101–21.

Blush, G., and Ross, K. (1987) 'Sexual Allegations in Divorce: The SAID Syndrome', *Conciliation Courts Review*, 25(1): 1–11.

Bruck, M., Ceci, S. J., and Melnyk, L. (1997) 'External and Internal Sources of Variation in the Creation of False Reports in Children', *Learning and Individual Differences*, 9(4): 289–316.

Butler, C. (2008) 'Mum Made Thousands of Hoax Rape Claims', *North Wales Daily Post*, 17 January. Available online at <http://www.dailypost.co.uk/news/north-wales-news/mum-made-thousands-hoax-rape-2849815> [accessed May 2016].

Butler-Sloss, E. (1988) *Report of the Inquiry into Child Abuse in Cleveland, 1987*, Cmnd 412, London: HMSO.

Ceci, S. J., Kulkofsky, S., Klemfuss, J., Sweeney, C. D., and Bruck, M. (2007) 'Unwarranted Assumptions about Children's Testimonial Accuracy', *Annual Review of Clinical Psychology*, 3(1): 311–28.

Cleave, L., and Gower, P. (2003) 'Ten Years of Guilt over for Rape Victim', *The New Zealand Herald*, 31 May. Available online at <http://www.nzherald.co.nz/nz/news/article.cfm?c_id=1&objectid=3504996> [accessed December 2014].

Clyde, J. (1992) *The Report of the Inquiry into the Removal of Children from Orkney in February 1991*, Edinburgh: HMSO.

Coy, M., Kelly, L., Elvines, F., Garner, M., and Kanyeredzi, A. (2013) '"Sex without Consent, I Suppose That Is Rape": How Young People in England Understand Sexual Consent', London: Office of the Children's Commissioner.

Crossley, L. (2014) 'Fantasist Jailed in 2003 for Falsely Claiming She Was Raped by Neil and Christine Hamilton, behind Bars for Lying Again after Wrongly Telling Police Her Boyfriend Attacked Her with a Samurai Sword', *Daily Mail*, 24 September. Available online at <http://www.dailymail.co.uk/news/article-2767792/Fantasist-jailed-2003-falsely-claiming-raped-Neil-Christine-Hamilton-bars-lying-wrongly-telling-police-husband-attacked-samurai-sword.html> [accessed May 2016].

Daily Mail Reporter (2010) 'Mother of Three Who Faked Elaborate Rape Scenes "for Attention" Jailed for Two Years', *Daily Mail*, 5 March. Available online at <http://www.dailymail.co.uk/news/article-1255594/Mother-faked-elaborate-rape-scenes-attention-jailed-years.html> [accessed May 2016].

Denfeld, R. (1995) *The New Victorians*, New York: Warner Books.

DiSanto, L. (2013) 'Woman Lies about Gang Rape to Cover for Cheating', *NBC Philadelphia, US*, 4 May. Available online at <http://www.nbcphiladelphia.com/news/local/Woman-Lies-About-Gang-Rape-to-Cover-for-Cheating-Police-206048611.html> [accessed May 2016].

Duell, M. (2012) 'Amy Winehouse's Ex-boyfriend Reg Traviss Hits out at "Lies" of Rape Accuser', *Daily Mail*, 16 December. Available online at <http://www.dailymail.co.uk/news/article-2248924/Amy-Winehouses-ex-boyfriend-Reg-Traviss-hits-lies-rape-accuser.html> [accessed May 2016].

Duffin, C. (2013) 'Woman Who Made a String of False Rape Allegations Is Jailed', *Telegraph*, 9 July. Available online at <http://www.telegraph.co.uk/news/uknews/wales/10169257/Woman-who-made-a-string-of-false-rape-allegations-is-jailed.html> [accessed May 2016].

Dworkin, A. (1987) *Intercourse*, New York: Free Press.

Engle, J., and O'Donohue, W. (2012) 'Pathways to False Allegations of Sexual Assault', *Journal of Forensic Psychology Practice*, 12(2): 97–123.

Fabra, M. (2014) 'El Supremo absuelve a un padre condenado por abusar de su hija', *El País*, 29 April. Available online at <http://sociedad.elpais.com/sociedad/2014/04/29/actualidad/1398763837_944898.html> [accessed May 2016].

Festinger, L. (1962) 'Cognitive Dissonance', *Scientific American*, 207(4): 93–107.

Findley, K., and Scott, M. (2006) 'The Multiple Dimensions of Tunnel Vision in Criminal Cases', *Wisconsin Law Review*, 2: 291–7.

Finkelhor, D., Williams, L. M., Burns, N., and Kalinowski, M. (1988) *Nursery Crimes: Sexual Abuse in Day Care*, Thousand Islands, CA: Sage.

Furedi, F. (2013) *Moral Crusades in an Age of Mistrust: The Jimmy Savile Scandal*, Basingstoke: Palgrave Macmillan.

Gardner, R. A. (1992) *True and False Accusations of Child Sex Abuse*, Cresskill, NJ: Creative Therapeutics.

Goodyear-Smith, F. (1993) *First Do No Harm: The Sexual Abuse Industry*, Auckland: Benton-Guy.

Goodyear-Smith, F. (1996) 'Victim-orientated Law Reforms: Advantages and Pitfalls', *Issues in Child Abuse Accusations*, 8(2): 87–93.

Goodyear-Smith, F. (2007) 'What Is the Evidence for Non-sexual Transmission of Gonorrhoea in Children after the Neonatal Period? A Systematic Review', *Journal of Forensic and Legal Medicine*, 14(8): 489–502.

Goodyear-Smith, F. (2015) *Murder that Wasn't: The Case of George Gwaze*, Dunedin: Otago University Press.

Goodyear-Smith, F., Laidlaw, T., and Large, R. (1997) 'Memory Repression and Recovery: What Is the Evidence?', *Health Care Analysis*, 5(2): 99–111.

Goodyear-Smith, F., Sharland, M., and Nadel, S. (2014) 'Think Hickam's Dictum not Occam's Razor in Paediatric HIV', *BMJ Case Reports*, 18 March. Available online at <http://casereports.bmj.com/content/2014/bcr-2013-202029.long> [accessed May 2016].

Govan, F. (2009) 'Woman Faces Jail for Lying about Rape to Get Abortion in Spain', *The Telegraph*, 19 August. Available online at <http://www.telegraph.co.uk/news/worldnews/europe/spain/6055338/Woman-faces-jail-for-lying-about-rape-to-get-abortion-in-Spain.html> [accessed May 2016].

Green, A. H. (1991) 'Factors Contributing to False Allegations of Child Sexual Abuse in Custody Disputes', *Child & Youth Services*, 15(2): 177–89.

Grometstein, R. (2007) 'Prosecutorial Misconduct and Noble-Cause Corruption', *Criminal Law Bulletin*, 43(1): 63–85.

HERBERT, I. (2006) 'Jailed for a Crime He Didn't Commit', *The Independent*, 8 June. Available online at <http://www.independent.co.uk/news/education/education-news/jailed-for-a-crime-he-didnt-commit-481421.html> [accessed May 2016].

HOPKINS, C. (1995) Testimony before the US Senate Committee on Labor and Human Resources, Subcommittee on Children and Families, Washington DC, 25 May 1995.

Innocence Project (2016) 'The Cases: Exonerated by DNA'. Available online at <http://www.innocenceproject.org/all-cases/> [accessed May 2016].

KANIN, E. J. (1994) 'False Rape Allegations', *Archives of Sexual Behavior*, 23(1): 81–92.

KASSIN, S. M. (2005) 'On the Psychology of Confessions: Does Innocence Put Innocents at Risk?', *American Psychologist*, 60(3): 215–28.

KEMPE, C. H., SILVERMAN, F. N., STEELE, B. F., DROEGEMUELLER, W., and SILVER, H. K. (1962) 'The Battered-Child Syndrome', *Journal of the American Medical Association*, 181(1): 17–24.

KUENZIE, J. (2012) 'Woman Faked Story about Rape Assault in Five Points', *WIS TV News*, 24 October. Available online at <http://www.wistv.com/story/19905381/police-woman-faked-story-about-rape-assault-in-five-points> [accessed May 2016].

LA FONTAINE, J. (1994) *The Extent and Nature of Organised and Ritual Abuse*, London: HMSO.

LANCASTER, R. (2011) *Sex Panic and the Punitive State*, Oakland, CA: University of California Press.

LANEY, C., and LOFTUS, E. F. (2008) 'Emotional Content of True and False Memories', *Memory*, 16(5): 500–16.

LANEY, C., and LOFTUS, E. F. (2013) 'Recent Advances in False Memory Research', *South African Journal of Psychology*, 43: 137–46.

LANNING, K. V. (1991) 'Ritual Abuse: A Law Enforcement View or Perspective', *Child Abuse & Neglect*, 15(3): 171–3.

LEO, R. A. (2009) 'False Confessions: Causes, Consequences, and Implications', *Journal of the American Academy of Psychiatry and the Law*, 37(3): 332–43.

LEON, C. (2011) *Sex Fiends, Perverts, and Pedophiles: Understanding Sex Crime Policy in America*, New York: New York University Press.

LINDSAY, S., and READ, D. (1994) 'Psychotherapy and Memories of Childhood Sexual Abuse: A Cognitive Perspective', *Applied Cognitive Psychology*, 8(4): 281–338.

LOFTUS, E. F. (1997a) 'Creating False Memories', *Scientific American*, 277(3): 70–5.

LOFTUS, E. F. (1997b) 'Memories for a Past that Never Was', *Current Directions in Psychological Science*, 6(3): 60–5.

MCCANN, J., VORIS, J., SIMON, M., and WELLS, R. (1989) 'Perianal Findings in Prepubertal Children Selected for Nonabuse: A Descriptive Study', *Child Abuse & Neglect*, 13(2): 179–93.

MCGEHAN, K. (1996) 'Rape Claim Victim Hits back at Police', *Waikato Times*, 17 October.

MCGEHAN, K. (1999) 'The Man Who Never Was...', *Waikato Times*, 20 February.

MCGREGOR, K. (2014) 'We Need to Better Understand Harm', Address to the Leading Justice Symposium, Parliament House, New Zealand, 29 April, reproduced in Ministry of Justice, New Zealand, *Leading Justice Symposium: Summary of Proceedings*. Wellington: Ministry of Justice.

MCLEOD, R. (1997) 'Sex, Lies and Men's Reputations', *The Daily News* [New Zealand], 8 February.

MEADOW, R. (1993) 'False Allegations of Abuse and Münchausen Syndrome by Proxy', *Archives of Disease in Childhood*, 68(4): 444–7.

MIKKELSEN, E. J., GUTHEIL, T. G., and EMENS, M. (1992) 'False Sexual-abuse Allegations by Children and Adolescents: Contextual Factors and Clinical Subtypes', *American Journal of Psychotherapy*, 46(4): 556–70.

Ministry of Justice (2014) *Report on Review of Ways to Reduce Distress of Victims in Trials of Sexual Violence*. Available online at <https://www.gov.uk/government/uploads/system/uploads/attachment_data/file/299341/report-on-review-of-ways-to-reduce-distress-of-victims-in-trials-of-sexual-violence.pdf> [accessed May 2016].

Ministry of Justice, The Netherlands (1994) *Report of the Working Group on Ritual Abuse*, The Hague: Ministry of Justice, The Netherlands. Available online at <http://www.skepsis.nl/rimi.html> [accessed December 2014].

MORRIS, S. (2014) 'Trainee Barrister Jailed for False Rape Claims', *The Guardian*, 26 June. Available online at <http://www.theguardian.com/uk-news/2014/jun/26/trainee-barrister-jailed-false-rape-claims> [accessed May 2016].

NASUWT (2012) 'OVER 97% of Allegations against Teachers Unsubstantiated', Press release, 9 April. Available online at <http://www.nasuwt.org.uk/Whatsnew/NASUWTNews/PressReleases/Over97OfAllegationsAgainstTeachersUnsubstantiated> [accessed May 2016].

O'BRIEN, B. (2009) 'Prime Suspect: An Examination of Factors that Aggravate and Counteract Confirmation Bias in Criminal Investigations', *Psychology, Public Policy, and Law*, 15(4): 315–34.

O'DONOHUE, W., and BOWERS, A. H. (2006) 'Pathways to False Allegations of Sexual Harassment', *Journal of Investigative Psychology and Offender Profiling*, 3(1): 47–74.

OFSHE, R., and WATTERS, E. (1995) *Making Monsters: False Memories, Psychotherapy, and Sexual Hysteria*, London: Andre Deutsch.

PARTON, N. (1985) *The Politics of Child Abuse*, London: Macmillan.

PETERS, S., WYATT, G., and FINKELHOR, D. (1986) 'Prevalence', in D. Finkelhor (ed.) *A Sourcebook on Child Sexual Abuse*, Beverly Hills, CA: Sage.

POWERS, A. (2012) 'A 10-year Nightmare over Rape Conviction is over: Brian Banks Spent Years in Prison, Branded a Rapist', *Los Angeles Times*, 25 May. Available online at <http://articles.latimes.com/2012/may/25/local/la-me-rape-dismiss-20120525> [accessed May 2016].

PRINCIPE, G. F., and SCHINDEWOLF, E. (2012) 'Natural Conversations as a Source of False Memories in Children: Implications for the Testimony of Young Witnesses', *Developmental Review*, 32: 205–23.

ROBIN, M. (1991) 'The Social Construction of Child Abuse and "False Allegations"', *Child & Youth Services*, 15(2): 1–34.

SCHREIER, H. (2004) 'Münchausen by Proxy', *Current Problems in Pediatric and Adolescent Health Care*, 34(3): 126–43.

SCHUMAN, D. (1986) 'False Allegations of Physical and Sexual Abuse', *Bulletin of the American Academy of Psychiatry and the Law*, 14(1): 15–21.

SHARPS, M. J., HESS, A. B., CASNER, H., RANES, B., and JONES, J. (2007) 'Eyewitness Memory in Context: Toward a Systematic Understanding of Eyewitness Evidence', *The Forensic Examiner*, 16(3): 20–7.

SPANOS, N. P., BURGESS, C. A., and BURGESS, M. F. (1994) 'Past-life Identities, UFO Abductions, and Satanic Ritual Abuse: The Social Construction of Memories', *International Journal of Clinical & Experimental Hypnosis*, 42(4): 433–46.

TAVRIS, C., and ARONSON, E. (2007) *Mistakes Were Made (But Not by Me)*, Orlando, FL: Harcourt.

Telegraph Reporters (2012) 'Nanny Jailed for Crying Rape after One-night Stand', *The Telegraph*, 21 November. Available online at <http://www.telegraph.co.uk/news/uknews/

crime/9692984/Nanny-jailed-for-crying-rape-after-one-night-stand.html> [accessed May 2016].

WATERHOUSE, R. (2000) *Lost in Care*, London: HMSO.

WEBSTER, R. (2005) *The Secret of Bryn Estyn: The Making of a Modern Witch Hunt*, Oxford, The Orwell Press.

WEEKS, J. (1989) *Sex, Politics and Society*, London/New York: Longman.

WEISS, K. J., and ALEXANDER, J. C. (2013) 'Sex, Lies, and Statistics: Inferences from the Child Sexual Abuse Accommodation Syndrome', *Journal of the American Academy of Psychiatry and the Law*, 41(3): 412–20.

WILLIAMS, A. (2012) '*X Factor* Judge Louis Walsh Settles £400,000 Libel Action against *The Sun* in Ireland over False Story that He Groped Man in Nightclub Toilets', *Daily Mail*, 28 November. Available online at <http://www.dailymail.co.uk/news/article-2239748/X-Factor-judge-Louis-Walsh-settles-400k-defamation-action-The-Sun-Ireland.html> [accessed May 2016].

9

THE COMPENSATIONS OF BEING A VICTIM

Barbara Hewson

This chapter examines certain powerful drivers that encourage claims of victimization in the present climate. Nothing in this chapter is intended to minimize the very real harms experienced by victims of serious crime, and their families, or the legitimate social objective of affording them justice. Much of my argument applies to genuine claims of victimization, although it also contributes to an explanation of why certain people may make false claims of being a victim. What I am concerned to examine are various internal and external motivators that may induce, or even impel, people to adopt the victim role, in a formal or quasi-formal sense, for example by disclosures in therapy, by joining a support group, by offering to counsel or support other victims, by going public with a claim, by initiating some legal process to seek redress, and so on. Not all victims choose to identify as such. Some object to the word 'victim' as connoting passivity (its Latin root means 'sacrifice'), preferring the term 'survivor'. The latter term is also open to criticism, given that many victims of crime have not experienced anything as severe as a life-threatening attack. To add to the complications, there are those who decline to define their experiences as abusive, leading to charges of false consciousness: in the fashionable slogan, 'they don't know they're victims'.

From a common-sense perspective, who would be the victim of a serious crime? For real victims, the status is involuntary. That much seems obvious. But, as with all common-sense propositions, it deserves interrogation. This chapter argues that acquiring the status or identity of 'victim' can bring a number of substantial benefits, both external and internal. These benefits may include psychological, financial, legal, social, and symbolic rewards. So, although it may superficially seem counterintuitive, there are considerable compensations in being a victim. This gives rise to some serious difficulties. One is that some people will claim to be victims when they are, in fact, pseudo-victims. The incentives for making false rape allegations, for instance, may include a desire for attention and sympathy, motives of anger or revenge, a wish for monetary compensation, or a need for an alibi (Hazelwood and Burgess, 2009). In addition, some allegations may be the product of mental illness.

A striking aspect of the inclusiveness of the modern victim identity is the extent to which men increasingly claim the role of victim, despite the fact that the position of victim has conventionally been a feminized one (Haaken, 1998). Another aspect is the benefit that some parties associated with victims can accrue as a result of a successful accusation ('vicarious benefits'). This consideration is particularly pertinent in the case of minors or incapacitated adults whom others allege have been victims of abuse. Thus, in custody disputes involving children, a mother may accuse a former partner of abuse in order to oust him from her child's life. Allegations of abuse (whether or not well-founded) typically also precipitate local authority intervention in the lives of families. On the wider social stage, 'victim stories come to serve as banners for various crusades and the self-advancement of others on the cultural scene' (Haaken, 1998: 196).

An abiding official concern with victims is enmeshed with a therapeutic and cultural climate that encourages victim self-identification. Victims today enjoy an elevated status, whilst (paradoxically) ever-widening categories of human experiences are termed abusive, making victimization a near-universal experience (Furedi, 2013). The extraordinary proliferation of historic sex abuse scandals in the UK in recent decades has also helped to forge a growing victim class, as well as an appetite on the part of the public for tales of victimhood (fostered by sensational and often irresponsible media coverage), and a desire on the part of politicians and policymakers to garner popular support by adopting the victim cause. The mass production of victims in a society preoccupied with victimhood may be seen as a product of a deeper societal and existential desire to make sense of life through a culturally sanctioned narrative about victims' survival of trauma and the ritual casting out of evil-doers (Webster, 2005; Lancaster, 2011; Furedi, 2013). To challenge this culturally sanctioned narrative in any way is deemed profoundly transgressive: critics are accused of showing insensitivity towards victims, of victim-blaming, and at worst of being 'rape-apologists', 'paedo-apologists', 'enablers', or even 'paedophiles' themselves. Such a highly doctrinaire reaction suggests that what we are dealing with here is a belief system—and a closed one, at that.

THE RISE AND RISE OF THE VICTIM

Sociologist Joel Best (1997) has described the ideology of victimization that had emerged by the 1970s as a spin-off of the civil rights movement. It has created what he calls 'a victim industry—a set of social arrangements that now supports the identification of large numbers of victims' (Best, 1997: 9). The language of rights and of victims' rights converged: 'Fighting for a right all too often means claiming a victim status' (Zur, 1995: 16). By the time the General Assembly of the United Nations issued its Declaration of Basic Principles of Justice for Victims of Crime and Abuse of Power in 1985, it was already using emotive language about victims. In paragraph 4(a), it spoke of 'victims in distress'; in paragraph 5(c), of the 'plight of victims' (United Nations, 1985). It defined victims as 'persons who have suffered harm... through acts or omissions that are violations of criminal laws' (United Nations, 1985: Principle 1). Crucially, it states that '[a] person may be considered a victim... regardless of whether the perpetrator is identified, apprehended, prosecuted or convicted...' (United Nations, 1985: Principle 2); thus the word can include a person making an allegation.

Proponents of human rights have helped to copper-fasten the modern fascination with victims. In the UK, a Labour government introduced the Human Rights Act 1998, ostensibly to 'bring rights home'; the Act has, however, also helped to reinforce the notion of victimhood domestically, terming human rights infringements as 'violations'. While, in terms of public international law, a violation means a state's breach of an international treaty obligation, the term is used domestically to convey an image of a violated individual, whose claim for compensation typically includes a claim for intangible 'moral damage'. Numerous critics of the human rights project (Chandler, 2006; Heyden, 2013; Sumption, 2013; Posner, 2014) have criticized the vagueness of human rights, the extent to which their application in practice enables the state to expand its powers over individuals in the name of protecting rights, and the influence of an elite cadre of human rights lawyers. Despite these critics, the human rights framework has unquestionably lent victims, and those advocating for them, an added moral authority.

By now, a powerful victim lobby has become well embedded in various institutional frameworks, insisting that systems of criminal justice be recalibrated to take account of their various needs. Victims are now increasingly powerful actors in their own right, both domestically and internationally (Hoyle, 2014). Yet—and perhaps incongruously—victims are constantly portrayed as needing more and more protection, support, and official intervention. The concomitant of the victim industry is the recovery movement, based on lay self-help groups, whose original model can be found in the US Alcoholics Anonymous (AA) movement, which espouses an explicitly religious worldview. A key component of the recovery movement's ethos is the imperative to identify as a person in need of help and to attend meetings of fellow sufferers. A problematic feature of the recovery movement's method, however, is the desire that it can instil in participants to compete with each other in telling tales of degradation—a tendency satirized in the *Monty Python* 'Four Yorkshiremen' sketch. The temptation to gild the lily is illustrated by former addict James Frey's (2003) controversial memoir, *A Million Little Pieces*, later exposed as part-fiction.

The language used to frame victims' needs has been explicitly therapeutic: victims are said to be at risk of secondary victimization and in need of support. Implicitly, this approach discounts individual resilience and agency in favour of a notion of continuing vulnerability (Best, 1997; Dineen, 1999; Furedi, 2004). A particularly influential idea has been that of 'testimony as recognition', or giving victims a voice, as a necessary precursor to recovery. This notion of speaking out has its roots in nineteenth-century evangelical Christianity, although it was vigorously promoted by second-wave feminists in the 1970s and 1980s, who sought to draw attention to the widespread problem, as they saw it, of rape and sexual abuse, and who appropriated the language of survivorship that was then being applied to victims of the Holocaust and their offspring (Jenkins, 2006; McLaughlin, 2012). Haaken (1998: 193) describes it as a 'moral and sacral discourse'. The notion of speaking out has been linked both to doing justice and individual healing—a process yoking together the personal and the societal realms. Thus feminist psychologist Judith Herman (1992: 1) argued that '[r]emembering and telling the truth about terrible events are pre-requisites both for the restoration of the social order and for the healing of individual victims'.

There is a certain irony in reading Herman's claim today, given that she was also an enthusiastic proponent of the contentious theory of 'recovered memory'. As Haaken (1998) notes, testifiers do not invariably speak the truth, no matter how virtuous they think they are. Because some of the literature on recovered memories is addressed elsewhere in this volume (see French and Ost, Chapter 11, and Belli, Chapter 19, in this volume), this chapter is not going to rehearse the extensive scientific research in this area (see also McNally, 2005). However, it should be noted at this juncture that concepts of remembering and truth-telling can be both slippery and resistive to analysis, especially when they evoke pre-modern concepts of good and evil. Philip Jenkins (2006: 258) has been particularly critical of this dimension of the victim narrative:

> Though expressed in psychological terms, the recovery movement had a powerful religious quality, with its core ideas of the loss of primal innocence through sexual sin and the recovery of an untarnished child-like state. The process by which the incest is recalled and the path to healing begun has much in common with the evangelical language of conversion: to recover is to be born again. Also recalling religious language is the emphasis on unquestioning faith, of belief in the testimony of others, even if it directly contradicts common sense. The children, external or internal, must be believed.

The idea of 'believing the victim' also derived support from an ethos of child protection originally developed in California in the 1970s, which took root in the British family courts in recent decades and is now firmly embedded in our criminal justice process (Jenkins, 1992; Webster, 2005). Both campaigning feminists, such as Susan Brownmiller, and a growing band of child protection professionals, such as social workers and child psychiatrists, encouraged belief in the ubiquity of sexual exploitation of women and children by male oppressors who were products of a patriarchal system (Jenkins, 1992; Lancaster, 2011). The Californian approach included an ideological taboo against disbelieving any allegation of child abuse, which was progressively taken up by professionals in the UK; thus 'an attitude of disbelief was replaced not by an open-minded willingness to investigate, but by a kind of systematic credulity' (Webster, 1998: 37). This notion of truth-telling has become increasingly influential in the criminal justice system. It is also an article of faith among certain campaigning groups and their supporters. According to former Director of Public Prosecutions (DPP) Sir Keir Starmer QC, who revised the Crown Prosecution Service (CPS) guidelines on the approach to assessing witness credibility in child abuse cases, it is 'more sophisticated' to 'start with the assumption that the victim is telling the truth' (Starmer, 2014).

This is now official policy in specialist police teams dealing with complainants, as illustrated by a recent controversy about Eleanor de Freitas, an educated young woman with bipolar disorder, who led a double life as a Tantric masseuse. She began seeing a young man in December 2012, whom she then accused of rape early in 2013. The police decided that her claim had too many factual inconsistencies to take forward. The accused man then initiated a private prosecution against her, which the CPS took over. She committed suicide three days before her trial. According to press reports, the specially trained police to whom she had made her original complaint adamantly refused to believe the case against her and even refused to cooperate with the CPS, which was forced to go over their heads to an assistant commissioner of the Metropolitan Police (Laville, 2014). The difficulty with this overtly victim-friendly approach is that collapsing the forensic distinction between a complainant and a victim in the narrow sense (meaning a person whose evidence has been accepted in court) has the problematic effect of creating a presumption of guilt (Goodyear-Smith, 1996; Webster, 2005; Conway, 2013). It creates an obvious risk of confirmation bias, and it turns public officials such as police and prosecutors, who should be impartial investigators, into advocates for complainants. The trend has penetrated the courtroom: in *R v Pooley*,[1] the Court of Criminal Appeal even suggested that an accused person had no right to put his or her case to an opposing witness who is deemed 'vulnerable' (meaning all minors, all persons with disabilities, and all complainants in sex cases). It proposed that defence advocates might like to presubmit a list of questions for a 'vulnerable' witness ahead of trial, for vetting by the judge.

A particular difficulty with this 'victims first' approach is that it ignores the potential for copycat complaints, inspired by a media frenzy. Just as some people can feel impelled to confess to crimes that they have not committed in the wake of intense media coverage of a high-profile crime (more than 200 confessed to the Lindbergh kidnapping and murder in 1932), so some people may feel inspired to claim a victim identity, in a peculiarly modern reworking of the Werther effect (that fashion for copycat suicides by young men which emerged in Europe, following the publication of Goethe's *The Sorrows of Young Werther* in 1774). Oscar Wilde (1891) described the Werther effect as life imitating art in his essay 'The Decay of Lying'.

High-profile sex scandals of the kind that have erupted in the UK involving children's care homes, or the late Jimmy Savile, are particularly striking instances of sensational stories of sexual degradation and victimization of vulnerable young people by authority figures: a kind of modern Gothic. These stories tend to follow a familiar trajectory, recounting tales of often sadistic abuse, which has been concealed for a prolonged period. In the aftermath of these scandals, large quantities of victims are urged to come forward by a variety of agencies, including campaigning charities, public relations (PR) agencies offering money in return for stories,[2] and the police. The media feeding frenzy that accompanies such scandals creates a kind of moral contagion—a sort of mental epidemic (Penrose, 1952; Coleman, 2004). The result is an explosion of similar stories, spreading in a viral fashion. Dawkins (1976: 192) called this viral effect a 'meme', while Marsden (1998) calls it a 'mind virus', which he says spreads by a Darwinian process of imitation. As Coleman (2004: 256)

---

[1] *R v Pooley; R v Lubemba* [2014] WLR (D) 472.   [2] Such as <http://www.talktothepress.co.uk>

puts it: 'Human behavior reporting impacts future human behaviors.' Such imitation could also be seen as a passive-aggressive form of social protest by those perceiving themselves as powerless, at a time of a widening gap between rich and poor, widespread voter apathy, and mistrust of political institutions. The victim narrative is especially seductive, because it privileges the victim, whose cry for vindication and (indeed) retribution is seen as a noble cause, often leading to a succession of moral crusades.

THE CONSOLATIONS OF VICTIMHOOD

Since the 1970s, then, the victim identity has become increasingly fashionable. Recovering victims are held up in popular culture as role models. There are victim-celebrities (professional victims who exploit their victim status for money and prestige), as well as celebrity-victims (famous people who disclose the experience of being a victim). This is part of a deeper cultural shift that values the public display of emotion (Furedi, 2004). Some victims derive a vocation from their experience, acquire qualifications as counsellors or psychologists, and develop careers tending to other victims. Others campaign, write memoirs or self-help books, or found self-help groups, some of which can acquire considerable influence and authority. They in turn set out to recruit other victims, often displaying considerable evangelical zeal. One such group, the Lantern Project, practises what it calls 'unstructured therapeutic disclosure', which involves a victim-turned-counsellor giving a client a 'graphic' account of his or her own experience of abuse, before expecting the client to 'disclose' his or her own experience (Scott, 2014). This particular practice is at odds with any professional concept of therapy. The same project also encourages clients to pursue compensation claims as part of the healing process. Thus therapy and law become inextricably intertwined.

Many campaigners and victim-advocates firmly believe that abuse is widespread and causes lifelong damage. The self-help survivors' bible, *The Courage to Heal*, states: 'Betrayal takes only a minute... After that the world is not the same' (Bass and Davis, 1988: 22). The theory of lifelong damage has been criticized for its mechanistic and determinist nature (Davis, 2005). But it is attractive to injury lawyers specializing in abuse claims: the greater the harm, the greater the damages that are potentially recoverable and the bigger the return on any litigation, in terms of legal fees. Unsurprisingly, such law firms continually use the media to solicit business and are regularly found waiting in the wings of modern sex scandals. There is a harsh economic logic to this: if multiple claims can be generated against institutions that are backed by insurers, the greater the pressure to settle, particularly when claims are as emotionally charged and as reputationally devastating as claims of childhood sexual abuse (CSA).

But, as psychologist Susan Clancy and others have shown, trauma need not be the default setting for many victims of CSA. Clancy (2009) noted that what is traumatic for a CSA victim is not necessarily the original experience, but the way in which others react to it later on. This is *not*, as she is at pains to point out, to condone abuse, but simply to recognize the reality that abuse per se need not traumatize. Some victims of rape also reject the trauma model. By what process are some individuals persuaded or converted into accepting a victim identity? Being reported to the authorities as a 'victim' by a third party is one; being contacted by a journalist, whistleblower, or would-be claimant may be another, as may contact with the therapy industry in one's later life.

There are some notorious examples of troubled souls who have constructed false victim identities over a period of years, such as the Swiss man calling himself 'Binjamin Wilkomirski', whose memoir of childhood in Auschwitz proved to be complete confabulation. Wilkomirski was contacted by another fake Holocaust survivor in the United States calling herself 'Laura Grabowski' and they claimed to have known each other in the concentration camp. Grabowski also claimed to have been a victim of Dr Joseph Mengele's brutal experiments. The two self-styled survivors then performed together at a concert for child Holocaust survivors in Los Angeles on 19 April 1998. Laura's history was even more remarkable: American-born under the name Laurel Willson, she had previously claimed to be the victim of satanic ritual abuse, about which she had published no fewer than three 'memoirs' under the name of 'Lauren Stratford'. 'I think only the individual can decide if he/she is a survivor', she wrote. It may be significant that both of these individuals were adopted in early childhood (Passantino, Passantino, and Trott, 1999).

Why do some people do this? Aside from a possible desire for monetary compensation, which is fuelled both by victims' groups insisting that this is a route to recovery and by claimant law firms offering free legal services under contingency fee arrangements, the status of victim carries more intangible psychological benefits. According to Davis (2005: 237), the victim/survivor account 'has great explanatory potential: It economically orders a wide range of confusing and troublesome experience, settles the question of self-blame, and is set within a discourse of hope for the future'. Other commentators, both psychologists and sociologists, share this view (Dineen, 1999; Clancy, 2005). Dineen (1999: 7) explains the psychological payoffs: in short, they relieve people of 'at least three of life's natural burdens: dealing with complexity, facing things beyond their control, and accepting personal responsibility for decisions and actions'. Lancaster (2011) itemizes the privileges of victimhood as the gaining of official empathy and indulgences of otherwise unreceptive authorities, and a disclaimer of personal responsibility. Moreover, '[t]he victim is the undisputed hero of his or her story. Victims' suffering bestows a sort of awe, an aura, a halo. This narrative, this nimbus can be leveraged against others' (Lancaster, 2011: 205).

Some people may assume a victim role, sometimes as a therapeutic rite of passage to the roles of survivor/thriver, irrespective of whether they have actual memories of abuse. Thus McNally (2005) reports that a number of women attended his memory research laboratory claiming to have been abused in childhood, although they had no actual memories of the abuse. He makes the pragmatic observation, '[i]f faced with a choice between being miserable and not knowing why, and being miserable and being able to blame someone else, many people will choose the latter' (McNally, 2005: 231). British cultural historian Richard Webster had—independently, it seems—reached a similar conclusion in his elaborate study of the 1990s scandals involving Welsh children placed in institutional care, some of whom made claims of abuse long after reaching adulthood. According to Webster (2005: 133, emphasis added):

> An allegation of abuse may also furnish a beguiling explanation for aspects of their lives which may previously have induced feelings of guilt. Broken relationships, sexual confusion, emotional difficulties, alcoholism, drug addictions and criminality can all be 'explained' by invoking a history of abuse. *Whether or not that history is true is all but irrelevant to its explanatory power and psychological potency.*

McNally's colleague Susan Clancy also reached the same conclusion in her study of people who believed themselves to be victims of alien abduction, invoking Donald Spence's distinction between historical and narrative truth: 'Believing that the narratives we create to explain our distress accurately reflect reality is both optimistic and naïve' (quoted in Clancy, 2005: 142). As she explains his approach, historical truth (or untruth) is irrelevant. The critical question is:

> Do our beliefs have *narrative* truth? Do they provide us with meaning and value? When people believe they were abducted by aliens, does this help them to understand perplexing or upsetting aspects of their lives? If so, the explanation is going to be persuasive, satisfying and resistant to argument.
>
> (Clancy, 2005: 143)

Haaken (1998: 95) argues that a hysterical current runs through the trauma model—that is, a battle for cultural recognition: women's accounts of suffering can at times be symbolic, with the more Gothic elements having 'less to do with actual events than with primitive currents in the human imagination'. She acknowledges that, for some women, sexual abuse is 'a metaphor for violations of the self' (Haaken, 1998: 250) and that even a lie may convey an emotional truth: 'The power of the story to stir others...depends on its felt truth and plausibility rather than on its mere facticity' (Haaken, 1998: 185).

In a more recent, small-scale, study, sociologist and researcher Jo Woodiwiss (2007) found that 'for many women a history of sexual abuse helps them to make sense of their lives and their present unhappiness and distress'. In her study of a cohort of sixteen women, of whom eleven had read *The Courage to Heal* (Bass and Davis, 1988), five had continuous memories of childhood abuse, six had 'recovered memories', and five had false memories. Intriguingly, some in the last group had resorted to a false memory critique, after their adoption of a sexual abuse narrative failed to produce a sufficient explanation or improvement for their symptoms. Woodiwiss (2010) blames a pervasive therapeutic self-help culture for the formation of these victim identities, which privileges looking inward and to the past for the cause of all one's life problems:

[W]omen themselves play an active role in constructing life stories based on CSA... That they ultimately construct themselves as victims of CSA tells us more about society, and the lack of alternative, social explanations for unhappiness, than it does about CSA, or indeed the science of memory.

The consolations of victimhood, then, are wide-ranging. But the lure of the victim narrative can sometimes create pseudo-victims, posing traps for investigators and the innocent accused, whenever fantasy and symbolism are mistaken for literal truth. Far from being sophisticated, the Starmer (2014) approach of 'believe the victim' appears somewhat quixotic, especially when the research set out above is taken into account, showing how some people may construct victim identities as a culturally validated response to the trials of life.

REFERENCES

BASS, E., and DAVIS, L. (1988) *The Courage to Heal: A Guide for Women Survivors of Child Sexual Abuse*, London: Cedar.
BEST, J. (1997) 'Victimization and the Victim Industry', *Society*, 34(4): 9–17.
CHANDLER, D. (2006) *From Kosovo to Kabul and beyond: Human Rights and International Intervention*, London/Ann Arbor, MI: Pluto Press.
CLANCY, S. (2005) *Abducted: How People Came to Believe They'd Been Abducted by Aliens*, Cambridge, MA: Harvard University Press.
CLANCY, S. (2009) *The Trauma Myth: The Truth about the Sexual Abuse of Children—and Its Aftermath*, New York: Basic Books.
COLEMAN, L. (2004) *The Copycat Effect: How the Media and Popular Culture Trigger the Mayhem in Tomorrow's Headlines*, New York: Paraview.
CONWAY, M. A. (2013) 'On Being a Memory Expert Witness: Three Cases', *Memory*, 21(5): 566–75.
DAVIS, J. E. (2005) *Accounts of Innocence: Sexual Abuse, Trauma and the Self*, Chicago, IL: University of Chicago Press.
DAWKINS, R. (1976) *The Selfish Gene*, Oxford: Oxford University Press.
DINEEN, T. (1999) *Manufacturing Victims: What the Psychology Industry Is Doing to People*, London: Constable.
FREY, J. (2003) *A Million Little Pieces*, London: John Murray.
FUREDI, F. (2004) *Therapy Culture: Cultivating Vulnerability in an Uncertain Age*, London: Routledge.
FUREDI, F. (2013) *Moral Crusades in an Age of Mistrust*, Basingstoke: Palgrave Macmillan.
GOETHE, J. W. VON (1774) *The Sorrows of Young Werther*, Leipzig: Weygand'sche Buchhanglung.
GOODYEAR-SMITH, F. (1996) 'Victim-oriented Law Reforms: Advantages and Pitfalls', *Issues in Child-abuse Accusations*, 8(2): 87–93.
HAAKEN, J. (1998) *Pillar of Salt: Gender, Memory, and the Perils of Looking Back*, New Brunswick, NJ: Rutgers University Press.
HAZELWOOD, R., and BURGESS, A. (2009) *Practical Aspects of Rape Investigation: A Multidisciplinary Approach*, Boca Raton, FL: CRC Press.

HERMAN, J. (1992) *Trauma and Recovery: The Aftermath of Violence—From Domestic Abuse to Political Terror*, New York: Basic Books.

HEYDEN, D. (2013) 'Are Bills of Rights Necessary in Common Law Systems?', Paper delivered at the Inner Temple Reader's Lecture Series, 21 January. Available online at <http://www.innertemple.org.uk/downloads/members/lectures_2013/lecture_heydon_2013.pdf> [accessed May 2016].

HOYLE, C. (2014) 'New Court, New Justice?', *Journal of International Criminal Justice*, 12(4): 681–703.

JENKINS, P. (1992) *Intimate Enemies: Moral Panics in Contemporary Great Britain*, New York: Aldine de Gruyter.

JENKINS, P. (2006) *Decade of Nightmares: The End of the Sixties and the Making of Eighties America*, Oxford: Oxford University Press.

LANCASTER, R. (2011) *Sex Panic and the Punitive State*, Berkeley, CA: University of California Press.

LAVILLE, S. (2014) 'Eleanor de Freitas Should Never Have Been Charged, Police Say', *The Guardian*, 9 December. Available online at <http://www.theguardian.com/uk-news/2014/dec/09/police-eleanor-de-freitas-rape-complaint-perverting-course-justice> [accessed May 2016].

MARSDEN, P. S. (1998) 'Memetics and Social Contagion: Two Sides of the Same Coin?', *Journal of Memetics: Evolutionary Models of Information Transmission*, 2(2): 171–85.

MCLAUGHLIN, K. (2012) *Surviving Identity: Vulnerability and the Psychology of Recognition*, London: Routledge.

MCNALLY, R. J. (2005) *Remembering Trauma*, Cambridge, MA: Belknap Press.

PASSANTINO, B., PASSANTINO, G., and TROTT, J. (1999) 'Lauren Stratford: From Satanic Ritual Abuse to Jewish Holocaust Survivor', *Cornerstone*, 28(117): 12–18.

PENROSE, L. (1952) *On the Objective Study of Crowd Behaviour*, London: H. K. Lewis & Co.

POSNER, E. (2014) 'The Case against Human Rights', *The Guardian*, 4 December. Available online at <http://www.theguardian.com/news/2014/dec/04/-sp-case-against-human-rights> [accessed May 2016].

SCOTT, M. (2014) 'Exaro News is Playing a Dangerous Game with Its Paedophile Murder Story', *Barrister Blogger*, 16 November. Available online at <http://barristerblogger.com/2014/11/16/exaro-news-playing-dangerous-game-paedophile-murder-story/> [accessed May 2016].

STARMER, K. (2014) 'Human Rights, Victims and the Prosecution of Crime in the 21st Century' *Criminal Law Review*, 11: 777–87.

SUMPTION, J. (2013) 'The Limits of Law', 27th Sultan Azlan Shah Lecture, 20 November. Available online at <https://www.supremecourt.uk/docs/speech-131120.pdf> [accessed May 2016].

TAVRIS, C., and ARONSON, E. (2007) *Mistakes Were Made (But Not by Me)*, Orlando, FL: Harcourt.

United Nations (1985) *Declaration of Basic Principles of Justice for Victims of Crime and Abuse of Power*, A/RES/40/34. Available online at <http://www.refworld.org/docid/3b00f2275b.html> [accessed February 2015].

WEBSTER, R. (1998) *The Great Children's Home Panic*, Oxford: The Orwell Press

WEBSTER, R. (2005) *The Secret of Bryn Estyn: The Making of a Modern Witch Hunt*, Oxford: The Orwell Press.

WILDE, O. (1891) 'The Decay of Lying: An Observation', in *Intentions*, London: James R. Osgood McIlvaine & Co.

WOODIWISS, J. (2007) 'Politics, Responsibility and Adult Victims of Child Sexual Abuse', *Sociological Research Online*, 12(2). Available online at <http://www.socresonline.org.uk/12/2/woodiwiss.html> [accessed May 2016].

WOODIWISS, J. (2010) 'Why Do Women Identify Themselves as Victims of Childhood Sexual Abuse?', *The Guardian*, 11 March. Available online at <https://www.theguardian.com/science/blog/2010/mar/10/women-victims-childhood-sexual-abuse> [accessed May 2016].

ZUR, O. (1995) 'Rethinking "Don't Blame the Victim": The Psychology of Victimhood', *Journal of Couple Therapy*, 4(3/4): 15–36.

10

HIS STORY; HER STORY
SEXUAL MISCOMMUNICATION, MOTIVATED REMEMBERING, AND INTOXICATION AS PATHWAYS TO HONEST FALSE TESTIMONY REGARDING SEXUAL CONSENT

J. Guillermo Villalobos, Deborah Davis, and Richard A. Leo

On 17 September 2009, alleged victim Kelli Kalisiak was receiving a one-and-a-half-hour massage in her home from her masseuse of three years, Joshua Lewis, whom Kalisiak described as like a 'family friend'. As she lay naked, covered only by a sheet, the massage departed from the usual procedure. Lewis began to touch Kalisiak's vagina and rub her clitoris. This continued for about 30 seconds, after which he continued to massage her thighs and to generally provide a more typical massage for another 15 minutes before stopping. During this time, Kalisiak lay unmoving and without comment. She responded to his requests to change position without comment. When it was over, Lewis asked her if she liked the massage or if it was 'too intense', and told her that if it was too intense, he would never do it again. Kalisiak told Lewis it was indeed too intense, and he said 'Okay' and left. The next day, Kalisiak and her mother called police to file charges of sexual assault.[1]

As often happens in cases of disputed sexual events, the two parties told stories with vastly different implications for whether there was or was not sexual consent. On the one hand, Lewis believed that he had consent, and even an invitation. He reported that Kalisiak often talked to him about how lonely she was and how difficult it was for her to find a romantic companion, as she was doing on that day. She had also talked that day about how she wanted him to 'be the boss', saying that he was the expert. She appeared to respond enthusiastically to his touch. He moved gradually from massaging her back, to massaging her thighs and systematically moving upward toward her vagina. The sheet was clearly not fully covering her buttocks or genitals and Lewis felt that was a signal of permission. She did nothing to indicate that he should stop as he

[1] *People of California v. Joshua Lewis*, Case No. 09SM04524 (2009).

moved toward her vagina, nor did she tell him to stop as he rubbed her clitoris. She allowed him to continue the massage for another 15 minutes or more—all the while saying nothing. She indicated no anger after it was over and said goodbye as usual. But, when asked after the fact, she said it was too intense and he said he would not do it again.

For her part, Kalisiak reported to police that she felt that she had been involuntarily assaulted—that she had done nothing to convey consent and that she clearly indicated that she did not want him to touch her genitals. But how did she convey this? Kalisiak knew that the sheet was not covering her genitals, and that Lewis was moving closer and closer to her vagina. But she did nothing to protest or stop the advance. She reported that she thought Lewis was gay (although this had never been discussed), that she regarded him as a friend, and that she trusted him. Her only reaction as he touched her clitoris was to stiffen. Kalisiak believed that Lewis would interpret her abrupt tensing as her displeasure and desire for him to quit (that is, as non-consent), even though she showed no other sign of protest and allowed the massage of other body areas to continue for more than 15 minutes until Lewis stopped voluntarily.

Although this event occurred in a professional context, wherein escalation to sexual intimacy might be expected to proceed differently from such contexts as dating, it reflects several failures of communication common to many cases involving disputed sexual interactions.

1. There was an honest disagreement: the male thought the female was interested and had no objection, whereas she actually was not interested and the sexual advances were unwanted.
2. There was no direct explicit communication: either of what the male wanted and intended to do, or of what the female wanted or did not want him to do.
3. The male relied on indirect indications of her interest, such as talking about her loneliness and desire for a relationship while naked, assigning him the role of 'boss', and the lack of expression of non-consent.
4. The male relied on gradual escalation of intimacy, proceeding until when (or if) he received a clear refusal.
5. The female relied on non-verbal behaviour to convey her non-consent—and, unfortunately, on non-verbal behaviour (that is, 'stiffening'), which could possibly be interpreted as excitement rather than discomfort. Moreover, this ambiguous indicator did not occur until after the deed was done.

Such scenarios are all too common. Although some interactions leading to first sexual contact between a couple are quite explicit, many take place in the form of hints, innuendo, mind reading (attempts to interpret the other person's interest and intentions), testing the waters indirectly, tentative attempts, and gradual escalation of intimacy toward the desired sexual outcome. Likewise, attempts to forestall sexual intimacy may be explicit. And yet many attempts to reject sexual advances are performed through hints, non-verbal signs of disinterest, ignoring advances, and other indirect signals of non-consent.

In part, this dance of ambiguity serves to protect both parties. The initiator can try to advance the sexual agenda, but with plausible deniability that can protect the ego in case the advance is rejected. The target can accept the sexual advance without having to explicitly admit it is wanted, or can reject it without explicitly rejecting the suitor. In this way, the relationship can be more easily maintained without insult or injury to the feelings of either. But, of course, there is a price for this protection: mistakes of interpretation can be made; opportunity may be lost when desire is not made clear; or unwanted advances or sexual intercourse may proceed unchecked because the target's non-consent is never clearly conveyed.

Clearly, disputed cases of sexual assault often involve deliberate and knowing violations of the victim's unambiguous non-consent. But determining sexual consent is not always an easy task,[2] although it is nonetheless usually the defining factor in legal allegations of sexual harassment and assault (Cook et al., 2011). Here, we explore the problems of communication leading to the subset of cases in which there is honest disagreement about whether (non-)consent was or was not conveyed.

THE NATURE AND VAGARIES OF CONSENT INTERACTIONS

A great deal of research has addressed the issue of how sexual consent interactions unfold; it has converged on the conclusion that most sexual encounters—particularly those involving first progression to intercourse—involve few explicit verbal statements, let alone explicit requests or denials. Instead, sexual interest and intentions, and sexual consent or refusal, tend to take place via hints, indirect verbal statements, non-verbal behaviours, and, crucially, failures to act (Davis and Villalobos, 2014).

Such indirect statements and behaviours are inherently, and by design, ambiguous and therefore easily misinterpreted. Moreover, they take place in a social context that directs their interpretation. This may be personal social context involving the parties, such as their previous dating history and history of intimacy, their general knowledge and expectations of one another, and so on. But the many indirect and non-verbal behaviours involved in sexual interactions are also interpreted in light of cultural sexual scripts specifying how people are expected to behave in sexual situations (Byers, 1996). Some such scripts directly promote misunderstanding, such as the idea that women conceal their actual interest in sex and often engage in initial refusals that are merely 'token' gestures, in order to avoid being perceived as promiscuous (Muehlenhard and Hollabaugh, 1988; Osman, 2003). Finally, many behaviours with implications for sexual interest have multiple meanings. They are the same as those reflecting liking or other kinds of interest in the other person, and/or they may be same as those designed to attract the romantic interest of the other party (rather than to invite an immediate sexual interaction). These triple issues of indirect communication, misleading sexual scripts, and multiple meaning contribute to honest discrepancies in understanding of sexual consent interactions.

---

[2] See Wertheimer (2003) for a review.

THE AMBIGUITIES OF NON-VERBAL AND INDIRECT COMMUNICATION

Despite the obvious risks of misunderstandings, initial communication of sexual desire often occurs through non-verbal cues such as eye contact, escalating physical proximity, suggestive movements, or non-sexual touching, which then may progress to more explicitly sexual touch, passionate kissing, undressing, and so on. Explicit verbal requests to engage in sexual activity are much less common, as are verbal requests for clarification or refusal of sexual advances (Perper and Weis, 1987; O'Sullivan and Byers, 1992; Hickman and Muehlenhard, 1999; Lim and Roloff, 1999).

Sexual communication is further complicated by the tendency to communicate refusal through indirect means, one of the most common being failure to resist (Perper and Weis, 1987; Hickman and Muelhenhard, 1999; Woodhams et al., 2012). Jordan (2005) argued that women tend to be socialized to be indirect and submissive when interacting with men, and to avoid aggressive responses during confrontations, which is reflected in part in the tendency to rely on indirect means to communicate their refusal to engage in sexual activities. Indeed, in a series of interviews of women aged 18–22, Fantasia (2011) found that even when the women really did not want to engage in sexual activities, most respondents considered not resisting their partners' sexual advances to be a form of consenting, for example 'he never asked but I never said no, so I guess he thought it was okay' (Fantasia, 2011: 125). Similarly, Hickman and Muelhenhard (1999) found that the most commonly reported signal to indicate consent, used roughly equally by both men and women, was simply not resisting the sexual advances of the other person (that is, expressing no response). Nevertheless, as illustrated by the experience of Kalisiak, lack of resistance to sexual advances could have very different meanings for the two interacting individuals. It might reflect reactions such as shock, confusion, shame, or fear of repercussions of refusal, among other things (Muehlenhard et al., 1992).

Woodhams and colleagues (2012) found that many victims' accounts of their own behaviours during sexual assaults did not adhere to the stereotypical myth of the 'resisting rape victim'. Some reported subtler forms of resistance, such as simply not responding to specific orders (such as removing her clothes) and choosing to remain stationary instead. Such weak signals of resistance are ambiguous and subject to misinterpretation as consent. Davis and Villalobos (2014) identified other ambiguous strategies, such as distancing herself from the subject through non-verbal means (for example stepping a few inches back, facing away from the subject), offering pretexts as to why she is unable to accept such invitations, or simply by pretending not to notice the subject's advances or hints. Given such indirect behaviours, it is entirely possible that a man may believe a woman to have consented to engage in sexual activities even when she believes she has made her refusal to do so very clear.

In addition to ambiguous behaviours, sexual communications often entail ambiguous, indirect statements. Lee and Pinker (2010) suggested that individuals are particularly likely to utilize indirect language to convey messages involving social risk. In their theory of the 'strategic speaker', the authors described 'off-record indirect speech acts' as statements the true meaning of which the hearer must infer through contextual cues and other circumstantial subtleties. The authors argued that speakers use off-record indirect speech primarily because such statements can be interpreted in more than one way, thereby providing plausible deniability of the intended message.

Lee and Pinker (2010) further suggested that speakers are more likely to use indirect statements when the intended message would suggest a substantial change in the nature of the relationship between speaker and hearer (for example from a platonic to a sexual relationship). Indeed, indirect speech is prevalent when the speaker attempts to avoid unambiguously stating illegal or potentially embarrassing intentions, such as sexual come-ons that may be rejected or interpreted as harassment. The speaker can retain some protection against legal or social consequences, because the message *can be* understood as the speaker originally intended, but it does not necessarily *have to be* interpreted that way. In this way, the speaker can maintain plausible deniability of his (or her) intentions, not only in case of rejection by the hearer, but also in case his (or her) message is scrutinized by a third party or is used to provide the basis of legal sanctions (Tiersma and Solan, 2012).

Arguably, most indirect speech is understood as intended by hearers (Lee and Pinker, 2010; Bergen and Grodner, 2012). Indeed, when one party to an interaction uses indirect speech, the other tends to 'line up pragmatically' and use indirect language as well (Roche, Dale, and Caucci, 2012). Use of indirect verbal and non-verbal behaviours is likely to be understood by both, and each is likely to actively interpret the indirect sexual meanings. Given that indirect verbal and non-verbal communication seems to be normative when initiating sexual advances, the mechanisms leading to misunderstandings and failures to interpret sexual cues adequately merit further investigation. In subsequent sections, we shall explore the roles of misleading sexual scripts, motivational biases, and multiple meanings in producing such misunderstandings.

MULTIPLE MEANING: GENERAL INTEREST, LIKING, AND ROMANTIC INTEREST VS SEXUAL INTENT

Attractive or sexually attractive attire, for example, may simply reflect a desire to appear attractive in general, to attract the interest of a potential partner, to compete with same-sex others, or to promote sexual activity, among other intentions. Similarly, verbal and non-verbal behaviours such as smiling, touch, expressions of liking, and intimate disclosures, among many others, may simply reflect the actor's liking of the target, may be intended to make the other person like oneself, and may reflect interest in the conversation or other goals.

These ambiguities in meaning open the door to misinterpretation of sexual intentions—a problem that can be exacerbated by sexual motivation. Likely because of their relatively greater sexual motivation, for example, men have been shown to perceive more sexual interest in women than women themselves intend to convey (through social clues such as friendliness, eye contact, smiling): a phenomenon known as the 'overperception bias' (Abbey, McAuslan, and Ross, 1998; Abbey, Jacques-Tiura, and LeBreton, 2011; Farris et al., 2008).[3] Error management theory (EMT) sug-

---

[3] See La France et al. (2009) for a meta-analysis and review.

gests an explanation for this phenomenon based on the notion that cognitive errors of inference are the result of adaptive biases that benefit reproductive goals (Haselton and Buss, 2000). From an evolutionary perspective, it was in men's best interests not to miss any opportunities for reproduction with any available woman, thus leading to an adaptive overperception of women's levels of sexual interest. However, while the bias is more prominent among men generally, sexual overperception tends to be more prominent among people with high sociosexuality—that is, those who report high interest in short-term and casual relationships—regardless of gender (Howell, Etchells, and Penton Voak, 2012). Regardless of gender, people tend to project their own desires for sex or commitment onto people with whom they are interacting (Henningsen and Henningsen, 2010).

Nevertheless, the gender bias in imputed sexual meaning tends to occur reliably. Thus Davis, Follette, and Merlino (1999) attempted to identify behaviours that might be interpreted most differently by the two genders. Men and women were presented with 72 behaviours and asked to make two ratings: whether women are more likely, equally likely, or less likely to engage in the behaviour when willing to have intercourse; and whether women never, sometimes, or often engage in the behaviour when not willing to have intercourse. Women answered for themselves personally and men answered with regard to women in general. Several results stood out. First, women reported that they were more likely to engage in many more behaviours when willing to have intercourse than when not willing. Second, however, many women also reported that they sometimes or often engaged in those same behaviours when *not* willing to have intercourse. For example, 70 per cent of women reported that they were more likely to dress in a sexually provocative manner when willing to have intercourse, but 55 per cent also reported that they sometimes or often do so when not willing. Third, women reported that they were equally likely to engage in many behaviours commonly viewed as reflecting sexual intentions regardless of whether they were willing to have intercourse or not (such as drinking or doing drugs with the male, hugging him, going to his residence alone with him, or smiling at him a lot).

Davis and colleagues (1999) also found considerable correspondence between women's reports of the meaning of their own behaviours and men's perceptions of that meaning. However, for a subset of the behaviours, there was a notable discrepancy between genders. The authors proposed the term 'rapeseed quotient' to define behaviours that women reported themselves as likely to engage in even when not willing (or equally likely whether willing or not), but which men think women either do *only* when willing or are much more likely to do when willing than when not willing to have intercourse. Some behaviours found to have the highest rapeseed quotients included dressing very sexily, allowing the man to touch her breasts or genitalia, and talking about sexual topics. Some were quite startling. For example, 40 per cent of men believed that women will perform oral sex if and only if willing to have intercourse, whereas 40 per cent of women said that they did so sometimes or often when not willing. These behaviours are some of those most likely to result in honest disagreements about consent and those that men are most likely to overperceive as reflecting consent.

MISLEADING SEXUAL SCRIPTS

A variety of 'scripts' for sexual interactions exist within cultures, specifying such details as how sexual interactions are to be initiated and by whom, the circumstances under which sex is expected to occur (such as at what point in the relationship and between what partners), expected behaviours for the two parties, how the interaction is to unfold over time, and the meaning of various behaviours, among many others. These scripts indicate how people ought to think and react in situations that could be considered sexual in nature, and shape expectations and behaviours in sexual situations (Simon and Gagnon, 1986; Gagnon, 1990).

Many such scripts concern the expected roles and behaviours of males versus females. Despite increasingly egalitarian gender roles and expectations in our culture, the media continue to portray sexual interactions predominantly in accord with traditional gender roles (Hust, Brown, and L'Engle, 2008; Hust et al., 2014), and most men and women continue to adhere to traditional gender roles when engaging in sexual activities (Jozkowski and Peterson, 2013; Masters et al., 2013). Prominent among these roles are those of males as the initiators of sex and women as the gatekeepers who determine whether sex will take place (Jozkowski and Peterson, 2013). Other scripts address the meaning of specific behaviours in consent interactions.

Among the most troubling of such scripts concerns the behaviour known as 'token resistance' to sex—that is, the expectation that a person will initially refuse sexual advances even if there is an actual desire to engage in sexual activities (Muehlenhard, 2011). Since women who consent too easily to sexual activity might be regarded as promiscuous, a woman may resist at first solely to manage impressions of her virtue, rather than because she truly does not want to engage in sex. Males believe that women engage in token resistance and a third to half of females report doing so (Muehlenhard and Hollabaugh, 1988; Sprecher et al., 1994). However, both men and women actually engage in such behaviours at similar rates and for a wide variety of reasons, including appearing 'hard to get', thinking that it is what 'is expected', and shame (Muehlenhard and Rodgers, 1998). This widespread belief in, and practice of, token resistance complicates the interpretation of even explicit refusals to engage in sex. The man might interpret rejection as the woman 'being a tease' or 'playing hard to get', and further pursue his sexual objectives, even in an aggressive manner (Murnen, Wright, and Kaluzny, 2002), often interpreting his sexual coercion as welcomed seduction (Farris et al., 2008).

The notion that even women who explicitly reject a sexual advance are sometimes actually receptive to sexual advances is troubling. There can be genuine ambiguity in the meaning of the woman's rejection, particularly when other behaviours are consistent with consent. But if the rejection is real, the woman may still be thought to have indicated consent. Such judgements may promote rape, as well as contribute to vindication of her rapist. Cultural scripts and predispositions often outweigh legal definitions of sexual consent when individuals make assessments of whether consent has been granted.[4]

---

[4] See Kahan (2010) for a review.

THE ROLE OF ALCOHOL IN NEGOTIATING SEXUAL CONSENT

The process of communicating and understanding sexual consent can be substantially affected by use of alcohol (or other drugs). A substantial number of cases involving alleged sexual assault or non-consensual sex involve the consumption of alcohol by one or both parties (Davis and Loftus, 2004; Abbey, 2011; Fantasia, 2011; Ward et al., 2012). In part, this may occur because the use of alcohol in sexual encounters can significantly impair interpretation and negotiation of sexual consent—that is, intoxicated men are less likely to interpret non-consent messages accurately. Similarly, compared to their non-intoxicated counterparts, intoxicated women tend to convey less emphatic signs of refusal of consent and tend to do so at a later time during the sexual encounter (Davis and Loftus, 2004; Abbey, 2011).

Both men and women perceive intoxicated others as more sexually aroused, easier to seduce, and more willing to consent (George et al., 1997)—a belief that is prominent even among professionals (Lee and Cheung, 1991). Moreover, mutual alcohol consumption is viewed as a sign of sexual intent or consent (Leigh, Arumburu, and Norris, 1992). Overall, on the one hand, these results suggest that intoxicated parties are likely to overperceive sexual interest and intent, and to recognize indicators of non-consent less effectively; on the other hand, when one party does not wish to engage in sex, efforts to convey non-consent will occur later in the sexual interaction, and be less clear and effective. Accordingly, the potential for both non-consensual sex, as well as for honest disagreements concerning whether consent did or did not occur, will be greater among intoxicated parties.

MEMORY FOR CONSENT INTERACTIONS

When sexual assault is alleged, both parties are asked to recount a wealth of detail, including (among many other things): details of the relationship and interactions leading up to the event in question; specific behaviours and statements made during the event; emotions and reactions to, and interpretations of, the other's behaviours and statements; and their own intentions and subjective thoughts. Many such details become important only in hindsight: they may not have been attended to at the time and therefore may never have been encoded into memory. Moreover, although the exact manner in which consent or refusal was conveyed is crucial in legal contexts, memory tends to be for the gist of what happened, rather than the exact details—and this is particularly true for memory for conversation. What is most likely to be remembered is each party's version of the gist of the events and their general reactions to, and interpretations of, their own and the other's actions. Thus the victim may report such gist characterizations as 'It was clear I didn't want to', whereas the accused may report his own gist summary as 'She obviously wanted it' or 'She didn't do anything to tell me to stop' (Davis and Friedman, 2007; Davis and Villalobos, 2014).

To complicate matters further, human memory is reconstructive in nature and not only fallible, but also malleable and susceptible to suggestion and bias (Loftus, 2005). It is possible, for example, to 'remember' saying things that one only thought about or intended to say at the time (Davis and Friedman, 2007). As a result, the woman might falsely remember saying things that she thought (but did not say) to stop the situation and for the man to falsely remember doing things that he did not do to verify the woman's consent. Furthermore, memories of past events also tend to be distorted so that they line up with one's beliefs about oneself, others, or how things work in general (Brainerd and Reyna, 2005). Indeed, both parties might forget some details of things that they believe they *would not have* done and falsely remember things that they believe they *would have done* in that situation, but did not. For example, a man might falsely remember explicitly asking the woman for consent because, in his mind, he would never engage in sexual activities with a woman without her consent. Likewise, the woman might remember explicitly telling the man that she did not want to have sex, because she believes that she would never reciprocate the sexual advances of a near-stranger.

Such false memories can be easily created through simple processes, such as continuous mental re-enactment of the contested events, the introduction of new information by witnesses, or suggestive questioning by investigative authorities (Loftus and Davis, 2006; Davis and Loftus, 2007). Alcohol-related cognitive impairments affecting memory encoding and retrieval can make such processes more likely. Alcohol tends to impair memory-encoding processes, making recollections of the disputed event poorer and more susceptible to external influences, such as recently learned information about the events or suggestive questioning (Soraci et al., 2007). If alcohol-induced memory loss is sufficiently severe, alleged rape victims or perpetrators with sketchy, or almost no, memories of the event may 'remember' details about how they behaved, based on what they believe they *would have done* in that situation under normal circumstances (Davis and Loftus, 2004).

It is important to note that, once an accusation is made, the pressures of interviewers' quest for details can both promote the tendency to answer based on assumptions about what the witness would have done and simultaneously influence answers through suggestion. Witnesses will often try to answer even when they do not remember clearly—and may, in effect, guess based on suggestive questions or comments of the interviewer, or on assumptions about what probably happened.

Reconstructive processes of memory can also be fuelled by motivation and emotions. Shame, for example, may prompt either party to reconstruct events to minimize shameful feelings—such as when a victim may remember a sexual interaction with a disreputable man as less voluntary to minimize the shame of having sex with such an undesirable character. Negative beliefs and emotions concerning the other party can lead to deliberate false reports, but can also lead to honest errors of memory. Original interpretations, as well as memory, of others' actions tend to be distorted toward consistency with other relevant beliefs.[5] In this way, changes in relationship status (such as

---

[5] See Davis and Loftus (2007) for a review.

a breakup) or relationship conflict can prompt reconstructive memories of sexual interactions with a partner one now dislikes or feels great anger toward.

FROM VOLUNTARY UNWANTED SEX TO RAPE

Before leaving the issue of memory for consent interactions, it is important to consider influences that may trigger the relabelling of sexual interactions after the fact. The issue of what constitutes consent has been widely discussed, is deeply complicated, and, unsurprisingly, has not yet been clearly settled.[6]

Among the difficult distinctions entailed in assessment of consent is the dimension of the desirability of a sexual interaction versus the voluntariness of the decision to engage in sex. Women widely report, for example, that they engage in voluntary unwanted sex (Sprecher et al., 1994; Davis, Follette, and Vernon, 2001; Impett and Peplau, 2002)—that is, the woman may have no actual desire to engage in sexual activity, and may prefer strongly not to do so, but nevertheless voluntarily do so. This may occur for a variety of reasons, including, among others, to please a partner, out of a sense of obligation, for fear of losing the partner if sex is refused, and for fear of repercussions of refusal (even though no threat or overt coercion has occurred). In hindsight, the woman may accurately remember that she did not like the interaction, but falsely assume that the accused knew she did not want to have sex. She may base such a belief on simple assumptions (such as that he would have 'just known' or that how she felt would clearly show), or on true or false memories of her own verbal or non-verbal behaviours varying in subtlety and directness in their communication of non-consent.

Some women feel that consent is implied once a certain point is reached (such as when the woman has agreed to go to the man's apartment, or has started to 'make out', or has talked about sexual topics) and will have unwanted sex because they feel they have given up the right to refuse by engaging in such behaviours (Fantasia, 2011). Most women in that study reported having engaged in sexual intercourse without expressing clear consent, conveying reasoning such as 'If you start making out, you know it will lead to sex' or 'I just went along with it' (Fantasia, 2011: 124). More troublingly, the women reported seeing non-consensual sex as normal—that is, they believed that having to engage in sexual activities once a certain threshold is reached (such as after 'making out' with a man at his apartment) or when a committed partner demands it is something that happens regularly to other women whom they know (Fantasia, 2011). Others report engaging in sex for fear that they will be raped if they do not participate voluntarily (Jensen, 2014). Perhaps for such reasons, Humphreys (2007) found that women perceived a series of scenarios involving potential sexual coercion as less consensual and more unclear than did men.

Such findings have made clear that much unwanted sex takes place in the absence of what would clearly constitute coercive behaviours, such as verbal threats or physical force. We suggest that this situation provides fertile ground for honest disagree-

---

[6] See Wertheimer (2003) for a detailed review of the issues involved in defining and determining sexual consent.

ments regarding whether sex was or was not consensual. Particularly if the woman resisted at all and the man tried to persuade her to have sex (without threats or force), the woman may report that she did not consent (or did not want to have sex), while the man believes that she did. In circumstances conducive to poor memory (such as intoxication), a woman's vague gist memories ('I didn't like it'; 'I didn't want to') might be quite accurate and suggest non-consent, even though the man's gist memories ('She seemed to like it'; 'She didn't say no') might also be accurate and suggest consent.

The broad continuum of situations in which women engage in unwanted sex has prompted some to suggest that there is rarely a bright line distinction between 'rape' or 'not rape', but rather a continuum of sexual intrusion (Jensen, 2014). The ambiguity of when sexual behaviour crosses the line between consensual and non-consensual, along with the tendency for women to engage in unwanted sex, creates circumstances under which women may well decide in hindsight that what they originally thought was voluntary, but unwanted, was actually rape.

CONCLUSIONS: ARE HONEST FALSE MEMORIES OF CONSENT INTERACTIONS MORE COMMON THAN EXPECTED?

Sexual communication is a wonderfully, and yet terrifyingly, complex process, proceeding through multiple verbal and non-verbal channels, and filled with intentional and unintentional misdirection and ambiguity. Even without external influence, interpretation of these communications is further complicated by the expectations, motivational biases, personal and relationship histories, and acute states of arousal or intoxication of the involved parties. The potential for honest differences in perception between the involved parties is already high—but when sexual interactions become subject to legal disputes, the memories of those involved become subject to both internal motivations and external sources of suggestion that can magnify the honest differences between them. Each party can report honestly, and yet quite falsely, what originally occurred. Involvement in the legal system tends to cast the parties into opposing camps as either 'innocent victim vs knowing perpetrator' or 'knowing false accuser vs falsely accused'. The research reviewed here suggests that a third possibility may be more common than previously recognized: genuine miscommunication and disagreements of memory between two honestly reporting parties.

REFERENCES

ABBEY, A. (2011) 'Alcohol's Role in Sexual Violence Perpetration: Theoretical Explanations, Existing Evidence and Future Directions', *Drug and Alcohol Review*, 30(5): 481–9.

ABBEY, A., JACQUES-TIURA, A. J., and LEBRETON, J. M. (2011) 'Risk Factors for Sexual Aggression in Young Men: An Expansion of the Confluence Model', *Aggressive Behavior*, 37(5): 450–64.

ABBEY, A., MCAUSLAN, P., and ROSS, L. (1998) 'Sexual Assault Perpetration by College Men: The Role of Alcohol, Misperception of Sexual Intent, and Sexual Beliefs and Experiences', *Journal of Social and Clinical Psychology*, 17(2): 167–95.

BERGEN, L., and GRODNER, D.J. (2012) 'Speaker Knowledge Influences the Comprehension of Pragmatic Inferences', *Journal of Experimental Psychology: Learning, Memory, and Cognition*, 38(5): 1450–60.

BRAINERD, C. J., and REYNA, V. F. (2005) *The Science of False Memory*, New York: Oxford University Press.

BYERS, E. S. (1996) 'How Well Does the Traditional Sexual Script Explain Sexual Coercion? Review of a Research Program', *Journal of Psychology and Human Sexuality*, 8(1–2): 7–25.

COOK, S. L., GIDYCZ, C. A., KOSS, M. P., and MURPHY, M. (2011) 'Emerging Issues in the Measurement of Rape Victimization', *Violence against Women*, 17(2): 201–18.

DAVIS, D., and FRIEDMAN, R. D. (2007) 'Memory for Conversation: The Orphan Child of Witness Memory Researchers', in M. P. Toglia, J. D. Read, D. F. Ross, and R. C. L. Lindsay (eds) *The Handbook of Eyewitness Psychology, Vol I: Memory for Events*, Mahwah, NJ: Lawrence Erlbaum Associates.

DAVIS, D., and LOFTUS, E. F. (2004) 'What's Good for the Goose Cooks the Gander: Inconsistencies between the Law and Psychology of Voluntary Intoxication and Sexual Assault', in W. T. O'Donohue and E. R. Levensky (eds) *Handbook of Forensic Psychology: Resource for Mental Health and Legal Professionals*, New York: Elsevier Science.

DAVIS, D., and LOFTUS, E. F. (2007) 'Internal and External Sources of Distortion in Adult Witness Memory', in M. P. Toglia, J. D. Read, D. R. Ross, and R. C. L. Lindsay (eds) *Handbook of Eyewitness Memory, Vol. 1: Memory for Events*, Mahwah, NJ: Lawrence Erlbaum Associates.

DAVIS, D., and VILLALOBOS, J. G. (2014) 'Language and the Law: Illustrations from Cases of Disputed Sexual Consent', in T. Holtgraves (ed.) *Handbook of Language and Social Psychology*, New York: Oxford University Press.

DAVIS, D., FOLLETTE, W. C., and MERLINO, M. L. (1999) 'Seeds of Rape: Female Behavior is Probative for Females, Definitive for Males', in *Psychological Expertise and Criminal Justice: A Conference for Psychologists and Lawyers*, Washington, DC: American Psychological Association.

DAVIS, D., FOLLETTE, W. C., and VERNON, M. L. (2001) 'Adult Attachment Style and the Experience of Unwanted Sex', Paper presented at the Meeting of the Western Psychological Association, Maui, Hawaii, May.

FANTASIA, H. C. (2011) 'Really Not Even a Decision Any More: Late Adolescent Narratives of Implied Sexual Consent', *Journal of Forensic Nursing*, 7(3): 120–9.

FARRIS, C., TREAT, T. A., VIKEN, R. J., and MCFALL, R. M. (2008) 'Sexual Coercion and the Misperception of Sexual Intent', *Clinical Psychology Review*, 28(1): 48–66.

GAGNON, J. H. (1990) 'The Explicit and Implicit Use of the Scripting Perspective in Sex Research', *Annual Review of Sex Research*, 1(1): 1–43

GEORGE, W. H., LEHMAN, G. L., CUE, K. L., MARTINEZ, L. J., LOPEZ, P. A., and NORRIS, J. (1997) 'Post-drinking Sexual Inferences: Evidence for Linear rather than Curvilinear Dosage Effects', *Journal of Applied Social Psychology*, 27(7): 629–48.

HASELTON, M. G., and BUSS, D. M. (2000) 'Error Management Theory: A New Perspective on Biases in Cross-sex Mind Reading', *Journal of Personality and Social Psychology*, 78(1): 81–91.

HENNINGSEN, D., and HENNINGSEN, M. (2010) 'Testing Error Management Theory: Exploring the Commitment Skepticism Bias and the Sexual Overperception Bias', *Human Communication Research*, 36(4): 618–34.

HICKMAN, S. E., and MUEHLENHARD, C. L. (1999) ' "By the Semi-mystical Appearance of a Condom": How Young Women and Men Communicate Sexual Consent in Heterosexual Situations', *Journal of Sex Research*, 36(3): 258–72.

HOWELL, E. C., ETCHELLS, P. J., and PENTON-VOAK, I. S. (2012) 'The Sexual Overperception Bias is Associated with Sociosexuality', *Personality and Individual Differences*, 53(8): 1012–16.

HUMPHREYS, T. (2007) 'Perceptions of Sexual Consent: The Impact of Relationship History and Gender', *Journal of Sex Research*, 44(4): 307–15.

HUST, S. T., BROWN, J. D., and L'ENGLE, K. (2008) 'Boys Will Be Boys and Girls Better Be Prepared: An Analysis of the Rare Sexual Health Messages in Young Adolescents' Media', *Mass Communication and Society*, 11(1): 3–23.

HUST, S. T., MARETT, E., REN, C., ADAMS, P. M., WILLOUGHBY, J. F., LEI, M., RAN, W., and NORMAN, C. (2014) 'Establishing and Adhering to Sexual Consent: The Association between Reading Magazines and College Students' Sexual Consent Negotiation', *Journal of Sex Research*, 51(3): 280–90.

IMPETT, E. A., and PEPLAU, L. A. (2002) 'Why Some Women Consent to Unwanted Sex With A Dating Partner: Insights from Attachment Theory', *Psychology of Women Quarterly*, 26: 360–70.

JENSEN, R. (2014) 'Rape, Rape Culture and the Problem of Patriarchy', *NWC NEWS: Media with Conscience*, 1 May. Available online at <http://mwcnews.net/focus/analysis/40143-rape-culture.html> [accessed May 2016].

JORDAN, J. (2005) 'What Would MacGyver Do? The Meaning(s) of Resistance and Survival', *Violence against Women*, 11(4): 531–59.

JOZKOWSKI, K. N., and PETERSON, Z. D. (2013) 'College Students and Sexual Consent: Unique Insights', *Journal of Sex Research*, 50(6): 517–23.

KAHAN, D. M. (2010) 'Culture, Cognition, and Consent: Who Perceives What, and Why, in Acquaintance-rape Cases', *University of Pennsylvania Law Review*, 158(3): 729–813.

LA FRANCE, B. H., HENNINGSEN, D. D., OATES, A., and SHAW, C. M. (2009) 'Social-sexual Interactions? Meta-analyses of Sex Differences in Perceptions of Flirtatiousness, Seductiveness, and Promiscuousness', *Communication Monographs*, 76(3): 263–85.

LEE, H. B., and CHEUNG, F. M. (1991) 'The Attitudes toward Rape Victims Scale: Reliability and Validity in a Chinese Context', *Sex Roles*, 24(9–10): 599–603.

LEE, J. J., and PINKER, S. (2010) 'Rationales for Indirect Speech: The Theory of the Strategic Speaker', *Psychological Review*, 117(3): 785–807.

LEIGH, B. C., ARAMBURU, B., and NORRIS, J. (1992) 'The Morning after: Gender Differences in Attributions about Alcohol-related Sexual Encounters', *Journal of Applied Social Psychology*, 22(5): 343–57.

LIM, G. Y., and ROLOFF, M. E. (1999) 'Attributing Sexual Consent', *Journal of Applied Communication Research*, 27(1): 1–23.

LOFTUS, E. F. (2005) 'Planting Misinformation in the Human Mind: A 30-year Investigation of the Malleability of Memory', *Learning and Memory*, 12(4): 361–6.

LOFTUS, E. F., and DAVIS, D. (2006) 'Recovered Memories', *Annual Review of Clinical Psychology*, 2: 469–98.

MASTERS, N., CASEY, E., WELLS, E. A., and MORRISON, D. M. (2013) 'Sexual Scripts among Young Heterosexually Active Men and Women: Continuity and Change', *Journal of Sex Research*, 50(5): 409–20.

MUEHLENHARD, C. L. (2011) 'Examining Stereotypes about Token Resistance to Sex', *Psychology of Women Quarterly*, 35(4): 676–83.

MUEHLENHARD, C. L., and HOLLABAUGH, L. C. (1988) 'Do Women Sometimes Say No when They Mean Yes? The Prevalence and Correlates of Women's Token Resistance to Sex', *Journal of Personality and Social Psychology*, 54(5): 872–9.

MUEHLENHARD, C. L., and RODGERS, C. S. (1998) 'Token Resistance to Sex: New Perspectives on an Old Stereotype', *Psychology of Women Quarterly*, 22(3): 443–63.

MUEHLENHARD, C. L., POWCH, I. G., PHELPS, J. L., and GIUSTI, L. M. (1992) 'Definitions of Rape: Scientific and Political Implications', *Journal of Social Issues*, 48(1): 23–44.

MURNEN, S. K., WRIGHT, C., and KALUZNY, G. (2002) 'If "Boys Will Be Boys", Then Girls Will Be Victims? A Meta-analytic Review of the Research that Relates Masculine Ideology to Sexual Aggression', *Sex Roles*, 46(11–12): 359–75.

O'SULLIVAN, L. F., and BYERS, E. (1992) 'College Students' Incorporation of Initiator and Restrictor Roles in Sexual Dating Interactions', *Journal of Sex Research*, 29(3): 435–46.

OSMAN, S. L. (2003) 'Predicting Men's Rape Perceptions Based on the Belief that "No" Really Means "Yes" ', *Journal of Applied Social Psychology*, 33(4): 683–92.

PERPER, T., and WEIS, D. L. (1987) 'Proceptive and Rejective Strategies of U.S. and Canadian College Women', *Journal of Sex Research*, 23(4): 455–80.

ROCHE, J. M., DALE, R., and CAUCCI, G. M. (2012) 'Doubling up on Double Meanings: Pragmatic Alignment', *Language and Cognitive Processes*, 27(1): 1–24.

SIMON, W., and GAGNON, J. H. (1986) 'Sexual Scripts: Permanence and Change', *Archives of Sexual Behavior*, 15(2): 97–120.

SORACI, S. A., CARLIN, M. T., READ, J. D., POGODA, T. K., WAKEFORD, Y., CAVANAGH, S., and SHIN, L. (2007) 'Psychological Impairment, Eyewitness Testimony, and False Memories: Individual Differences', in M. P. Toglia, J. D. Read, D. F. Ross, and R. C. L. Lindsay (eds) *The Handbook of Eyewitness Psychology, Vol. I: Memory for Events*, Mahwah, NJ US: Lawrence Erlbaum Associates.

SPRECHER, S., HATFIELD, E., CORTESE, A., POTAPOVA, E., and LEVITSKAYA, A. (1994) 'Token Resistance to Sexual Intercourse and Consent to Unwanted Intercourse: College Students' Dating Experiences in Three Countries', *Journal of Sex Research*, 31: 125–32.

TIERSMA, P. M., and SOLAN, L. M. (2012) 'The Language of Crime', in L. Solan and P. Tiersma (eds) *The Oxford Handbook on Language and Law*, Oxford: Oxford University Press.

WARD, R., MATTHEWS, M. R., WEINER, J., HOGAN, K. M., and POPSON, H. C. (2012) 'Alcohol and Sexual Consent Scale: Development and Validation', *American Journal of Health Behavior*, 36(5): 746–56.

WERTHEIMER, A. (2003) *Consent to Sexual Relations*, Cambridge: Cambridge University Press.

WOODHAMS, J., HOLLIN, C. R., BULL, R., and COOKE, C. (2012) 'Behavior Displayed by Female Victims during Rapes Committed by Lone and Multiple Perpetrators', *Psychology, Public Policy, and Law*, 18(3): 415–52.

11

BELIEFS ABOUT MEMORY, CHILDHOOD ABUSE, AND HYPNOSIS AMONG CLINICIANS, LEGAL PROFESSIONALS, AND THE GENERAL PUBLIC

Christopher C. French and James Ost

In criminal trials involving allegations of abuse, it is highly likely that the main—possibly the only—form of evidence to be considered will be the written or spoken reports of those involved. In other words, guilt or innocence will often be decided upon the basis of the reliability or otherwise of human memory. It is obvious therefore that the beliefs about memory held by legal professionals and members of the jury can play a crucial role in determining the verdict that is reached. It is of considerable interest to assess whether legal professionals' beliefs about memory accord with current scientific findings relating to memory. The same is true of the beliefs of members of the general public who will constitute the juries in such trials.

Other professional groups that may play a central role in such cases, especially in cases of alleged non-recent abuse, are psychiatrists, clinical psychologists, and therapists. In some cases, the alleged victim may have entered into therapy with no memory whatsoever of ever being the victim of childhood sexual abuse. As therapy proceeds, however, apparent memories of such abuse, typically at the hands of the patient's own parents, can emerge as a result of the use of various techniques (see, for example, Loftus and Ketcham, 1994; McNally, 2003; Mair, 2013). In addition to their role in actually producing such accounts, these professionals may well appear in court cases or alternatively submit written reports arguing for the veracity of the accounts themselves on the basis of their clinical experience. Once again, it is important to assess the degree to which their views about how memory works accord with the best available scientific evidence on this topic.

Fortunately, data are now available from a number of surveys indicating the degree to which beliefs about memory held by the general public (that is, potential and actual jurors), clinicians and therapists, and legal professionals accord with those of experts in the scientific study of memory. Unfortunately, such surveys typically reveal that although common beliefs about memory do sometimes coincide with expert opinion, serious misconceptions about the nature of memory are also not uncommon in all of these groups. The main aim of this chapter is to summarize the findings from a representative sample of these studies (see also Patihis et al., 2014; Ost and French, 2016).

A comprehensive review of the scientific research on memory is well beyond the scope of one short chapter. It is, however, important to give a broad-brush summary of our current scientific understanding of those aspects of memory that are particularly relevant to claims of childhood abuse. Although leading memory researchers still disagree on some issues, and we are still a long way from a detailed and comprehensive understanding of the neurobiological aspects of how memories are laid down, retrieved, distorted, and forgotten, there is general agreement on many aspects of the nature of autobiographical memory based upon replicable findings from hundreds of well-controlled studies (see, for example, Kassin et al., 2001).

Among the relevant findings that are generally accepted by memory experts and supported by strong empirical evidence are that:

(1) in general, traumatic events are much more likely to be remembered than non-traumatic events;
(2) traumatic events are more likely to be remembered than forgotten;
(3) memory for specific details of traumatic events can sometimes be distorted;
(4) under some circumstances, traumatic events (especially mildly traumatic events) can be forgotten altogether through the normal processes;
(5) the accuracy of eyewitness testimony can be affected by factors present at the time an event was witnessed (such as conditions and duration of observation, whether or not the event was unexpected, the allocation of attentional resources, etc.);
(6) the accuracy of eyewitness testimony can be affected by events that take place after the witnessed event (such as post-event misinformation);
(7) entirely false memories of events that never took place at all can arise spontaneously or as a result of the actions of third parties (such as inappropriate interviewing techniques, deliberate experimental manipulations, etc.);
(8) such false memories can be as detailed and subjectively compelling as memories of real events;
(9) memory is a constructive process that does *not* work like a video camera, accurately recording all details of experiences;
(10) neither the confidence of witnesses nor the amount of detail in eyewitness reports provide reliable guides to the veracity of testimony; and
(11) it is not possible to recall accurate and detailed memories from the first years of life (a phenomenon known as 'childhood, or infantile, amnesia').

Many aspects of this account of what is known about the nature of memory do not fit well with another influential view about how memory works under certain circumstances—that is, the view derived from Freudian psychoanalytic theory. According to this approach, if an individual suffers an extreme trauma, such as childhood sexual abuse, an automatic and involuntary psychological defence mechanism known as 'repression' kicks in and pushes the memory of the trauma out of conscious awareness.[1] No matter how hard the individual tries to recollect the traumatic event in question, he or she will be unable to do so.[2] This does not mean, however, that the repressed memories cannot cause any further psychological damage; on the contrary, they can allegedly produce a wide range of adult psychological problems in the affected individual.

It is further claimed that such repressed memories can sometimes re-emerge into consciousness spontaneously years, or even decades, later; more commonly, they are said to be recovered by the use of various so-called memory recovery techniques employed in a clinical context. Some psychiatrists, clinical psychologists, and therapists (but by no means all) believe that the only way in which to eliminate certain psychological problems is for these repressed memories to be recovered and 'worked through'. Needless to say, this is an intensely painful process and, inevitably, families are often torn apart as a result. Furthermore, alleged offenders can find themselves facing serious criminal charges. Despite the widespread acceptance of the notion of repression, most of the world's leading memory scientists (for example Loftus, 1993; Loftus and Ketchum, 1994; McNally, 2003) have serious doubts about whether repression of this sort ever actually occurs at all.

In the following review of beliefs about the nature of memory, the first section deals with studies that have assessed such beliefs in various samples of the general public. The following two sections deal with assessments of memory-related beliefs in clinicians and therapists, and in legal professionals, respectively. Studies that include specific comparisons between the views of the public and those of particular professional groups will be presented in the section dealing with the relevant professional group.

THE GENERAL PUBLIC'S BELIEFS ABOUT MEMORY

Golding, Sanchez, and Sego (1996) reported the results of a survey of 613 undergraduate students specifically regarding their belief in, and experience of, ostensibly repressed memories. Responses indicated that, in general, the students did believe in the existence of repressed memories, but also that therapy can sometimes result in false memories. They believed that evidence based upon recovered memories should sometimes be allowed in court. Some of the respondents (13 per cent) believed that they had themselves recovered a repressed memory (although usually not through therapy) and 22 per cent reported that they personally knew someone who had recalled a repressed memory. Female students reported stronger belief in repressed memories and less belief in the possibility of therapy resulting in false memories.

Magnussen and colleagues (2006) asked two representative samples of adult Norwegians (totalling 2,000 individuals) various questions about human memory

[1] 'The ordinary response to atrocities is to banish them from consciousness' (Herman, 1992: 1).
[2] Freud himself was equivocal about whether this mechanism was conscious (i.e., voluntary and deliberate on the part of the client) or unconscious (i.e., involuntary and outside the client's awareness and control). See, e.g. Brewin and Andrews (2014); Patihis et al. (2014). Here, we are referring to the involuntary form of repression.

and reported that, in some respects (such as age of earliest memories, accuracy of dramatic versus ordinary memories), the views of their samples were in line with the general scientific consensus. On other issues, though, there was significant divergence from the views of memory experts. For example, a majority of the respondents wrongly believed that the recall facility of small children was at least as good as that of adults and a large proportion of the sample believed that memory for traumatic events is repressed. Belief in repression actually increased as level of education increased in this sample, resulting in around 40 per cent of respondents with a college degree agreeing that murderers can repress memories of their crime (a view that was upheld by a Norwegian court in 2001).

More recently, Simons and Chabris (2011) assessed beliefs about memory in a large representative sample of the US population by means of a telephone survey. In their words:

> Substantial numbers of respondents agreed with propositions that conflict with expert consensus: Amnesia results in the inability to remember one's own identity (83% of respondents agreed), unexpected objects generally grab attention (78%), memory works like a video camera (63%), memory can be enhanced by hypnosis (55%), memory is permanent (48%), and the testimony of a single confident eyewitness should be enough to convict a criminal defendant (37%).
>
> Simons and Chabris (2011: 1)

Simons and Chabris (2012) also reported a replication attempt using Amazon Mechanical Turk (MTurk). Once results from the telephone survey and the MTurk survey had been appropriately weighted to reflect 2010 Census data, the two surveys produced very similar results.

Patihis and colleagues (2014: Study 1) surveyed beliefs about memory in a sample of 390 undergraduates. They found that 81 per cent believed that traumatic memories are often repressed, 70 per cent believed that repressed memories can be retrieved in therapy accurately, 44.6 per cent believed that hypnosis can accurately retrieve memories that previously were not known to the person, 66.7 per cent believed that memory of everything experienced is stored permanently in the brain, even if we cannot access all of it, 87.7 per cent believed that some people have true 'photographic memories', and 15.1 per cent believed that, with effort, we can remember events back to birth.

This study also assessed a number of individual difference variables to evaluate which ones correlated with particular belief measures. Beliefs in repression, memory recovery in therapy, and the notion that all experiences are stored in memory were more prevalent in women than in men. In contrast to Magnussen and colleagues' (2006) survey of the general Norwegian population, number of years of education was correlated with greater scepticism towards the notion of repression. Students taking psychology-related subjects reported beliefs that were more in line with the scientific literature than those taking other subjects. Both intelligence, as assessed via SAT scores, and critical thinking ability were significantly associated with more accurate beliefs about memory. A number of personality measures were also found to correlate with beliefs about memory. Specifically, proneness to fantasy and absorption tended to be correlated with various mistaken beliefs about memory, although empathy was the only personality variable that correlated with the belief that traumatic memories are often repressed. One unexpected finding was that dissociativity was *negatively* correlated with the belief that repressed memories can be accurately recovered through therapy or hypnosis.

Studies such as these reveal that, despite the fact that a broad consensus exists among memory researchers regarding basic aspects of memory, a very large proportion of the general public continues to endorse a wide range of misconceptions in this area. Because juries consist of members of the public, this clearly implies that evidence relating to memory will often be misunderstood, possibly leading to wrongful convictions.

CLINICIANS' AND THERAPISTS' BELIEFS ABOUT MEMORY

Yapko (1994a, 1994b) surveyed psychotherapists' views on the nature of memory and hypnosis. He summarized his findings as follows:

> Survey data regarding hypnosis and suggestibility indicate that while psychotherapists largely view hypnosis favorably, they often do so on the basis of misinformation. A significant number of psychotherapists erroneously believe, for example, that memories obtained through hypnosis are more likely to be accurate than those simply recalled, and that hypnosis can be used to recover accurate memories even from as far back as birth. Such misinformed views can lead to misapplications of hypnosis when attempting to actively recover memories of presumably repressed episodes of abuse, possibly resulting in the recovery of suggested rather than actual memories.
>
> (Yapko, 1994a: 163)

Poole and colleagues (1995) surveyed the opinions, practices, and experiences of both American and British psychotherapists regarding the recovery of memories of childhood sexual abuse. Results indicated that the majority (71 per cent) had engaged in memory recovery efforts directed at suspected childhood sexual abuse, using, for example, hypnosis and dream interpretation. Having said that, the vast majority also acknowledged that it is possible for a client to come to 'believe that she was sexually abused as a child if no abuse had actually occurred' (Poole et al., 1995: 432). However, of those who agreed that such false memories were possible, 91 per cent reported that such cases had never, or had only rarely, occurred among their own clients.

A Dutch sample of therapists endorsed many misconceptions regarding the nature of memory, as did a sample of Dutch health services undergraduates (Merckelbach and Wessel, 1998). Of the therapists, 96 per cent believed that repression exists, as did 94 per cent of the students; 84 per cent of the therapists believed that repressed memories cause psychological problems, as did 90 per cent of the students; 43 per cent of therapists believed that repressed memories should be reactivated, compared to 60 per cent of the students. (Note that sample sizes were small in this study.)

Three different types of mental health professional in Quebec were surveyed by Legault and Laurence (2007): psychiatrists, clinical psychologists, and social workers. Although it had been anticipated that the psychologists would demonstrate the highest level of research-based knowledge about the nature of memory, this was not in fact found to be the case. A consistent pattern emerged showing the psychiatrists to be the most informed group and the social workers, the least. The psychologists scored in the middle. The social workers were most likely to endorse popular misconceptions supportive of the use of memory recovery techniques and the psychiatrists were least likely to do so.

A number of other interesting findings were also noted by Legault and Laurence (2007). Female respondents were more likely to express views supportive of the validity of recovered memory techniques than were males. Respondents were asked to indicate which of twenty-four common symptoms (such as sexual difficulties, poor self-esteem, night terrors) were either possibly or definitely indicative of a history of sexual abuse. No symptom was more frequently chosen than others. However, more than half (53 per cent) of social workers incorrectly believed that at least one of the symptoms was a definite indication of past abuse, compared to only 24 per cent of psychologists and 36 per cent of psychiatrists.

Many of the agreement rates to individual items in Legault and Laurence's (2007) study are striking (SW = social workers, Psy = psychologists, MD = psychiatrists):

- 'Hypnotically obtained memories are less reliable than simple remembering' (true: SW = 16 per cent, Psy = 47 per cent, MD = 71 per cent);
- 'Everything one experiences is permanently recorded in one's brain' (false: SW = 84 per cent, Psy = 71 per cent, MD = 51 per cent);
- 'Hypnosis can be used to recover memories of actual events from as far back as birth' (false: SW = 80 per cent, Psy = 67 per cent, MD = 46 per cent);
- 'The real experts on traumatic memory are not the researchers who study memory but the victims themselves' (false: SW = 73 per cent, Psy = 52 per cent, MD = 27 per cent);
- 'A primary motivation for the statement that recovered memories are unreliable is to establish a legal defence for sexual abuse' (false: SW = 71 per cent, Psy = 51 per cent, MD = 30 per cent).

It should therefore be noted that a sizeable proportion of even the most informed group endorsed many inaccurate beliefs regarding the true nature of memory.

Such relatively poor understanding of the nature of memory by psychologists was also found in a survey of 858 Norwegian psychologists, the vast majority of whom worked in hospitals, clinical institutions, or private practice by Magnussen and Melinder (2012). Surprisingly, the psychologists, all of whom would have taken courses in cognitive psychology covering memory processes in their university training, failed to outperform either lay people or trial judges on issues relating to eyewitness testimony. A large majority of the psychologist sample believed that memories recovered during therapy were mostly real and a sizeable minority believed that murderers sometimes repress memories of their crimes. One important message consequently emphasized by the authors of this report is that simply being a professional psychologist is not enough, in and of itself, to guarantee expert knowledge regarding memory issues in legal trials.

Mirandola and colleagues (2013) used translated versions of the same items as those used by Magnussen and Melinder (2012) in their own survey of psychology students' and professors' knowledge about memory functioning. This study took into account both level of education (comparing introductory students, advanced students, and professors) and subject orientation (comparing the effects of training in experimental psychology with psychodynamic clinical psychology training). Professors specializing in memory research were excluded. A very clear pattern of results emerged. No differences were found between introductory students enrolled on the experimental course and the clinical course, but advanced students on the experimental course had a better understanding of the nature of memory than did advanced students on the clinical course. This difference was even more pronounced in favour of the experimentalists amongst the professors. Having said that, the rate of correct responses was not impressive within any group, ranging from about 45 per cent to 65 per cent across the six subgroups. A sizeable proportion of responses fell into the 'don't know' or 'uncertain' categories, the frequency of correct responses rarely exceeding 50 per cent. The superiority of the experimentalists over the clinicians was even found for items that might be considered to be of particular relevance to the latter, such as items dealing with children's recall, infantile amnesia, repression, and recovered memories.

Chartered clinical psychologists and hypnotherapists in the UK were surveyed by Ost and colleagues (2013) regarding the psychologists' and hypnotherapists' experience of cases involving ostensible recovered memories, satanic abuse, dissociative identity disorder, and false memories. Cases of ostensibly recovered memories were reported by 20 per cent of the clinical psychologists and 39.8 per cent of the hypnotherapists, with 17.6 per cent of respondents reporting that they believed such memories to be 'usually' or 'always' essentially accurate. Cases of alleged satanic/ritualized abuse were reported by 37.9 per cent of the clinical psychologists and 24.5 per cent of the hypnotherapists, with 26.4 per cent of respondents believing such memories to be 'usually' or 'always' essentially accurate. Almost two-fifths of the sample (39.6 per cent) reported that they had seen a case meeting the criteria for diagnosis of multiple personality disorder/dissociative identity disorder, with 19.5 per cent believing that such reports are essentially accurate 'usually' or 'always'. Clinical psychologists were less likely to report encountering cases of suspected false memories than the hypnotherapists, but the majority of both samples acknowledged that false memories of repeated sexual abuse were possible. Perhaps unsurprisingly, belief in the possibility of false memories was negatively correlated with belief in the essential accuracy of claims of satanic/ritualistic abuse and the diagnosis of multiple personality disorder/dissociative identity disorder.

Pelisoli, Herman, and Dell'Aglio (2015) assessed knowledge of research findings relevant to the forensic evaluation of child sexual abuse allegations amongst American and Brazilian professionals and non-professionals (that is, introductory psychology students), using an eighteen-item multiple-choice test. The average score for the non-professionals (44 per cent) did not exceed the expected score for random guessing (45 per cent), but even the average score of the highest scoring subgroup, US psychologists, was only 76 per cent. The average score of a combined 'other professionals' subgroup (consisting of Brazilian BA-, MA-, and PhD-level psychologists, and US caseworkers, social workers, nurses, and physicians) was 55 per cent. All subgroups had either gaps in their knowledge or, even more worryingly, firmly held, but mistaken, beliefs. For example, the statement, 'At least 10% of 5–10-year-olds who experience severe sexual abuse repress all memories of the abuse' was endorsed by 33 per cent of the US psychologists, 67 per cent of the other professionals, and 73 per cent of the non-professionals.

This study also revealed that a large proportion of all groups except the US psychologists were either unfamiliar with, or resistant to accepting, robust empirical evidence that shows that child abuse professionals are typically overly confident in their own judgements. For example, whereas 90 per cent of the US psychologists correctly endorsed the statement 'Mental health professionals and social workers are not very good at detecting when children are recounting false memories generated by suggestive interviews versus when they are recounting true memories based on actual events', only 38 per cent of the non-professionals and 42 per cent of the other professionals shared that view. Similarly, whereas 87 per cent of the US psychologists correctly rejected the claim that, 'In general, clinical judgments made by experienced mental health professionals and social workers are more accurate than judgments based on mechanical calculations made according to rigid statistical formulas', only 19 per cent of the non-professionals and 18 per cent of the other professionals did so.

An important issue that Patihis and colleagues (2014: Study 2) addressed was whether or not views regarding repressed and recovered memories had become any more sceptical over recent years in light of more recent findings from experimental studies of memory suggesting that such scepticism is warranted. This was achieved by comparing survey results from 2011–12 (from samples of research-oriented psychologists, clinical practitioners, and the general public) with similar samples surveyed in previous research (Yapko, 1994a, 1994b; Golding et al., 1996; Gore-Felton et al., 2000). The good news is that, in general, it appears that there has been a shift towards greater caution regarding recovered memories.

For example, among mainstream PhD psychotherapists, there was a significant reduction in the percentage who agreed with the statement 'Hypnosis can be used to recover memories of actual events as far back as birth', from 48.2 per cent in 1992 to 9.4 per cent in 2011–12. There was also a significant increase in the level of agreement with the statement 'It is possible to suggest false memories to someone who then incorporates them as true memories', from 86.2 per cent to 96.2 per cent (Patihis et al., 2014). Clinical psychologists' responses to a recovered-memory vignette from 1996–97 were compared with clinical psychologists' responses to the same vignette in 2011–12. Again, there was evidence of greater caution among the more recent sample. With respect to undergraduates, although there was no significant difference in the accuracy ratings of repressed memories as assessed in 1995 compared with 2011, there was a significant reduction (from 24 per cent to 12 per cent) in the proportion who felt that therapists who encourage individuals to recover repressed memories are employing legitimate methods. There was also an increase from 3 per cent to 6 per cent in the percentage who thought that such therapists implant false memories. (It should be noted, however, that 6 per cent is still a very low percentage.)

The bad news from this study is that there still exists a substantial gap between practitioners and the general public, on the one hand, and memory researchers, on the other, with respect to their beliefs about the nature of memory (Patihis et al., 2014: Study 2). Fewer than 30 per cent of the researchers believed that traumatic memories are often repressed, whereas at least 60 per cent of all other participant groups endorsed this notion. Similarly, whereas fewer than 25 per cent of the researchers agreed that repressed memories can be retrieved accurately through therapy, agreement levels were at least 43 per cent across other groups.

Clinicians potentially have two central roles to play in the context of non-recent cases of alleged childhood sexual abuse: first, it is often during therapy sessions employing dubious 'memory recovery' techniques that such memories arise in the first place; and second, clinicians may be called as expert witnesses to give their opinions regarding the validity of such recovered memories. Given these central roles, it is of great concern that surveys have repeatedly shown that clinicians' views are often at odds with the findings from scientific research. Furthermore, it appears that—with the possible exception of some psychiatrists and experimental memory researchers—non-clinical psychologists generally share many of the same misconceptions.

LEGAL PROFESSIONALS' BELIEFS ABOUT MEMORY

Magnussen and colleagues (2008) surveyed a sample of 157 Norwegian judges regarding their knowledge and beliefs about eyewitness testimony, and were able to compare their findings with a previous survey of 160 American judges by Wise and Safer (2004). The Norwegian judges were slightly better informed than the American judges, but both groups held many misconceptions regarding memory. For example, only 31 per cent of the Norwegian judges and 33 per cent of the American judges correctly disagreed with the statement 'At trial, an eyewitness's confidence is a good predictor of his or her accuracy in identifying the defendant as the perpetrator of a crime'. Similarly, only 31 per cent of the Norwegian judges and 23 per cent of the American judges correctly disagreed with the statement 'A witness's ability to recall minor details about a crime is a good indicator of the accuracy of the witness's identification of the perpetrator of the crime'.

Wise, Safer, and Maro (2011) surveyed 532 American law enforcement officers on their knowledge and beliefs regarding factors affecting the accuracy of eyewitness testimony, as well as collected data regarding how they conducted eyewitness interviews and identification procedures. Their sample was divided into eighty-three officers working in departments that had implemented reforms to eyewitness procedures and the remaining officers, who worked in departments that had not implemented such reforms. Once again, respondents showed limited knowledge of eyewitness factors. For example, only 19 per cent of the officers in the unreformed departments and 30 per cent of those in the reformed departments responded correctly to the statement 'At trial, an eyewitness's confidence is a good predictor of his or her accuracy in identifying the defendant as the perpetrator of a crime'. Similarly, only 12 per cent and 22 per cent, respectively, responded correctly to the statement 'A witness's ability to recall minor details about a crime is a good indicator of the accuracy of the witness's identification of the perpetrator of the crime'. In general, the two groups did not differ in their knowledge of eyewitness factors. Furthermore, both groups reported departing from official guidelines when conducting interviews and identification procedures.

Houston and colleagues (2013) surveyed a sample of ninety-nine judges in Scotland with respect to factors affecting the accuracy of eyewitness testimony. As in previous studies, a high degree of variability was found regarding the extent to which the judges' beliefs matched those of experts. For example, whereas 97 per cent agreed with the experts regarding the effects of alcohol intoxication on eyewitness accuracy, only 40 per cent agreed with the experts regarding the phenomenon of weapon focus (whereby the attention of victims threatened with weapons is so fixated on the weapon involved that they cannot remember the perpetrator's face). Other topics showing poor agreement between the judges' and expert opinions included the effects of exposure duration, and the relationship between confidence and accuracy. Overall consistency across all survey items was 67 per cent compared to 61 per cent for a sample of the general Scottish public.

CONCLUSION

The available evidence overwhelmingly supports the view that misconceptions regarding the true nature of memory are widely held not only by members of the general public, but also by professionals working in clinical and legal contexts. The negative implications of this situation with respect to the possibility of miscarriages of justice are obvious. There is an urgent need for knowledge transfer from memory experts to other professionals, but, to date, this has met with only limited success. It is perhaps not surprising that clinicians sometimes show resistance to accepting the latest insights from memory research: not only may one professional group understandably resent being told by another professional group that its understanding of the nature of memory is mistaken, but also there is the implicit acknowledgement that the former's methods (a) may have not been achieving anything positive, but (b) may actually have been causing a great deal of unnecessary harm.

The lack of awareness of the true nature of memory on the part of legal professionals is perhaps more difficult to understand. If it reflects nothing more than the failure of memory experts to ensure that appropriate training in these matters is provided within the legal professions, this is disappointing, but can be rectified. It may be, however, that it reflects a widely shared, but totally misguided, attitude on the part of many within the legal field that simply because everyone has memories, everyone knows how memory works and therefore special training in this area is not required.[3] We hope that this chapter will contribute to changing such ill-informed attitudes.

REFERENCES

Brewin, C. R., and Andrews, B. (2014) 'Why It Is Scientifically Respectable to Believe in Repression: A Response to Patihis, Ho, Tingen, Lilienfeld, and Loftus (2014)', *Psychological Science*, 25(10): 1964–6.

Golding, J. M., Sanchez, R. P., and Sego, S. A. (1996) 'Do You Believe in Repressed Memories?', *Professional Psychology: Research and Practice*, 27(5): 429–37.

Gore-Felton, C., Koopman, C., Thoresen, C., Arnow, B., Bridges, E., and Spiegel, D. (2000) 'Psychologists' Beliefs and Clinical Characteristics: Judging the Veracity of Childhood Sexual Abuse Memories', *Professional Psychology: Research and Practice*, 31(44): 372–7.

Herman, J. (1992) *Trauma and Recovery: From Domestic Abuse to Political Terror*, London: Pandora.

Houston, K. A., Hope, L., Memon, A., and Read, J. D. (2013) 'Expert Testimony on Eyewitness Evidence: In Search of Common Sense', *Behavioral Sciences and the Law*, 31(5): 637–51.

Kassin, S. M., Tubb, V. A., Hosch, H. M., and Memon, A. (2001) 'On the "General Acceptance" of Eyewitness Testimony Research: A New Survey of the Experts', *American Psychologist*, 56(5): 405–16.

Keane, A. (2010) 'The Use at Trial of Scientific Findings Relating to Human Memory', *Criminal Law Review*, 1(1): 19–30.

Legault, E., and Laurence, J.-R. (2007) 'Recovered Memories of Childhood Sexual Abuse: Social Worker, Psychologist, and Psychiatrist Reports of Beliefs, Practices, and Cases', *Australian Journal of Clinical and Experimental Hypnosis*, 35(2): 111–33.

Loftus, E. (1993) 'The Reality of Repressed Memories', *American Psychologist*, 48(5): 518–37.

Loftus, E., and Ketcham, K. (1994) *The Myth of Repressed Memory*, New York: St Martin's Press.

Magnussen, S., and Melinder, A. (2012) 'What Psychologists Know and Believe about Memory: A Survey of Practitioners', *Applied Cognitive Psychology*, 26(1): 54–60.

Magnussen, S., Andersson, J., Cornoldi, C., De Beni, R., Endestad, T., Goodman, G. S., Helstrup, T., Koriat, A., Larsson, M., Melinder, A., Nilsson, L.-G., Rönnberg, J., and Zimmer, H. (2006) 'What People Believe about Memory', *Memory*, 14(5): 595–613.

Magnussen, S., Wise, R. A., Raja, A. Q., Safer, M. A., Pawlenko, N., and Stridbeck, U. (2008) 'What Judges Know about Eyewitness Testimony: A Comparison of Norwegian and US Judges', *Psychology, Crime, and Law*, 14(3): 177–88.

Mair, K. (2013) *Abused by Therapy: How Searching for Childhood Trauma Can Damage Adult Lives*, Kibworth Beauchamp: Matador.

McNally, R. J. (2003) *Remembering Trauma*, Cambridge, MA: Harvard University Press.

Merckelbach, H., and Wessel, I. (1998) 'Assumptions of Students and Psychotherapists about Memory', *Psychological Reports*, 82(3): 763–70.

---

[3] For example, Keane (2010: 23–4) claims that, 'in some respects at least, the scientific findings are the same as, or very similar to, commonly held beliefs, common experience and common sense, and . . . this *may* make expert evidence or guidance otiose'.

Mirandola, C., Ferruzza, E., Cornoldi, C., and Magnussen, S. (2013) 'Beliefs about Memory among Psychology Students and Their Professors in Psychodynamic Clinical and Experimental Study Programs', *Revue Européenne de Psychologie Appliquée/European Review of Applied Psychology*, 63(5): 251–6.

Ost, J., and French, C. C. (2016) 'How Misconceptions about Memory May Undermine Witness Testimony', in P. Radcliffe, G. Gudjonsson, A. Heaton-Armstrong, and D. Wolchover (eds) *Witness Testimony in Sex Cases*, Oxford: Oxford University Press.

Ost, J., Wright, D. B., Easton, S., Hope, L., and French, C. C. (2013) 'Recovered Memories, Satanic Abuse, Dissociative Identity Disorder and False Memories in the UK: A Survey of Clinical Psychologists and Hypnotherapists', *Psychology, Crime & Law*, 19(1): 1–19.

Patihis, L., Ho, L. Y., Tingen, I. W., Lilienfeld, S. O., and Loftus, E. F. (2014) 'Are the "Memory Wars" over? A Scientist–Practitioner Gap in Beliefs about Memory', *Psychological Science*, 25(2): 519–30.

Pelisoli, C., Herman, S., and Dell'Aglio, D. D. (2015) 'Child Sexual Abuse Research Knowledge among Child Abuse Professionals and Laypersons', *Child Abuse & Neglect*, 40: 36–47.

Poole, D. A., Lindsay, D. S., Memon, A., and Bull, R. (1995) 'Psychotherapy and the Recovery of Memories of Childhood Sexual Abuse: U.S. and British Practitioners' Opinions, Practices, and Experiences', *Journal of Consulting and Clinical Psychology*, 63(3): 426–37.

Simons, D. J., and Chabris, C. F. (2011) 'What People Believe about How Memory Works: A Representative Survey of the U.S. Population', *PLoS ONE*, 6(8): e22757.

Simons, D. J., and Chabris, C. F. (2012) 'Common (Mis)Beliefs about Memory: A Replication and Comparison of Telephone and Mechanical Turk Survey Methods', *PLoS ONE*, 7(12): e51876.

Wise, R. A., and Safer, M. A. (2004) 'What U.S. Judges Know and Believe about Eyewitness Testimony', *Applied Cognitive Psychology*, 18(4): 427–43.

Wise, R. A., Safer, M. A., and Maro, C. M. (2011) 'What U.S. Law Enforcement Officers Know and Believe about Eyewitness Factors, Eyewitness Interviews and Identification Procedures', *Applied Cognitive Psychology*, 25(3): 488–500.

Yapko, M. D. (1994a) 'Suggestibility and Repressed Memories of Abuse: A Survey of Psychotherapists' Beliefs', *American Journal of Clinical Hypnosis*, 36(3): 163–71.

Yapko, M. D. (1994b) *Suggestions of Abuse: True and False Memories of Childhood Sexual Trauma*, New York: Simon & Shuster.

12

TO CATCH A SEX OFFENDER

POLICE, TRAWLS, AND PERSONAL INJURY SOLICITORS

David Rose

In an academic book, this chapter is an oddity: a contribution by a journalist, which attempts to be both an analysis and a memoir of work that has occupied some of my time over the past fifteen years. I can remember the exact moment when alleged 'historic' abuse and false allegations first entered my consciousness, because it happened to be the day of my wedding on 1 July 2000 to Professor Carolyn Hoyle, now director of University of Oxford's Centre for Criminology. One of our guests was the criminal barrister Andrew Hall QC. He thrust a copy of Richard Webster's first book on the subject (Webster, 1998) into my hands and told me I had to read it. A few months later, my BBC *Panorama* programme, 'In the Name of the Children',[1] was the result.

OPERATION GRANITE

The *Panorama* film drew general conclusions, but mainly focused on a single case: that of Roy Shuttleworth, who had been a teacher at an approved school in Cheshire, Greystone Heath. He was convicted and sentenced to twelve years' imprisonment in 1996, on the evidence of eight former inmates who said he had abused them in the 1970s, more than twenty years before his trial (Rose and Horne, 2000). Greystone Heath was one of many institutions in the northwest of England that were the subject of 'trawl' police inquiries. In each, the method was the same. Following an initial allegation against a former member of staff, the police would contact as many former pupils or inmates as they could. This could run to many hundreds for each institution concerned. Detectives would ask them whether they had been abused, sexually or physically, and those who said they had been often became witnesses at subsequent trials.

Many of those to whom the police spoke had been in care as children or given custodial sentences as juveniles, and many had later been convicted and imprisoned as

[1] See <http://news.bbc.co.uk/1/hi/programmes/panorama/archive/1031559.stm>

adults. All of the 'victims' who gave evidence against Shuttleworth had convictions as adults for crimes of dishonesty and three were in prison during his trial. According to Richard Webster (2005: 468–9), the officers who conducted Operation Granite, the Cheshire police investigation into Greystone Heath and other institutions, made special arrangements with the prison authorities to take such men out of their jails and interview them in the relative comfort of police station rape suites. Meanwhile, word spread rapidly along prison landings that for those who alleged they had been abused as children, there was compensation to be had, either from the Criminal Injuries Compensation Authority or through civil damages claims. Unless there was compelling evidence that their stories were false, complainants were treated as, and categorized only as, 'victims'.

As I delved into the Shuttleworth case, it became clear that important interactions between police and their eventual witnesses were often poorly recorded, or not recorded at all. In many cases, I discovered, police had met alleged victims several times before their statements were produced and signed, but did not create any reliable record of such pre-statement interviews. None were audio-taped, let alone recorded on video. There were thus risks that witnesses might be 'led' to their statements, that inconvenient details that did not fit other, verifiable, facts could be changed or excised before they were committed to paper, and that claims from one complainant might be fed to another. This might lead to an appearance of corroboration, whereby the reality was a mutual collusion to tell lies.

The House of Lords had set a precedent that multiple allegations that were not 'strikingly similar' could be held to be mutually corroborating even if there were no other supporting evidence.[2] Professor Mike McConville, then of Warwick University, described this in an unbroadcast portion of his interview for *Panorama* as a 'wigwam', with 'allegations propping each other up, like drunken men'.

In regard to Roy Shuttleworth, my colleagues and I were able to cast factual doubt on every allegation against him, mainly by showing that central details of the statements of the 'victims' flew in the face of other, externally verifiable, facts. The most surprising moment in our research came when I interviewed one of the complainants, who had given evidence that, after Shuttleworth forcibly subjected him to anal sex in the Greystone Heath showers, he escaped by jumping from a first-floor window in his accommodation block and then ran across the grounds to the headmaster's office. He claimed that, naked and bleeding from his anus, he had covered a distance of about 400 yards in full view of a busy road, without any motorists or pedestrian passers-by noticing. On arriving at the head's study, he went on, he was not only disbelieved, but caned on his naked buttocks.

By the time we made the programme, Greystone Heath had long been abandoned and was semi-derelict. But I managed to gain access to the buildings and inspected the windows of the block where the 'victim' said he had jumped through the first-floor window. All the windows in the block were barred with thick slats of solid steel. I measured the gap between each slat: 3 inches. I asked the witness if he remembered

---

[2] *DPP v P* (1990) 93 Cr App R 267.

this and how he had managed to fit through. He replied: 'That's right, but I was skinny, weren't I.'

Like many trawl investigations, Operation Granite began in 1993 with allegations to police that were almost certainly genuine: Alan Langshaw, the former teacher who was their object, pleaded guilty (Webster, 2005: 465–6). Inspired by the recent example of inquiries into historic abuse in North Wales, which had attracted immense, national publicity, the police began their trawl.

The apparent credibility of complainants who could not possibly be telling the truth was impressive. One former Greystone Heath pupil told me that, among other assaults by Shuttleworth, he had been forced to masturbate him when they took a shower together. He was quite insistent, saying that he had made a statement after the police showed him photographs of former members of staff and he recognized Shuttleworth as the man who had abused him. No doubt he would have given evidence at Shuttleworth's trial, had not the police, at a very late stage, discovered an inconvenient fact: this supposed victim had left Greystone Heath in 1967—seven years before Shuttleworth started working there. Even when I put this to him, he stuck to his bogus story, telling me: 'It did happen. He was there. He was there, Shuttleworth.'

The complainant also revealed that he had made a claim for compensation through a firm of solicitors, which had enrolled him as a client and obtained legal aid. Now that the discrepancy in dates had emerged, he said he had been compelled to withdraw this claim. In his view, this was a grave injustice.

Long before the trials of Shuttleworth and others, several law firms were putting together a class civil action, which eventually included more than 700 complainants. In this, there was no one more energetic than Peter Garsden of the Cheadle Hulme firm Abney Garsden McDonald (now Abney Garsden). By the time I interviewed him in the autumn of 2000, he had 350 clients in this single class action. He was also a founder of the Association of Child Abuse Lawyers, of which, at time of writing in 2015, he is president and media relations officer. The *Panorama* programme's time restrictions meant that only a small proportion of Garsden's interview was broadcast, so most of what follows here, taken from the transcript of the recorded interview, is published now for the first time.

A FIGHT BETWEEN GOOD AND EVIL

Garsden was candid about the closeness of his relationship with the police, saying: 'It very quickly became apparent that it was important for us and the police to have a symbiotic relationship with each other. They depended on us and we depended on them.' That meant 'the police would want us to refer any new complaints of abuse that they didn't know about to them, because it would help them in their process'. In turn:

> [W]e depended on them, because we wanted from them as much information about the pending criminal trials as possible, so that we could attend court, take notes of evidence; we wanted statistical information about allegations of abuse, who was abused at which home.

He admitted that the 'two systems', criminal and civil, were therefore 'running in parallel'. But he said he was confident that there was no danger of this 'symbiosis' contaminating the criminal process. His reason was that the police made it clear that they wanted the solicitors to 'do as little as possible' before criminal trials. Witnesses would not therefore be giving criminal evidence when civil proceedings were already current—although they were, of course, in prospect.

As a Merseyside detective superintendent, John Robbins was in charge of Operation Care, a trawl investigation into homes and schools that saw twenty former staff convicted for historic abuse—as well as the acquittal, a few weeks after 'In the Name of the Children' was broadcast, of David Jones, former manager of Wolverhampton Wanderers Football Club. (He had worked in an institution in Liverpool as a young man.) Meanwhile, Robbins had joined Peter Garsden's law firm. In an interview with me, he admitted he was now helping to support the civil damages claims of some of the same individuals whom he had previously come across as alleged victims in criminal trials. But, like Garsden, he insisted that there was no danger that the prospect of compensation could contaminate police inquiries: 'I sleep easy in my bed. We were searching for the truth,' he said. As for the advice he had given to personal injury lawyers not to lodge claims until criminal trial were complete, he commented: 'My advice was designed to avoid creating the impression they [alleged victims] were in it only for the money.'

Arguably, that impression could have been said to be misleading.

Thanks to generous legal aid funding, it was evident that fighting claims on behalf of alleged abuse victims was good business. When we met in 2000, Garsden's firm's historic abuse department was employing sixteen people, including six solicitors and three assistants. But the money he was making was not, he said, his primary motive; rather, he said, he believed that he was, quite literally, doing the work of the Lord, while some of his opponents—those who defended historic abuse law suits or suggested that innocent people might be convicted of abusing children—were agents of Satan:

> I believe that really, we're messing with the Devil, because you know, child abuse is evil, and the people that get involved in it are powerful, manipulative people. They will do their level best to stop us succeeding and stop us getting justice for the victims.

I asked Garsden: 'Is this the Devil at work?' He replied:

> It is, it is, and that was something that never occurred to me before I became involved with a Christian pressure group. And it was them that said this to me. I mean, within the umbrella of abuse is Satanic Abuse. And that is a lot more closely associated with the Devil than this [historic school and care home abuse] is, but it, but this is still an evil force, definitely.

Convinced of the righteousness of his cause, Garsden refused to accept that anyone who claimed to have been a victim of historic abuse might be lying: 'Nobody in this world is going to put themselves through what these people have to put themselves through, if they're telling a pack of lies. It's absolute nonsense.' It was true, he averred, that there had been occasions on which a 'survivor' had made allegations against people who turned out not to have been working at an institution at the same time as he or she was an inmate—but this was exactly the sort of discrepancy that defence counsel liked to exploit to discredit a witness: 'Defence teams will play games with these sorts of discrepancies, that's their job. Their job is to suggest that the account is "unreliable".'

Yet this, Garsden said, did not 'shake the truth' of the central allegation of abuse. In his view, such discrepancies could invariably be explained by the passage of time:

> You find that the peripheral details are sometimes inaccurate, because it happened so long ago. But the central memory of the abuse stays with them. It comes back to them in nightmares on a daily basis… Everything else sort of surrounds that and is, you know, detail.

OPERATION LENTISK

Garsden was far from unique. Solicitors in other parts of the country were equally assiduous in generating historic abuse lawsuits and in working closely with the police. One example I examined some months after making the programme was that of Forde Park School in Devon, where the law firm Woollcombe Beer Watts had been collaborating with another police inquiry, Operation Lentisk (Rose, 2002).

Lentisk—which led to several criminal convictions and lengthy sentences—owed its very origins to the search for compensation. In the autumn of 1996, long before Lentisk started, a former pupil named Andy Kershaw formed the Forde Park Survivors' Group. He told me its express purpose was to press for damages from Devon County Council, the local education authority, not only for alleged abuse, but also for its supposed failure to provide a 'decent education'.

Kershaw said that he believed that, to stand a chance of success, he needed corroborative evidence from other former pupils: 'The only way forward, as I saw it, was I had to speak to other people.' He said he used local radio and newspapers to 'advertise' (his word) for other alleged victims. By early 1997, he went on, about sixty-five former pupils had contacted him. He wrote to all of them, urging them to try to start legal proceedings, and they agreed that Kershaw would try to get legal aid. If successful, the other members of the group would follow his example and sue.

Kershaw also lobbied the police. At first, he said, they were not prepared to launch an inquiry because of the three decades that had elapsed since the alleged abuse. Their disdain meant that the survivors group was 'concerned we weren't being taken seriously. So we contacted the press.' A series of media features about Forde Park ensued. Some made outlandish allegations—such as that pupils were forced to endure brain operations without their consent. The group also organized lobbies of Parliament. Finally, in 1998, Kershaw said, the police agreed to begin Operation Lentisk.

Meanwhile, Kershaw got his legal aid. By the time the police inquiry started, the survivors' group had employed a solicitor, Woollcombe Beer Watts's Penny Ayles. Between December 1999 and April 2001, Ayles organized several meetings for the survivors at an Exeter hotel. There, it was explained that they could expect different levels of damages for different kinds of abuse: up to £50,000 for buggery, but significantly less for mere physical assaults.

When I interviewed Ayles, she confirmed that some of her clients had spoken to the police only after making statements to her. But, like Peter Garsden, she denied that the civil and criminal legal processes had become dangerously blurred, creating a risk of false allegations. Again like Garsden, she believed the traumatic impact of 'disclosing' the alleged historic abuse to be simply too great to be feigned: 'I would think it highly unlikely, having met the clients and seen the devastating effects [of their alleged abuse] on them.'

My investigations into Forde Park focused on the case of Brian Ely, a former teacher and scout troop leader, whom I met, after his conviction, in the forbidding setting of Dartmoor prison. Sentenced to fifteen years, he protested his innocence throughout.

I found one piece of evidence that supported his assertion: a man whose own family claimed he had lied about Ely and Forde Park after contact with the survivors' group. Both his partner and mother-in-law told me that the claimant had 'come forward' only after seeing a television news item about Forde Park. Afterwards, he had gone to a group meeting, and only then announced that he intended to concoct a bogus story. 'As far as I am concerned,' his mother-in-law said, 'he is lying when he says he was abused and is doing it for compensation.' Of course, as with any alleged victim of a sexual offence, the protection afforded by the Sexual Offences Act 1992[3] means that the claimant's name could not be published. This restriction lasts for the lifetime of the claimant, no matter how strong the evidence is that he or she has lied.

PARLIAMENTARY INQUIRY INTO ABUSE INVESTIGATIONS

By the time of the 2001 general election, awareness of the dangers of false allegations and convictions was spreading. Former Merseyside Labour MP Claire Curtis-Thomas had displayed considerable political courage by giving a forthright interview about these risks for 'In the Name of the Children' and went on to found the All-Party Group for Abuse Investigations to press for reform. After the group's inaugural meeting, then Lord Chief Justice Lord Woolf said, in an interview, that there might well have been wrongful convictions in historic abuse cases. The evidence given by some complainants 'may not be accurate', he said, especially when they were 'tempted' by compensation awards. The dangers were especially great when solicitors and police conducted trawls, asking 'Did anything happen to you?' (Rozenberg, 2001).

After the election, Labour MP Chris Mullin was appointed chairman of the Commons Select Committee on Home Affairs. Before he became a Member of Parliament, he had worked for the ITV programme *World in Action* and had led its eventually successful attempts to find new evidence that would undermine the wrongful convictions of the Birmingham Six. I wrote to him, and urged him to hold an

[3] Sexual Offences (Amendment) Act 1992, s. 5.

inquiry into trawl inquiries and historic abuse. Later, along with Richard Webster and Bob Woffinden, a doyen among investigative reporters concerned with miscarriages of justice, I gave evidence to the Committee. Its fourth question for potential witnesses at the outset of the inquiry was 'Is there a risk that the advertisement of prospective awards of compensation in child abuse cases encourages people to come forward with fabricated allegations?' (Home Affairs Select Committee, 2002a). In our evidence, all three of us answered this in the affirmative.

The Committee's 2002 report, among the signatories to which was future Prime Minister David Cameron, was an outstanding document, warning that trawl inquiries into historic abuse had produced 'a new genre of miscarriages of justice'. Mullin said at its launch: 'I am in no doubt that a number of innocent people have been convicted and that many other innocent people, who have not been convicted, have had their lives ruined.'

The report made many recommendations designed to reduce these dangers. Rejecting the argument made to me by Peter Garsden that discrepancies between the details of victims' claims and other, verifiable, facts did not 'shake the truth' of a complainant's allegations, it recommended that complainant's claims be subjected to 'statement validity analysis' as a tool for assessing their credibility (Home Affairs Select Committee, 2002b: para. 50). It also recommended that allegations that were more than ten years old should proceed only with the permission of the court (Home Affairs Select Committee, 2002b: para. 92), while the requirement that similar fact evidence could constitute corroboration only when there were 'striking similarities' between different allegations against the same individual should be restored (Home Affairs Select Committee, 2002b: para. 97).

Peter Garsden had given evidence denying that solicitors' relationships with the police were (as he had earlier told me) 'symbiotic'. He told the Committee that, in fact, the police regarded him as a 'pain in the neck'. Nevertheless, the Committee stated that it was deeply concerned about the absence of rules governing relationships between the police and personal injury solicitors in historic abuse inquiries. It recommended that the Home Office should issue clear guidelines, to be drawn up in consultation with the Association of Chief Police Officers (Home Affairs Select Committee, 2002b: para. 108). The report's conclusion added:

> The potential for compensation to act as an inducement for giving false or exaggerated evidence during investigations of this kind, is another area of real concern. To minimise this risk, we have recommended that the working relationship between personal injury solicitors and the police be guided by a 'model relationship', to be drawn up by the Home Office.
> (Home Affairs Select Committee, 2002b: para. 141)

Nevertheless, 'much can be done to improve the conduct of future investigations and prosecutions' (Home Affairs Select Committee, 2002b: para. 142).

On 16 October 2002, Claire Curtis-Thomas succeeded in holding a Commons debate to discuss the Committee report, in which Conservative Shadow Attorney-General Edward Garnier QC acknowledged the risks of miscarriages of justice, citing the cases of two of his own constituents (Webster, 2002). It appeared that the dangers of false convictions were beginning to be recognized by both main parties.

The following year, the Labour government's response showed that such optimism was unjustified. Trawling was henceforth to be rebranded as 'dip-sampling', but the only important Committee recommendation that the government accepted was that all interactions between witnesses and police should be recorded. The Committee's proposals on similar fact evidence, statement validity analysis, and cases that were more than ten years old were all rejected. Underlying the Committee's report had been the assumptions that there had been many false allegations and wrongful convictions, the response said. However, while the 'government...respect[ed] the views of the Committee', it '[did] not share its belief in the existence of large numbers of miscarriages of justice' (Home Office, 2003: para. 10).

The response's comments about personal injury solicitors and the lure of compensation refused to recognize that this might be a problem—adding that, in any case, relationships between the police and lawyers were already covered by a 2002 Home Office circular, *Complex Child Abuse Investigations: Inter-agency Guidance*. Paragraph 68 of the government's response was the most negative of all:

> The Government does not think that the existence of a problematic relationship between police forces and firms of solicitors has been substantiated, and therefore specific guidelines are not justified. The assumptions that civil compensation claims have driven false allegations, or that impropriety has existed in relationships between police forces and firms of solicitors is not supported by any evidence.
>
> (Home Office, 2003: para. 68)

INSTITUTIONAL AMNESIA

Despite the government's rejection of the most of the Committee's report, I fondly imagined that awareness of the risks of false convictions had become widespread and that the worst of the great children's home panic was over. My confidence was misplaced.

The extent of my complacency became apparent in November 2012, when I watched the BBC *Newsnight* report on abuse in North Wales that was, only a week after its broadcast, to force the resignation of the Corporation's director-general, George Entwistle. The programme claimed that abusers at institutions such as Bryn Estyn had shared their victims with outside paedophiles, including a leading member of the Conservative Party. Although it did not name him, the programme contained enough clues for viewers to point the finger at the former Party Treasurer, the late Lord McAlpine, who duly sued for libel. Less than two weeks after the broadcast, the BBC agreed to pay him damages of £185,000 (BBC News, 2012a). Later, Sally Bercow, wife of Commons Speaker John Bercow, was forced to pay a further undisclosed sum in respect of an ill-considered tweet (Press Association, 2013).

However, the really remarkable aspect of the *Newsnight* film was that it was based on a single, uncorroborated source: a former Bryn Estyn resident named Stephen

Messham. To those of us who had followed these matters over time, Messham was no stranger (Rose, 2012a). To my lasting regret, my own name had been one of three on a story published by *The Observer* in 1993, which made unsupported claims derived mainly from Messham's testimony about Gordon Anglesea, a former North Wales police officer. Anglesea sued for libel, and eventually won damages of £375,000 and costs of £1 million against *The Observer*, *The Independent*, and *Private Eye* (Rose, 2012a).

Messham's behaviour at the trial was bizarre. Before he agreed to give evidence, he had insisted that *Private Eye* pay him £60,000, on the grounds that it had previously published an article that had damaged him. Surprisingly, the magazine did pay him £4,500. Moreover, Messham had changed his story about the abuse that he said Anglesea inflicted on him, his allegations becoming more serious over time. When all of this was put to him, he took an overdose of tranquilizers in court and collapsed in the witness box. He was taken to hospital, but the judge insisted that he resume his evidence next day.

In 1997, Messham gave evidence again, this time to the judicial inquiry into historic abuse in North Wales chaired by Sir Ronald Waterhouse. In all, he said, he had been sexually abused as a child in care by forty-nine different men and women. He explicitly named a 'McAlpine' as one of them—although in such a manner that it was apparent to Sir Ronald and his colleagues that his claims could not possibly be true. (After the *Newsnight* film in 2012, Messham stated for the record that Lord McAlpine had never abused him at all.)

Meanwhile, Messham was cross-examined at the inquiry by Anthony Jennings QC. Jennings started to press him about a damaging admission: that parts of an interview he had given to *The Independent on Sunday* were untrue. First, Messham refused to answer his questions. Then, according to the inquiry transcript, he got out of the witness box and 'moved towards' Mr Jennings. He yelled:

> Excuse me, I will not have it from you ever, Jennings, right? Because one thing I don't like is a little bastard, right? You don't push it, right? You are sick just like your client. Don't push me, don't fucking push me you little... I'll tell you now, you bastard.

Messham then leapt at Jennings and started throwing punches at him. A security officer intervened. When the inquiry reconvened the following Monday, Messham was warned that any repetition of this behaviour would be treated as a serious contempt of court and he would be sent to prison.

On the one hand, Messham certainly exhibited the distress that lawyers such as Peter Garsden insisted should be taken as evidence that a 'victim' was telling the truth. On the other hand, to take anything he said at face value was clearly extremely dangerous. Indeed, in 1993, the Crown Prosecution Service (CPS) had concluded: 'Reliance ought not to be placed on [Messham's] evidence for the purpose of prosecuting any alleged abuser.' To this, Gerard Elias QC, counsel to the Waterhouse inquiry, added in his closing speech:

> In certain respects Messham's evidence was demonstrably untrue and some of his allegations are wholly inconsistent with earlier statements made by him to the police. In these circumstances we submit it is plain that his evidence must be approached with care.

Nevertheless, when it came to the *Newsnight* broadcast, all of this was ignored. What had produced this institutional amnesia? Part of the answer was the recent broadcast by ITV of a documentary claiming that Sir Jimmy Savile, the late celebrity disc jockey, had been a prodigious, serial paedophile and, worse, the disclosure that *Newsnight* had cancelled a film that would have made these allegations the previous year.

In 2012, Messham's allegations unravelled speedily enough. But, by the time they did, Prime Minister David Cameron had already ordered a 'review' of the Waterhouse inquiry, and asked the Serious and Organised Crime Agency (now the National Crime Agency) to begin again digging well-tilled soil—that is, allegations of historic abuse in schools and care homes in North Wales. At the time of writing in January 2015, pending prosecutions make it impossible to add further comment.

The resurfacing of Stephen Messham and his stories about 'paedophile rings' involving senior politicians reminded me of the Hollywood film *Groundhog Day*, in which a TV weatherman played by the actor Bill Murray is doomed to repeat the same day of his life in a seemingly endless loop. Messham and North Wales were not, however, the only example of this process.

OPERATION RENO

Back in 2005, I had written in *The Observer* about an inquiry by Humberside police into St Williams, an approved school for convicted juvenile offenders at Market Weighton, near Hull (Rose, 2005). As with Operation Granite and Greystone Heath, this had started with genuine allegations, made spontaneously to police, not as a result of a trawl: allegations made against James Carragher, the former principal. He had already been charged with, and pleaded guilty to, sexual offences in 1993. He pleaded guilty a second time in 2004 and was jailed for fourteen years. By this time, Operation Aldgate, a classic trawl, was in full swing.

It ended in fiasco. Although five men who had worked at St Williams were charged, juries found two of them not guilty, while the CPS dropped the charges against the other three. Some of their accusers were suffering from serious mental illness and all had numerous convictions. One of those acquitted—of physical, not sexual, abuse—was the school's former deputy head, Noel Hartnett: the very man who had first notified the police about the abusive behaviour of Carragher back in the 1990s. The judge at Hartnett's trial was highly critical of aspects of the police inquiry, saying that officers had 'not investigated professionally' and had 'not investigated to discover the truth' (Rose, 2005).

Hartnett and some of the others acquitted after Operation Aldgate complained to the Independent Police Complaints Commission (IPCC), which was concerned enough to order a major investigation by an outside police force, West Yorkshire. Three years later, this investigation, known as Operation Gullane, delivered its report. It contained more than 400 separate criticisms of Operation Aldgate's conduct. Aldgate, the report said, had not been 'robust'. Officers had believed accusers' stories without checking them and had adopted an overly credulous 'mindset' that had led them to hound innocent people. There had been a 'failure to pursue reasonable lines of inquiry which could have helped prove/disprove witness and suspect accounts' and a 'failure to seek corroboration in respect of allegations made' (IPCC, 2007: 8).

The IPCC made 126 recommendations for future abuse inquiries nationally to ensure that such mistakes were not repeated. It was particularly scathing about the role played by some solicitors, highlighting the examples of six alleged victims who had all been in Holme House prison near York at the same time and shared a personal injury lawyer. They had, the report concluded, 'colluded' in making their statements, and so produced allegations on which no court could rely (Rose, 2012b).

However, in December 2004, after the last of the Aldgate acquittals, when Operation Gullane was only just starting, an advertisement appeared in *Inside Time*, a newspaper published by a charitable trust that is distributed free to all prison inmates. Placed by David Greenwood of Jordans firm of solicitors of Dewsbury, it asked: 'Were you at St William's care home 1970-88?' The firm, it went on, was coordinating civil damages claims by former residents, and it was 'important that potential claimants enforce their legal rights as soon as possible. Especially those who have been contacted by Operation Aldgate at Hull Central police station' (Rose, 2005). This advert was the first of many published 2004-09.

At the same time, Greenwood wrote to Humberside Police, requesting their co-operation. He said that he hoped soon to be able to announce that he had been given a 'block' legal aid grant to act as coordinating solicitor in a class action for victims of abuse at St Williams. He said that he needed details of all of the suspects the police had investigated and what charges had been laid. 'This will greatly assist our claimants', Greenwood wrote.

Greenwood—who left Jordans in 2013 and is now a partner at Yorkshire firm Switalskis—was already experienced in this field. By 2012, the historic abuse section of Jordans' website stated that the firm represented clients from eighty different schools and care homes. Few of these claimants would ever be required to face cross-examination in civil trials, because the institutions themselves, or the insurance companies that usually defend such actions, normally settled out of court. Jordans' website advised potential clients, 'Over 98 per cent of abuse cases handled by Jordans are settled out of court, making it very unlikely that it will be necessary for you to go to court' (Rose, 2012a).

The *Inside Time* advertisements worked. By 2010, Greenwood had more than 100 clients, all claiming that they had been horrifically abused, most of them sexually, at St William's. The class action had received extensive and entirely uncritical publicity in local media. That September, Greenwood again contacted Humberside Police—but, this time, he was asking to supply information rather than to receive it. His class action had, he said, generated fresh evidence of offences at St William's, which the police must investigate. He held meetings with Detective Chief Superintendent Colin Andrews, one of the force's most experienced detectives. The result was Operation Reno: a new investigation covering the same ground as Operation Aldgate. As with Operation Pallial in North Wales, groundhog day had arrived—and a personal injury solicitor had been instrumental in getting the new inquiry started.

As Operation Reno got under way, four of the men who had already been acquitted in trials arising from Operation Aldgate again found themselves suspects. But the allegations against them were now much more serious: Noel Hartnett, for example, had been accused in 2004 of physical abuse, but now it was claimed he had committed multiple acts of the most extreme sexual assaults.

Hartnett was suffering from the terminal lung condition pulmonary fibrosis, but he was determined to fight back. Lawyers acting for the De La Salle Brotherhood, the Catholic order that had run St Williams, had given him statements served by Greenwood in respect of his civil compensation action and asked him to analyse them. He already had much of the documentation generated as a result of his earlier trial, including the school's attendance and employment records, as well as the full text of the 3,000-page IPCC report on Operation Aldgate.

The consequences were devastating. In a total of fifty-four cases, he was able to provide persuasive evidence that those now making allegations were lying. Some had not been at the school at the same time as their supposed abusers worked there; others accused people who did not exist. Most worryingly, there were multiple allegations against a handful of the same fictitious individuals, suggesting that the claimants must have colluded in making false claims or adopted bogus allegations supplied by some third party. Still others made claims that could easily be refuted from other, verifiable, sources, such as medical records and plans of the school buildings. Some of those making new allegations had already been described as deeply unreliable by Operation Gullane.

Thanks to the detailed forensic memos that Hartnett composed about most of those accused during Operation Reno, he and the others who had already been found not guilty in 2004 were told there would be 'no further action' against them. However, by this time, they had lived for a further two years or so under the cloud of being paedophilia suspects. The police later confirmed that several alleged St Williams victims were being investigated for possible fraud and, eventually, files on at least three were sent to the CPS. Moreover, Hartnett had been able to analyse several versions of the same complainants' statements. This meant that he was able to show that the claims of some had grown steadily more lurid—apparently, because they believed that the more serious their allegations, the more compensation they would eventually be paid.

Finally, in the autumn of 2012, Greenwood advised his clients to stop cooperating with Operation Reno, the criminal inquiry that he had himself triggered. The immediate result was that fifty-three separate police case files, which had been close to completion, had to be withdrawn from consideration by the CPS. More than twenty full-time CID officers had been working for years on inquiries that had now proven futile. The cost, needless to say, was immense.

Yet this was not the end of Operation Reno. Indeed, in the wake of the documentary that claimed to expose Jimmy Savile as a serial paedophile, as the issue of historic abuse began to occupy ever more news airtime and space in newspapers, both the St Williams civil action and the criminal inquiry continued to grow in scope. Noel Hartnett told me that, by the summer of 2014, the action had attracted well over 200 claimants.

CONCLUSION: THE FLIGHT FROM REASON

A detailed analysis of the cultural forces that have shaped historic abuse investigations is beyond the scope of this chapter. Readers will find this explored in the work of Richard Webster, especially in the concluding sections of *The Secret of Bryn Estyn* (Webster, 2005: 536*ff*).[4] In essence, Webster believed that inquiries into historic abuse had come to share many of the characteristics of the early modern witch hunt. Such offences were not being seen as mere crimes, but as evidence of dark, secret conspiracies, as manifestations of a titanic struggle between Good and Evil, and as precursors of the final battle to come. He further considered that they had been made all the more dangerous because most people were convinced that such irrational impulses belonged to the past and that reason had triumphed. As Webster put it on the homepage of his website, where many of his essays can still be found:

> The most fervent modern advocates of reason and of science have often suggested or implied that we are no longer generally susceptible to dangerous delusions such as gripped the minds of learned men in the great European witch-hunt of the sixteenth and seventeenth centuries. This is, I believe, but another example of the dangers of rationalism. For if we accept and allow ourselves to be guided by a view of cultural history which denies the very possibility of a witch-hunt taking place in our midst, we have created the ideal conditions for one to take place in front of our eyes without our even noticing what is happening.[5]

In his interview, quoted in this chapter, Peter Garsden appeared to confirm the validity of Webster's diagnosis: it is not often that one meets a solicitor who states his conviction that, in representing alleged victims of historic abuse, he is battling with the Devil. But while Garsden is unusual in being willing to express such a view, the widespread acceptance, especially by the media, of some of the most extreme and disturbing conspiratorial abuse narratives suggests that he is not alone in his analysis.

Christian religious observance, it need hardly be stated, has been in decline in Britain for many decades. Deprived of the legend of the Fall, some have come to look elsewhere for stories about the loss of innocence, as if (as Webster argued) such stories fill an unacknowledged need. The sexual abuse of needy children by those appointed by society to take care of them speaks directly to this.

This, I suggest, explains two associated phenomena. The first is the vitriol poured on anyone who challenges mainstream narratives—and here, unfortunately, I write as a frequent recipient. Blogs have claimed that I am 'linked to paedophiles', simply because I have written articles defending those wrongly accused.[6] Using language that Webster would have recognized as an example of the conspiratorial worldview that once underlay witch hunts, another blogger commented that my article describing the past of Stephen Messham in the aftermath of the McAlpine *Newsnight* scandal was 'clearly an attempt on the part of sections of the British establishment to strike back at allegations which potentially could bring down some of its most powerful members' (Pride, 2012).

---

[4] See also Part II of this volume. [5] Online at <http://www.richardwebster.net>
[6] See, e.g., <http://google-law.blogspot.co.uk/2012/11/is-david-rose-who-vilified-messham.html>

The second phenomenon, exhibited by many police officers, lawyers, and, regrettably, journalists, is the refusal to consider allegations of historic child abuse according to the same standards that would normally be applied to other criminal claims. Peter Garsden would not admit that significant factual discrepancies between complainants' statements and externally verifiable facts affected the core truth of his clients' claims. The government response to the Select Committee report simply denied that there was evidence that alleged victims' hopes for compensation might affect the safety of criminal convictions. The strangest thing of all is that police officers, usually so sceptical of the stories told by convicted criminals, have sometimes accepted them wholesale without conducting basic checks if they happen to concern claims of historic abuse.

Far too often, the media have given this process a free pass. One of the most dramatic examples in my own career was the sensational disclosure in 2008 that a children's home on Jersey, Haut de la Garenne, had been a charnel house of not only abuse, but also murder. After local CID chief Lenny Harper announced that 'human remains' had been found there, in the shape of a 'fragment' of part of a child's skull, the story went round the world. Stoked by further briefings from Harper, reporters suggested that many more murdered victims would soon come to light. As the *Guardian* front page put it on 25 February 2008:

> Six more bodies may be buried at a former children's home in Jersey where a youngster's remains were found by detectives investigating allegations of widespread child abuse on the island, police said yesterday. The remains were found under a thick concrete floor inside the Victorian mansion, beside scraps of fabric, a button and what appeared to be a hair clip. It is believed the child's skull was among the remains found.
>
> (Pidd and Morris, 2008: 1)

Some weeks later, I broke the surprising story that scientific experts from the University of Oxford and the British Museum had established that the 'skull fragment' was, in reality, a piece of an old coconut shell (Rose, 2008a). Worse, Harper continued to tell both the press and local politicians that there was 'no scientific dispute' that the 'skull' was human, weeks after he had been informed by scientists via email 'It ain't bone' (Rose, 2008b). Eventually, after Harper retired, a seasoned detective from Lancashire, Mick Gradwell, took over the case and eventually revealed that all Harper's headline-grabbing claims had been bogus: there were no bodies, no murders, no missing children, nor, for that matter, 'torture chambers' and 'abuse pits' in the home's basement—indeed, the building did not even *have* a basement (Rose, 2009).

But the point is: the factual corrective to Harper's narrative of Evil received only a fraction of the attention given the original, bogus, allegations. For weeks after my first article about the coconut had appeared, newspapers continued to run stories about finds of 'burnt' milk teeth being discovered by Harper's excavations, implying that there had been an organized attempt to conceal the evidence of murders by incinerating their victims.

In the case of Jersey, rationality and empiricism eventually supervened. But since the Jimmy Savile scandal broke, such correctives have become rarer. Metropolitan Police Commander Peter Spindler set the tone in October 2012, soon after launching Operation Yewtree, the inquiry into alleged abuse by Savile and some of his associates.

The investigation, he said, was a 'watershed moment' and Savile, 'undoubtedly' one of the most prolific sexual offenders who had ever lived.

Spindler added: 'We have to believe what they [the victims] are saying because they are all saying the same thing independently.' Meanwhile, 'Scotland Yard sources'—that is, press officers speaking on a non-attributable basis—were saying that the police were also looking at 'figures of high standing' who 'might have helped Savile, helped organise abuse, cover it up or taken part in assaults' (BBC News, 2012b).

Some of the discrepancies that I was able to expose in articles about the Savile case in the autumn of 2014 had been canvassed in the blogosphere for months, by Susanne Cameron-Blackie[7] and others. But although one other national newspaper journalist did become interested, he backed off, having told at least two of his sources that to publish material casting doubt on the prevailing narrative would be 'career suicide'.

Meanwhile, the High Court had established a compensation scheme: a means of paying damages to 'victims' from what was left of Savile's estate, administered by his executors, NatWest. It allowed for only the most cursory scrutiny of allegations' veracity. The assumption underlying it was, self-evidently, that most of them must be true.

If the Savile case marked a new high point in credulousness, it was about to be surpassed. Late in 2014, the website Exaro News began to publish stories of truly extreme abuse and sexual murder by Tory MPs and 'senior military officers' during the 1970s and 1980s.[8] The site, edited by Mark Watts, a former employee of Iranian propaganda channel Press TV, had been drip-feeding claims of this nature for months. So far, so unremarkable—but they were then taken up by BBC Home Affairs Correspondent Tom Symonds and, despite the absence of missing children, the police. By the end of the year, Scotland Yard was investigating no fewer than three supposed murders—although it had no victims' names. Moreover, all of this had emanated from a single source: an anonymous 'survivor' named 'Nick', whom the senior investigating officer had publicly declared was 'credible and true'. It was left to the barrister Matthew Scott (2015) to point out some of the obvious dangers:

> The first effect of broadcasting Nick's detailed allegations is that anybody wishing to make a false allegation has now been given not just rumours, which in truth have been flying around on the internet for years, but a detailed and apparently first-hand description of exactly how another witness says the abuse took place. This, of course, flies in the face of good policing practice in which the account of one witness is never given to other potential witnesses precisely because of the danger of contamination … If Nick's account is *untrue*, then to broadcast it is to feed a monstrous hysteria.[9]

'Hysteria' is the right word. On some days now, when one opens a newspaper, one will find half a dozen articles about some aspect of alleged child sexual abuse. It is as if child abuse has become our greatest social ill, especially if it took place long ago. But since the Savile and 'Nick' allegations, public discourse has had few, if any, limits. Richard Webster (2005: 555) concluded *The Secret of Bryn Estyn* by warning that, without

---

[7] See the 'Duncroft/Savile' section of blog *Anna Raccoon*, online at <http://annaraccoon.com/category/duncroftsavile/>

[8] See, e.g., Watts and Conrad (2014).

[9] Since the time of first writing, the Yard has admitted that this was a serious error, while the inquiry triggered by 'Nick's' allegations has effectively collapsed.

action 'to reintroduce reason and restraint into our system of justice', future historians would come to view the hunts for actual witches in the early modern era 'as nothing' compared to the contemporary child abuse panic. It seems to me that, since he wrote those words in 2005 and especially since his tragically early death in 2011, we have come significantly closer to making that baleful vision a reality.

REFERENCES

BBC News (2012a) 'BBC Reaches Settlement with Lord McAlpine', 15 November. Available online at <http://www.bbc.co.uk/news/uk-20348978> [accessed January 2015].

BBC News (2012b) 'Jimmy Savile: Number of Victims Reaches 300, Police Say', 25 October. Available online at <http://www.bbc.co.uk/news/uk-20081021> [accessed May 2016].

Home Affairs Select Committee (2002a) Minutes of Evidence, 14 May. Available online at <http://www.publications.parliament.uk/pa/cm200102/cmselect/cmhaff/836/2051401.htm> [accessed January 2015].

Home Affairs Select Committee (2002b) *The Conduct of Investigations into Past Cases of Abuse in Children's Homes: Fourth Report of Session 2001–02*, London: HMSO. Available online at <http://www.publications.parliament.uk/pa/cm200102/cmselect/cmhaff/836/83602.htm> [accessed May 2016].

Home Office (2002) *Complex Child Abuse Investigations: Inter-agency Guidance*. Available online at <http://www.workingtogetheronline.co.uk/documents/Complex_abu.pdf> [accessed May 2016].

Home Office (2003) *The Conduct of Investigations into Past Cases of Abuse in Children's Homes: The Government Reply to the Fourth Report from the Home Affairs Committee Session 2001–02, HC 836*, Cm 5799, April. Available online at <https://www.gov.uk/government/uploads/system/uploads/attachment_data/file/251046/5799.pdf> [accessed May 2016].

Independent Police Complaints Commission (IPCC) (2007) *Operation Gullane: Report on the IPCC Managed Investigation Undertaken by West Yorkshire Police into Complaints Emanating from Operation Aldgate*. Available online at <https://www.ipcc.gov.uk/sites/default/files/Documents/investigation_commissioner_reports/operation_gullane_exec_sumary.pdf> [accessed May 2016].

PIDD, H., and MORRIS, S. (2008) 'Six More Bodies Feared Buried in Jersey Home', *The Guardian*, 25 February. Available online at <http://www.theguardian.com/uk/2008/feb/25/jersey.child.bodies> [accessed May 2016].

Press Association (2013) 'Lord McAlpine Libel Row with Sally Bercow Formally Settled in High Court', *The Guardian*, 22 October. Available online at <http://www.theguardian.com/uk-news/2013/oct/22/lord-mcalpine-libel-row-sally-bercow> [accessed May 2016].

PRIDE, T. (2012) 'Child Abuse Scandal Can of Worms: Just Who Is *Daily Mail* Reporter David Rose?', 11 November. Available online at <https://tompride.wordpress.com/2012/11/11/child-abuse-scandal-can-of-worms-just-who-is-daily-mail-reporter-david-rose/> [accessed May 2016].

ROSE, D. (2002) ' "Abuser" Was Netted in Police Trawl—But Is He Innocent?', *The Observer*, 6 January. Available online at <http://www.theguardian.com/society/2002/jan/06/2> [accessed May 2016].

Rose, D. (2005) 'Child Abuse Police Left Me a Broken Man', *The Observer*, 12 June. Available online at <http://www.theguardian.com/society/2005/jun/12/childrensservices.childprotection1> [accessed May 2016].

Rose, D. (2008a) ' "Human Bone" at Centre of Jersey Children's Home Inquiry Is Actually a Piece of Wood or Coconut Shell', *Mail on Sunday*, 18 May. Available online at <http://www.dailymail.co.uk/news/article-567013/Human-bone-centre-Jersey-childrens-home-inquiry-actually-piece-wood-coconut-shell.html> [accessed May 2016].

Rose, D. (2008b) 'Jersey Police Failed to Reveal that Tested "Skull" Was Coconut', *Mail on Sunday*, 24 May. Available online at <http://www.dailymail.co.uk/news/article-1021722/Jersey-police-failed-reveal-tested-skull-coconut.html> [accessed May 2016].

Rose, D. (2009) 'Bungled Jersey Child Abuse Probe Branded a "£20 Million Shambles" ', *Mail on Sunday*, 4 October. Available online at <http://www.dailymail.co.uk/news/article-1217863/Bungled-Jersey-child-abuse-probe-branded-20million-shambles.html> [accessed May 2016].

Rose, D. (2012a) 'A Victim of His Delusions: Astonishing Story the BBC *Didn't* Tell You about Its Troubled Star Witness', *Mail on Sunday*, 11 November. Available online at <http://www.dailymail.co.uk/news/article-2231212/Steven-Messham-Astonishing-story-BBC-DIDNT-tell-troubled-star-witness.html> [accessed May 2016].

Rose, D. (2012b) 'The Deputy Head Teacher Falsely Accused of Child Abuse and the Ambulance-chasing Lawyer Who Advertises for "Victims" in Prisons', *Mail on Sunday*, 1 December. Available online at <http://www.dailymail.co.uk/news/article-2241628/The-deputy-head-teacher-falsely-accused-child-abuse-ambulance-chasing-lawyer-advertises-victims-prisons.html> [accessed May 2016].

Rose, D., and Horne, G. (2000) 'Abuse Witch-Hunt Traps Innocent in a Net of Lies', *The Guardian*, 26 November. Available online at <http://www.theguardian.com/society/2000/nov/26/socialcare.childrensservices> [accessed January 2015].

Rozenberg, J. (2001) 'Lord Woolf Urges Care over Paedophile Cases', *The Telegraph*, 24 November. Available online at <http://www.telegraph.co.uk/news/uknews/1363288/Lord-Woolf-urges-care-over-paedophile-cases.html> [accessed January 2015].

Scott, M. (2015) 'Exaro News Is Playing a Dangerous Game with Its Paedophile Murder Story', *Barrister Blogger*, 16 November. Available online at <http://barristerblogger.com/2014/11/16/exaro-news-playing-dangerous-game-paedophile-murder-story/> [accessed May 2016].

Watts, M., and Conrad, M. (2014) ' "Nick" Tells of How Much MPs Liked to Inflict Pain during Abuse', *Exaro News*, 5 November. Available online at <http://www.exaronews.com/articles/5396/video-nick-tells-of-how-mps-liked-to-inflict-pain-during-abuse> [accessed May 2016].

Webster, R. (1998) *The Great Children's Home Panic*, Oxford: The Orwell Press.

Webster, R. (2002) 'A Change of Course for the Home Office?'. Available online at <http://www.richardwebster.net/homeaffairscommittee.html> [accessed January 2015].

Webster, R. (2005) *The Secret of Bryn Estyn: The Making of a Modern Witch Hunt*, Oxford: The Orwell Press.

PART IV
INTERROGATION; PROSECUTION; CONVICTION; APPEAL

HOW COULD THE JUSTICE SYSTEM GET IT SO WRONG?

13

WHEN EXONERATION SEEMS HOPELESS

THE SPECIAL VULNERABILITY OF SEXUAL ABUSE SUSPECTS TO FALSE CONFESSION

Deborah Davis and Richard A. Leo

In May 2006, 10-year-old Shawnae Matthews reported to police that her uncle Mario Matthews had sexually molested her for approximately a year. The molestation allegedly occurred three years earlier, when she was aged 7, between January and December 2003. Shawnae reported that her uncle Mario had forced her to have intercourse between ten and twenty times, and had digitally penetrated her on other occasions.

On 22 March 2007, almost a year after the initial allegations, Mario Matthews was brought to a San Bernardino police station, where he was interrogated for roughly an hour. Few would imagine that his interrogation was of the type likely to induce a false confession. It was short. There was no physical intimidation nor were there explicit verbal threats seemingly sufficient to cause him to confess falsely.

Yet Mario Matthews did confess falsely. Although he denied everything at first, he later admitted to all of the allegations his niece had made. He did so relatively quickly, within an hour, and with no apparent coercion. And, as a result, Matthews went to jail, where he spent several years awaiting trial. It was only when the case went to trial that his false confession was discovered. When the victim was asked in court whether the person sitting at the defence table was her molester, she responded 'No.' When challenged with the fact that she had explicitly reported that it was her uncle Mario Matthews who had molested her, she responded that indeed it was her uncle Mario Matthews, but she had two uncle Mario Matthews, and it was the other one who had molested her.

Had Matthews' false confession not been so dramatically revealed in open court, he would almost certainly have been convicted and spent much of his life in jail. But *why* did he falsely confess? And why did he do so in response to such a seemingly non-coercive interrogation? Are there features of the interrogation that are much more powerful than one would expect? Or could Matthews himself have been vulnerable in some way that led him to succumb to the influence of the interrogator? As developed in the following sections, we suggest the answer may lie, in part, in the nature of the crime of which he was accused.

Mario Matthews is just one among a steadily growing number of proven false confessors. Systematic analyses of wrongful convictions have revealed that between 14 per cent and over 60 per cent of the wrongfully convicted had falsely confessed (Leo, 2008). Other cases of false confession have been documented in individual case accounts (Connery, 1977; Edds, 2003; Burns, 2011) and in compilations of cases involving false confessions (such as Drizin and Leo, 2004). Most proven false confessions involve serious crimes such as murder, rape, robbery, arson, and kidnapping, among others (Drizin and Leo, 2004). Notably underrepresented among these proven false confessions, however, are those involving child sex abuse, date rape, or other 'he said, she said' sexual allegations relying heavily, if not exclusively, on the testimony of the alleged victims and perpetrators. Although there have been many false confessions to rape, the issue is the identity of the perpetrator (rather than consent) and the false confessors have been exonerated primarily through DNA. Other than Mario Matthews, comparably few proven false confessions to child sexual abuse have been documented, and many of these occurred in notorious day care centre cases entailing multi-child false allegations of abuse and other fantastic activities such as satanic abuse.[1] We have been unable to locate many other proven false confessions involving child sex abuse, and few false confessions in sexual assault cases involving the issue of consent rather than identity and relying primarily on victim testimony in the absence of physical evidence against the suspect.

Nevertheless, we suggest that false confessions to sexual abuse, such as that of Mario Matthews (and to other 'he said, she said' sexual allegations), are likely to be much more common than most would assume. At the same time, they are much more likely to go unrecognized. Unless strong physical evidence exists to support claims of abuse or other sexual offences, those who judge must rely heavily (sometimes exclusively) upon the word of the alleged victim versus that of the alleged perpetrator. If the alleged perpetrator confesses, this contest of credibility is seemingly resolved: who, after all, would falsely confess to a crime likely to send him or her to prison for decades, or even for life? And no evidence exists to contradict the confession and prove the confessor innocent; only the belated retraction by the confessor provides the suggestion of possible innocence. But such a retraction is likely to be viewed as dishonest—as only an effort to avoid the severe consequences of confession. In a few instances, the complainants have recanted.[2] But, in the absence of such recantations, DNA or other concrete evidence is often unavailable to support the exoneration of the defendant. Had Mario Matthew's niece not exonerated him so definitively in open court, his claims of innocence almost certainly would not have been believed, he would almost certainly have been convicted, and he would have spent decades in prison. Most false confessors to sexual abuse, and to other 'he said, she said' sexual allegations, are not so lucky.

In the remainder of this chapter, we first explore sources of vulnerability to false confession among sexual abuse suspects. We then turn to consideration of the relative

---

[1] See the National Registry of Exonerations, online at <http://www.law.umich.edu/special/exoneration/Pages/detaillist.aspx>
[2] Ibid.

difficulty of identifying a false confession to sexual abuse versus offences involving more, and more concrete, available evidence.

INTERROGATION AND THE INNOCENT ABUSE SUSPECT

Interrogation-induced false confessions occur primarily for three reasons: the fact, length, and severity of the pressures of interrogation; distress intolerance and confession simply to escape the interrogation; and the mistaken belief that false confession will result in the best long-term legal outcomes.[3] Enhanced vulnerability to false confession is therefore best understood by considering how these outcomes may apply to sexual abuse suspects. We focus our discussion on child sexual abuse suspects, noting, however, that similar considerations apply to other sexual assault suspects whose cases rely primarily on the alleged victim's testimony, absent other forms of evidence.

ENHANCED LIKELIHOOD, PRESSURES, AND PERSISTENCE

Interrogation-induced false confessions become possible only when suspects are subject to interrogation—and they become more likely the more prolonged the interrogation and the more pressures toward confession exerted by the interrogator.[4] Why, if at all, might sexual abuse suspects be more likely and more vigorously interrogated?

Criminal suspects are often asked to come to the police station 'voluntarily' to 'help with the investigation' or to 'discuss' the accusations against them—a request that is difficult to ignore, particularly when the alleged events involve one's own family or children. Once the suspect agrees to be questioned (with or without a *Miranda* warning), police often look for verbal and non-verbal cues that they have been taught are diagnostic of lying, and thus of guilt (Zulawski and Wicklander, 2002; Inbau et al., 2011). Much of what interrogators are taught regarding detection of deceit is directly contradicted by scientific studies identifying actual cues to deception.[5] These behavioural analysis assessments for deception rely heavily on cues reflecting anxiety and arousal, assuming that they reflect deception. Moreover, the manuals teach that various other postural, speech, and non-verbal cues reflect deception—many of which are either not related to deception at all, are related to deception in the opposite manner to that taught in the manuals, or have not been scientifically tested.[6] In reviewing scientific studies of lie detection, Vrij and colleagues noted that no lie-detection tool based on analysis of verbal or non-verbal behaviour is accurate (Vrij, 2008; Vrij et al., 2010); rather, such tools impair accuracy relative to untrained controls, while simultaneously increasing confidence in judgements (DePaulo and Pfeifer, 1986; Porter,

---

[3] See Davis and O'Donohue (2004), Leo (2008), and Kassin et al. (2010) for reviews.
[4] Ibid.
[5] See Vrij (2008) and Vrij, Granhag, and Porter (2010) for reviews.
[6] See Vrij (2008) for review of cues thought to reflect deception versus actual indicators of deception.

Woodworth, and Birt, 2000; Meissner and Kassin, 2002; Garrido, Masip, and Herrero, 2004).[7]

Adding to the problems of the basic inaccuracy of the cues central to interrogators' behavioural analysis protocols, interrogators make their assessments of deception in the context of the existing expectations of guilt that led them to target the suspect for interrogation. The assessments are subjective, and are based on the subset of cues that the detective remembers and is able to attend to in the moment, and, as such, they reflect the unsystematic use and weighting of the cues that are noticed, as opposed to all cues recommended by behavioural analysis protocol—that is, much less proper attention to, and weighting of, actual cues to deception. This situation renders judgements of deception highly subjective, unreliable, and susceptible to the biases and expectations of the detective conducting the interview. Likely to experience anxiety under the circumstances, all suspects are thus at risk of being judged deceptive, based on the flawed behavioural analysis indicators of deception, as employed by interrogators who use them selectively and unsystematically, in the context of expectations of guilt. But are some classes of suspects—and sexual abuse suspects, in particular—at increased risk of being judged deceptive and therefore at increased risk of being interrogated?

We suggest that sexual abuse suspects may be more likely to be judged deceptive than many other classes of suspects. Stereotypes link some suspects' social categories with sexual abuse, for example stepfathers, priests, boy scout leaders, previously suspected or convicted sex offenders, and, to some extent, simply being a male relative or acquaintance of the victim. Such stereotypes can impact both suspect and interrogator. As discussed in the following sections, awareness of stereotypes linking their social category to sexual abuse—that is, 'stereotype threat' (Steele and Aronson, 1995)—can lead suspects to feel that they will be presumed guilty, to experience greater arousal and anxiety as a result, and therefore to appear more deceptive according to behavioural analysis criteria. Such stereotypes may also magnify the presumption of guilt that interrogators already entertain as the result of the accusations against the suspect and any evidence appearing to support them, thereby affecting their effort and persistence in attempts to induce a confession.

STEREOTYPE THREAT AND THE APPEARANCE OF DECEPTION

A number of scholars have noted that defendants belonging to social categories stigmatized by stereotypes linking them to criminal behaviour may tend to appear more deceptive than other suspects when assessed by means of procedures relying on reflections of anxiety and arousal—that is, awareness of stereotypes linking their social category to criminal behaviour can lead such suspects to experience increased anxiety, to manifest behavioural cues of anxiety, and therefore to misleadingly appear more deceptive. Such a possibility has been supported by the extensive literature on 'stereotype threat'.

---

[7] See also Nahari's Chapter 18 on lie detection in this volume.

Steele and Aronson (1995) defined stereotype threat as awareness of stereotypes linking an individual's social category to specific behaviours or traits, and the resulting concerns that the individual may be perceived as manifesting traits or behaviours consistent with the stereotypes and/or that one might involuntarily act in such a way as to apparently confirm the stereotypes. The authors first investigated the effects of stereotype threat with regard to stereotypes of inferior intelligence applied to African Americans—showing, for example, that African Americans performed more poorly than white Americans on tests they believed to assess intelligence, but performed no differently on the same tests if the tests were not described as assessing intelligence. Later research has shown that the stereotype threat experienced by African Americans when taking a test relevant to their 'intelligence' impairs performance through effects on arousal and anxiety, as well as the increased cognitive load required to manage the thoughts and emotions provoked by concerns about confirming or being thought to confirm stereotypes of inferior intelligence.[8]

The relevance of these effects of stereotype threat to assessments of deception was first discussed in a National Academy evaluation of the polygraph in 2003 (National Research Council of the National Academies, 2003). The report noted that groups subject to criminal stereotypes, such as African American males, are likely to experience 'identity threat' (which includes stereotype threat) during interrogation or polygraph testing. Noting that polygraph assessment relies on physiological indices of arousal and anxiety, the authors suggested that such groups may be subject to false positives for deception because of identity-threat-induced anxiety. The implications of this problem for both physiological and behavioural methods of lie detection in interrogation, as well as the end result of false confession, have since been more fully developed by ourselves and others (Najdowski, 2011; Davis and Leo, 2012; Davis et al., 2014).

Crucially, while the National Research Council report and others (such as Najdowski, 2011) focused on race-related criminal stereotypes and their effects for racial minority defendants, we have suggested that criminality-related stereotype threat applies to many classes of suspects whose social category is stereotypically associated with crime generally (such as those with criminal records) or with specific types of crime (such as stereotypes associating stepfathers and sex abuse—Davis and Leo, 2012; Davis et al., 2014). To the extent that awareness of any such stereotypes magnifies anxiety that one will be presumed guilty, it can also magnify the appearance of deception when one is interviewed or interrogated. Moreover, it is important to note that although our discussion has focused on the effects of stereotype-threat-related cues of anxiety on assessments of deception recommended by interrogation trainers, cognitive effects of stereotype threat can also affect valid cues of deception. For example, just as stereotype threat imposes increased cognitive load on those subject to it,[9] so lying imposes increased cognitive load on liars.[10] Accordingly, even valid methods for assessment of deception, some relying on reflections of cognitive load, can produce inflated rates of false positives among suspects subject to stereotype threat.

---

[8] See Inzlicht and Schmader (2011) and Steele (2011) for reviews.   [9] Ibid
[10] See Vrij et al. (2010) for a review.

Stereotype-threat-related arousal, anxiety, and increased cognitive load have important effects on whether and how the suspect is interrogated. The aforementioned initial assessment of deception, for example, can affect whether the interrogator elects to proceed to the accusatory interrogation or not. Theoretically, if the suspect is assessed as honest, the interrogator should not interrogate (see Inbau et al., 2011, for example). To the extent that stereotype threat leads abuse suspects to appear more deceptive, the interrogator should be more likely to proceed to interrogation. In practice, however, once suspects are brought in for questioning, it is highly likely that the detective will choose to interrogate—regardless of the appearance of deception. Nevertheless, the assessment of deception can exert important effects on the subsequent conduct of the interrogation.

Among the most important of these effects is the operation of confirmation biases among interrogators. Laboratory research has shown, for example, that where interrogators expect suspects are guilty, they ask more guilt-presumptive questions, use more interrogation techniques, and exert more pressure to get a confession. Notably, these effects are stronger for innocent than guilty suspects—presumably a result in part of increased resistance to confession among innocent suspects. Moreover, interrogator expectations affect suspect performance such that suspects questioned by interrogators with greater expectations of guilt are rated as more defensive and somewhat more guilty by neutral observers of the taped interrogations (for example Kassin, Goldstein, and Savitsky, 2003).

Interrogation manuals instruct interrogators to be sensitive to indications that the suspect might not be guilty, and to step down and eventually terminate the interrogation if the suspect appears to be innocent (for example Inbau et al., 2011). But, as suggested by the substantial literature on confirmation biases generally (Nickerson, 1998)[11] and studies of confirmation biases specific to interrogation (for example Meissner and Kassin, 2002; Kassin et al., 2003), recognition of innocence is made more difficult by forces encouraging the presumption of guilt. Suspects are targeted for interrogation when evidence (however strong or weak) exists to suggest guilt—and sometimes simply on the basis of a theory or hunch. Accordingly, interrogators begin the interrogation with at least some expectation of suspect guilt, which can in turn bias their initial assessments of deception.[12]

These assessments are likely to further solidify confidence in the suspect's guilt and to set in motion a reciprocal cycle of confirmatory processes through which expectations of guilt affect interrogator behaviours, some of which influence suspects to experience greater anxiety and to appear more deceptive, which further promotes interrogator presumptions of guilt, interrogation effort, and persistence. As a result, suspects are highly likely to be interrogated if they are interviewed. Moreover, interrogators' abilities to recognize innocence among interrogated suspects are compromised, leading them to persist in interrogating, to interrogate more forcefully, and, as a result, to enhance the risk of false confession among innocents. Stereotypes associating suspect social categories with the crime of which they are suspected may mag-

---

[11] See Findley and Scott (2006) for a review.
[12] See Meissner and Kassin (2002) regarding guilt bias in assessments of deception by trained investigators.

nify these processes among interrogators and suspects alike—that is, the stereotypes themselves may encourage the initial and continuing presumption of guilt among interrogators. And the stereotype threat experienced by suspects throughout the initial interview and the interrogation can magnify verbal and non-verbal behaviours perceived by their interrogators and others to reflect deception, enhancing the risk that claims of innocence will go unrecognized in the moment by the interrogator and later by others reacting to taped interrogations.[13]

DISTRESS, DISTRESS INTOLERANCE, AND CONFESSION TO ESCAPE INTERROGATION

Among the most prominent causes of confession, both true and false, is distress intolerance and confession to escape the pressures of interrogation.[14] Accordingly, factors that either enhance suspects' experience of distress or impair their distress tolerance can increase the likelihood of stress-induced confession. We have elsewhere offered a detailed analysis of the effects of interrogation-related regulatory decline (IRRD) on distress, distress intolerance, and the decision to confess (Davis and Leo, 2012). We reviewed evidence that the stresses of interrogation lead to ego-depletion and self-regulation failure, and therefore to impaired emotion regulation and impulse control. Impaired emotion regulation, in turn, renders suspects more vulnerable to distress—and impaired impulse control renders them more distress intolerant and likely to succumb to the impulse to do anything to escape the interrogation (including confessing). Moreover, we reviewed substantial evidence that, through its effects on self-regulation, stereotype threat can affect performance in interrogation (Davis and Leo, 2012). It impairs self-regulation of emotion and impulse control (thereby enhancing the risk of stress-induced confession) and control of cognition (thereby increasing suggestibility and the risk of becoming convinced that confession will serve one's long term legal interests—the subject of the next two sections).

Accordingly, sex abuse suspects may suffer enhanced distress in interrogation as the result of the increased interrogator effort and persistence discussed in the previous section, as well as stereotype-threat-related regulatory decline and its effect on emotion regulation. Stereotype-threat-related regulatory decline can likewise cause abuse suspects to experience enhanced impairment in impulse control, thereby enhancing the likelihood of true or false confession through the double whammy of greater distress and lesser impulse control.

BELIEVING THE UNBELIEVABLE: CONFESSION IS IN YOUR BEST INTERESTS

Interrogation manuals and trainers acknowledge that the goal of interrogation is to convince suspects that confession is in their best interests: '[F]or a suspect to acknowledge a criminal act involving negative consequences requires that the suspect believe

---

[13] See Najdowski (2011) and Davis and Leo (2012) for reviews.
[14] See Kassin et al. (2010) for a review.

a confession is in his best interest' (Jayne and Buckley, 1999: 207). But how to convince the suspect of something so seemingly obviously unbelievable?

Broadly, interrogation entails a two-step process of persuasion. In the first phase, called 'positive confrontation' (Inbau et al., 2011), the suspect is confronted with the accusation and with the absolute confidence of the interrogator(s) in his or her guilt. In addition, the interrogator may present true or false 'evidence' against the suspect to support the accusation. The effectiveness of this first phase is crucial to the elicitation of a confession, in that both laboratory and field studies have shown that the likelihood of both true and false confession is strongly affected by the perceived strength of evidence against the suspect. Indeed, interrogator use of false evidence has been strongly implicated in real-life instances of proven false confession.[15]

If the first phase of interrogation is successful, the suspect will have become convinced that his or her guilt is clearly established. But the tactics of the first phase are repeated as necessary throughout the interrogation to handle any suspect denials or arguments for innocence. If innocent—and particularly if the interrogator has presented false or mistaken, but seemingly convincing, evidence against him or her—the suspect may have become convinced that he or she is hopelessly implicated, that he or she will not be able to demonstrate his or her innocence, and that he or she cannot convince others (judges and juries included) of his or her innocence. This sense of hopelessness tends to focus suspects' attention on how to minimize the consequences of guilt, rather than on attempts to establish innocence. It also renders suspects more vulnerable to the second step of persuasion, in which the interrogator misrepresents the consequences of the suspect's guilt as flexible, himself or herself as possessing the authority to affect those consequences (as well as the desire to 'help' the suspect), and confession as the way in which to achieve the best legal outcomes.[16] We suggest that sex abuse suspects may be more susceptible to both the sense of hopelessness promoted by the positive confrontation phase of interrogation and to persuasion that confession is best during the second broad phase of persuasion.

TO WALK IN THEIR SHOES: WHY WOULD AN INNOCENT ABUSE SUSPECT FEEL PARTICULARLY HOPELESS?

It takes little imagination to anticipate common reactions among innocent persons accused of sexual abuse. Among them may be shock, confusion, surprise, and anger or outrage toward the accuser. But following closely behind will be shame, fear, and hopelessness: expectations of loss of reputation and perhaps family, friends, and employment; fear of being labelled a predator or pervert; fears of conviction and incarceration; and the sense that even if he or she is exonerated, some people will nevertheless assume his or her guilt and others will always harbour doubt. The credibility of an alleged victim may seem impossible to overcome. Once the accusation is made, the suspect may feel presumed guilty—that is, as though he or she has been tried, judged, and convicted even before legal proceedings begin. Some suspects, such as gay men, Catholic priests,

---

[15] See Kassin et al. (2010) for a review.

[16] For reviews, see Davis and O'Donohue (2004); Leo (2008); Davis (2010); Davis, Leo, and Follette (2010); Kassin et al. (2010).

or stepfathers, may have felt that they had always been presumed guilty—viewed as paedophiles before they were even accused, and convicted by common stereotypes associating their social category with sexual molestation.

Before entering interrogation, these suspects may have experienced a host of adverse reactions from others, such as accusations and conflict within the family, other altered social interactions of various sorts, perhaps even dismissal by employers or other groups, adverse publicity, and much more. They are likely to experience unremitting stress, anxiety, and worry, and to become more and more hopeless as the reactions of all but their closest and most loyal supporters appear to reflect an uncompromising presumption of guilt. Such reactions leading into interrogation increase vulnerability to confession through multiple pathways, including distress, self-regulation failure, hopelessness, impaired cognition, and vulnerability to persuasion (Davis and Leo, 2012). But how, one might ask, is this different from the reactions of suspects generally and innocents accused of other crimes?

The answer, we suggest, lies largely in the evidentiary situation facing sex abuse suspects, which has implications both for social reactions and likely legal outcomes of the accusations: that the sum total of direct evidence is often the informal accounts and formal testimony of the alleged victim. There may be other indirect evidence, such as observers' characterizations of the relationship between suspect and victim, or of each's behaviour or personality, and so on. In some cases, there may be physical evidence that abuse took place, with or without evidence that could identify the perpetrator (such as semen or other sources of DNA).

But for a large subset of cases of sexual abuse there is no physical evidence. As was true for Mario Matthews, the alleged abuse may have taken place sufficiently far in the past so that no DNA is available for testing. Injuries may be healed or may never have occurred. Much alleged abuse entails no penetration and no potential for injury. Moreover, many accusations involve indefinite time frames and often repeated instances of abuse. As a result, the suspect is placed in a contest of credibility with a child and with no means to provide a specific alibi or to otherwise prove innocence.

Indeed, Mario Matthews experienced exactly this situation. He was faced with an allegation from a seemingly credible child, for which no physical evidence existed. His interrogation occurred four years after the alleged events and the child's allegation was made three years after the events. No physical evidence was available. The events were alleged to have taken place over a span of a year with no definite dates and thus no alibi was possible. When interrogated, Matthews denied culpability at first, but the interrogator emphasized the contest of credibility between him and the child. Throughout the interrogation, he reiterated that the child had specifically said that Matthews had abused her and there was no reason to doubt her. At one point, the interrogator lied to Matthews and told him that the child had been shown a line-up of suspects and had picked him out of the line-up:

> It was you. All the physical evidence I've read, or all the physical evidence I sent to the crime lab, comes back to you. And when I showed her the picture, she said 'That's the person.' You kind of stand out. 'That's the person right there.' 'Are you positive?' 'That's

him. That's who did all that stuff to me, multiple times.' That's why I went to the judge... Good enough for me...[17]

Matthews' response was telling: 'So, I don't have no way... I don't have no way!'

As it seemed to do for Matthews, this evidentiary situation may create an enhanced sense of hopelessness in abuse suspects—that is, we suggest that sexual abuse claims (as well as some rape claims) are often characterized by an evidentiary situation consisting of (a) seemingly credible claims of one or more victims, (b) against a suspect for whom stereotypes associate his social category with a propensity to sexually abuse, (c) lack of concrete physical evidence that could exonerate the suspect, and (d) testimony of professional and non-professional witnesses in seeming support of the occurrence of the abuse and often the suspect's guilt, which likewise cannot be refuted by concrete evidence. There is therefore reason to believe that child sexual abuse suspects will be *less* likely than most other innocent suspects to expect (e) that their claims of innocence will be believed in the absence of concrete proof of innocence, (f) that there will be evidence to prove their innocence, or even (g) that there will be a way to effectively cast doubt on the validity of the alleged victim's (or victims') claims of guilt or other apparently abuse supportive testimony. As noted earlier, a primary goal of interrogation tactics is to instil in suspects such a sense of hopelessness, which then makes it easier for the interrogator to convince him or her that confession will result in better legal outcomes than denial. For many sexual abuse suspects, this goal has been effectively met before they enter interrogation.

It is clear that there exist good reasons for many sexual abuse suspects to feel hopeless. But what evidence exists that this is actually the case? While we cannot easily study this issue with actual sexual abuse suspects, we have conducted several studies examining reasoning regarding false confession to abuse by asking participants to role play—asking each to imagine that he is an innocent person accused of sexual abuse, to read a transcript of the interrogation, and to report his reasoning concerning what he should do. Should he continue to deny? Should he invoke his rights to silence or to an attorney? Or should he falsely confess? Why?

Participants in three studies read a case background describing the allegations of a 6-year-old girl against her step-grandfather. They were told to assume either that the grandfather was guilty or that he was innocent, and that he was being interrogated by police and must decide what to do. They then read an approximately six-page interrogation transcript in which the interrogator firmly accused the grandfather of guilt, emphasized the testimony of the little girl, and otherwise used common interrogation tactics to try to encourage the grandfather to confess (specific combinations of tactics were varied). Upon completing the transcript, participants were asked to indicate whether the grandfather should (a) refuse to talk further and ask for an attorney, (b) continue to answer questions, but not confess, (c) confess to accidentally touching his granddaughter while asleep, thinking she was his wife (the scenario suggested by the interrogator), or (d) confess to deliberate molestation—and to explain their choices. Participants were asked a number of additional questions regarding their perceptions

---

[17] Interview of Mario Mathews by Detective Cunningham, 22 March 2007, Case No. 930607346, Rialto, CA, Police Department, Interrogation transcript, pp. 72–3.

of the strength of evidence against the suspect, the likelihood that the suspect would be convicted only on the basis of the child's testimony, and others.

Several aspects of the results highlight the potential vulnerability of sexual abuse suspects to the feeling of hopelessness. First, recommendations that the suspect should falsely confess were startlingly high. In the first study, roughly 16 per cent recommended that the suspect should falsely confess to achieve the best long-term legal outcomes. When asked in the second two studies what, specifically, would result in the least likelihood of being charged with a crime, 20 per cent and 26 per cent recommended false confession for the innocent, whereas 20 per cent and 20 per cent recommended false confession to minimize the likelihood of being convicted if charged, and 45 per cent and 58 per cent recommended false confession to minimize the seriousness of the charges, if any (Davis, Leo, and Follette, 2008, 2010; Davis et al., 2010). That these recommendations were fuelled at least in part by the sense that establishing innocence would be hopeless for the suspect was reflected in participants' responses to the other questions.

Although not suspects themselves, participants recognized the likelihood that a child will be believed over the suspect and the high likelihood of conviction. Mean ratings of the likelihood that the child's testimony would be believed (on a nine-point scale) ranged across studies from 6.9 to 7.6, whereas ratings of the likelihood that the suspect could convince the jury of his innocence ranged from 2.1 to 3.6. Ratings of the likelihood that the suspect would be convicted ranged from 6.7 to 7.4. Consistent with research indicating that perceived strength of the evidence strongly predicts the likelihood of confession, an index of the strength of evidence against the suspect (consisting of the aforementioned questions and others) was significantly correlated with the perceived wisdom of false confession across all three studies. Moreover, across studies, the majority of those who recommended that the suspect should falsely confess cited certainty that the child would be believed, or that no one would believe that the abuse did not happen, as the main reason to falsely confess. Many explained that it would be better to tell a good story about why it happened than to deny that it happened at all and be thought a liar.

But how might an abuse suspect come to this conclusion? The answer lies in the remaining interrogation tactics deployed against the suspect.

CONVINCING THE SUSPECT THAT CONFESSION IS BEST: ARE ABUSE SUSPECTS PARTICULARLY PERSUADABLE?

Once the interrogator has confronted the suspect with accusations against him, absolute confidence in his guilt, and the strength of the evidence against him (largely the believability of the alleged victim), the interrogator is likely to tell the suspect that he or she is not there to find out *whether* the suspect committed the abuse, but rather to find out *why* it happened and *what kind of person* the suspect is. This is followed by a tactic that we have dubbed the 'sympathetic detective with a time-limited offer' (Davis et al., 2010). The detective flatters the suspect, tells him that he or she does not believe the suspect to be a 'predator' or 'molester', but rather that this was a mistake or one-time occurrence that might have been unintentional. The detective expresses his or her desire to help the suspect, but reminds the suspect throughout that he or she cannot help if the suspect denies the incident happened.

This is repeated as necessary throughout the interrogation and is supplemented by the process of 'theme development',[18] in which the interrogator suggests ways in which the abuse might have happened that are seemingly not intended as sexual or which otherwise appear to minimize the seriousness (and apparent legal consequences) of the suspect's behaviour. The interrogator may then state that if this is what happened, 'that's no big deal', 'I can understand that', or 'we can work with that'. The suggested scenario and the evaluative statements give the impression that there is a version of the incident to which the suspect can admit that might not be criminal, which might result in no serious charges, or which might result in counselling instead of jail (a possibility that interrogators are taught to bring up toward the beginning of the interrogation—see Inbau et al., 2011).

If the suspect admits to the suggested minimized version of the incident, the interrogator will then deploy other tactics to move the suspect to more serious admissions, until the suspect admits to the version the interrogator actually believes to be true (usually the version reported by the victim). Throughout this process, the interrogator will remind the suspect of the credibility of the victim, and bring up likely reactions of judges and juries to someone who straight out lies to them and denies what happened versus to someone who stands up 'like a man', admits his mistakes, and expresses his remorse.

In effect, because of the evidentiary situation apparently facing sexual abuse suspects, the interrogation as a whole may function much more for them as a preview of reactions of the judge and jury at trial. The interrogator expresses unremitting complete confidence in the suspect's guilt and the credibility of the victim, and likewise promotes the perception that judges and juries will not believe him, and will look upon and treat him harshly for lying. The contest of credibility between suspect and alleged victim—the primary issue—is won by the alleged victim: a result that the interrogator has argued persuasively will be repeated at trial. This is the result that suspects are likely to expect even before they are interrogated, as our research has suggested. The interrogation may serve only to reinforce these expectations and to magnify suspects' fears.

The nature of the persuasive tactics used for abuse suspects is conceptually the same for other suspects—although particular types of minimizing scenario and specific enactments of general strategies differ in detail. We suggest that they may, however, be more effective for abuse suspects for two reasons. First, as mentioned earlier, the sense of hopelessness regarding establishing innocence may be greater for abuse suspects, given their evidentiary situation. This may render them more susceptible to any suggestion or hint of how they might minimize the consequences of being perceived guilty.

Second, we suggest that the identity threat posed by an accusation that one is a paedophile or child sexual abuser (particularly for an innocent, who is not) is among the most aversive that one can experience. While suspects will be generally subject to

---

[18] See Inbau et al. (2011) for details of the full recommended tactics.

identity threat as alleged thieves, embezzlers, drug users and pushers, and even murderers, abuse of children is viewed as worse by many—even by other criminals. To the extent that this is true for a suspect, he may be particularly susceptible to flattery and suggestions by the interrogator that he is not a predator or molester, but rather a nice guy in a bad situation, who just made a one-time mistake and needs help. The interrogator solidifies this characterization by offering the minimized scenarios (such as accidental touching, touching the child while asleep thinking it was his girlfriend, etc.), giving the suspect a way in which to admit the guilt that others will inevitably assume, and yet deny the real intent and perversion (and hence identity) of the child molester. Recall in this light the explanations of our study participants for their recommendations of false confession that it is better to tell a seemingly understandable or excusable story about how it happened than simply to be thought a remorseless intentional predator and liar.

CHALLENGES OF DETECTING FALSE CONFESSIONS OF ABUSE

False confessions inevitably produce a cocktail of adverse consequences for the suspect. They are difficult to recognize for a variety of reasons:[19] prosecution is more likely; charges are more serious; defence attorneys tend to disbelieve claims of false confession and encourage clients to plead; and, ultimately, between 73 per cent and 81 per cent are convicted if they go to trial (Leo and Ofshe, 1998; Drizin and Leo, 2004). The case is unlikely to be further investigated in a way that might exonerate the innocent confessor.[20]

We suggest that false confessions to sexual abuse and to other 'he said, she said' sexual accusations are particularly unlikely to be recognized, and that false confessors are particularly unlikely to be exonerated at trial or in post-conviction proceedings. For many other false confessors, exonerating evidence may be available if it is tested or sought; for those who falsely confess to sexual abuse or other 'he said, she said' offences, exonerating evidence is unlikely to exist. The case was a contest of credibility that was seemingly resolved by the confession. The false confessor's best hope is likely to lie in the victim's recantation of the charges.

If the false confessor wishes to dispute the confession, concrete evidence of innocence is, of course, most effective. But most who go to trial will be faced with the necessity of convincing the jury that the confession was false without the benefit of such evidence. Typically, this must be done by attorney arguments and/or expert testimony explaining how and why false confessions occur. Judges and juries alike possess a number of beliefs that make this difficult, particularly for abuse suspects. Many do not believe that false confessions occur; others believe that only the mentally defi-

---

[19] See Davis and Leo (2012) for a review.
[20] See Leo and Davis (2010) for a review of these consequences.

cient would falsely confess and many believe that what are thought of as coercive tactics are necessary to produce a false confession (Leo, 2008).

Most false confessors, however, are mentally normal. Moreover, what jurors think of as most likely to result in false confessions (such as physical coercion, threats, etc.) are not actually necessary. Mario Matthews, for example, confessed in less than an hour in response to seemingly very mild tactics. The sense of hopelessness that we have argued is so central to the vulnerability of abuse suspects is not among the factors that lay persons regard as crucial causes of false confession.[21]

CONCLUSIONS

We have provided an initial exploration of the unique situation of sexual abuse suspects in interrogation. Unfortunately, while there is a great deal of evidence to support the importance and nature of the basic processes forming the basis of our analysis (such as the nature and effects of stereotype threat, of self-regulation failure, and of the use of specific interrogation tactics, the causes of false confession, and so on), there is a dearth of empirical evidence in the specific context of allegations of sexual abuse. We hope this chapter has raised awareness of the potentially unique vulnerability of sexual abuse and other 'he said, she said' assault suspects to false confession, and has served as a call to arms for other researchers to join in the investigation of the issues we have identified.

REFERENCES

BLANDON-GITLIN, I., SPERRY, K., and LEO, R. (2011) 'Jurors Believe Interrogation Tactics Are not Likely to Elicit False Confessions: Will Expert Witness Testimony Inform Them Otherwise?', *Psychology, Crime & Law*, 17(3): 239–60.

BURNS, S. (2011) *The Central Park Five: A Chronicle of a City Wilding*, New York: Alfred A. Knopf.

CHOJNACKI, D. E., CICCHINI, M. D., and WHITE, L. T. (2008) 'An Empirical Basis for the Admission of Expert Testimony on False Confessions', *Arizona State Law Journal*, 40(1): 1–45.

CONNERY, D. (1977) *Guilty until Proven Innocent*, New York: G. P. Putnam's Sons.

COSTANZO, M., SHAKED-SCHROER, N., and VINSON, K. (2010) 'Juror Beliefs about Police Interrogations, False Confessions, and Expert Testimony', *Journal of Empirical Legal Studies*, 7(2): 231–47.

DAVIS, D. (2010) 'Lies, *Damned Lies*, and the Path from Police Interrogation to Wrongful Conviction', in M. H. Gonzales, C. Tavris, and J. Aronson (eds) *The Scientist and the Humanist: A Festschrift in Honor of Elliot Aronson*, New York: Psychology Press.

---

[21] For surveys of lay beliefs about the existence and causes of false confession, see Chojnacki, Cicchini, and White (2008); Henkel, Coffman and Dailey (2008); Costanzo, Shaked-Schroer, and Vinson (2010); Blandon-Gitlin, Sperry, and Leo (2011).

DAVIS, D., and LEO, R. A. (2012) 'To Walk in Their Shoes: The Problem of Missing, Misrepresented and Misunderstood Context in Judging Criminal Confessions', *New England Law Review*, 46(4): 737–67.

DAVIS, D., and O'DONOHUE, W. T. (2004) 'The Road to Perdition: "Extreme Influence" Tactics in the Interrogation Room', in W. T. O'Donohue and E. Levensky (eds) *Handbook of Forensic Psychology*, New York: Elsevier.

DAVIS, D., HERNANDEZ, J., FOLLETTE, W. C., and LEO, R. A. (2010) 'Interrogation through Pragmatic Implication: Communicating Beneficence and Promises of Leniency', Presentation to the Society for Personality and Social Psychology, Las Vegas, Nevada, January.

DAVIS, D., LEO, R. A., and FOLLETTE, W. C. (2008) 'Recommending False Confession for the Innocent', Presentation to American Psychology Law Society, Fort Lauderdale, FL, March.

DAVIS, D., LEO, R. A., and FOLLETTE, W. C. (2010) 'Selling Confession: Setting the Stage with the "Sympathetic Detective" with a Time-limited Offer', *Journal of Contemporary Criminal Justice*, 26(4): 441–57.

DAVIS, D., WILLIAMS, M. J., OGUNDIMU, O., and HYATT, M. (2014) 'Stereotype Threat In Police Interrogation: Effects on Memory for *Miranda* Warnings', Unpublished manuscript.

DEPAULO, B. M., and PFEIFER, R. L. (1986) 'On-the-job Experience and Skill at Detecting Deception', *Journal of Applied Social Psychology*, 16(3): 249–67.

DRIZIN, S., and LEO, R. A. (2004) 'The Problem of False Confessions in the Post-DNA World', *North Carolina Law Review*, 82: 891–1007.

EDDS, M. (2003) *An Expendable Man: The Near Execution of Earl Washington Jr*, New York: New York University Press.

FINDLEY, K., and SCOTT, M. (2006) 'The Multiple Dimensions of Tunnel Vision in Criminal Cases', *Wisconsin Law Review*, 2: 291–398.

GARRIDO, E., MASIP, J., and HERRERO, C. (2004) 'Police Officers' Credibility Judgments: Accuracy and Estimated Ability', *International Journal of Psychology*, 39(4): 254–75.

HENKEL, L. A., COFFMAN, K. A. J., and DAILEY, E. M. (2008) 'A Survey of People's Attitudes and Beliefs about False Confessions', *Behavioral Sciences & the Law*, 26(5): 555–84.

INBAU, F. E., REID, J. E., BUCKLEY, J. P., and JAYNE, B. C. (2011) *Criminal Interrogation and Confessions*, 5th edn, Gaithersburg, MD: Aspen.

INZLICHT, M., and SCHMADER, T. (2011) *Stereotype Threat: Theory, Process, and Application*, New York: Oxford University Press.

JAYNE, B., and BUCKLEY, J. (1999) *The Investigator Anthology: A Compilation of Articles and Essays about the Reid Technique of Interviewing and Interrogation*, Chicago, IL: John E. Reid & Associates.

KASSIN, S. M., DRIZIN, S. A., GRISSO, T., GUDJONSSON, G. H., LEO, R. A., and REDLICH, A. D. (2010) 'Police-induced Confessions: Risk Factors and Recommendations', *Law and Human Behavior*, 34(1): 3–38.

KASSIN, S. M., GOLDSTEIN, C. C., and SAVITSKY, K. (2003) 'Behavioral Confirmation in the Interrogation Room: On the Dangers of Presuming Guilt', *Law and Human Behavior*, 27(2): 187–203.

LEO, R. A. (2008) *Police Interrogation and American Justice*, Cambridge, MA: Harvard University Press.

LEO, R. A., and DAVIS, D. (2010) 'From False Confession to Wrongful Conviction: Seven Psychological Processes', *Journal of Psychiatry and Law*, 38(1–2): 9–56.

LEO, R. A., and OFSHE, R. J. (1998) 'The Consequences of False Confessions: Deprivations of Liberty and Miscarriages of Justice in the Age of Psychological Interrogation', *Journal of Criminal Law & Criminology*, 88(2): 429–96.

MEISSNER, C. A., and KASSIN, S. M. (2002) ' "He's guilty!" Investigator Bias in Judgments of Truth and Deception', *Law and Human Behavior*, 26(5): 469–80.

NAJDOWSKI, C. J. (2011) 'Stereotype Threat in Criminal Interrogations: Why Innocent Black Suspects Are at Risk for Confessing Falsely', *Psychology, Public Policy & Law*, 17(4): 562–91.

National Research Council of the National Academies (2003) *The Polygraph and Lie Detection*, Washington, DC: National Academies Press.

NICKERSON, R. S. (1998) 'Confirmation Bias: A Ubiquitous Phenomenon in Many Guises', *Review of General Psychology*, 2(2): 175–220

PORTER, S., WOODWORTH, M., and BIRT, A. R. (2000) 'Truth, Lies, and Videotape: An Investigation of the Ability of Federal Parole Officers to Detect Deception', *Law and Human Behavior*, 24(6): 643–58.

STEELE, C. M. (2011) *Whistling Vivaldi: How Stereotypes Affect Us and What We Can Do*, New York: W. W. Norton.

STEELE, C. M., and ARONSON, J. (1995) 'Stereotype Threat and the Intellectual Test Performance of African Americans', *Journal of Personality and Social Psychology*, 69(5): 797–811.

VRIJ, A. (2008) *Detecting Lies and Deceit: Pitfalls and Opportunities*, 2nd edn, Chichester: John Wiley & Sons.

VRIJ, A., GRANHAG, P. A., and PORTER, S. (2010) 'Pitfalls and Opportunities in Nonverbal and Verbal Lie Detection', *Psychological Science in the Public Interest*, 11(3): 89–121.

ZULAWSKI, D., and WICKLANDER, D. (2002) *Practical Aspects of Interview and Interrogation*, Boca Raton, FL: CRC Press.

14

COMPLAINTS OF SEXUAL ABUSE AND THE DECLINE OF OBJECTIVE PROSECUTING

Luke Gittos

The argument of this chapter is that the last decade has seen a shift away from what I will call 'objectivity' in the prosecution of sex cases. This shift has taken three primary forms. The first is the passing of new evidential rules that have placed the experience of the complainant as a more central consideration in the trial process. The second is a prosecutorial focus on complainant experience,[1] which encourages prosecutors to make decisions in order to improve public perceptions rather than to effect a fair outcome. The third is the development of tribunals whose focus is primarily the delivery of therapeutic closure to complainants over and above the objective administration of justice, and a stronger connection between these tribunals and criminal investigations. The primary example of the third of these trends is the relationship between criminal investigations and the public inquiry into historic allegations of child abuse, which has emerged as an alternative forum for criminal complainants where a decision is taken not to proceed with a criminal prosecution. These three factors taken together constitute a new therapeutic trend within the prosecutorial process—one that prioritizes the provision of 'closure' over and above more traditional goals of public justice, including establishing the truth, and ensuring the fairness and impartiality of proceedings.

This shift is not unique to the UK. In the United States, a departure from due process and established procedure is becoming more common in relation to cases across college campuses involving allegations of sexual abuse in favour of delivering closure to complainants. The existence of campus rape tribunals to respond to rape complaints has been described as an 'alternative' to criminal prosecution in rape cases, precisely because they are comparatively free from the high burdens of proving a criminal case.[2] Internationally, advocates for rape victims routinely argue that altering established due process allows for the courts to correct the established 'rape culture' in Western societies (Halley, 2015).

The shift away from objective prosecuting towards emphasizing the need for a complainant's closure heightens the possibility of miscarriages of justice in criminal cases.

---

[1] Often mistakenly described as 'victim experience'.
[2] See 'Know Your IX', online at <http://knowyourix.org/title-ix/title-ix-the-basics/>

The usual protections for those accused are compromised or, in civil cases, denied, and an innocent person wrongly accused of sexual assault is more likely to be found guilty. Justice itself becomes a subsidiary purpose to the delivery of a particular result. To illustrate this point, this chapter will consider recent high-profile investigations in the UK around sexual abuse and changes in prosecutorial policy in response to these investigations.[3]

EVIDENTIAL RULES

The most significant reform around the trial process has arguably been the legal restrictions placed on a defendant's questioning of the complainant. In 1975, Miss Justice Heilbron headed a committee to examine the law around evidence in rape trials. The Heilbron Report expressed concerns 'about the extent to which, in a rape trial, the personal history and character of a rape victim can be introduced' (Home Office, 1975: para. 89), and declared that such evidence not only caused distress and humiliation to the victim, but was also 'inimical to the fair trial of the essential issues' (Home Office, 1975: para. 92). So while complainant experience was a partial influence in the initial restrictions on sexual history evidence, the inclusion of such evidence was also considered 'inimical' in the jury's judgement of the evidence. The Heilbron Committee concluded 'that the previous sexual history of the alleged victim with third parties is of no significance so far as credibility is concerned and is only rarely likely to be relevant to issues directly before the jury' (Home Office, 1975: para. 131).

The Heilbron Report was influential in the enactment of section 2 of the Sexual Offences (Amendment) Act 1976. This Act was the first piece of legislation to restrict the use of evidence relating to a complainant's sexual history. Section 2 forbade any evidence to be adduced, and any question to be asked in cross-examination, by or on behalf of any defendant about any of the complainant's sexual experiences other than with the defendant himself, but permitted the defence to apply, in the absence of the jury, for leave to do so. The Act also introduced the right of anonymity for complainants in rape cases.

The efficacy of section 2 became subject to debate and 'growing dissatisfaction' (Kelly, Temkin, and Griffiths, 2006: 12). A number of cases were thought to have given the section a wide reading, allowing for sexual history evidence to be deemed 'admissible' in a wide range of circumstances.[4] Academic studies demonstrated that 'irrelevant' questions were still being asked about sexual history and that section 2 had been interpreted in a way that rendered it ineffective at restricting irrelevant questioning (Kelly et al., 2006). This growing dissatisfaction was resolved in 1999 with the passing of the Youth Justice and Criminal Evidence Act, which introduced a statutory rule forbidding any questions regarding sexual history to be asked of a complainant,[5] with limited exceptions.[6]

---

[3] See also Gittos (2015).   [4] See, e.g., the Court of Appeal case of *Viola* [1982] 3 All ER 73.
[5] Youth Justice and Criminal Evidence Act 1999, s. 41.
[6] The extent of these exemptions is considered in Youth Justice and Criminal Evidence Act 1999, s. 42.

The new law quickly raised a conflict with the defendant's right to a fair trial.[7] In 2001, the restrictions enacted in the 1999 Act were made the subject of a challenge to the House of Lords. In *R v A*,[8] the defence sought to adduce evidence of a previous sexual relationship between the complainant and the defendant as evidence of the complainant's consent. The provisions of the 1999 Act gave no clear route to having the material deemed admissible. The defence argued before the Lords that the Act was incompatible with Article 6 of the European Convention of Human Rights on the basis that it denied the defendant the right to adduce evidence that was plainly relevant to his defence. The Lords did not declare the Act incompatible, but instead interpreted the provisions in a manner that made it compatible with Article 6. They read into the provisions an exemption for evidence to be deemed admissible where it was 'so relevant to the issue of consent that to exclude it would endanger the fairness of the trial under Article 6'.[9] Today, evidence of a previous sexual relationship between a complainant and a defendant is arguably more likely to be deemed admissible than prior to *R v A*, but the Court of Appeal has since dismissed appeals seeking to argue that the exclusion of such material rendered their trials unfair. This shows that the Court of Appeal has, to some extent, endorsed a restrictive reading of the exemption read into the Act in *R v A*.

The experience of rape victims in court has similarly been subject of reform. In the 1990s, there was a degree of consensus that the justice system did too little to accommodate the experiences of complainants. Home Office research published in 2006 suggested that it had become a 'cliché' to point out that the justice system took 'little heed of the needs and concerns of victims and witnesses' (Burton, Evans, and Sanders, 2006: 1). Widely cited research into complainants' experiences of rape trials revealed that complainants thought of a trial of their case as a 'second assault' (Lees, 1996; Victim Support, 1996).

Victim-centred justice became a driving force of the New Labour government's policy around the justice system (Burton et al., 2006). Shortly after its election in 1997, the government convened an interdepartmental working group to undertake a review into the experiences of witnesses and complainants in the criminal court. The outcome was a report entitled *Speaking up for Justice* (Home Office, 1998). The report argued that reforms that had been enacted throughout the 1980s and 1990s to cater for children in the trial process should be expanded to protect other vulnerable groups, 'including complainants and witnesses in sex cases'.

This led to the introduction of special measures into criminal trials by the Youth Justice and Criminal Evidence Act 1999. These provisions were extended by section 101 of the Coroners and Justice Act 2009, which allowed for automatic admissibility of a video-recorded statement as complainant's evidence-in-chief, unless this would not be in the interests of justice. Today, such applications are made as a matter of course in rape trials and are routinely granted. Achieving best evidence (ABE) interviews are now widely deployed in rape trials. While recent research has suggested that such

---

[7] All defendants have the right to a fair trial, but in this chapter we are particularly concerned with the implications for innocent defendants who have been wrongly accused.
[8] [2001] UKHL 25.   [9] [2001] UKHL 25, [46].

measures have no impact on jury considerations in rape cases, many have acknowledged that the regime marked a new position for the emotional well-being of complainants as a consideration in criminal proceedings.

From a practitioner perspective, these reforms complement long-standing facts about the justice system in England and Wales that make trials involving rape and sexual abuse cases vulnerable to passing miscarriages of justice. There is no corroboration requirement for rape and child sexual abuse cases.[10] This means that uncorroborated allegations are capable of forming the subject of a prosecution. It is no longer unusual for a case to proceed solely on the evidence of the complainant. Cases often turn on two unsupported accounts. Defendants are consistently left to answer questions about the complainant's motivations[11] for making the allegation in the first place, a question that a falsely accused defendant is often ill-equipped to answer.[12]

The recent reforms have moved beyond preventing juries from hearing evidence that is 'inimical to the fair trial of the essential issues' (Home Office, 1975: para. 92), and have focused on protecting complainants and witnesses from emotional harm in the course of trial proceedings. While undoubtedly these reforms have worked to improve the quality of evidence in particular cases, they have also raised the potential for miscarriages of justice by placing higher burdens on defendants to prove why a particular area of questioning, for example with regards to sexual history, should be admissible. Concerns have also been raised that special measures could create an uneven ground between the defendant and the complainant in the jury's consideration of the evidence (Burton et al., 2006; Milne, Shaw, and Smith, 2009; Stern, 2010). From a defence perspective, the assumption behind the imposition of a screen—that the defendant is sufficiently robust to give evidence without assistance[13] where a complainant is sufficiently vulnerable to require protection—has been said to create impressions in the jury's perception of the evidence before either the defendant or the complainant has given evidence. Because sexual abuse prosecutions often rest entirely on witness evidence—especially in cases of alleged historical abuse, where delay limits access to defence evidence—'the right to a fair trial is particularly curtailed if such evidence is given using special measures—no effective cross-examination of the prosecution's principal evidence can occur and the defendant is unable to rebut the prosecution's case against them' (Sutton, 2014).

With regard to verdicts, some reassurance is offered by recent research using mock juries, which found there to be no clear or consistent impact on jury decisions as a result of these special measures and which suggests that concerns about the influence on juries may be overstated (Ellison and Munro, 2013). It is significant, though, that funded research and official publications on this issue have been in the context of policies to increase conviction rates for rape and sexual offences, and to improve the

---

[10] In Scotland, the current law requires corroboration for each key element of the offence. This is currently subject to criticism in the form of a review by Lord Carloway (Scottish Government, 2012). For discussion on whether or not corroboration should be retained, see also Davidson and Ferguson (2014).

[11] Motivations and the various factors that give to wrongful allegations are discussed in Chapter 8.

[12] In the case of allegations of non-recent abuse that allegedly occurred one or more decades ago, an innocent defendant may not know or remember the complainants.

[13] Trials are likely to be particularly harrowing for innocent defendants who are facing the prospect of imprisonment.

experience of complainants and victims, rather than in the context of possibly innocent defendants facing the prospect of years in prison.

These reforms have occurred concurrently with a prosecutorial focus on reducing the attrition rate in rape cases. The perceived need to prevent cases 'dropping out' before they reach court has led to prosecutorial policy that encourages lawyers to charge cases that once would have been discontinued.

ACTION PLAN TO INCREASE PROSECUTION OF SEXUAL OFFENCES

As well as making sex trials more victim-centred, the investigation process has been reformed in favour of charging more defendants. Recent statistics on rape in England and Wales were published in the 2014–15 annual performance report on violence against women and girls (VAWG) of the Crown Prosecution Service (CPS, 2015). In the twelve months covered by the report, more people had been prosecuted for rape and sexual abuse than ever before: 88,359 (68.5 per cent)—a rise of 11,833 (15.5 per cent) from 2013–14 and the highest ever. The report notes that the 'rise in volumes indicates the success of the work undertaken across the police and CPS to improve referral processes for domestic abuse and all sexual offences' (CPS, 2015: 6). The figures also reveal that while more people are being prosecuted and convicted of rape overall (a 17 per cent increase in prosecutions and a 10 per cent increase in convictions), the rate of convictions to acquittals has now reduced to 57 per cent, its lowest level since 2007 (CPS, 2015: 9). This means that prosecutorial policy in recent years has led to more failed prosecutions.

The reaction to these statistics was interesting. Whereas previous falls in the conviction rate for rape have been treated with 'serious concern' by prosecutors, the most recent drop has instead caused the CPS to refocus its reporting around the volume of people convicted of rape overall. This number, in 2015, is at an all-time high.

The increase in prosecutions reflects official concern with the number of cases 'dropping out' of the system at the investigation stage, leading to an allegedly high attrition rate.[14] Reports into the operation of the justice system have variously blamed inaccurate police reporting (HMIC, 2014), 'attitudinal issues', and unfair evidential burdens for cases 'dropping out' of the system and not reaching court (Kelly, Lovett, and Regan, 2005).

The high attrition rate[15] for rape has certainly received renewed prosecutorial attention in recent years, with the CPS becoming keener to prosecute rape as a means of atoning for the mistakes of the past. High-profile cases in which suspects have not been charged have been the subject of official apologies, coupled with public indications

---

[14] Whether the attrition rate for rape is in fact high is subject to debate (see, e.g., Stern, 2010; Reece, 2013), depending on whether it measures the gap between prosecution and conviction, or between reporting and convictions, and, in the latter case, whether all of the reported crimes are equated with actual crime.

[15] Defined as the ratio between allegations made and eventual convictions, which has remained around 6 per cent in recent years.

that the authorities will proceed with cases that once would have been discontinued.[16] And this need for a 'fundamental shift' in how the prosecutorial authorities view rape and sexual abuse allegations has led to two significant pieces of prosecutorial reform that have driven up the number of people charged with rape and sexual abuse.

In 2013, the CPS published new guidelines on the prosecution of childhood sexual abuse cases. It encouraged lawyers to adopt a 'merits-based approach' to deciding whether or not to charge allegations of child sexual abuse (CPS, 2013: para. 60). Prosecutors were instructed to ignore past experience of juries being less willing to convict where a complainant had been drinking or where there was a long delay in reporting the case. The guidelines instructed lawyers to consider the views of a 'notional jury' that is wholly unaffected by any 'myths' surrounding the credibility of complainants (CPS, 2013: para. 61). These guidelines also suggested that lawyers should be focusing on the 'credibility of the allegation rather than focusing solely on the victim' (CPS, 2013: para. 41). The fact that the guidelines followed a significant report into prosecutorial failings around child abuse investigations in Rotherham and Rochdale (Jay, 2014) suggested that the CPS was using the guidelines as a means of preventing such perceived failures being repeated. In the weeks after the reports were published, Keir Starmer (2013) warned against the justice system being 'over cautious' in its prosecution of sexual abuse cases.

Allegations of adult rape have similarly been made subject of reform targeted at increasing the number of people charged. Most recently, this has focused on the amended definition of consent under the Sexual Offences Act 2003. Under the 2003 Act, whether or not a defendant had a reasonable belief in the complainant's consent should be assessed 'having regard to all the circumstances, including any steps A has taken to ascertain whether B consents'.[17] This definition has been described as creating a new agreement-based model of consent, which requires the seeking of agreement over and above acquiescence and/or the use of force (Munro, 2008).

The CPS and Metropolitan Police Service (2015) Action Plan on Rape sought to address issues with attrition by 'correcting' certain myths that existed around this definition. The Action Plan stated that a 'key finding' of the CPS's scrutiny panel, which had been convened to analyse the CPS's treatment of rape cases, was that improvement was required in prosecutorial understanding of consent. The document said that prosecutors 'must focus their case on the behaviour of the accused, not the complainant' (CPS and MPS, 2015: 2)—that the panel had uncovered 'pervasive myths' among the police and prosecutors, as well as 'society as a whole'.

In a speech to Women's Aid in July 2015, Director of Public Prosecutions (DPP) Alison Saunders was keen to emphasize how the new Action Plan on Rape placed greater 'focus' on the actions of defendants when deciding whether to charge:

> In the last year we have implemented a National Rape Action plan culminating in our launch of a number of new tools for prosecutors. You may have heard about our work on 'consent'—in January we launched a toolkit for police, prosecutors and advocates as

---

[16] For example, the former DPP's announcement in November 2012 regarding the 'failure' to prosecute Liberal MP Cyril Smith (Dodd and Syal, 2012).
[17] Sexual Offences Act 2003, s. 1(2).

well as a public leaflet on consent—explaining the importance of challenging whether victims of rape had the freedom or capacity to consent and developing a focus more on the steps taken by the alleged offender to gain consent.

(Saunders, 2015)

One of the actions anticipated by the Plan was the launch of aides-mémoire and toolkits on consent that were to be distributed to all CPS lawyers (CPS and MPS, 2015).

The consent toolkits and aides-mémoire reiterated the need to focus prosecutorial attention on the behaviour of the accused rather than on the complainant. The aides-mémoire even set out the appropriate steps that CPS lawyers may take when ascertaining whether a defendant had a reasonable belief in consent, including:

- enquiring as to how the suspect knew or believed the complainant was consenting to sex and that he or she continued to consent;
- investigating whether the suspect targeted or exploited the victim at a time when he or she was most vulnerable;
- recognizing or ignoring any signs from the complainant that he or she did not want sexual activity; and
- checking if consent was given for all of the sex acts and not only one or some, such as consent for sexual intercourse, but not oral sex.[18]

Public reporting of these toolkits perhaps exaggerated their impact by tending to suggest that a defendant would now be required to 'prove' that his partner consented to sex (Raynor and Gardner, 2015). This was not the case: the burden remained on the Crown to prove all aspects of its case. However, the toolkits were implemented under perceived pressure to 'push up' the number of people charged with rape. The 'steps' identified in the aides-mémoire arguably make it more likely that a defendant who had not taken such steps would be charged where once he may have faced no further action.

The credence paid to complainants in prosecutorial decision-making is evident in the CPS's introduction of a new 'right to review' (CPS, 2014). The right was introduced under the terms of the Victim's Code, first issued by the Secretary of State in 2006 'as part of the wider Government strategy to transform the criminal justice system by putting victims first' and since revised (Ministry of Justice, 2013: para. 1). Among numerous other entitlements, this Victims' Code gave complainants the right to have the decision of any CPS lawyer reviewed by an independent reviewing lawyer where the initial decision had been made not to charge a defendant with an offence. By introducing the threat of external review, the 2013 Victims Code placed lawyers under additional pressure to charge those defendants who may have previously not been prosecuted on grounds of lack of evidence or public interest.[19]

The fact that the volume of convictions has increased with no concurrent rise in the conviction rate should give cause for concern, given that it suggests that more people are now the subject of failed prosecutions than ever before. From a feminist perspective

---

[18] See CPS (undated*b*).

[19] These represent the two stages of the Full Code Test for Crown Prosecutors, which must be passed before a prosecution can be authorized: (1) sufficient evidence must be present to charge; and (2) a prosecution must be in the public interest.

that treats all allegations as true, there is concern that this reflects the continuing influence of 'rape myths' on jurors' decisions. It is likely that these factors apply in some cases in which a guilty offender is acquitted; it is likely that, in other cases, innocent people have been wrongly prosecuted and jurors reach the correct decision. Whereas prosecution and policing guidelines now steer investigators away from questioning the credibility and reliability of complainants (CPS, 2013; CPS and MPS, 2015), juries are likely to be even-handed in their debates about the reliability of evidence and about who is telling the truth. The police have been instructed to institutionalize a presumption that the victim should always be believed (HMIC, 2014). The Report of the Independent Review in the Investigation and Prosecution of Rape in London (Angiolini, 2015: 59) recommends removal of a section in the Crime Recording Information System requiring consideration be given to whether an allegation is false—yet, based on knowledge of large-scale miscarriages of justice that have previously followed adherence to 'believe the victim' policies[20] and especially in cases that are reliant on verbal testimony, it is reasonable to assume that these failed prosecutions include innocent defendants who were, erroneously or knowingly, falsely accused.

THERAPEUTIC TRIBUNALS

These shifts have coincided with an elevation of complainant emotional satisfaction in a series of high-profile investigations into childhood sexual abuse. The most widely cited example is Operation Yewtree. In October 2012, a UK television channel broadcast a programme about sexual allegations that had been made against deceased celebrity and disc jockey Jimmy Savile. Following the broadcast, the Metropolitan Police, in partnership with a leading UK children's charity, began investigating the claims made in the programme, as well as 'hundreds' of other complaints that had been reported after the programme was aired (Furedi, 2013). Operation Yewtree has been variously understood in the UK as a 'turning point' or 'sea change'[21] moment in the authorities' treatment of allegations of rape and sexual abuse. This, in turn, has triggered a new onset of sexual abuse allegations to the police, which has become known as the 'Yewtree effect' (HMIC, 2014; ONS, 2016).

When the MPS published its report into Jimmy Savile in 2013, it was entitled *Giving Victims a Voice* (Gray and Watt, 2013). The report acknowledged that because Savile was dead, none of the allegations could be tested in the normal way; instead, the complainants' allegations would be treated as 'proven' evidence. This meant that the report would not refer to those making allegations as 'complainants', as would be normal in a criminal case until a conviction had been obtained, but rather as 'victims'. The change in language signified that the word of the complainants was going to be treated as true, or 'proven', notwithstanding the fact that it could not be tested in the normal way. The

---

[20] Discussed especially in Chapters 3, 4, and 12 of this book. See also Seigel (2009) and Beck (2015).
[21] Dominic Grieve, Attorney General, cited in *Yorkshire Post* (2013).

spread of this elision between complainants and victims today is striking: today, the words 'victim' and 'complainants' are often elided by prosecutors when discussing sex cases.[22]

In the UK, a number of recent high-profile official investigations into sexual allegations have evidenced the shift towards providing therapeutic closure for victims over and above the objective establishment of truth. The most prominent recent example of this is the Independent Inquiry into Child Sexual Abuse (IICSA), which commenced in 2015. In commencing the Inquiry, its chair said that child abuse had left 'scars not only on the victims themselves but on society as a whole'. The chair assumed that the persons giving evidence were, in fact, 'victims' rather than 'witnesses', and that their experiences, the truth of which was unquestioned, had made an impact both at the social and individual levels. The Inquiry represented, according to the chair, a 'historic opportunity' to confront the mistakes of the past and to confront those responsible, and to make recommendations for changes in the future. The chair routinely made reference to 'victims and survivors', echoing the elision between complainants and victims that was evident in the Savile report.

As well as therapy directing the language of the Inquiry, its therapeutic role has been acknowledged explicitly. The terms of reference for the Inquiry indicated that part of its purpose was, among other things, to:

> ...consider the extent to which State and non-State institutions have failed in their duty of care to protect children from sexual abuse and exploitation' and 'providing opportunities for them (survivors of sexual abuse) to bear witness to the Inquiry, having regard to the need to provide appropriate support in doing so.[23]

The focus on 'survivors' 'bearing witness' to the Inquiry as a means of seeking closure led it to become an alternative forum for complainants to give evidence where related criminal investigations have not been prosecuted. The use of therapeutic language in the public-orientated material surrounding the court further demonstrated the emotional remit of the Inquiry. A section on the website called 'Share Your Experience' provided a link to a tick-box form allowing 'survivors' to make allegations of sexual abuse by entering very basic details into a database. The idea that those complaining to the Inquiry were not 'alleging' or 'accusing', but merely 'sharing' an 'experience', reflected the therapeutic outlook of the inquiry.

The status of this child abuse inquiry as primarily a therapeutic institution was reflected in the turmoil that surrounded the appointment of a chair. A prominent member of the judiciary in England and Wales, Baroness Butler-Sloss, was initially instructed to lead the inquiry in July 2014. Shortly following her appointment, 'survivor groups' made complaints that she was not sufficiently removed from the British establishment to be able to make an objective judgment. Baroness Butler-Sloss acknowledged the concerns and stepped down four days after her appointment. Prominent British solicitor Dame Fiona Woolf was appointed shortly after, but similarly stood down when it was revealed that she had lived on the same street as Lord

---

[22] CPS policy documents regularly refer to individuals in the stage of making an allegation as 'victims'. See, e.g., CPS (undated*a*: ch. 5).

[23] See IICSA Terms of Reference, online at <https://www.iicsa.org.uk/about-us/terms-of-reference>

Brittan, who was the subject of allegations being investigated by the Inquiry. The complaints of the survivor groups were consistently reiterated by prominent members of the legal profession, including a former Lord Justice of Appeal and former Solicitor General Vera Baird, who both emphasized the need for survivors to feel as though 'justice had been seen to be done' (Watt, 2014). The primacy of survivors' experience of the tribunal in the consideration of the appropriate chair shows that the provision of closure and emotional satisfaction is a central and highly influential concern of the Inquiry.

This therapeutic turn in policing and prosecuting has increased the risk of miscarriage of justice—more specifically, the risk of prosecuting and convicting innocent people, or of subjecting them and their families to drawn-out investigation processes with long-term damaging effects. This is evident in recent failed prosecutions involving high-profile individuals. They are arguably more susceptible to historical allegations of abuse because their whereabouts and characteristics at particular times are more likely to be publicly known.[24] Public appeals for information by prosecutors can encourage complainants to come forward with evidence that is then used as corroboration for an original complaint.[25] While this approach to investigating historical offences is often necessary, given the likely paucity of available evidence, it increases the possibility that defendants will be charged on evidence that lacks credibility when considered on its own terms. Actor William Roache was prosecuted and acquitted of two rapes and four indecent assaults, all of which were alleged to have occurred between 1965 and 1971 (Brown, 2014). The complainants in that case were found to be lacking in credibility with regards to significant aspects of their evidence. Member of Parliament Nigel Evans was also prosecuted and acquitted for a series of alleged child sex offences in 2014 (Evans, 2014). A number of commentators suggested that the evidence in the case raised questions about why he had been prosecuted. A number of other high-profile individuals have been arrested, with a great deal of public exposure, purportedly for the purpose of allowing other victims to 'come forward'. This has led to popular scepticism with regards to the Savile effect—and even concessions by leading police officers that investigators may have taken the need to 'believe' complainants too seriously (Hogan-Howe, 2016).

CONCLUSION

The last decade has seen a shift in the UK justice system away from objective prosecuting towards providing therapeutic closure for complainants. Recent reforms around prosecuting rape and child sexual abuse have focused on improving the experience of victims

---

[24] This point was raised by Paul Gambaccini following the announcement that his case would not be prosecuted after a year on bail, and is discussed in his later book. which provides a journalized account of the experience (Gambaccini, 2015).

[25] During previous child abuse scandals, this process—applied by police and personal insurance solicitors—was referred to as 'trawling' for complainants, a method criticized by the Home Affairs Select Committee (2002) as likely to lead to some wrongful prosecutions and convictions.

and witnesses, encouraging them to report offences with confidence and protecting them from the ordeal of giving evidence. A prosecutorial focus on complainant experience has led to more defendants being charged, while the conviction rate for sexual offences falls. This shows that the move away from what we may call 'objective' prosecuting has been bad for the effective administration of justice. There is a real risk that the drive to charge more people, the relaxation of traditional protections for defendants, and the development of new tribunals that seek to deliver therapeutic 'closure' over and above a just result will mean a higher proportion of innocent people being wrongly prosecuted, and sometimes convicted, in allegations involving sexual abuse.

REFERENCES

ANGIOLINI, E. (2015) *Report of the Independent Review into the Investigation and Prosecution of Rape in London*, London: Metropolitan Police.

BECK, R. (2015) *We Believe the Children: A Moral Panic in the 1980s*, New York: Public Affairs.

BROWN, J. (2014) 'William Roache: *Coronation Street* Star Found not Guilty of All Sexual Abuse Charges, *The Independent*, 6 February. Available online at <http://www.independent.co.uk/news/uk/crime/william-roache-coronation-street-star-found-not-guilty-of-all-sexual-abuse-charges-9111654.html> [accessed December 2015].

BURTON, M., EVANS, R., and SANDERS, A. (2006) *Are Special Measures for Vulnerable and Intimidated Witnesses Working? Evidence from the Criminal Justice Agencies*, Home Office Online Report 01/06. Available online at <http://collection.europarchive.org/tna/20080205132101/homeoffice.gov.uk/rds/pdfs06/rdsolr0106.pdf> [accessed August 2015].

Crown Prosecution Service (CPS) (undated*a*) *Rape and Sexual Offences*, Guidance. Available online at <http://www.cps.gov.uk/legal/p_to_r/rape_and_sexual_offences/> [accessed May 2016].

Crown Prosecution Service (CPS) (undated*b*) 'What is Consent?', Aide-memoire. Available online at <http://www.cps.gov.uk/publications/equality/vaw/what_is_consent_v2.pdf> [accessed May 2016].

Crown Prosecution Service (CPS) (2013) *Guidelines on Prosecution Cases of Child Sexual Abuse*. Available online at <http://www.cps.gov.uk/legal/a_to_c/child_sexual_abuse/> [accessed August 2015].

Crown Prosecution Service (CPS) (2014) *Victims' Right to Review Scheme*. Available online at <http://www.cps.gov.uk/victims_witnesses/victims_right_to_review/index.html> [accessed August 2015].

Crown Prosecution Service (CPS) (2015) *Violence against Women and Girls Crime Report 2014–2015*. Available online at <http://www.cps.gov.uk/publications/docs/cps_vawg_report_2015_amended_september_2015_v2.pdf> [accessed August 2015].

Crown Prosecution Service and Metropolitan Police Service (CPS and MPS) (2015) *Joint CPS and Police Action Plan on Rape*. Available online at <http://www.cps.gov.uk/publications/equality/vaw/rape_action_plan_april_2015.pdf> [accessed August 2015].

DAVIDSON, F. P., and FERGUSON, P. R. (2014) 'The Corroboration Requirement in Scottish Criminal Trials: Should It Be Retained for Some Forms of Problematic Evidence?' *International Journal of Evidence and Proof*, 18(1): 1–27.

DODD, V., and SYAL, R. (2012) 'Cyril Smith Abuse Claims: "Decision not to Prosecute Would not Be Made Today"', *The Guardian*, 27 November. Available online at <http://www.theguardian.com/society/2012/nov/27/cyril-smith-claims-decision-prosecute> [accessed December 2015].

ELLISON, L. E., and MUNRO, V. E. (2013) 'A "Special" Delivery? Exploring the Impact of Screens, Live-links and Video-recorded Evidence on Mock Juror Deliberation in Rape Trials', *Social Legal Studies*, 23(1): 3–29.

EVANS, M. (2014) 'Nigel Evans: Should "Weak Case" Have Been Brought?', *The Telegraph*, 10 April. Available online at <http://www.telegraph.co.uk/news/uknews/crime/10755913/Nigel-Evans-should-weak-case-have-been-brought.html> [accessed December 2015].

FUREDI, F. (2013) *Moral Crusades in an Age of Mistrust: The Jimmy Savile Scandal*, Basingstoke: Palgrave Macmillan.

GAMBACCINI, P. (2015) *Love, Paul Gambaccini: My Year under the Yewtree*, London: Biteback.

GITTOS, L. (2015) *Why Rape Culture is a Dangerous Myth: From Steubenville to Ched Evans*, Exeter: Imprint Books.

GRAY, D., and WATT, P. (2013) *Giving Victims a Voice: A Joint MPS and NSPCC Report into Allegations of Sexual Abuse Made against Jimmy Savile under Operation Yewtree*, London: Metropolitan Police Service/NSPCC.

HALLEY, J. (2015) 'Trading the Megaphone for the Gavel in Title IX Enforcement', *Harvard Law Review Forum*, 128: 103–21.

HM Inspectorate of Constabularies (HMIC) (2014) *Crime Recording: Making the Victim Count*. Available online at <https://www.justiceinspectorates.gov.uk/hmic/wp-content/uploads/crime-recording-making-the-victim-count.pdf> [accessed August 2015].

HOGAN-HOWE, B. (2016) 'Suspected Sex Offenders Have Rights the Police Must Respect', *The Guardian*, 10 February. Available online at <http://www.theguardian.com/commentisfree/2016/feb/10/accused-sex-crimes-anonymous-until-charged-reputations-police-complaint> [accessed February 2016].

Home Affairs Select Committee (2002) *The Conduct of Investigations into Past Cases of Abuse in Children's Homes*, London: HMSO. Available online at <http://www.publications.parliament.uk/pa/cm200102/cmselect/cmhaff/836/836.pdf> [accessed May 2016].

Home Office (1975) *Report of the Advisory Group on the Law of Rape*, Cmnd 6352, London: HMSO (the 'Heilbron Report').

Home Office (1998) *Speaking up for Justice: Report of the Interdepartmental Working Group on the Treatment of Vulnerable or Intimidated Witnesses in the Criminal Justice System*, London: HMSO.

JAY, A. (2014) *Independent Inquiry into Child Sexual Exploitation in Rotherham, 1997–2013*, Rotherham: Rotherham Metropolitan Borough Council (the 'Jay Report').

KELLY, L., LOVETT, J., and REGAN, L. (2005) *A Gap or a Chasm? Attrition in Reported Rape Cases*, London: Home Office Research, Development and Statistics Directorate.

KELLY, L., TEMKIN, J., and GRIFFITHS, S. (2006) *Section 41: An Evaluation of New Legislation Limiting Sexual History Evidence in Rape Trials*, London: HMSO.

LEES, S. (1996) *Carnal Knowledge: Rape on Trial*, London: Hamish Hamilton.

MILNE, R., SHAW, G., and SMITH, K. (2009) *Achieving Best Evidence in Criminal Proceedings: Guidance on Interviewing Victims and Witnesses, and Using Special Measures*, London: CPS.

Ministry of Justice (2013) *Code of Practice for Victims of Crime*, London: HMSO. Available online at <http://www.cps.gov.uk/publications/docs/victims_code_2013.pdf> [accessed May 2016].

MUNRO, V. (2008) 'Constructing Consent: Legislating Freedom and Legitimating Constraint in the Expression of Sexual Autonomy', *Akron Law Review*, 41(4): 923–56.

Office for National Statistics (ONS) (2016) *Focus on Violent Crime and Sexual Offences: Year Ending March 2015*. Available online at <http://www.ons.gov.uk/peoplepopulationandcommunity/crimeandjustice/compendium/focusonviolentcrimeandsexualoffences/yearendingmarch2015> [accessed May 2016].

RAYNOR, G., and GARDNER, B. (2015) 'Men Must Prove a Woman Said "Yes" under Tough New Rape Rules', *The Telegraph*, 28 January. Available online at <http://www.telegraph.co.uk/news/uknews/law-and-order/11375667/Men-must-prove-a-woman-said-Yes-under-tough-new-rape-rules.html> [accessed August 2015].

REECE, H. (2013) 'Rape Myths: Is Elite Opinion Right and Popular Opinion Wrong?', *Oxford Journal of Legal Studies*, 33(3): 445–73.

SAUNDERS, A. (2015) 'Violence against Women and Girls', DPP speech to Women's Aid, 1 July. Available online at <http://www.cps.gov.uk/news/articles/violence_against_women_and_girls_-_dpp_speech_to_women_s_aid:july_2015_/> [accessed August 2015].

Scottish Government (2012) *Reforming Scots Criminal Law and Practice* (the 'Carloway Report'). Available online at <http://www.scotland.gov.uk/Resource/0039/00396483.pdf> [accessed August 2015].

SEIGEL, M. (ed.) (2009) *Race to Injustice: Lessons Learned from the Duke Lacrosse Rape Case*, Durham, NC: Carolina Academic Press.

STARMER, K. (2013) 'The Criminal Justice Response to Child Sexual Abuse: Time for a National Consensus', 6 March. Available online at <http://www.cps.gov.uk/news/articles/the_criminal_justice_response_to_child_sexual_abuse_-_time_for_a_national_consensus/> [accessed December 2015].

STERN, V. (2010) *A Report by Baroness Vivien Stern CBE of an Independent Review into How Rape Complaints Are Handled by Public Authorities in England and Wales*, London: HMSO.

SUTTON, S. (2014) 'A New Vision for Victims, but Are Defendants Being Left out in the Cold?', *Tuckers Solicitors Blog*, 1 October. Available online at <https://www.tuckerssolicitors.com/case/new-vision-for-victims-defendants-cold/> [accessed December 2015].

Victim Support (1996) *Women, Rape and the Criminal Justice System*, London: Victim Support.

WATT, N. (2014) 'Ex-Solicitor General Urges Butler-Sloss to Stand down from Child Abuse Inquiry', *The Guardian*, 14 July. Available online at <http://www.theguardian.com/society/2014/jul/14/former-solicitor-general-butler-sloss-child-abuse-inquiry> [accessed August 2015].

Yorkshire Post (2013) 'Minister Hails "Sea Change" in Sex Abuse Approach', 22 November. Available online at <http://www.yorkshirepost.co.uk/news/minister-hails-sea-change-in-sex-abuse-approach-1-6260019> [accessed May 2016].

15

'IN DENIAL'

THE HAZARDS OF MAINTAINING INNOCENCE AFTER CONVICTION

Daniel S. Medwed

Innocent people convicted of child abuse or sexual offences face a classic 'catch-22' situation that has ramifications on their prospects for parole and for exoneration in court. If prisoners continue to maintain their innocence while imprisoned, then corrections officials may interpret this behaviour as demonstrating a key trait of sex offenders—'denial'—and make them ineligible for treatment programmes that are a prerequisite for parole in many jurisdictions. Even if they are technically eligible to apply for parole, inmates who claim innocence before parole boards harm their chances for release based on the belief that those unable to admit guilt are likely to reoffend; they are perceived as lacking in remorse and failing to address their offending behaviour (Medwed, 2008: 491).

Prisoners who pursue their innocence through post-conviction litigation also face an uphill climb. This is attributable in part to cognitive biases that affect how prosecutors treat innocence claims in the aftermath of conviction and all too often lead them to discount their potential legitimacy (Medwed, 2012: 123–32). Considering the hazards that inmates encounter in maintaining their innocence in parole and post-conviction litigation settings, there is reason to think that many of them are not in denial, but rather the victims of profound miscarriages of justice. This chapter will explore this conundrum in these two settings, before concluding with some thoughts on reform.

PAROLE RELEASE DECISION-MAKING AND THE INNOCENT PRISONER'S DILEMMA

As a threshold matter, prisoners convicted of sex offences often must participate in 'sex offender treatment programmes' in order even to be eligible for release on parole. A fundamental requirement of such programmes is that inmates must accept responsibility for their behaviour by 'admitting guilt'. American courts have upheld this practice, finding that it neither inherently coerces prisoners nor violates their constitutional rights (Brar, Wortsel, and Martinez, 2012: 775).

This naturally poses an obstacle for innocent people convicted of sex crimes. In the 'San Antonio Four' case from Texas, for example, a group of women were accused of sexually assaulting two girls in their care and steadfastly refused to accept plea deals before trial that would have spared them incarceration. Convicted of aggravated sexual assault of a child, the four received stiff sentences: fifteen-year prison terms for three of them, and thirty-seven-and-a-half years for the purported ringleader. The case against them rested on the inconsistent testimony of the two girls and the faulty expert opinion statements of a doctor. The case crumbled years later, in 2013, after a court acknowledged the glaring errors in the expert's testimony. A sad footnote to this saga is that only one of them had been paroled prior to these events; the remaining three had bypassed the chance for release by refusing to participate in a sex offender treatment programme. As of 2014, all four are free, awaiting an opportunity to formally prove their innocence (Rodriguez McRobbie, 2013; Chammah, 2014).

In situations where innocent prisoners convicted of sex crimes are permitted to seek parole, they still must tread carefully in light of the premium that parole boards place on admissions of guilt. Parole boards consider a wide range of variables in their release decisions (Cromwell et al., 1985: 199; Palacios, 1993: 567, 579). Among those variables, 'evidence of rehabilitation'—as perceived by parole commissioners during the live hearing part of the release process—has historically played an instrumental role in the release decision (Medwed, 2008: 512). Most notably, the parole hearing provides an opportunity for a face-to-face meeting between the prisoner and parole officials, allowing the latter 'to search for such intuitive signs of rehabilitation as repentance, willingness to accept responsibility, and self-understanding' (Cromwell et al., 1985: 200). Purely from a risk management perspective, parole boards value an admission of guilt as reassurance that the inmate is aware of his or her past indiscretions and perhaps unlikely to reoffend.

This search for signs of rehabilitation has links to (a) modern psychology and (b) Judeo-Christian theology. In the eyes of many psychologists, a 'sick' prisoner can be 'cured' only if he or she accepts and openly acknowledges his or her involvement in criminal activity. And a person can do this, or so many think, only if he or she is not 'in denial'—a concept that relates to Sigmund Freud's ground-breaking psychological research in the area of disavowal and repression. The psychological discourse about denial emphasizes that a person can experience a positive mental and spiritual transformation only after coming to terms with past misdeeds (Medwed, 2008: 533–4). Similarly, Judeo-Christian theology treats the admission of sinful conduct and apology for such conduct as integral in atoning for sins. Under ancient Jewish law, rehabilitation and atonement were the pillars of punishment theory. The parole process's dependence on remorse and responsibility also mirrors the Christian sacrament of penance: 'contrition, confession, the act of penance, and absolution' (Celichowski, 2001: 239, 249; Cohen, 2005: 247; Medwed, 2008: 532–3).

Perhaps it is no surprise that parole boards, influenced by the rehabilitative origins of parole, along with prevailing psychological beliefs and theological traditions, want to hear inmates admit guilt—that is, that, to gain release from the *peniten*tiary, inmates must essentially display evidence of their penitence (Schimmel, 2002: 182). Quantitative and qualitative data confirm that (a) parole boards attach tremendous importance to inmate statements that take responsibility for the crime underlying their conviction and (b) the refusal to admit guilt diminishes the likelihood of parole (Medwed, 2008: 514–15). Specifically, statistics from the UK in one year studied, 2003, indicated that 51 per cent of parole applications were granted overall, but that only 24 per cent of applicants who maintained their innocence received parole (Naughton, 2005: 1–2).

The true value of acceptance of responsibility in measuring an inmate's worthiness for release may be minimal, especially in the case of those whose denial is related to innocence. A 2002 study of 144 inmates convicted of sex offences in England revealed that while offenders perceived to be 'in denial' by the parole board (about one third of the sample) were much more likely to be rated 'high risk' than those who accepted responsibility, only one 'high-risk denier' was subsequently reconvicted of a sex crime, as compared with seventeen of the ninety-seven 'non-deniers' (Hood et al., 2002: 371, 387, n. 5; Shute, 2004: 315, 324). How many of those 'high-risk' deniers were actually innocent?

To be clear, some convicted sex offenders who claim innocence at parole hearings almost certainly are in denial, sometimes in the face of irrefutable evidence of guilt. Social scientists have observed that people typically make choices that maximize their 'positive self-image'. Individuals are often reluctant to acquire or divulge information that counters the affirmative view they hold of themselves. As a consequence, guilty prisoners may be hesitant to admit guilt for fear of damaging their vision of themselves as 'good'. Inmates may also have practical reasons for refusing to acknowledge guilt, for instance sex offenders who worry that admitting culpability could imperil them within the prison (Sigler, 2006: 561, 567; Medwed, 2008: 539).

But it is dangerous to underestimate the strong possibility that assertions of innocence at parole hearings reflect the truth. Even more dangerous is the chance that an innocent prisoner's resolve may flag over the years—that the desperation to improve the chances for earlier release may eventually prove hard to resist. Consider the internal dialogue that an innocent prisoner must experience before facing the parole board. Should he or she continue to maintain innocence and hinder his or her parole prospects? Should he or she falsely accept responsibility to boost his or her odds for release? Even if the admission of guilt prompts the parole board to release him or her, the confession now belongs in the inmate's parole file, which may be accessible to police and prosecutors. If the defendant were to pursue his or her innocence claim through post-conviction litigation, prosecutors may rely on the inculpatory statement in devising their response. And what about the inmate who vacillates, claiming innocence in one appearance before the board and guilt in another? Or who admits to a lesser crime (say, indecency), but protests the greater offence (rape)? Such is the 'innocent prisoner's dilemma' when encountering the parole board (Medwed, 2008: 539–41).

LITIGATING POST-CONVICTION INNOCENCE CLAIMS

The parole process is not the only mechanism through which an innocent prisoner may seek his or her freedom. The court systems in the UK and the United States provide an array of post-conviction options for proving innocence. These options, though, are littered with procedural, substantive, and strategic barriers.

Newspaper headlines notwithstanding, most criminal cases lack biological evidence suitable for DNA testing. This large category of 'non-DNA' cases includes many cases involving child or intimate partner abuse in which there have been delays in reporting the allegations to law enforcement and, accordingly, no opportunity to retrieve potentially incriminating biological evidence. In such cases, as in the San Antonio Four saga, it is usually the purported victim's statements, coupled perhaps with some expert opinion testimony about physical and/or psychological trauma, that comprise the evidence against the accused. Most prisoners therefore must resort to subjective, non-DNA evidence to prove their innocence. That evidence often consists of statements by new witnesses, the discovery of information that casts doubt on the honesty of key prosecution witnesses, or recantations by trial participants. Finding this evidence is challenging; persuading courts to take it seriously is just as burdensome (Medwed, 2012: 125–6).

After the conviction of a defendant, it becomes increasingly difficult to prompt courts to explore the accuracy of that outcome. In the United States, defendants may file a motion for a new trial in the aftermath of a conviction. Although these motions typically allow for the presentation of new evidence, they have strict time restrictions. Chances are remote that a defendant can assemble enough newly discovered evidence to prove his or her innocence before the time runs out on a new trial motion. Defendants also invariably challenge their conviction in a procedure called the 'direct appeal', but the issues that courts review at this stage are relatively narrow. For the most part, appellate courts consider only issues and evidence previously presented to the trial judge, not anything new, during the direct appeal (Medwed, 2012: 125–6). The appellate procedure in England and Wales, while quite different, contains its own roadblocks.[1]

Limitations on direct appeals and new trial motions put many defendants at the mercy of a jurisdiction's post-conviction procedures, such as writs of habeas corpus or error coram nobis, or their statutory analogues. These are not direct attacks on the judgment, but rather indirect or 'collateral' challenges whereby petitioners may introduce evidence never heard before. Even though every jurisdiction in the United States permits the presentation of newly discovered evidence through some sort of collateral procedure, legislators and judges are notoriously sceptical of these claims. The post-conviction process reflects this scepticism through rigid statutes of limitations,

---

[1] In England and Wales, there is no direct appeal as of right; instead, the intermediate appellate court, the Court of Appeal, has the power to grant permission to appeal. The standard for reversal on appeal is that the Court must find the conviction 'unsafe'. If the Court of Appeal agrees to hear a case, then defendants may present new evidence in the interest of justice, but the Court is notoriously wary of entertaining this evidence (Griffin, 2001: 1241, 1267–70).

onerous burdens of proof for defendants, and deferential standards of review for judicial decisions denying petitions (Medwed, 2012: 125).

It may be particularly hard to prove innocence based on recantation evidence where the primary accuser has repudiated his or her trial testimony and now asserts that the defendant did not commit the underlying offence (Medwed, 2005: 655, 658, n. 13). Many innocence claims in sex abuse cases depend on this form of evidence, but courts tend to be hostile toward it—and understandably so. If the witness swore under oath that the defendant perpetrated the crime, how can we believe the witness now when he or she 'swears' that the former testimony was untrue? As the Mississippi Supreme Court once proclaimed, '[n]o form of proof is so unreliable as recanting testimony'.[2]

It should go without saying that, occasionally, recantation evidence is meritorious. Consider the case of Brian Banks, a prominent California high-school athlete who was accused of raping an acquaintance on campus.[3] Facing a sentence of forty-one years to life imprisonment, Banks pled guilty in 2002. Moreover, the accuser sued the school district and ultimately procured a US$1.5 million settlement. Years later, while Banks was on parole as a registered sex offender, his accuser contacted him via Facebook, met with him, and admitted that she had fabricated her account. With this admission caught on tape, Banks's legal team sought his exoneration in court. The judge who had presided over the original plea overturned the conviction in 2012 (Hiserman, 2012).

Given judicial aversion to recantation evidence in general and the procedural obstacles embedded in the post-conviction process, a key factor in a defendant's ability to make any progress with a post-conviction innocence claim often lies in the prosecution's reaction. Prosecutorial resistance can stop a case in its tracks, or at least make the process much more arduous for the defendant. To be fair, many prosecutors react admirably to innocence claims. Some even take proactive measures to correct wrongful convictions. But prosecutors do not always exhibit an open mind in the post-conviction arena when faced with evidence of innocence; on the contrary, many prosecutors fight these claims with vigour. One common situation is that in which prosecutors, confronted with a potential wrongful conviction, hatch revised theories of the case that bear little resemblance to the stance at trial, to support the continued incarceration of a defendant (Medwed, 2012: 125).

Why do some prosecutors respond this way? Numerous explanations come to mind, including resource constraints, belief in the finality of verdicts, the absence of firm ethical rules, and political considerations. Let us now turn to the most significant and mysterious source of prosecutorial opposition: cognitive bias (Medwed, 2012: 127–9).

The scholarship on cognitive bias offers many findings that apply to the conduct of post-conviction prosecutors. The term 'confirmation bias' refers to the propensity of people to value information that reinforces, rather than undermines, their initial hypotheses. This bias flourishes in the post-conviction context. The factfinder, usually a jury, has validated the prosecutor's theory of the case in the form of a guilty verdict.

[2] *Yarborough v. State*, 514 So.2d 1215, 1220 (Miss. 1987).
[3] See 60 *Minutes*, 'Blindsided: The Exoneration of Brian Banks', aired on 24 March 2013, script available online at <http://www.cbsnews.com/news/blindsided-the-exoneration-of-brian-banks/>

That theory is further validated when a court affirms the conviction on direct appeal. At this point, an offshoot of the confirmation bias (known as the 'status quo bias') surfaces. Once external actors have corroborated a decision, it requires extensive contrary data to push the stakeholders in that decision (including prosecutors) away from that point of reference. As information emerges, these stakeholders may process it selectively by overvaluing data in favour of the status quo and discounting findings that defy it. In other words, the presumption of guilt grows 'stickier' for prosecutors after conviction (Medwed, 2012: 127).

The status quo bias affects many prosecutors who handle post-conviction innocence claims. Where post-conviction petitions are distributed to the *same* prosecutor who tried the case, the impact of the status quo bias is pronounced: people are particularly reluctant to second-guess their own choices. The status quo bias lingers even when innocence claims are allocated to prosecutors with no explicit link to the original trial. Studies indicate that people within an organization may respect the decisions of their peers because of the power of the 'conformity effect'—that is, a wish to act in line with a colleague. The pressure to conform can spur post-conviction litigators to defer to their predecessors or look at the new evidence with a dubious eye (Medwed, 2012: 127–8).

One's aversion to 'cognitive dissonance'—that is, the disturbing realization that one's actions do not reflect one's self-image—also comes into play. Convicting an innocent person undermines an ethical prosecutor's belief that charges should be made only against the guilty and that his or her office would not press charges otherwise. To avoid cognitive dissonance, prosecutors may latch onto the original theory of guilt as a way in which to reconcile their beliefs with their actions. This partially explains why prosecutors can seem indifferent to wrongful convictions: they simply cannot confront the possibility that they or their office helped to generate one; the cognitive burden is too heavy to bear (Medwed, 2012: 128).

ON THE HORNS OF THE INNOCENT PRISONER'S DILEMMA: AN EXAMPLE

The following case exemplifies the hazards for defendants claiming innocence during the parole and post-conviction processes.

Bruce Dallas Goodman was convicted in Utah for the rape and murder of a young woman with whom he had been romantically involved. The crime occurred in a rural part of the state near a highway exit. The only physical evidence that could identify the perpetrator was a cigarette butt located nearby, which was later found to have been smoked by a type 'A' secretor. It also appears as though the victim had engaged in sex with a type 'A' secretor—that is, with someone with type 'A' blood who secretes 'A' antigens into body fluids. Testimony at Goodman's trial suggested that 32 per cent of the population falls into this category. At the time, more accurate methods of testing biological evidence, such as DNA testing, were in their infancy (Medwed, 2008: 523).

The other evidence against Goodman, like the blood evidence, was largely circumstantial. He was last observed with the victim miles away from the crime scene and roughly five hours before the discovery of her body. On direct appeal, the Utah Supreme Court conceded that '[w]ithout question this was a close case', but affirmed Goodman's conviction. Justice Stewart's dissent proclaimed that '[t]he evidence in this case falls far short of proving that the defendant committed the crime charged' (Medwed, 2008: 524).[4]

Goodman had always claimed innocence, and continued to do so after his conviction and loss on appeal. Yet, in 2000, Goodman 'admitted' his culpability at a hearing before the Utah Board of Pardons and Parole in the hope of gaining favour. His comments failed to have the desired effect: the Board denied him parole (Medwed, 2008: 524–5).

Goodman's wish for freedom came to pass four years later through the work of the Rocky Mountain Innocence Center (RMIC), a Salt Lake City group that investigates and litigates post-conviction claims of innocence. The Center sought to subject the biological evidence from the Williams murder to DNA testing. After it obtained the evidence and sent it for testing, the results proved that none of the material belonged to Goodman; rather, the DNA evidence proved that *two other* people had left these samples (Medwed, 2008: 525).

The RMIC then analysed how to present this new discovery in court. One option involved filing a motion under Utah's post-conviction DNA statute. Under that remedy, a judge may dismiss the charges 'with prejudice' if the defendant proves actual innocence, and prosecutors would be barred from retrying him. The Center alternatively considered the state habeas corpus remedy, which allows courts to overturn convictions when presented with newly discovered evidence that undermines confidence in the verdict, but permits a retrial. I had recently joined the RMIC's board of directors and engaged in the discussions. We decided to contact the prosecutors and gauge their feelings (Medwed, 2008: 525–6).

The prosecution's stance all along had been that Goodman had killed Williams by himself; the DNA findings destroyed that theory of the case. Even so, prosecutors involved with the litigation did not conclude that Goodman was innocent. A new prosecution theory evolved to justify the conviction: that Goodman was one of several perpetrators who took part in the Williams murder and that the absence of his biological evidence from the crime scene did not prove his innocence. This theory emerged despite the lack of evidence that Goodman had acted in concert with others, let alone that he was even present at the crime scene (Medwed, 2008: 524, 526).

In their conversations with us, the prosecutors cited Goodman's admission of guilt at his parole hearing as one reason for their reluctance to deem him innocent. We explained the pressures that prisoners face in applying for release, particularly when they know that proclamations of innocence damage their parole outlook. But the prosecution would not stray from its belief that Goodman was entangled in the crime and indicated it would oppose a filing under the DNA statute. So we compromised: the prosecutors stipulated that they would vacate the conviction under the habeas corpus procedure and not pursue a retrial (Medwed, 2008: 527–8).

[4] *State v. Goodman*, 763 P.2d 786, 788–90 (1988).

Goodman was released in 2004, but not formally exonerated—a casualty I ascribe to the one–two punch of a flawed parole process and prosecutorial intransigence to post-conviction innocence claims. Without the imprimatur of a court-ordered exoneration, the consequences of Goodman's wrongful murder conviction will dog him, presenting barriers in his search for state compensation or any form of employment. And yet the Goodman story is, in many respects, a happy one: he was released. What about the scores of innocent prisoners convicted of sexual abuse whose cases lack DNA evidence—and whose plaintive cries of innocence fall on the deaf ears of parole officials and prosecutors?

THOUGHTS ON POSSIBLE REFORMS

Having outlined the hazards that convicted sex offenders may face in claiming innocence during the parole and post-conviction processes, I will now use my remaining pages to ponder some potential remedies designed to make it easier for the truly innocent to obtain freedom.

PAROLE

Presupposing that the current norm in which prisoners are penalized for claiming innocence at parole hearings rests on a flimsy policy and ethical foundation, the question is: what can be done to ameliorate this flaw? As an initial point, parole boards could be educated about the 'innocent prisoner's dilemma' and exhorted to discount the overarching importance of inmate statements regarding guilt or innocence as factors in their release decisions (Medwed, 2008: 543–6). I have urged parole boards to adopt this approach in a handful of cases. This strategy has occasionally appeared to help.

Beyond encouraging parole boards to discount the significance of inmate statements about guilt or innocence, another possible reform might involve banning prosecutors from formally using such statements in subsequent post-conviction proceedings. This could advance a number of desirable goals. For one thing, it might remove any disincentive for prisoners to convey empathy for the victim for fear that the statement would be interpreted as an admission of guilt and deployed against them in later litigation. For another, innocent prisoners would no longer pay a direct price in the post-conviction setting for admitting guilt before parole officials solely in the hopes that it might generate a positive outcome. Further, in light of the pressure to 'admit' guilt to appease parole officials, these statements may lack credibility and have little value as evidence at a post-conviction proceeding (Medwed, 2008: 542).[5]

Instead of ignoring inmate statements on the topic of guilt or innocence, or limiting the ensuing impact of such statements, parole boards could take an entirely different

---

[5] To be fair, curtailing the subsequent use of these statements at post-conviction proceedings could further incentivize inmates to lie: an innocent prisoner could 'admit' guilt at a parole hearing with few, if any, direct costs and thereby increase the odds of a parole grant. This might, in turn, further erode the integrity of the parole hearing (Medwed, 2008: 542–3).

approach and view them as issues worthy of scrutiny. Parole boards could be told—and empowered—to engage in more thorough factual investigations about innocence claims, provided that such inquiries are limited to the issue of suitability for release on parole and not a formal determination of guilt or innocence. To aid parole boards in this endeavour, three ideas rise to the fore:

(1) altering the structure of parole release hearings where innocence is at issue to permit inmates a greater opportunity to clarify the basis of their claim;[6]
(2) augmenting the resources of parole boards to conduct investigations; and
(3) advising parole boards to refer innocence claims to organizations better positioned to evaluate them (Medwed, 2008: 546–55).

In no way would these proposals usurp the court's function in adjudicating legal questions of guilt or innocence (Medwed, 2008: 546).

Courts appear to be gradually recognizing the problems wrought by this dilemma. Three US appellate courts have cited my research in this area.[7] Yet without greater recognition of this problem and the implementation of concrete reforms to rectify it, the 'innocent prisoner's dilemma' will linger—to the detriment of the innocent and the integrity of our system of justice.

POST-CONVICTION LITIGATION

The cognitive biases of prosecutors can profoundly affect their responses to post-conviction innocence claims in sex abuse cases and, as a result, influence the outcome of the litigation. My chief recommendation is to implement structural reforms within prosecutors' offices to create distance between the original decision maker and the post-conviction reviewer of the claim to allow for a new look at an old choice—or at least to permit the possibility of such a look.

For prosecutors, one reform might entail asking them to establish internal divisions to investigate post-conviction innocence claims. Prosecutors' offices are well positioned to investigate post-conviction innocence claims. First, prosecutors have access to lots of case files. This is an advantage in analysing an innocence claim revolving around an assertion that the main prosecution witness lied and it turns out that the witness has testified in other matters. Second, prosecutors can tap into a group of veteran investigators (the police) who have a powerful information network of their own (Medwed, 2012: 136).

Prosecutors in these divisions would become specialists in post-conviction innocence cases, making them better evaluators of a claim's merit than generalist lawyers from other units. Moreover, structural separation between the trial bureau and the attorneys entrusted with reviewing post-conviction petitions could minimize the

---

[6] Specifically, I would propose modifying the format of parole hearings to allow prisoners to provide advance notice about their desire to claim innocence; with such notice, parole boards could adjust their hearing schedules to allow more time for these inmates to make their presentations, and to permit expanded rights to make their arguments by calling witnesses and even drawing on the assistance of counsel (Medwed, 2008: 548–9).

[7] *In re Personal Restraint of Dyer*, 189 P.3d 759 (2008) (*Dyer II*; in dissent); *Newman v. Beard*, 617 F.3d 775, 786 (3d Cir. 2010); *Steele v. State*, 291 P.3d 466, 473 (Idaho Ct. App. 2012).

impact of the status quo bias. Consolidating responsibility for post-conviction innocence claims might also nurture productive relationships between individual attorneys in the unit and lawyers affiliated with innocence projects. Stronger relationships of this nature could yield increased cooperation in presenting innocence claims to the courts. This in turn could spawn greater openness from judges in reviewing claims in which the defence and the prosecution appear united (Medwed, 2012: 136–7).

There are, however, downsides to my proposed reforms. The power of conformity effects would persist: a post-conviction prosecutor might hesitate to second-guess the trial decisions of a peer in his or her office. Lawyers might abhor assignments to the innocence unit, envisioning the group as akin to a police internal affairs bureau that 'rats out' colleagues. Attorneys in an innocence unit could have a hard time gathering information or may fear professional repercussions. Political considerations also augur against these entities: prosecutors might worry about voters viewing an innocence unit as a sign of 'weakness' and holding it against them on election day. Resource constraints, too, may make the enterprise impractical, especially in smaller offices (Medwed, 2012: 137).

Still, on balance, promoting the growth of innocence units at prosecutors' offices would lead to more exonerations of wrongfully convicted prisoners, including purported sex offenders, and more consistent treatment of inmate petitions within each jurisdiction. This is a good thing in my view and in the eyes of many increasingly sceptical observers of the Anglo-American criminal justice system (Medwed, 2012: 137).

CONCLUSION

Convicted sex offenders are among the most reviled members of society. They are branded as 'predators' and 'deviants', particularly those accused of preying upon children. Although many convicted sex offenders no doubt deserve such disdain, what about the strong possibility that some do not—that some are actually innocent?

For that unknown, but potentially sizable, segment of the population, the avenues available to correct this error after conviction are fraught with problems. Parole boards rely heavily on 'admissions of guilt' as a precondition for release and, during post-conviction litigation, prosecutors often resist innocence claims with all their might, making prisoners' chances for success exceedingly slim. This chapter has sought to describe some of the failings of those procedures and to offer some modest reforms—changes aimed at allowing those wrongfully deemed 'the worst of the worst' the best opportunity for justice.

REFERENCES

BRAR, L. G., WORTSEL, H. S., and MARTINEZ, R. (2012) 'Mandatory Admission of Guilt in Sex Offender Programs', *Journal of the American Academy of Psychiatry and the Law*, 40(3): 433–5.

CELICHOWSKI, J. (2001) 'Bringing Penance back to the Penitentiary: Using the Sacrament of Reconciliation as a Model for Restoring Rehabilitation as a Priority in the Criminal Justice System', *Catholic Lawyer*, 40(3): 239–70.

CHAMMAH, M. (2014) 'The Mystery of the San Antonio Four', *Texas Observer*, 7 January. Available online at <https://www.texasobserver.org/mystery-san-antonio-four/> [accessed May 2016].

COHEN, J. R. (2005) 'The Culture of Legal Denial', *Nebraska Law Review*, 84: 247–312.

CROMWELL, P. F., KILLINGER, G. G., KERPER, H., and WALKER, C. (1985) *Probation and Parole in the Criminal Justice System*, Eagan, MN: West Publishing Co.

GRIFFIN, L. (2001) 'The Correction of Wrongful Convictions: A Comparative Perspective', *American University International Law Review*, 16(5): 1241–308.

HISERMAN, M. (2012) 'Rape Conviction of Brian Banks is Overturned', *Los Angeles Times*, 24 May. Available online at <http://articles.latimes.com/2012/may/24/sports/la-sp-brian-banks-20120524> [accessed May 2016].

HOOD, R., SHUTE, S., FEILZER, M., and WILCOX, A. (2002) 'Sex Offenders Emerging from Long-term Imprisonment: A Study of Their Long-term Reconviction Rates and of Parole Board Members' Judgments of Their Risk', *British Journal of Criminology*, 42(2): 371–94.

MEDWED, D. S. (2005) 'Up the River without a Procedure: Innocent Prisoners and Newly Discovered Non-DNA Evidence in State Courts', *Arizona Law Review*, 47(3): 655–718.

MEDWED, D. S. (2008) 'The Innocent Prisoner's Dilemma: Consequences of Failing to Admit Guilt at Parole Hearings', *Iowa Law Review*, 93(2): 491–557.

MEDWED, D. S. (2012) *Prosecution Complex: America's Race to Convict and Its Impact on the Innocent*, New York: New York University Press.

NAUGHTON, M. (2005) 'Why the Failure of the Prison Service and the Parole Board to Acknowledge Wrongful Imprisonment Is Untenable', *Howard Journal of Criminal Justice*, 44(1): 1–11.

PALACIOS, V. J. (1993) 'Go and Sin No More: Rationality and Parole Release Decisions by Parole Boards', *South Carolina Law Review*, 45(3): 567–615.

RODRIGUEZ MCROBBIE, L. (2013) 'How Junk Science and Anti-lesbian Prejudice Got Four Women Sent to Prison for More than a Decade', *Slate*, 4 December. Available online at <http://www.slate.com/blogs/outward/2013/12/04/san_antonio_four_junk_science_and_anti_lesbian_prejudice_sent_them_to_prison.html> [accessed May 2016].

SCHIMMEL, S. (2002) *Wounds not Healed by Time: The Power of Repentance and Forgiveness*, New York: Oxford University Press.

SHUTE, S. (2004) 'Does Parole Work? The Empirical Evidence from England and Wales', *Ohio State Journal of Criminal Law*, 2(1): 315–31.

SIGLER, M. (2006) 'Just Deserts, Prison Rape, and the Pleasing Fiction of Guideline Sentencing', *Arizona State Law Journal*, 38(2): 561–80.

16

WHEN JURIES FIND INNOCENT PEOPLE GUILTY
STRENGTHS AND LIMITATIONS OF THE APPELLATE SYSTEM IN ENGLAND AND WALES

Michael Zander QC

Sometimes, the jury gets it wrong. For whatever reason, it finds someone guilty who is innocent. Trials for historical sex abuse cases are perhaps the category of case in which the jury is the most likely to get it wrong. Commonly, there is little or no evidence beyond the accusations of the alleged victims. The jurors are told by the judge that they must be sure 'beyond a reasonable doubt' before they reach a verdict of guilty. But the jurors are all too likely to be influenced by a climate of opinion that today recognizes the possibility of sex abuse that, years ago, would have been considered unthinkable. The jury believes the accusations of the complainants, rather than the defendant's denials—and it is wrong. He is completely innocent. What then? Until 1907, the convicted innocent defendant in the UK had no recourse other than to seek a pardon from the Home Secretary under the royal prerogative of mercy. But repeated attempts in the nineteenth century to get a criminal appeal court established finally resulted in the setting up of the Court of Criminal Appeal under the Criminal Appeal Act 1907.[1] The most consistent and most influential opponents of the introduction of a right of appeal were the judges (Pattenden, 1996).

Since its establishment more than 100 years ago, the Court of Appeal has basically refused to exercise the jurisdiction given to it by Parliament to consider whether it disagrees with the jury's verdict sufficiently to quash the decision. Changing the statutory language has made no difference. The Criminal Cases Review Commission (CCRC) understandably works within the guidelines laid down by the Court of Appeal. That could change, but one has to be pessimistic as to the likelihood of it happening.

---

[1] Between 1844 and 1906, there were no fewer than 30 failed parliamentary Bills aimed at setting up an appeal system for criminal cases. For the history, see Pattenden (1996). For the history elsewhere, see especially Marshall (2011); see also Berger (2005: 7–8).

THE ROLE OF THE COURT OF APPEAL

The Court's remit in regard to jury decisions was originally established by section 4 of the 1907 Act, which required it to quash the conviction 'if [it thinks] that the verdict of the jury should be set aside on the ground that it is unreasonable or cannot be supported having regard to the evidence... or that on any ground there was a miscarriage of justice'. This could reasonably be interpreted as giving the Court full power to substitute its view of the evidence for that of the jury. Sir John Walton, the Attorney General who guided the Criminal Appeal Bill through the House of Commons, stated that the objective was to give the Court the same power to rehear evidence as the Court of Appeal had in civil cases. He envisaged that the new Court would set aside a conviction 'where there was some element of doubt, where there was some disturbing factor'.[2]

However, at the very first sitting of the new Court in 1908, Lord Chief Justice Lord Alverstone made it very clear that this is not how the judges saw the new jurisdiction:

> It must be understood that we are not here to re-try the case where there was evidence proper to be left to the jury upon which they could come to the conclusion at which they arrived.... Here there was evidence on both sides, and it is impossible to say that the verdict is one which the jury could not properly have arrived at.[3]

Lord Chief Justice Lord Goddard expressed the same proposition in a classic statement in 1949.[4] He dealt first with the situation in which the trial judge disagrees with the jury's verdict:

> It is fair and right to say that from a very early period in the history of this court it has been laid down, and has been laid down frequently since, that the fact that the trial judge was dissatisfied with the verdict, although it is a matter to be taken into account in this court, must not be taken as a ground by itself for quashing the conviction. If it were, it would mean that we should be substituting the opinion of the judge for the opinion of the jury, and that is one of the things that this court will never do.

That proposition has never been disputed. Lord Goddard dealt then with the situation in which it was the appeal judges that did not share the jury's view of the evidence:

> In just the same way it has been held from an equally early period in the history of this court that the fact that some members or all the members of the court think that they themselves would have returned a different verdict is again no ground for refusing to accept the verdict of the jury, which is the constitutional method of trial in this country. If there is evidence to go to the jury, and there has been no misdirection, and it cannot be said that the verdict is one which a reasonable jury could not arrive at, this court will not set aside the verdict of guilty which has been found by the jury.

A JUSTICE Committee in 1964 suggested that 'it seems absurd and unjust that verdicts which experienced judges would have thought surprising and not supported by

---

[2] House of Commons, Hansard, 31 May 1907, col. 232. [3] *R v Williamson* (1908) 1 Cr App R 3.
[4] *R v Hopkins-Husson* (1949) 34 Cr App R 47.

really adequate evidence, should be allowed to stand for no other reason than that they were arrived at by a jury'.[5] In 1965, the Donovan Committee agreed:

> Under the terms of s 4(1), if it is strictly construed, there is, in the case of an innocent person who has been wrongly identified and in consequence wrongly convicted, virtually no protection conferred by his right to appeal ... We think that this defect should be remedied.
>
> (Donovan Committee, 1965: para. 45)

The Committee recommended the adoption of a broader formula—one originally proposed by F. E. Smith, later Lord Chancellor, during the debates on the Criminal Appeal Bill: that the Court should quash a conviction where the verdict, in its opinion, was 'under all the circumstances of the case unsafe or unsatisfactory'. This was the formula adopted in the Criminal Appeal Act 1966, which was then incorporated into the Criminal Appeal Act 1968 as section 2(1)(a).

A year later, in 1969, the Court of Appeal decided the case of *Cooper*,[6] in which it famously gave voice to 'the lurking doubt' test—one entirely different from the traditional approach. Lord Justice Widgery (as he then was), having acknowledged that, prior to the 1966/1968 Acts, it was almost unheard of for the Court to interfere with a jury's verdict, went on:

> However now our powers are somewhat different, and we are indeed charged to allow an appeal against conviction if we think that the verdict of the jury should be set aside on the ground that under all the circumstances of the case it is unsafe or unsatisfactory. That means that in cases of this kind the court must in the end ask itself a subjective question, whether we are content to let the matter stand as it is, or whether there is not some lurking doubt in our minds which makes us wonder whether an injustice has been done. This is a reaction which may not be based strictly on the evidence as such; it is reaction which can be produced by the general feel of the case as the court experiences it.

The 'lurking doubt' test, as expressed in *Cooper*, must have given hope to many appellants, but that hope will usually have been dashed by the Court's unwillingness to apply it.

Research carried out for JUSTICE almost twenty years later stated that only six cases had been found in which a conviction had been quashed on the ground of a lurking doubt about the jury's decision when there was no new evidence.[7] Lord Justice Lawton, a vastly experienced criminal appeal judge, explained this reluctance in his evidence to the Runciman Royal Commission on Criminal Justice (1993). The 'lurking doubt' test, he said, meant that the Court could quash a conviction if it had a hunch that there had been an injustice. This cannot be a sound way of administering criminal justice; and since 1969 the judges seem to have appreciated that it was not because only six appeals have been allowed on this ground. In other words, the judges did not apply the test because they thought it was fundamentally wrongheaded.

---

[5] JUSTICE (1964: para. 59).   [6] *R v Cooper* [1969] 1 QB 267.

[7] The research, carried out for JUSTICE by Kate Malleson, was published in *Miscarriages of Justice* (Malleson, 1969). It was referred to in the Runciman Report (Royal Commission on Criminal Justice, 1993: para. 45).

This was the position considered by the Runciman Commission (of which I was a member). In its report, the Commission said that it had received conflicting evidence about the 'lurking doubt' case. Some, like Lord Justice Lawton, pointed to the fact that there were very few cases in which the test had been applied; others suggested that the Court sometimes applied the test without acknowledging the fact—quashing the conviction, even though there was no new evidence and no error of law or procedure, where:

> ...nevertheless the combined experience of the three members of the court leads them to conclude that there may have been an injustice in the trial and in the jury's verdict... There is no real difference between this approach and an application of the 'lurking doubt' principle.
>
> (Royal Commission on Criminal Justice, 1993: para. 45, n. 9)

The Royal Commission had been set up directly as a result of the quashing of the convictions in a slew of high-profile Irish Republican Army (IRA) terrorism cases, culminating in that of the Birmingham Six. The Commission was fully conscious of the expectation that it would make recommendations aimed at preventing the conviction of innocent persons. On the attitude of the Court of Appeal towards jury decisions, the Commission wanted to encourage the judges to be more robust in their approach. At the start of the chapter dealing with appeals, it said:

> We are all of the opinion that the Court of Appeal should be readier to overturn jury verdicts than it has shown itself to be in the past. We accept that it has no means of putting itself in the place of the jury as far as seeing the witnesses is concerned. Nevertheless, we argue in this chapter that the court should be more willing to consider arguments that indicate that the jury might have made a mistake.
>
> (Royal Commission on Criminal Justice, 1993: para. 3, n. 9)

It added:

> We fully appreciate the reluctance felt by judges sitting in the Court of Appeal about quashing a jury's verdict. The jury has seen the witnesses and heard their evidence; the Court of Appeal has not. Where, however, on reading the transcript and hearing argument the Court of Appeal has a serious doubt about the verdict, it should exercise its power to quash. We do not think that quashing the jury's verdict where the court believes it to be unsafe undermines the system of jury trial.
>
> (Royal Commission on Criminal Justice, 1993: para. 46, n. 9)

It urged that this should be made clear in a redraft of section 2(1)(a) of the Criminal Appeal Act 1968. Section 2 *was* redrafted, but the redraft did not give effect to this recommendation; rather, the Court was now required to quash a conviction 'if [it thinks] that the conviction is unsafe'.

In *ex p Pearson*,[8] in 2000, 'lurking doubt' received a degree of affirmation from then Lord Chief Justice Lord Bingham, when he said that there were:

> ...cases in which the Court, although by no means persuaded of an appellant's innocence, is subject to some lurking doubt or uneasiness whether an injustice has been

---

[8] *R v Criminal Cases Review Commission, ex p Pearson* [2000] 1 Cr App R 141 (DC).

done... If, on consideration of all the facts and circumstances of the case before it, the Court entertains real doubts whether the appellant was guilty of the offence of which he has been convicted, the Court will consider the conviction unsafe.[9]

But in *Pope*,[10] in 2012, Lord Judge (then Lord Chief Judge) put the matter very differently:

> As a matter of principle, in the administration of justice when there is trial by jury, the constitutional primacy and public responsibility for the verdict rests not with the judge, nor indeed with this court, but with the jury. If therefore there is a case to answer and, after proper directions, the jury has convicted, it is not open to the court to set aside the verdict on the basis of some collective, subjective judicial hunch that the conviction is or maybe unsafe. Where it arises for consideration at all, the application of the 'lurking doubt' concept requires reasoned analysis of the evidence or the trial process, or both, which leads to the inexorable conclusion that the conviction is unsafe. It can therefore only be in the most exceptional circumstances that a conviction will be quashed on this ground alone, and even more exceptional if the attention of the court is confined to a re-examination of the material before the jury.[11]

Lord Judge said that the Court had read an 'interesting' article by Professor Leonard Leigh considering the Court of Appeal cases in which the phrase 'lurking doubt' had been invoked (Leigh, 2006). Professor Leigh's thesis was that while a court might entertain a doubt about the safety of a conviction based on the general feel of the case, there had to be some combination of evidence and circumstance that led the court to that conclusion. The cases did not support the proposition that a verdict could be characterized as unsafe based simply on a feeling of uneasiness. The cases that suggested a wider approach, he wrote, 'were in fact decided on considerations which were capable of and were closely analysed: they did not rely on a mere visceral or inchoate reaction' (Leigh, 2006: 809–10).

The decision in *Pope* may be the end of the suggestion that a conviction can be quashed solely on the basis of a 'subjective hunch', the 'general feel of the case', or a 'lurking doubt'. In launching such a proposition, Lord Widgery in *Cooper* arguably went too far. Lord Justice Lawton was surely right to say that it is not a sound basis for quashing a conviction. Professor Leigh's proposition that there has to be some combination of evidence and circumstance that leads the court to the conclusion that the verdict should be quashed seems sounder. That is what the Runciman Commission meant when it said that a conviction should be quashed where 'on reading the transcript and hearing argument the Court of Appeal has a serious doubt about the verdict'. But in saying that there has to be a reasoned analysis leading to 'an inexorable conclusion that the conviction is unsafe', Lord Judge set the bar higher: if that is the test, very few cases will even get a hearing. That presumably was the Court's purpose in putting the matter as it did: it simply does not want to engage with these difficult and deeply troubling cases.

---

[9] *Ex p Pearson*, 146. [10] *R v Pope* [2012] EWCA Crim 2241.
[11] *Pope*, [14].

One understandable reason is the realistic fear that it would increase the Court's already heavy workload.[12] The Court is seriously overworked.[13] Taking a view as to whether the jury got it wrong, quite apart from its inherent difficulty, may require the judges to consider the whole of the transcript of a trial that lasted days, or even weeks, and may involve the hearing of new evidence.

That reason, however, is not one given by the judges; the reason they normally give is that it would usurp the constitutional role of the jury. This is far less persuasive. The jury's role is to give a verdict at the trial. From 1907, the Court of Appeal has had a statutory power to quash the jury's verdict. The formulation of the power was expressed in three different ways in the 1907, 1968, and 1995 Acts. But the history from 1907 to the present shows that the different formulations made no difference. Save in exceptional cases, the judges have refused to take on the task of assessing whether the jury got it wrong on the facts. Changing the way in which the power is expressed—so far, at least—has proven useless. If there is nothing new and no error of law or process defect, the Court of Appeal is unlikely to interfere with the jury's decision.

THE ROLE OF THE CRIMINAL CASES REVIEW COMMISSION

The CCRC was established on the unanimous recommendation of the Runciman Commission. It was based on the view of almost everyone who submitted evidence on the issue that there should be a new independent body to take over consideration of alleged miscarriages of justice.

The CCRC's remit was established under the Criminal Appeal Act 1995. Its function is to receive and to consider applications, and to refer to the Court of Appeal cases in which it 'considers that there is a real possibility that the conviction, verdict, finding or sentence would not be upheld were the reference to be made...because of an argument, or evidence, not raised in the proceedings which led to it'.[14] A reference must therefore generally be based on something new, although that has been interpreted by the Commission to include only slightly new, as well as new evidence on some argument previously made.

But section 13(2) of the 1995 Act gives the CCRC a discretion to make a reference even if there is nothing new 'if it appears to the Commission that there are exceptional

---

[12] According to Professor John Spencer (2006: 677, 693), overwork was 'the reason why the Criminal Division of the Court of Appeal, like the Court of Criminal Appeal before it, has always done its best to avoid getting involved in appeals that turn on disputed facts, and particularly those that require the hearing of witnesses: one of the consequences of which is that the defendant is in a weak position to appeal where he was wrongly convicted.... Appeals on the basis of "I simply didn't do it!" are particularly time-consuming, and if the Court of Appeal were obliged to handle anything but a trivial number of them, this would seriously retard the task of dealing with appeals against sentence: a task that must be given high priority, if the court is to hear the appeal before the sentence has been served.'

[13] Sir Robin Auld (2001: 642) said of the judges who sit on criminal appeals: 'Five or six hours' preparation a day in addition to normal sitting hours, sometimes longer, and much of the weekend is not unusual.'

[14] Criminal Appeal Act 1995, s. 13(1).

circumstances which justify making it'. If there is nothing new and there was no defect in the trial, it follows that it is one of those cases in which one can say that the reference is on the basis that the jury got it wrong. Section 13(2) was itself something new: in that subsection, Parliament recognized the concept of the 'exceptional case'. Presumably, it intended the concept to have some practical meaning.

The 'real possibility' test in section 13(1) means that the CCRC is constrained by what it considers to be the reference's chances of success.[15] Commentators have criticized this dependence on the Court of Appeal (Naughton, 2009). It was not prescribed by the Runciman Royal Commission on Criminal Justice (1993). There was actually nothing in the Commission's report regarding the grounds on which the new body should refer cases to the Court of Appeal. Indeed, so far as I have been able to see from my Commission papers, the position papers prepared by the Secretariat, and the minutes of meetings, the topic was never even discussed by the Commission. All that the Commission's report said on the subject was:

> When, therefore an investigation is completed whose results the Authority believes should be considered by the Court of Appeal, we recommend that it should refer the case to the court, together with a statement of its reasons for so referring it.
>
> (Royal Commission on Criminal Justice, 1993: para. 16, n. 9)

Since it did not deal with the question, I am necessarily speculating, but I believe that the Royal Commission would have agreed with the basic approach of section 13(1), which stipulates that a referral should be based on some new argument or evidence that makes a significant difference—as well as with section 13(2), which allows that, exceptionally, it need not be something new.

As to section 13(1), I believe that the Royal Commission would have taken the view that it makes no sense to suggest that the CCRC should refer conviction cases in which it did *not* think there was a real possibility that the conviction would be reconsidered. It would have agreed with Professors Richard Nobles and David Schiff (2009: 158):

> Sending cases that had no hope of success would raise false hopes for appellants and delay the Court of Appeal Criminal Division's hearing of cases which were going to succeed, resulting in longer periods of imprisonment for wrongfully convicted prisoners.

Would a different test be better? It is suggested by some that the Commission should refer a case if it thinks the applicant is, or at least might be, innocent. I am strongly against that. If that were the sole ground of referral, the Commission would make hardly any referrals. Innocence is extraordinarily difficult to establish. If it were to be added to the existing grounds, it would imply that others referred were not innocent. We would have first- and second-class referrals. And the appeal would then be heard by a Court of Appeal required to consider only whether the conviction was safe.

---

[15] In *R v Criminal Cases Review Commission, ex p Pearson* [2000] 1 Cr App R 141, 146, Lord Bingham said the test is 'imprecise but plainly denotes a contingency which, in the Commission's judgment, is more than an outside chance or a bare possibility but which may be less than a probability or a likelihood or a racing certainty. The Commission must judge that there is at least a reasonable prospect of a conviction, if referred, not being upheld.'

The Scottish CCRC has been given what sounds like a more open-ended remit: it can refer a case to the appellate court on the ground that it believes that a miscarriage of justice[16] may have occurred and that it is in the interests of justice.[17] Does this mean that the Scottish Commission is readier to make a referral than the English Commission? I am not aware that anyone has been able to establish that that is the case. Certainly, it is wrong to think that the Scottish Commission makes referrals without regard to the appellate court's likely response. Both its practice and case law show that the Scottish Commission operates in the same way as the English Commission in using the appellate court's approach as the guide to its referral decisions.

The Runciman Commission's main reason for the proposal to set up the new body to replace the Home Office's 'C3 Division'[18] was that it would be a better vehicle for investigation of possible cases of wrongful convictions than C3. There is nothing in the Commission's report to suggest that the new body should refer cases by reference to a new principle; the nearest the Commission got to a new principle was in suggesting, as has been seen, that the Court of Appeal should be ready to quash the verdict if it had 'a serious doubt'.

It is understandable that the judges of the Court of Appeal should be very careful about following that recommendation, but where it applies, they should follow it. The conviction should be quashed, where appropriate, subject to a retrial. If the Court of Appeal were to be readier to act on that recommendation, many of the concerns raised by critics of the CCRC would be resolved. The Court has always been too worried that taking a different view of the evidence from that of the jury would undermine the system of jury trial. I believe that there is no danger whatever of the system of jury trial being undermined if the Court were prepared to be more robust in quashing jury decisions. This, as noted above, was also the view of a unanimous Royal Commission on Criminal Justice when it said in terms, 'We do not believe that quashing the jury's verdict where the court believes it to be unsafe undermines the system of jury trial' (Royal Commission on Criminal Justice, 1993: para. 46, n. 9).

---

[16] The phrase 'miscarriage of justice' is also the basis of the right of appeal in Scotland. Section 106(3) of the Criminal Procedure (Scotland) Act 1995 (inserted by the Crime and Punishment (Scotland) Act 1997, s. 17) permits a person to appeal 'against any alleged miscarriage of justice in which he was convicted', including any miscarriage on the basis of evidence not heard at the trial or on the basis that the jury's verdict was one that no reasonable jury, properly directed, could have returned. The two Commissions are therefore both working to the same formula as their respective appeal courts.

[17] Criminal Procedure (Scotland) Act 1995, s. 194C, inserted by the Crime and Punishment (Scotland) Act 1997, s. 25. The CCRC has said that it would not wish for a wider remit. In its first report on the CCRC in March 1999, the House of Commons Home Affairs Committee said that the Commission had submitted some observations on ideas for amending the statutory test for referral: 'They suggested that the phrase "miscarriage of justice" would itself be unclear as a test' and that 'it made sense for the Commission's test to be based on the same concepts as the Court of Appeal's test, if the situation was to be avoided where cases were referred under one set of criteria but then had to be rejected by the Court on different criteria' (House of Commons Home Affairs Committee, 1999: para. 23).

[18] The principal functions of the C3 Division of the Home Office were to assist ministers in discharging the Home Secretary's duties and powers (a) under mental health legislation in relation to offenders detained in psychiatric hospitals, and (b) in relation to the royal prerogative or referrals to the Court of Appeal (HL Deb. 17 May 1993, vol. 545, col. 75WA).

USING FAIL-SAFE RESORTS

It is right that the Court of Appeal is not a trial court and it is also right that, constitutionally, we place great value on the verdict of the lay jury. There is general agreement that a Crown court conviction should require at least ten members of the jury prepared to say that they are sure that the prosecution has proved its case beyond a reasonable doubt. But no one denies that juries do sometimes get it wrong. The Court of Appeal is there as a fail-safe protection, but it has only been willing to act at half-cock. Where a sufficient argument can be mounted that scrutiny of the jury's decision is justified, the Court should not shirk that task on the constitutional ground that it must abide by the jury's decision. It need not do so. From a constitutional point of view, there is a very great difference between saying that a person should not be convicted in the Crown court save by a jury and saying that a person on appeal should not have a doubtful conviction quashed because he or she was convicted by a jury.[19]

If the Court declines to quash a conviction that the CCRC is strongly persuaded is unsafe, the CCRC has the power to refer the case again—and again. The CCRC has only twice used the power to refer a case a second time.[20]

In the final analysis, section 16(2) of the Criminal Appeal Act 1995 also allows the CCRC to refer a case to the Home Secretary on the ground that it justifies exercise of the prerogative power of mercy. It is surprising that there has not been a single conviction case in which the Commission has made such a referral.[21] Using this power would be an important signal that the Commission feels fully confident in deploying its full range of possibilities. It would be a signal, too, that the Commission acknowledges the reality that there are cases in which the Court of Appeal has not been able or has not been willing to do what, in justice, is required.

Given the existence of the Commission and of its power under section 16(2), it is highly unlikely that a Home Secretary would exercise the prerogative of mercy on his or her own initiative. The Commission is now, in practice, the only gateway to the exercise of this prerogative power. A pardon, of course, is not an ideal outcome for an innocent person—but better to be pardoned for something you did not do than to continue to stand convicted.

REFERENCES

AULD, R. (2001) *Review of the Criminal Courts of England and Wales: Report*, London: HMSO.
BERGER, B. L. (2005) 'Criminal Appeals as Jury Control: An Anglo-Canadian Historical Perspective on the Rise of Criminal Appeals', *Canadian Criminal Law Review*, 10(1): 1–41.

---

[19] See the two articles by Rupert Grist (2012a, 2012b).
[20] The case of Anthony Stock—which was referred first by the Home Secretary and twice by the CCRC, but which conviction was, however, upheld (*R v Stock* [2008] EWCA Crim 1862) and the case of Z referred for the second time in March 2014 (*R v Z*).
[21] The CCRC's 2010/11 Annual Report said that the Commission had used the power under s. 16(2) to recommend the use of the royal prerogative in relation to the sentence of an applicant who had provided valuable help to the authorities after sentence and appeal (CCRC, 2011: 22).

Criminal Cases Review Commission (CCRC) (2011) *Annual Report and Accounts 2010/11*. Available online at <https://www.gov.uk/government/uploads/system/uploads/attachment_data/file/247333/1225.pdf> [accessed May 2016].

Donovan Committee (1965) *Report of the Interdepartmental Committee on the Court of Criminal Appeal*, Cmnd 2755, London: HMSO.

GRIST, R. (2012a) 'The CCRC: Real Possibilities and Lurking Doubts', *Criminal Law & Justice Weekly*, 176 (January): 9.

GRIST, R. (2012b) 'Lurking Doubts Remain', *Criminal Law & Justice Weekly*, 176 (May): 313.

House of Commons Home Affairs Committee (1999) *The Work of the Criminal Cases Review Commission: First Report*, HC 106 (1998–99), London: HMSO.

JUSTICE (1964) *Criminal Appeals*, London: JUSTICE.

LEIGH, L. (2006) 'Lurking Doubt and the Safety of Convictions', *Criminal Law Review*, 809–16.

MALLESON, K. (1969) *Miscarriages of Justice*, London: JUSTICE.

MARSHALL, P. D. (2011) 'A Comparative Analysis of the Right to Appeal', *Duke Journal of Comparative and International Law*, 22(1): 1–25.

NAUGHTON, M. (ed.) (2009) *The Criminal Cases Review Commission: Hope for the Innocent?* Basingstoke: Palgrave Macmillan.

NOBLES, R., and SCHIFF, D. (2009) 'After Ten Years: An Investment in Justice', in M. Naughton (ed.) *The Criminal Cases Review Commission: Hope for the Innocent*, Basingstoke: Palgrave Macmillan.

PATTENDEN, R. (1996) *English Criminal Appeals 1894–1994: Appeals against Conviction and Sentence in England and Wales*, Oxford: Oxford University Press.

Royal Commission on Criminal Justice (1993) *Report*, Cm 2263, London: HMSO ('Report of the Runciman Commission').

SPENCER, J. R. (2006) 'Does Our Present Criminal Appeal System Make Sense?', *Criminal Law Review*, 677–94.

PART V
FINDING WAYS FORWARD
WHAT'S TO BE DONE?

17

REDUCING HARM RESULTING FROM FALSE ALLEGATIONS OF CHILD SEXUAL ABUSE

THE IMPORTANCE OF CORROBORATION

Steve Herman

Criminal prosecutions based on false allegations of child sexual abuse (CSA) have sent innocent people to prison for many years, resulted in the suicide of wrongly accused adults, and caused irreparable harm to non-abused children (Nathan and Snedeker, 2001; Rabinowitz, 2003; Bensussan, 2011). Wrongful substantiations of false allegations by child protection caseworkers can result in severe harm, sometimes leading to the traumatic forced separation of young children from their parents (Besharov, 1994; Bernet, 1997). Even when CSA investigations do not ultimately result in wrongful substantiations or wrongful convictions, the investigations themselves can have grave negative consequences for non-abused children and for those who are wrongly suspected of committing sexual abuse (Pillai, 2002; Nathan, 2005; Burnett, Chapter 2, in this volume).

There is little doubt that false allegations of CSA occur and that their consequences can be disastrous. However, there is considerable controversy about their prevalence, how often they result in erroneous confirmations by the authorities, and what should be done about them. This chapter describes research that casts light on the magnitude of the problem of false allegations. It is argued that a major reform of current investigative and adjudicative procedures is necessary to reduce the risk of severe harm posed by erroneous confirmations of false allegations. Specifically, obtaining strong corroboration for reports of CSA should become the central priority in most investigations. Reports of sexual abuse that cannot be corroborated should rarely be substantiated by child protection agencies and should never be criminally prosecuted.

Readers may be confused by the way that the words 'substantiation' and 'corroboration' are used in this chapter. In English, 'to substantiate' means 'to establish by proof or competent evidence',[1] which is close to the meaning of 'corroborate'. However,

---

[1] See <http://www.merriam-webster.com/dictionary/substantiate>

in child protection contexts, the meaning of 'substantiate' is closer to the meaning of the word 'believe', since the 'substantiation' of a sexual abuse allegation often amounts to little more than a child protection caseworker's affirmation that he or she believes that a child is telling the truth. For the sake of readability and simplicity, this idiosyncratic usage is adopted in this chapter, while the word 'corroboration' is used throughout to refer to hard, corroborative evidence, such as conclusive medical evidence, eyewitness evidence, physical evidence, and perpetrator confessions. This usage is consistent with the way in which the term is used in most social science research reports and by law enforcement. However, in legal contexts, the word may be used in a more general sense, to refer to *any* evidence that supports—or appears to support—a legal hypothesis. For example, the fact that a child protection caseworker or parent strongly believes that a child is telling the truth could be described as corroboration by those who (wrongly) believe that caseworkers are able to accurately discriminate between true and false verbal reports of abuse in the absence of any hard evidence.

The research reviewed in this chapter focuses on cases of suspected CSA that are investigated and evaluated by mental health, social work, and medical professionals and paraprofessionals (MHPs), because there is more research about these investigations than about investigations conducted by law enforcement personnel and other legal professionals. Also, because errors often cascade from one stage of an investigation to the next, initial errors by child protection caseworkers often lead to subsequent erroneous confirmations of false allegations in law enforcement, civil litigation, and criminal justice contexts. Although the focus of this chapter is on investigations by MHPs, the problems that are described are also relevant to investigations conducted by police, prosecutors, and the courts.

THE MAGNITUDE OF THE PROBLEM

Sexual abuse of children is common, affecting approximately 18 per cent of girls and 8 per cent of boys worldwide (Stoltenborgh et al., 2011). Child sexual abuse is underreported: many true cases of CSA never come to the attention of the authorities. Self-report surveys indicate that approximately 60 per cent of sexually abused children never tell anyone about their abuse and, when children do disclose sexual abuse, only about 25 per cent of their disclosures are reported to the authorities (London et al., 2008).[2] At the same time, CSA is also overreported: approximately 50 per cent of reports of suspected sexual abuse that are reported to child protection agencies in the United States are not based on true cases of CSA (Herman, 2005). The assertion that CSA is both under- and overreported is not a contradiction—that is, the fact that many sexually abused children never disclose their abuse is not inconsistent with the fact that many reported cases of suspected CSA turn out to be based on false reports or erroneous suspicions.

[2] As London et al. (2008) note, data on the prevalence of CSA disclosures based on retrospective reports by adults may be unreliable for a number of reasons, including difficulties in accurately recalling events that occurred in the distant past.

Although there are some false allegations of sexual abuse that are supported by seemingly strong evidence, especially false confessions (see Davis and Leo's Chapter 13, in this volume), the focus of this chapter is on the cases that entail the greatest risk of error: cases that include an uncorroborated or weakly corroborated report of sexual abuse by a child or adult. For simplicity, both weakly corroborated and uncorroborated cases will be referred to as 'uncorroborated'.

Research shows that most uncorroborated reports of sexual abuse by children are substantiated by MHPs and that many of these cases are criminally prosecuted. A review of five US field studies of a total of 894 forensic CSA evaluations conducted by MHPs found that 36 per cent of the cases included an uncorroborated report of sexual abuse by a child (Herman, 2010). Approximately 82 per cent of the uncorroborated cases that included a child's report of sexual abuse were substantiated by MHPs. About 50 per cent of uncorroborated cases investigated by MHPs are charged by prosecutors, according to another study of 329 forensic CSA evaluations (Walsh et al., 2010). Strongly corroborated cases—approximately 40 per cent of the cases investigated by MHPs—are those that include a perpetrator confession, photographs or videos of the abuse, a reliable eyewitness, incontrovertible medical evidence such as pregnancy, or similarly strong evidence. Approximately 95 per cent of strongly corroborated cases are substantiated by MHPs and approximately 85 per cent are charged by prosecutors (Herman, 2010; Walsh et al., 2010).

Some MHPs defend their decisions to substantiate children's uncorroborated reports of sexual abuse by reassuring legal decision-makers that most reports of sexual abuse by children are true, citing research that supposedly shows that only 2–8 per cent of children's reports of sexual abuse are false (Everson and Boat, 1989). These figures are misleading for at least two reasons. First, the cited studies generally focus on deliberate lies by either children or adults—but *deliberate* lies do not appear to be the most common cause of false reports of sexual abuse by children, especially younger children; instead, most false reports by younger children appear to be the result of repetitive suggestive questioning by well-intentioned, but misguided, adults (Ceci and Bruck, 1995; also DeYoung, Chapter 3, and Goodyear-Smith, Chapter 8, in this volume). Second, field studies do not provide estimates of the rate of false reports; instead, they provide estimates of the rate of *detected* false reports. However, when a false report is detected, no error is made, because the report is not substantiated. What legal decision-makers and policymakers want to know is the error rate for MHPs' decisions to substantiate uncorroborated reports—that is, they want to know how many false reports are not detected and, consequently, are substantiated.

Consider the implications of a study of investigations of 1,249 cases of suspected CSA conducted by child protection caseworkers (Everson and Boat, 1989). The overall substantiation rate was 56 per cent. Information about the percentage of cases in which a child made a report of sexual abuse during formal interviews, the percentage of cases that included strong corroboration, and the percentage of cases of each type that were substantiated is not available in the report, but can be estimated using data from Herman (2010) and Walsh and colleagues (2010) as follows:

- 28 per cent of cases included neither a report nor corroboration, fewer than 1 per cent of which were substantiated;
- 36 per cent of cases included strong corroboration with or without a report, of which 83 per cent were substantiated; and
- 36 per cent of cases included an uncorroborated report, 72 per cent of which cases were substantiated.

In addition, it can be estimated that children made reports of sexual abuse during formal interviews in approximately 60 per cent of all cases.

The child protection caseworkers who participated in the Everson and Boat (1989) study estimated that approximately 5 per cent of the cases they investigated included a false report of sexual abuse by a child. Children made reports of sexual abuse in 60 per cent of cases. This means that approximately 8 per cent (that is, 5 per cent/60 per cent) of all reports made by children were detected false reports. If we assume that none of the detected false report cases included strong corroboration, then 14 per cent (5 per cent/36 per cent) of the uncorroborated reports (the only reports that are likely to be false) were detected as false reports.

If 14 per cent of uncorroborated reports were *detected* false reports, what percentage were likely to have been *undetected* false reports? In other words, what was the ratio of undetected to detected false reports? An important study by Hershkowitz and colleagues (2007) casts some empirical light on this question. In that study, experienced child abuse investigators read transcripts of real forensic interviews in which children had made reports of sexual abuse, half of which were later determined to be almost certainly true and half of which were later determined to be almost certainly false on the basis of independent evidence. On the basis of the transcripts alone, participants in the Hershkowitz and colleagues (2007) study judged that 44 per cent of the false reports were 'very likely' or 'quite likely' to be true, suggesting that about half of all false reports made by children during forensic interviews are likely to be believed by investigators (Herman, 2009). If the authors' results can be generalized, they suggest that a false report by a child has about a 50–50 chance of being believed and substantiated by child protection caseworkers. The hypothesis that caseworkers and other MHPs are unable to reliably recognize false reports of sexual abuse made by children during forensic interviews is supported by hundreds of studies showing that few professionals or laypersons have any reliable ability to correctly discriminate between true and false reports of past events made by either children or adults (for example Bond and DePaulo, 2006, 2008; Edelstein et al., 2006; Talwar et al., 2006).

If MHPs do detect only about 44 per cent of children's false reports of sexual abuse and the other estimates shown above are approximately correct, then about 14 per cent of the uncorroborated reports in Everson and Boat (1989) were detected and 11 per cent were undetected (erroneously substantiated) false reports. This means that 15 per cent (11 per cent/72 per cent) of the participants' decisions to substantiate uncorroborated reports (in that study), or 7 per cent ((11 per cent × 36 per cent)/56 per cent) of all of their decisions to substantiate (including decisions about corroborated cases), were false positive errors.[3] If this analysis is correct, then what Everson and Boat (1989) and the other studies cited actually imply is not that 5 per cent of children's investigated reports are false, but that about 15 per cent ((25 per cent × 36 per cent)/60 per cent) of all investigated reports are false and about 25 per cent of reports in the most problematic subset of cases, the uncorroborated report cases, are false. Only about half of these false reports are detected.

Two other analyses of data from empirical studies have resulted in estimates of evaluator error rates that are consistent with the above estimates. Herman (2005) estimated that at least 24 per cent of MHPs' judgements about the veracity of uncorroborated CSA allegations were errors, either false positives or false negatives. Herman and Freitas (2010) estimated that the median participant in a study of 110 MHPs who engage in forensic CSA evaluations made false positive errors in at least 12 per cent of all cases that they classified as substantiated. These error rate estimates are not precise. Nevertheless, three different approaches to estimating error rates using different datasets and methodologies produce convergent results, and suggest that judgement error rates are significantly higher than most practitioners and researchers realize. For example, the typical MHP assessed by Herman and Freitas (2010) estimated that she made false positive errors in only about 5 per cent of all of the cases she substantiated.

There are some clinician-researchers, legal scholars, and professional organizations who reject the conclusion that the reliability, validity, and accuracy of MHPs' judgements about uncorroborated CSA allegations are too low for these judgements to serve as the basis for potentially catastrophic legal interventions in the lives of children and adults (Berliner and Conte, 1993; American Academy of Child and Adolescent Psychiatry, 1997; Faller and Everson, 2012; Lyon, Ahern, and Scurich, 2012). These clinician-researchers and organizations have not yet made any empirically based arguments to support their belief that MHPs are able to make accurate, valid, or even reliable judgements about the validity of uncorroborated CSA allegations; instead, they make a wholly negative argument, which consists of unconvincing attacks on the external validity of the numerous, diverse, empirical studies that provide convergent, and remarkably consistent, empirical evidence for the poor reliability, validity, and accuracy of MHPs' judgements about uncorroborated allegations (Realmuto, Jensen, and Wescoe, 1990; Finlayson and Koocher, 1991; Horner and Guyer, 1991a, 1991b; Horner, Guyer, and Kalter, 1992, 1993a, 1993b; McGraw and Smith, 1992; Realmuto and Wescoe, 1992; Jackson and Nuttall, 1993; Shumaker, 2000; Hershkowitz et al., 2007; Everson and Sandoval, 2011).[4] The arguments made by Everson and his colleagues might be somewhat more convincing if they could point to a *single* empirical study that tended to support their belief that child abuse professionals' judgements about uncorroborated CSA allegations are accurate, valid, or even reliable. But no such study exists.

---

[3] A false positive error occurs when a false allegation is judged to be true. A false negative error is the opposite, i.e. when a true allegation is judged to be false.

[4] See Herman (2005, 2009) for reviews.

REDUCING HARM RESULTING FROM FALSE ALLEGATIONS OF CHILD SEXUAL ABUSE

The focus of this chapter is on the harm that can result from investigations of suspicions of sexual abuse in cases in which no abuse has actually occurred or the wrong person has been identified as the perpetrator. However, investigations of true allegations can also cause harm to abused children and their families, especially when the authorities fail to validate the true allegations. There are a variety of reforms that could reduce harm to innocent children and adults in cases of suspected CSA. Some reforms could reduce harm resulting from investigations of false allegations and, at the same time, reduce harm resulting from investigations of true allegations; others could reduce harm resulting from false allegations, but have little or no impact on the risk of harm resulting from true allegations. Finally, there are reforms that would reduce harm resulting from false allegations at the cost of an increase in the risk that some true allegations will not be detected.

In general, the accuracy and outcomes of human judgements about cases of suspected CSA can be improved in two ways. Some reforms can reduce the risk of harm as a result of investigative or adjudicative processes themselves, without necessarily affecting the accuracy of the legal decisions, for example taking steps to protect the anonymity of children and adults during investigations, and allowing child witnesses to testify via closed-circuit television (CCTV) to avoid forcing them to face their abusers in open court.

Some changes to investigative and adjudicative procedures can increase the accuracy of forensic judgements either by increasing the quantity and quality of evidence collected during investigations, or by improving the judgement process itself. Many of these procedures are already supported by a majority consensus among CSA researchers and practitioners, and represent current best practices. These best practices should be implemented in all jurisdictions in order to increase the accuracy of legal decisions, and failure to follow them should be emphasized in defending against false allegations. Best practices include the following.

- All forensic interviews with children and adults should be video-recorded, from start to finish. Ideally, recordings should show both the interviewer and the child. Video recording reduces the need for repeated interviews of children and addresses the problem of interviewers' imperfect memory (Ceci and Bruck, 2000; Berliner and Lieb, 2001).
- Evidence-based forensic child interview protocols should be used to increase the likelihood that the maximum amount of useful information will be obtained and to reduce the likelihood that suggestive or leading questions from the interviewer will contaminate the child's report or memory. The protocol with the most research support is that of the US National Institute of Child Health and Human Development (NICHD) (Lamb et al., 2007). This is a public domain protocol that has been translated into a number of languages.[5]

---

[5] The original NICHD protocol, numerous translations, and training materials are available online at <http://nichdprotocol.com/>

- Ongoing training and supervision of forensic child interviewers prevent the degradation of interview skills after training workshops. A number of studies show, surprisingly, that intensive interviewing workshops have no significant long-term impact on participants' interviewing skills in the absence of ongoing supervision and corrective feedback (Stevenson, Leung, and Cheung, 1992; Lamb et al., 2002; Warren and Marsil, 2002).
- The number of forensic child interviews should be minimized. Between one and three interviews should suffice in most cases (American Academy of Child and Adolescent Psychiatry, 1997; Quinn, 2002).
- The same person should not be both a forensic interviewer and child psychotherapist, because the two roles are incompatible (Kuehnle and Connell, 2009).

There are other promising techniques and procedures that are in use in some jurisdictions, but not yet endorsed or accepted by the majority of researchers and practitioners, and so cannot yet be described as best practices. One such method is the use of the polygraph testing to evaluate suspects' veracity. The polygraph is already used effectively in many jurisdictions, often more as a tool to elicit confessions than as an actual lie detector (Staller and Faller, 2010). Narrative analysis techniques such as content-based criterion analysis (CBCA) are designed to distinguish between children's true and false narratives. Although the accuracy of both polygraph testing and techniques such as CBCA is not as high as one would like, given the extremely poor performance of both professionals and laypersons in studies of the ability of unaided human judges to discriminate between true and false statements, these tools may deserve a closer look from researchers and practitioners (but compare Vrij, 2005).

Bakken makes an intriguing proposal in his chapter in this volume (Chapter 20) that would be likely to increase the rate at which false allegations are correctly identified. He suggests that persons accused of sexual abuse and other forms of person abuse should be allowed to enter an 'innocence' plea, which, unlike a 'not guilty' plea, would require the authorities to undertake a more in-depth investigation of the case against the defendant, with the defendant's cooperation.

THE IMPORTANCE OF CORROBORATION

Many practitioners and researchers believe that most true reports of sexual abuse by children are uncorroborated. For example, one group of prominent researchers writes that 'in the vast majority of sexual abuse cases, the primary, and often the only, evidence is the child's verbal allegation and testimony' (Lamb et al., 2008: 182).[6] This widespread belief is simply not supported by the empirical research, which shows that approximately 40 per cent of all cases of recent alleged sexual abuse investigated by MHPs in the United States include strong corroborative evidence (Haskett et al., 1995; Herman, 2010; Walsh et al., 2010). In contrast, strong corroboration is less common in

[6] For additonal illustrative quotations from publications by prominent CSA researchers, see Herman (2010: 191).

the litigation of historical sexual abuse cases based on adults' reports of sexual abuse that occurred in the distant past.

All of the cases included in the sample studied by Lippert and colleagues (2010) were considered to be likely to represent true cases of CSA by at least one of the agencies or evaluators involved (Lippert, personal communication, 5 April 2010). The assumption that corroborative evidence is rare in contemporaneous cases of alleged CSA is so axiomatic for most CSA researchers that it is endorsed even by those whose own empirical research directly contradicts it. For example, Staller and Vandervort (2010: 3) state that 'one of the law's most difficult tasks [is]: proving a criminal case of child sexual abuse beyond a reasonable doubt' in a book that is an in-depth case study of one US jurisdiction that obtains confessions in 64 per cent of criminal CSA cases that are accepted for prosecution and in which 75 per cent of charged cases end in convictions (Faller and Henry, 2000). The conviction rates found by Faller and Henry (2000) are—contrary to their assertion—comparable to conviction rates for other types of felony; one meta-analysis found that 71 per cent of all felony cases charged by prosecutors resulted in convictions (Cross, Whitcomb, and De Vos, 1995). The erroneous assumptions that corroborative evidence is absent in the vast majority of investigated CSA cases and that these cases are particularly difficult to prosecute thus spring from ideologies that prevent some researchers from seeing even their own data clearly.

Most child protection caseworkers and other MHPs are not trained in law enforcement procedures, which focus on the elicitation, collection, and preservation of corroborative evidence. The systematic pursuit of corroboration is the essence of law enforcement investigations, but is often dismissed or ignored by MHPs. Kenneth Lanning, a former FBI agent who specialized in CSA cases, has cogently articulated the 'law enforcement perspective' on CSA investigations and contrasted it with the perspective of many MHPs as follows:

> The law-enforcement perspective deals with criminal activity and legally defensible fact-finding. The process must, therefore, focus *more on*
>
> - admissible evidence of *what* happened than on emotional belief that *something* happened...
> - objective than on subjective reality
> - neutral investigation than on child advocacy
>
> In their desire to convince society that child sexual victimization exists and children do not lie about it, some professionals interpret efforts to seek corroboration for alleged sexual victimization as a sign of denial or disbelief. Corroboration, however, is essential. Investigators cannot just accept that something sexual happened to a child and ignore the context details that are necessary if it is to be proven in a court of law. When the only evidence offered is the word of a child against the word of an adult, child sexual victimization can be difficult to prove in a court of law. It is not the job of law-enforcement officers to believe a child or any other victim or witness. The child victim should be carefully interviewed. The information obtained should be assessed and evaluated, and appropriate investigation should be conducted to corroborate any and all aspects of a victim's statement. The investigator should always be an objective

fact-finder considering all possibilities and attempting to determine what happened with an open mind.

(Lanning, 2001: 102)

Despite the fact that MHPs often dismiss or ignore the need for corroboration, strong corroborative evidence is already available in approximately 40 per cent of all CSA evaluations conducted by MHPs. This suggests an important question: could rates of corroboration be increased to even higher levels if corroboration were to be made the central priority in all investigations of cases of suspected CSA?

The best available evidence that a law-enforcement-centric response to allegations of sexual abuse may result in higher rates of corroborated cases is anecdotal and comes from an in-depth case study of one rural US jurisdiction, St. Joseph County,[7] in the state of Michigan, which has been remarkably successful in obtaining confessions in CSA cases (Staller and Faller, 2010). Prosecutors, law enforcement, and child protection caseworkers in St. Joseph County follow a detailed written protocol for responding to cases of alleged sexual abuse. The protocol emphasizes the need for a speedy videotaped interview of the child. If the child discloses abuse, then the alleged perpetrator is interrogated by law enforcement personnel as soon as possible—often on the same day. If necessary, some of the videotape of the child's disclosure is shown to the suspect during the interrogation and proven interrogation techniques, including deception and psychological manipulation, are used to elicit confessions. If the suspect denies committing abuse, he (or she) is offered a polygraph test. Many additional confessions are obtained during the polygraph tests.

A key feature of the St. Joseph's County approach is the emphasis on speed: suspects who have the time to obtain legal counsel may be much less likely to agree to interrogation, less likely to make confessions, and more likely to be able to destroy evidence. A study of a sample of 323 criminal CSA cases in St. Joseph County found a 64 per cent confession rate (Faller and Henry, 2000). This is double the confession rate found in studies of prosecution samples in other US jurisdictions (for example Cross et al., 1995; Lippert et al., 2010).

One underlying reason why those who make legal and policy decisions in the United States and other countries continue to accept a child protection system in which allegations of serious crimes are initially investigated by child protection caseworkers is the arguably erroneous assumption that strong corroborative evidence is unobtainable in most true cases of CSA. If key legal decision-makers and policymakers were to be made aware that strong corroboration is already available in many investigations of true CSA allegations and, even more importantly, that speedy, competent, law-enforcement-centric responses to suspected CSA could result in the collection or elicitation of strong corroborative evidence in many more cases, then the status quo would be more difficult to defend.

Although reforms that increase the rate at which true allegations of CSA are corroborated may lower the false negative rate, by themselves they are unlikely to have a significant positive impact on the false positive rate, because it is usually difficult, or impossible, to find evidence that can clearly prove a universal negative—that a specific

[7] The pseudonym 'St. Mary County' is used in Staller and Faller (2010).

child was *never* sexually abused. There is a marked logical asymmetry in the types of evidence that can be used to prove that CSA never occurred versus the types of evidence that can prove that it did occur at least once. For example, a suspect's denial is not usually considered to be evidence that abuse did not occur, but a confession is strong evidence that it did; the fact that no third party witnessed even a single incident of abuse is not strong evidence that abuse did not occur, whereas a third-party witness to a single incident is strong evidence that it did; lack of medical evidence is not strong evidence that abuse did not occur, whereas certain types of medical evidence provide very strong evidence of sexual abuse—and so on.

The single most effective way in which to reduce false positive errors in forensic CSA evaluations would be to raise the evidentiary bar for the substantiation and criminal prosecution of allegations of CSA. In the United States, prior to the 1980s, there were numerous jurisdictions that required corroborative evidence as a prerequisite to the pursuit of criminal prosecution of cases of alleged CSA. In response to the perception that these requirements resulted in an inability to prosecute some child molesters, these corroboration requirements were abolished in the 1980s (Lane, 1986). Scotland has traditionally required at least one form of corroboration for the prosecution of any crime (not only sexual abuse), but the corroboration requirement has come under attack in Scotland by police and prosecutors concerned specifically about sexual assault and domestic violence cases, and, by the time you read this, the corroboration requirement in Scotland may have already been definitively abolished. On the one hand, heated arguments about the negative effects of the corroboration requirement in Scotland are not based on clear empirical evidence that the requirement restricts the ability of prosecutors to obtain convictions in true cases of sexual assault (Nicolson and Blackie, 2013). On the other hand, it seems quite likely that Scotland's corroboration requirement does—or did—prevent a significant number of wrongful convictions in cases in which the only evidence is the false or erroneous—but believable—testimony of an alleged victim.

There are indications that US appellate courts and legislators are starting to become aware of the risks of wrongful criminal convictions in CSA cases that are based on uncorroborated allegations. For example, the US Supreme Court recently overturned a death sentence in a CSA case,[8] in part because it realized that false positive errors are more likely in professional and lay judgements about the validity of uncorroborated CSA allegations than in judgements about other types of allegation of criminal conduct:

> The problem of unreliable, induced, and even imagined child testimony means there is a 'special risk of wrongful execution' in some child rape cases...Studies conclude that children are highly susceptible to suggestive questioning techniques like repetition, guided imagery, and selective reinforcement...Similar criticisms pertain to other cases involving child witnesses; but child rape cases present heightened concerns because the central narrative and account of the crime often comes from the

[8] *Kennedy v. Louisiana*, 128 S.Ct. 2641 (2008).

child herself. She and the accused are, in most instances, the only ones present when the crime was committed.[9]

The Oregon Supreme Court has ruled that expert opinion testimony by a physician that he has diagnosed a child as sexually abused should not be considered legally admissible unless it is firmly based on physical evidence of abuse, because the potential for prejudicial impact from opinions based on assessments of psychosocial evidence far outweighs their limited probative value.[10]

The California State Legislature has recently amended the Family Code in response to legitimate concerns that uncorroborated allegations of sexual abuse in custody cases create a serious risk of harm to non-abused children and their parents:

> As a prerequisite to considering allegations of abuse [in a child custody proceeding], the court may require substantial independent corroboration, including, but not limited to, written reports by law enforcement agencies, child protective services or other social welfare agencies, courts, medical facilities, or other public agencies or private nonprofit organizations providing services to victims of sexual assault or domestic violence.
>
> (California Family Code, § 3011)

In many US jurisdictions, statutes require only a preponderance of the evidence for the substantiation of CSA (and other child maltreatment) allegations. 'Preponderance of the evidence' is the lowest evidentiary standard in use in the US legal system (two higher standards are 'clear and convincing evidence' and 'beyond a reasonable doubt'), and is often interpreted as meaning that the evidence is sufficient to conclude that there is a greater than 50 per cent chance that the legal hypothesis in question is true (Myers, 2009). Because of the potentially severe risk of harm that false allegations pose to the wrongly accused and to children who make false reports of sexual abuse as a result of suggestive questioning, this standard seems too lax to many observers (Herman, 2009). McMahon (1999) has argued that the use of this standard to substantiate CSA in custody disputes is a violation of the accused parent's constitutional due process rights.

In summary, to protect non-abused children and those who are wrongly accused of sexual abuse from potentially severe harm at the hands of the state, it is time for legal decision-makers and policymakers to follow the lead of the US and Oregon Supreme Courts and the California State Legislature, and to raise evidentiary bars for the substantiation of CSA allegations in child protection contexts and their prosecution in criminal justice contexts. If the raising of evidentiary thresholds is combined with reforms designed to refocus CSA investigations on the collection and elicitation of corroboration, and away from a focus on the evaluation of children's believability, then it might be possible to significantly reduce false positives without any corresponding increase in false negatives.

---

[9] *Kennedy*, 2663.   [10] *State v. Southard*, 347 Or 127 (2009).

REFERENCES

American Academy of Child and Adolescent Psychiatry (1997) 'Practice Parameters for the Forensic Evaluation of Children and Adolescents Who May Have Been Physically or Sexually Abused', *Journal of American Academy of Child and Adolescent Psychiatry*, 36(10): 423–42.

BENSUSSAN, P. (2011) 'Forensic Psychiatry in France: The *Outreau* Case and False Allegations of Child Sexual Abuse', *Child and Adolescent Psychiatric Clinics of North America*, 20(3): 519–32.

BERLINER, L., and CONTE, J. R. (1993) 'Sexual Abuse Evaluations: Conceptual and Empirical Obstacles', *Child Abuse and Neglect*, 17(1): 111–25.

BERLINER, L., and LIEB, R. (2001) *Child Sexual Abuse Investigations: Testing Documentation Methods*, Olympia, WA: Washington State Institute for Public Policy.

BERNET, W. (1997) 'Case Study: Allegations of Abuse Created in a Single Interview', *Journal of American Academy of Child and Adolescent Psychiatry*, 36(7): 966–70.

BESHAROV, D. J. (1994) 'Responding to Child Sexual Abuse: The Need for a Balanced Approach', *The Future of Children*, 4(2): 135–55.

BOND, C. F. JR., and DEPAULO, B. M. (2006) 'Accuracy of Deception Judgments', *Personality and Social Psychology Review*, 10(3): 214–34.

BOND, C.F. JR., and DEPAULO, B. M. (2008) 'Individual Differences in Judging Deception: Accuracy and Bias', *Psychological Bulletin*, 134(4): 477–92.

CECI, S. J., and BRUCK, M. (1995) *Jeopardy in the Courtroom: A Scientific Analysis of Children's Testimony*, Washington, DC: American Psychological Association.

CECI, S. J., and BRUCK, M. (2000) 'Why Judges Must Insist on Electronically Preserved Recordings of Child Interviews', *Court Review*, 37(2): 10–12.

CROSS, T. P., WHITCOMB, D., and DE VOS, E. (1995) 'Criminal Justice Outcomes of Prosecution of Child Sexual Abuse: A Case Flow Analysis', *Child Abuse & Neglect*, 19(12): 1431–42.

EDELSTEIN, R. S., LUTEN, T. L., EKMAN, P., and GOODMAN, G. S. (2006) 'Detecting Lies in Children and Adults', *Law and Human Behavior*, 30(1): 1–10.

EVERSON, M. D., and BOAT, B. W. (1989) 'False Allegations of Sexual Abuse by Children and Adolescents', *Journal of American Academy of Child and Adolescent Psychiatry*, 28(2): 230–5.

EVERSON, M. D., and SANDOVAL, J. M. (2011) 'Forensic Child Sexual Abuse Evaluations: Assessing Subjectivity and Bias in Professional Judgements', *Child Abuse and Neglect*, 35(4): 287–98.

FALLER, K. C., and EVERSON, M. D. (2012) 'Contested Issues in the Evaluation of Child Sexual Abuse Allegations: Why Consensus on Best Practice Remains Elusive', *Journal of Child Sexual Abuse*, 21(1): 3–18.

FALLER, K. C., and HENRY, J. (2000) 'Child Sexual Abuse: A Case Study in Community Collaboration', *Child Abuse & Neglect*, 24(9): 1215–25.

FINLAYSON, L. M., and KOOCHER, G. P. (1991) 'Professional Judgment and Child Abuse Reporting in Sexual Abuse Cases', *Professional Psychology: Research and Practice*, 22(6): 464–72.

HASKETT, M. E., WAYLAND, K., HUTCHESON, J. S., and TAVANA, T. (1995) 'Substantiation of Sexual Abuse Allegations: Factors Involved in the Decision-making Process', *Journal of Child Sexual Abuse*, 4(2): 19–47.

HERMAN, S. (2005) 'Improving Decision Making in Forensic Child Sexual Abuse Evaluations', *Law and Human Behavior*, 29(1): 87–120.

HERMAN, S. (2009) 'Forensic Child Sexual Abuse Evaluations: Accuracy, Ethics, and Admissibility', in K. Kuehnle and M. Connell (eds) *The Evaluation of Child Sexual Abuse Allegations: A Comprehensive Guide to Assessment and Testimony*, Hoboken, NJ: John Wiley & Sons.

HERMAN, S. (2010) 'The Role of Corroborative Evidence in Child Sexual Abuse Evaluations', *Journal of Investigative Psychology and Offender Profiling*, 7(3): 189-212.

HERMAN, S., and FREITAS, T. R. (2010) 'Error Rates in Forensic Child Sexual Abuse Evaluations', *Psychological Injury and Law*, 3: 133-57.

HERSHKOWITZ, I., FISHER, S., LAMB, M. E., and HOROWITZ, D. (2007) 'Improving Credibility Assessment in Child Sexual Abuse Allegations: The Role of the NICHD Investigative Interview Protocol', *Child Abuse & Neglect*, 31(2): 99-110.

HORNER, T. M., and GUYER, M. J. (1991a) 'Prediction, Prevention, and Clinical Expertise in Child Custody Cases in which Allegations of Child Sexual Abuse Have Been Made: I. Predictable Rates of Diagnostic Error in Relation to Various Clinical Decision Making Strategies', *Family Law Quarterly*, 25(2): 217-52.

HORNER, T. M., and GUYER, M. J. (1991b) 'Prediction, Prevention, and Clinical Expertise in Child Custody Cases in which Allegations of Child Sexual Abuse Have Been Made: II. Prevalence Rates of Child Sexual Abuse and the Precision of "Tests" Constructed to Diagnose It', *Family Law Quarterly*, 25(3): 381-409.

HORNER, T. M., GUYER, M. J., and KALTER, N. M. (1992) 'Prediction, Prevention, and Clinical Expertise in Child Custody Cases in which Allegations of Child Sexual Abuse Have Been Made: III. Studies of Expert Opinion Formation', *Family Law Quarterly*, 26(2): 141-70.

HORNER, T. M., GUYER, M. J., and KALTER, N. M. (1993a) 'The Biases of Child Sexual Abuse Experts: Believing Is Seeing', *Bulletin of the American Academy of Psychiatry and the Law*, 21(3): 281-92.

HORNER, T. M., GUYER, M. J., and KALTER, N. M. (1993b) 'Clinical Expertise and the Assessment of Child Sexual Abuse', *Journal of American Academy of Child and Adolescent Psychiatry*, 32(5): 925-31.

JACKSON, H., and NUTTALL, R. (1993) 'Clinician Responses to Sexual Abuse Allegations', *Child Abuse & Neglect*, 17(1): 127-43.

KUEHNLE, K., and CONNELL, M. (eds) (2009) *The Evaluation of Child Sexual Abuse Allegations: A Comprehensive Guide to Assessment and Testimony*, Hoboken, NJ: John Wiley & Sons.

LAMB, M. E., HERSHKOWITZ, I., ORBACH, Y., and ESPLIN, P. W. (2008) *Tell Me What Happened: Structured Investigative Interviews of Child Victims and Witnesses*, Hoboken, NJ: John Wiley & Sons.

LAMB, M. E., ORBACH, Y., HERSHKOWITZ, I., ESPLIN, P. W., and HOROWITZ, D. (2007) 'A Structured Forensic Interview Protocol Improves the Quality and Informativeness of Investigative Interviews with Children: A Review of Research Using the NICHD Investigative Interview Protocol', *Child Abuse & Neglect*, 31(11-12): 1201-31.

LAMB, M. E., STERNBERG, K. J., ORBACH, Y., ESPLIN, P. W., and MITCHELL, S. (2002) 'Is Ongoing Feedback Necessary to Maintain the Quality of Investigative Interviews with Allegedly Abused Children?', *Applied Developmental Science*, 6(1): 35-41.

LANE, L. (1986) 'The Effects of the Abolition of the Corroboration Requirement in Child Sexual Assault Cases', *Catholic University Law Review*, 36: 793-808.

LANNING, K. (2001) *Child Molesters: A Behavioral Analysis for Law-Enforcement Officers Investigating the Sexual Exploitation of Children by Acquaintance Molesters*, 4th edn, Alexandria, VA: National Center for Missing & Exploited Children.

LIPPERT, T., CROSS, T. P., JONES, L. M., and WALSH, W. A. (2010) 'Suspect Confession of Child Sexual Abuse to Investigators', *Child Maltreatment*, 15(2): 161-70.

LONDON, K., BRUCK, M., WRIGHT, D. B., and CECI, S. J. (2008) 'Review of the Contemporary Literature on How Children Report Sexual Abuse to Others: Findings, Methodological Issues, and Implications for Forensic Interviewers', *Memory*, 16(1): 29–47.

LYON, T. D., AHERN, E. C., and SCURICH, N. (2012) 'Interviewing Children vs. Tossing Coins: Accurately Assessing the Diagnosticity of Children's Disclosures of Abuse', *Journal of Child Sexual Abuse*, 21(1): 19–44.

MCGRAW, J. M., and SMITH, H. A. (1992) 'Child Sexual Abuse Allegations amidst Divorce and Custody Proceedings: Refining the Validation Process', *Journal of Child Sexual Abuse*, 1(1): 49–62.

MCMAHON, C. (1999) 'Due Process: Constitutional Rights and the Stigma of Sexual Abuse Allegations in Child Custody Proceedings', *The Catholic Lawyer*, 39: 153–99.

MYERS, J. E. B. (2009) 'Expert Psychological Testimony in Child Sexual Abuse Trials', in B. L. Bottoms, C. J. Najdowski, and G. S. Goodman (eds) *Children as Victims, Witnesses, and Offenders: Psychological Science and the Law*, New York: The Guilford Press.

NATHAN, D. (2005) 'I'm Sorry: A Long-delayed Apology from One of the Accusers in the Notorious McMartin Pre-school Molestation Case', *Los Angeles Times*, 30 October. Available online at <http://articles.latimes.com/2005/oct/30/magazine/tm-mcmartin44> [accessed May 2016].

NATHAN, D., and SNEDEKER, M. (2001) *Satan's Silence: Ritual Abuse and the Making of a Modern American Witch Hunt*, Lincoln, NE: Authors Choice Press.

NICOLSON, D., and BLACKIE, J. (2013) 'Corroboration in Scots Law: "Archaic Rule" or "Invaluable Safeguard"?' *Edinburgh Law Review*, 17(2): 152–83.

PILLAI, M. (2002) 'Allegations of Abuse: The Need for Responsible Practice', *Medical Science and the Law*, 42(4): 149–59.

QUINN, K. M. (2002) 'Interviewing Children for Suspected Sexual Abuse', in D. Schetky and E. P. Benedek (eds) *Principles and Practice of Child and Adolescent Forensic Psychiatry*, Washington, DC: American Psychiatric Association.

RABINOWITZ, D. (2003) *No Crueler Tyrannies: Accusation, False Witness, and Other Terrors of Our Times*, New York: Free Press.

REALMUTO, G. M., and WESCOE, S. (1992) 'Agreement among Professionals about a Child's Sexual Abuse Status: Interviews with Sexually Anatomically Correct Dolls as Indicators of Abuse', *Child Abuse & Neglect*, 16(5): 719–25.

REALMUTO, G. M., JENSEN, J. B., and WESCOE, S. (1990) 'Specificity and Sensitivity of Sexually Anatomically Correct Dolls in Substantiating Abuse: A Pilot Study', *Journal of American Academy of Child and Adolescent Psychiatry*, 29(5): 743–6.

SHUMAKER, K. R. (2000) 'Measured Professional Competence between and among Different Mental Health Disciplines when Evaluating and Making Recommendations in Cases of Suspected Child Sexual Abuse', Unpublished PhD thesis. Available from ProQuest Dissertations and Theses database (UMI No. 9950748).

STALLER, K. M., and FALLER, K. (eds) (2010) *Seeking Justice in Child Sexual Abuse: Shifting Burdens and Sharing Responsibilities*, New York: Columbia University Press.

STALLER, K. M., and VANDERVORT, F. E. (2010) 'Professional Practitioners' Views on Videotaping: Capturing and Conveying a Child's Story', in K. M. Staller and K. Faller (eds) *Seeking Justice in Child Sexual Abuse: Shifting Burdens and Sharing Responsibilities*, New York: Columbia University Press.

STEVENSON, K. M., LEUNG, P., and CHEUNG, K. M. (1992) 'Competency-based Evaluation of Interviewing Skills in Child Sexual Abuse Cases', *Social Work Research and Abstracts*, 28(3): 11–16.

STOLTENBORGH, M., VAN IJZENDOORN, M. H., EUSER, E. M., and BAKERMANS-KRANENBURG, M. J. (2011) 'A Global Perspective on Child Sexual Abuse: Meta-analysis of Prevalence around the World', *Child Maltreatment*, 16(2): 79–101.

TALWAR, V., LEE, K., BALA, N., and LINDSAY, R. C. L. (2006) 'Adults' Judgments of Children's Coached Reports', *Law and Human Behavior*, 30(5): 561–70.

VRIJ, A. (2005) 'Criteria-based Content Analysis: A Qualitative Review of the First 37 Studies', *Psychology, Public Policy, & Law*, 11(1): 3–41.

WALSH, W. A., JONES, L., CROSS, T., and LIPPERT, T. (2010) 'Prosecuting Child Sexual Abuse: The Importance of Evidence Type', *Crime and Delinquency*, 56(3): 436–54.

WARREN, A. R., and MARSIL, D. F. (2002) 'Why Children's Suggestibility Remains a Serious Concern', *Law and Contemporary Problems*, 65(1): 127–47.

18

ADVANCES IN LIE DETECTION

LIMITATIONS AND POTENTIAL FOR INVESTIGATING ALLEGATIONS OF ABUSE

Galit Nahari

Suppose a woman goes to the police station and complains that, a month ago, on Saturday night, she was raped by her next-door neighbour in the car park of their building. The woman claims that she was shocked and embarrassed after the event, and thus told nobody about it. There are no witnesses to the alleged rape and there is no evidence to support the complaint of the woman. The police interrogate the neighbour, who denies raping the woman or ever having had a sexual relationship with her, and claims that he was out of town on that specific night, sitting on a beach alone. Obviously, it is impossible that both of them are telling the truth and quite likely that one of them is lying. Since there is no evidence to support the woman's complaint or the neighbour's alibi, this is a classic case of one person's word against another's. Can we tell who is lying?

This 'word against word' situation is only one example of the types of case in which detecting lies is a critical component in the forensic setting. In other situations, one may suspect the veracity of a key testimony in court or of a confession (such as when an interviewee claims that he or she confessed under pressure). An erroneous judgment regarding veracity in such cases might lead to acquitting guilty suspects or—arguably, even more seriously—to conviction of innocents. In the current chapter, I will first discuss our ability to discriminate between truths and lies without the use of tools. Subsequently, I will review, from a bird's-eye view, a variety of tools for lie detection and interrogation strategies, and describe their advantages, pitfalls, and limitations. Finally, I will raise a few suggestions for improving our ability to detect lies.

ONE CAN(NOT) TELL WHEN SOMEONE LIES

What would you say if the interrogator who interviews the neighbour and the woman in the rape case were to suggest flipping a coin to decide whether his interviewees are lying or telling the truth? You would probably argue, rightly, that it is absurd and unacceptable to rely on the turn of a coin in making such an important decision. One should note, therefore, that an attempt to distinguish a lie from truth, without using tools, is often not much more reliable than flipping a coin. A meta-analysis of 206 studies (Bond and DePaulo, 2006) showed an average accuracy rate of only 54 per cent. Vrij (2008), who compared the results of seventy-nine studies, concluded that, compared to laypersons, professionals (such as law enforcement personnel) are more confident, but only slightly more accurate (55.9 per cent compared to 54.3 per cent) in detecting lies.

Why are we so poor at detecting lies? There are several potential explanations, some of which relate to the interviewees and others, to the observers.

REASONS RELATED TO THE INTERVIEWEES

Subtle differences between liars and truth-tellers Differences in verbal and non-verbal behaviours between liars and truth-tellers are small and unreliable. DePaulo and colleagues' (2003) comprehensive meta-analysis, which was based on 120 independent samples, examined 158 cues to deception (behaviours or impressions). Most of those deception cues showed no links, or only weak links, to deception. An unequivocal cue, such as Pinocchio's growing nose, does not exist in reality (Vrij, Granhag, and Porter, 2010). The scarcity of objective cues to deception makes the task of lie detection difficult.

Embedded lies and concealments Liars often embed their lies within truthful details (Vrij, 2008; Leins, Fisher, and Ross, 2013). Instead of telling an outright lie (that is, one in which all details are falsehood), they change only specific details in a truthful account (Vrij et al., 2010) or simply conceal vital details in the account (DePaulo et al., 1996). Differences between embedded or concealed lies and truths are small, and thus it is difficult to detect these kind of lies.

Control of behaviour Liars may attempt to make a credible impression, by suppressing behaviours that are related to deception, while showing behaviours that are related to honesty. For example, to give a credible impression, liars might try to look calm and relaxed (Hartwig et al., 2010), to seek eye contact (Mann et al., 2012), or to provide many details (Nahari, Vrij, and Fisher, 2012). These attempts to look honest make the task of uncovering lies harder.

REASONS RELATED TO THE OBSERVER

Wrongful theories and beliefs People have beliefs about how liars behave. Some of these beliefs are wrong. For example, one of the most popular beliefs, internationally, is that liars look away while talking (Global Deception Research Team, 2006; Vrij, 2008), although that is an unreliable cue for deception (DePaulo et al., 2003). Obviously, using unreliable cues may lead to wrong decisions.

Different rules for different cases Interviewees differ in their behaviours while lying. For example, African Americans and Hispanic citizens display higher levels of avoiding eye contact and hand gestures than do Caucasians (R. R. Johnson, 2006), and highly fantasy-prone individuals are better at creating a sense of authenticity than low fantasy-prone individuals (Schelleman-Offermans and Merckelbach, 2010). Moreover, deception behaviours vary also across situations. For example, some deceptions cues (such as increase in blinking) appear only in high-stakes situations (DePaulo et al., 2003). Consequently, using a cue without considering who the interviewee is and what the situation is might be useless for lie detection, or may even impair it.

What you see is not always what you get One can observe only the external behaviour, but never its internal cause, and thus may wrongly interpret the observed behaviour. For example, a suspect who provides an alibi that is poor in detail might be a truth-teller who barely remembers the alibi events (Olson and Charman, 2012) or a liar who is afraid to provide details that will uncover his or her lie (Nahari et al., 2012). This phenomenon of attributing a mistaken interpretation to a behaviour was termed 'Othello's error' by Ekman (2001), based on Othello's mistaken assumption that Desdemona's expression of fear was the reaction of a woman caught in betrayal.

Judgemental biases Human judgements are vulnerable to a host of biases (Gilovich, Griffin, and Kahneman, 2002). Lie detection, as a specific case of human judgement, is no exception in this sense. There is empirical evidence for cognitive biases in credibility judgements—notably, the confirmation bias (that is, the tendency to unconsciously seek and interpret behavioural data in a way that verifies the first impression or prior expectations about the object in question). For example, Kassin, Goldstein, and Savitsky (2003) showed that mock interrogators, manipulated to expect that the suspect is guilty, selected more guilt-presumptive questions, used more interrogation techniques, exerted more pressure to get a confession, and judged the suspect to be guilty more often, as compared with mock interrogators manipulated to expect the suspect to be innocent. Levine, Asada, and Park (2006) showed that participants who were told that an interviewee was lying attributed to the interviewee less eye contact during the interview as compared with participants who did not know whether the interviewee lied or told the truth. Finally, Porter, ten Brinke, and Gustaw (2010) demonstrated that participants required less evidence to arrive at a guilty verdict and were more confident in their verdict for defendants whom they considered had an untrustworthy appearance[1] than for those whom they considered to appear trustworthy.

Subjective glasses for judgements People may differ from each other in the way in which they perceive and interpret the deceptive cues, and consequently make different judgements in the very same case (Nahari, Glicksohn, and Nachson, 2010). For example, Nahari (2012) demonstrated that the same statement was assessed by professional lie detectors (such as police officers) as being poor in detail and by laypersons (students) as being rich in detail, while Baker, ten Brinke, and Porter (2013) showed that emotionally intelligent people are easily fooled by deceivers. Judgements, therefore, can be biased by the personal characteristics of the observer, such as experience, personality, or attitudes.

---

[1] Based on information about an individual's character gleaned from facial expressions and features. Porter, ten Brinke, and Gustaw (2010) note that assessments of trustworthiness based on the face alone are often instantaneous, but highly fallible.

TOOLS FOR DETECTING LIES

To improve our poor ability to uncover lies, scientists and forensic experts have attempted, for many years, to develop lie detection instruments and methods. The polygraph is probably the most widely known and used instrument in criminal investigations, but there are many other, old and new, lie detection tools. Some of the tools are based on verbal behaviours, some on non-verbal behaviours, and others on psycho-physiological responses. There are also initial attempts to develop behavioural tools for detecting lies and for interrogation strategies. I will briefly present here prime examples of tools for lie detection.

VERBAL TOOLS

Verbal tools ignore the non-verbal and paraverbal behaviours, and focus only on content: What do the interviewees say? How do they say it? The common ground of verbal tools for lie detection is that they are all based on the assumption that truths and lies differ in their content, and suggest a content criteria to distinguish between them.

Criteria-based content analysis (CBCA) (Steller and Kohnken, 1989) This tool consists of nineteen criteria that are assumed to apply in truthful accounts more than in false accounts. For example, truthful accounts are expected to be coherent and consistent, but to be provided in a non-chronological sequence. The criteria are based on the assumption that real experiences are difficult to fabricate and that liars who are keen to impress as honest show behaviours (such as avoid admitting lack of memory) that they wrongly perceive as consistent with truthfulness. The averaged accuracy rate of CBCA, as has been examined in twenty-four studies, was 71 per cent for detecting truths and 71 per cent for detecting lies (Vrij and Ganis, 2014). As part of the statement validity analysis (SVA) tool, CBCA is accepted as evidence in some North American and European jurisdictions' courts, including Germany, the Netherlands, and Sweden (Vrij, 2008).

Reality monitoring (RM) (Sporer, 2004) Reality monitoring is the only verbal tool with a strong theoretical framework (M. K. Johnson, 2006). Originally, the concept of 'reality monitoring' referred to the process through which a person goes when he or she determines the origin of his or her *own* memory as a perceptual experience (that is, a memory of an event that happened in reality) or as self-generated thought or imagination (that is, a memory of an event that did not happen in reality) According to RM, the former are characterized by more contextual attributes (such as where and when the event took place), and perceptual attributes (such as what he or she felt, smelt, or saw when the event took place), whereas the latter are characterized by more cognitive operational attributes (such as thoughts and reasons). Empirical evidence (M. K. Johnson, 2006) shows that people use the same indications for determining the origin of *others'* memories (interpersonal reality monitoring) as true or false, and thus the potential of RM as a lie detector tool was recognized by scholars investigating deception.

The RM lie detection tool consists of a set of content criteria for assessing the presence of contextual, perceptual, and cognitive operation attributes, as well as the realism of the described event, the general clarity of the description, and the ability to reconstruct the event based on the given information. Vrij (2008), who reviewed ten laboratory RM studies, reported an average accuracy rate of 72 per cent for truths and 66 per cent for lies (see also Masip et al., 2005). These are encouraging results for its value as a tool in the criminal interrogation setting, although to date we are not aware of it being used by 'professional lie catchers' practitioners for this purpose.

Scientific content analysis (SCAN) (Sapir, 2000) This tool was developed by Avinoam Sapir, a former polygraph examiner in the Israeli police. It is a popular tool among practitioners and used worldwide. The tools draws on many criteria, some of which are indicators for truth (such as denial of allegation) and others of which are indicators for lie (such as spontaneous corrections). However, few studies have examined the validity of SCAN. In one laboratory experiment, SCAN did not distinguish truths from lies (Nahari, Vrij, and Fisher, 2012).

Verifiability approach (Nahari, Vrij, and Fisher, 2014a, 2014b) The verifiability approach suggests examining the extent to which the interviewee provides details that can be checked. According to this approach, when liars try to provide many details so as to make an honest impression, they prefer to provide details that are difficult to verify (such as 'I saw a black Audi driving in Shenkin Street') rather than to provide details that are easy to verify (such as 'I phoned my friend Fred at 10.30 this morning'). In support of the verifiability approach, Nahari and colleagues (2014a, 2014b) showed that it is possible to differentiate between liars and truth-tellers by means of the verifiability criterion.

NON-VERBAL TOOLS

Two well-known non-verbal tools will be presented: one focuses on face expressions; the other focuses on body language in general (not only facial expressions).

Facial emotional expressions (Ekman, 2003) Micro-expressions are very brief facial expressions that occur when a person either deliberately or unconsciously conceals a feeling. According to Ekman (2003), micro-expressions are very useful signs of concealed emotions. However, facial emotional expression is not appropriate for discriminating true and false forensic accounts, such as alibis or confessions. As Ekman (2003: 218–19) emphasized:

> [A] mistake is to presume that concealed emotion is evidence that a person is lying about the topic of interest to the interviewer. We need to be careful to avoid what I have called Othello's error... The fear of being disbelieved looks the same as the fear of being caught... Lying about the topic of interest should be the last, not the first, explanation of why a micro expression has occurred.

Behavioural analysis interview (BAI) (Inbau et al., 2013) This tool is unique in that it considers both verbal and non-verbal responses. Its interview protocol includes behaviour-provoking questions. It assumes that liars feel more nervous and uncomfortable than truth-tellers in an interrogation situation, and thus will show more nervous behaviours, such as crossing their legs and shifting about in their chairs, and will provide answers that sound less sincere. Truth-tellers, assumed to be relaxed and thus to establish eye contact, lean forward, etc. The few lab experiments that have tested BAI have, however, refuted its principal value, finding it unreliable as a tool for detecting lies—and even as impairing lie detection accuracy (Vrij and Ganis, 2014). The main criticism of this tool is that it lacks theoretical backing and is based on behavioural cues already regarded as not valid for detecting lies (such as averting gaze).

PSYCHO-PHYSIOLOGICAL DETECTION METHODS

Psycho-physiological detection methods rely on physiological responses associated with deception. These methods differ in two general parameters: the *physiological channels* that are measured; and the *paradigm*, or *questioning protocol*, which is used to produce these physiological responses.

Physiological channels Each of the various psychophysiological detection methods provide different measures. Some methods measure the activity of the autonomic nervous system (such as skin conductance, perspiration, blood pressure, and breathing patterns), while other methods measure the activity of the central nervous system (brain activity).

Paradigm There are two main prototype paradigms (see Ben-Shakhar, 2012). The first is designed for detecting deception by means of direct questions about the involvement in a crime ('Did you kill Mrs Smith on Thursday night?') and is mostly associated with the comparison questions technique (CQT). In the CQT (Raskin, 1989), the psychological responses for two main question types are compared: *relevant questions*, which are specific questions that tap into the issue of interest ('Did you do X?'); and *comparison questions*, which are vague and refer to long time periods ('Have you ever done X?'). The general assumption in using the CQT is that truth-tellers produce more physiological arousal to the comparison questions relative to the relevant question, while liars show less arousal to the comparison questions relative to the relevant questions.

The second paradigm is suitable for detecting concealed knowledge ('Did Mrs Smith wear a blue skirt on the night she was murdered?'), and has been labelled 'guilty knowledge test' (GKT) or 'concealed information test' (CIT). The CIT (Lykken, 1959) utilizes a series of multiple-choice questions, each having one relevant alternative (such as a feature of the crime under investigation) and several neutral (control) alternatives. These relevant items are significant only for knowledgeable (guilty) individuals. Significant stimuli elicit enhanced physiological responses (that is, orienting responses), and thus if the suspect's physiological responses to the relevant alternative are consistently more marked than to the neutral alternatives, knowledge about the event (that is, the crime) is inferred.

Polygraph The polygraph instrument provides autonomic nervous system measures and is typically applied by law-enforcement agencies alongside the CQT questioning protocol. Yet CQT is considered by most researchers as lacking scientific foundation (see, for example, Ben-Shakhar, 2012). The main criticism against using the CQT is that both guilty and innocent examinees are highly aroused by the relevant questions

('Did you do it?'), and thus may display similar physiological responses to these questions. The validity of the polygraph test using CQT is thus controversial. Vrij (2008) summarized published reviews of CQT and showed that, in laboratory studies, 74–82 per cent of guilty examinees and 60–66 per cent of innocent examinees were correctly classified; in field studies, 83–89 per cent of guilty examinees and 53–75 per cent of innocent examinees were correctly classified. Although accuracy rates for guilty detection seem reasonable, the low accuracy for innocence detection is worrying. Yet CQT studies themselves suffered from a host of methodological problems (Ben-Shakhar, 2002; Vrij, 2008) and thus it is difficult to draw generalizations from them.

Polygraph measurement is applied also by using the CIT paradigm, mostly by academic researchers. The CIT has a stronger theoretical underpinning than the CQT and intensive laboratory studies support its validity. Vrij (2008), who summarized reviews of CIT laboratory studies, reported accuracy rates that ranged from 76 per cent to 86 per cent among guilty examinees and from 83 per cent to 99 per cent among innocent examinees. In comparison to the CQT, in CIT applications, the danger of incriminating innocents is lower. However, the external validity of CIT studies is questionable. For example, unlike laboratory studies, in realistic criminal investigations, polygraph tests are often administered after a relatively long delay. Time delay affects the memory of guilty examinees and decreases the effectiveness of the test (Nahari and Ben-Shakhar, 2011). Other than in Japan, where the CIT is routinely applied by the national police, the application of the CIT by law enforcement agencies is rare and limited (Ben-Shakhar, 2012). The main criticism of CIT relates to its applicability to real criminal investigations, among others, because of the difficulty in identifying a sufficient number of silent relevant items that are known only to the investigators and the perpetrator.

Neuroscience techniques Investigators have recently begun using the CIT protocol (or variants of CIT) in combination with neuroscience techniques. For two decades, there has been extensive research using CIT with electroencephalography (EEG) and lately a few attempts have been made to apply CIT also with functional magnetic resonance imaging (fMRI).

Event-related potential (ERP) is an electrophysiological reaction, which appears in the EEG in response to the occurrence of a discrete event (a stimulus). The P300 is a special ERP component that results whenever a meaningful and rare stimulus is presented, and is used in CIT to detect concealed knowledge.[2] Functional MRI measures the changes in regional cerebral blood flow, which indicate anatomical location of brain activation in a certain task.[3]

Measuring brain activity may provide us with a better understanding of the cognitive process that underlies deception behaviour and this is a sufficient reason to conduct more deception research with these neuroscience technologies. Yet one should note that the limitations of the CIT cannot be solved simply by changing the measurement channel (central rather peripheral nervous system) and that CIT that is applied alongside neuroscience techniques is no more accurate than CIT that is applied in

---

[2] For a review, see Rosenfeld (2011). [3] For a review, see Gamer (2011).

combination with the polygraph instrument (Ben-Shakhar, 2012). Neuroscience techniques (especially fMRI) are, however, more complex and expensive to conduct than the polygraph test, and also raise novel ethical issues (for example a brain scan can expose medical information). Thus, when considering their application for forensic purposes, a significant advantage of the former over the latter is needed. We may reach that point in the future, but we are definitely not there yet.

BEHAVIOURAL TOOLS

There are initial attempts to develop behavioural methods for detecting lies. I present here one example, which is based on CIT.

Symptom validity test (SVT) The SVT is based on asking examinees, who deny knowledge of some critical items (that is, concealed information), to guess these items. Examinees are presented with a series of questions regarding critical items. Each question has two alternative answers (one alternative is the correct answer). Thus an unknowledgeable individual is expected to guess the answers on the SVT and thus give about 50 per cent correct answers (chance level), while a knowledgeable individual will be unable to ignore his or her knowledge and will consequently deviate from chance-level performance (that is, 50 per cent). The technique has been used to detect malingering in various contexts and was recently successfully adopted for detecting concealed information (Meijer et al., 2007; Nahari and Ben-Shakhar, 2011).

GENERAL ASSESSMENT OF LIE DETECTION TOOLS

In principle, tools can provide us with more objective, systematic, and standard means for making veracity judgements. No tool is 100 per cent accurate, but taking into account that the accuracy rate of detecting lies without using tools is only slightly above chance, accuracy rates of 70 per cent or 80 per cent are considerable. Yet it is still appropriate to question whether or not the existing tools overcome the problems, raised in the preceding section, regarding the veracity of judgements that are made without them.

Subtle differences between liars and truth-tellers One significant advantage of using tools over detecting lies without tools is the potential ability of the former to measure behaviours and responses that are difficult (such as level of richness in detail) or impossible (such as skin conductance) to assess without them. In this way, tools enable us to observe deceptive and truthful behaviours that are difficult to spot with the 'naked eye'.

Researchers have not stopped there, in *measuring* existing differences, but have recently suggested interrogation strategies that have a differential influence on liars and truth-tellers, and consequently *actively increase* the existing differences between the groups. For example, differences between liars and truth-tellers increased when suspects were asked to provide their accounts in a reverse chronological order (Vrij et al., 2012), or when suspects were warned that the verifiability of their accounts would be checked (Nahari et al., 2014b).

Embedded lies and concealments By their nature, embedded lies and concealments contain truthful content details (that is, perceptual details), and thus affect directly the efficiency of verbal tools. Yet providing truthful details may affect also non-verbal tools, *indirectly*, because providing truthful details is not expected to be accompanied by non-verbal cues of deception.

Control of behaviour When liars are aware of the mechanism of the method applied, they may try to countermeasure it and consequently decrease its efficiency to detect their lies. Evidence for the destructive effect of physical (such as pressing the toe to the floor) and mental (such as counting in reverse) countermeasures were found regarding CQT and CIT applied with polygraphs (Honts and Kircher, 1994; Honts et al., 1996) and CIT applied with EEG (Rosenfeld et al., 2004) or fMRI (Ganis et al., 2011). Informing participants regarding the working of the CBCA decreased its efficiency (Vrij et al., 2004). There are a few successful attempts to develop methods that are resistant to countermeasures, including in relation to the CIT applied in combination with EEG (Rosenfeld, 2011) and the verifiability approach (Nahari et al., 2014b).

Theoretical and empirical weaknesses Most of the lie detection tools lack a theoretical underpinning. One may argue that, from a practical perspective, this is not a problem as long as the tool is effective in discriminating between lies and truths. Yet the validity of most of the tools that are in use by practitioners to date was rarely or never examined empirically—or, worse, was examined and found unreliable. There are, however, tools that were supported empirically (such as RM, CIT), but were never or only rarely applied in practice.

Different rules for different cases When applying a tool, one must take into account the mechanism of the tool and its limitations. For example, when there has been a long period of time past between the investigation and the criminal event, one may avoid using tools that are based on memory (such as RM and CIT), and when a suspect has difficulties in language, one may avoid using verbal tools. Ignoring the limitations of tools may lead to erroneous decisions.

What you see is not always what you get There is no tool that can measure deception directly. Tools can measure only *correlates* of deception (such as physiological changes, presence of contextual details). This understanding is critical for a valid interpretation of the tool's output. For example, CIT examines knowledge of concealed information (rather than deception), based on the assumption that only the criminal holds concealed knowledge. However, concealed information can be leaked to innocents (Nahari and Ben-Shakhar, 2011). Awareness that CIT examines *knowledge* rather than *deception* leads to consideration of alternative explanations to recognition of concealed knowledge.

Judgemental biases Using a tool to make a decision may have the face validity of objectiveness, but, in fact, most of the tools involve a human decision-making process (such as interpretation of plots); thus judgements that are based on tools are not free from biases. Indeed, assessment of RM criteria found them to be influenced by the first impression of participants regarding richness in details of the account (Nahari and Ben-Shakhar, 2013) or by extra-domain information (Bogaard et al., 2014), and the interpretation of polygraph test outputs were influenced by prior expectations regarding the guiltiness of the examinee (Elaad, Ginton, and Ben-Shakhar, 1994).

Subjective glasses for judgements I believe that personal characteristics, such as attitudes and personality traits, may affect decision-making that is based on tools as much as they affect decision-making that is not. Unfortunately, despite its importance, studies in this area are scarce. One example is the recent study of Nahari and Vrij (2014), in which the authors showed that people assess the RM criteria in accordance with their own experience in telling stories: the richer in detail their own stories were, the more critical they were in judging others' stories.

TAKE-HOME MESSAGES FROM THE RESEARCH

The current chapter has offered a glance through the lie-detection literature. It has reviewed, and discussed, old and new methods and directions for detecting lies, and has indicated their accuracy, pitfalls, and advantages. To close the chapter, I will raise several points and suggestions that I consider to be essential for improving our ability to detect lies and to reduce judgemental errors.

Use and not abuse Using tools, when done properly, might improve lie detection. Yet one should apply only those tools that have been tested empirically and found reliable, should consider the limitations of the tools, and their suitability to the specific situation and interviewee, and should take into account alternative explanations for their results.

Active awareness of judgemental biases The danger of biases, whether judgements are made with tools or without them, must be kept in mind. It is difficult to avoid biases, but there are several actions that can (and should) be applied to reduce their influence (such as, when possible, using *independent* and *blind* evaluations of a tool's outputs)

Generating, rather than measuring, deception cues More efforts should be invested in developing interrogation strategies for increasing the differences between liars and truth-tellers. Applying such strategies together with tools may increase the efficiency of the latter.

Exploiting liars' strategies One may use strategies that are employed by liars 'against' them, as an indicator for deception. For example, when liars provide detailed accounts as a strategy, they usually provide unverifiable details. One can use the appearance of many unverifiable details as an indicator of possible deception.

REFERENCES

Baker, A., ten Brinke, L., and Porter, S. (2013) 'Will Get Fooled Again: Emotionally Intelligent People Are Easily Duped by High-stakes Deceivers', *Legal and Criminological Psychology*, 18(2): 300–13.

BEN-SHAKHAR, G. (2002) 'A Critical Review of the Control Questions Test (CQT)', in M. Kleiner (ed.) *Handbook of Polygraph Testing*, London: Academic Press.

BEN-SHAKHAR, G. (2012) 'Current Research and Potential Applications of the Concealed Information Test: An Overview', *Frontiers in Psychology*, 3: 1–11.

BOGAARD, G., MEIJER, E. H., VRIJ, A., BROERS, N. J., and MERCKELBACH, H. (2014) 'Contextual Bias in Verbal Credibility Assessment: Criteria-based Content Analysis, Reality Monitoring and Scientific Content Analysis', *Applied Cognitive Psychology*, 28(1): 79–90.

BOND, C. F., and DEPAULO, B. M. (2006) 'Accuracy of Deception Judgments', *Personality and Social Psychology Review*, 10(3): 214–34.

DEPAULO, B. M., KASHY, D. A., KIRKENDOL, S. E., WYER, M. M., and EPSTEIN, J. A. (1996) 'Lying in Everyday Life', *Journal of Personality and Social Psychology*, 70(5): 979–95.

DEPAULO, B. M., LINDSAY, J. J., MALONE, B. E., MUHLENBRUCK, L., CHARLTON, K., and COOPER, H. (2003) 'Cues to Deception', *Psychological Bulletin*, 129(1): 74–118.

EKMAN, P. (2001) *Telling Lies: Clues to Deceit in the Marketplace, Politics, and Marriage*, New York: Norton & Co.

EKMAN, P. (2003) 'Darwin, Deception, and Facial Expression', *Annals of the New York Academy of Sciences*, 1000: 205–21.

ELAAD, E., GINTON, A., and BEN-SHAKHAR, G. (1994) 'The Effects of Prior Expectations and Outcome Knowledge on Polygraph Examiners' Decisions', *Journal of Behavioral Decision Making*, 7: 279–92.

GAMER, M. (2011) 'Detecting of Deception and Concealed Information Using Neuroimaging Techniques', in B. Verschuere, G. Ben-Shakhar, and E.Meijer (eds) *Memory Detection: Theory and Application of the Concealed Information Test*, Cambridge: Cambridge University Press.

GANIS, G., ROSENFELD, J. P., MEIXNER, J., KIEVIT, R. A., and SCHENDAN, H. E. (2011) 'Lying in the Scanner: Covert Countermeasures Disrupt Deception Detection by Functional Magnetic Resonance Imaging', *Neuroimage*, 55(1): 312–19.

GILOVICH, T., GRIFFIN, D., and KAHNEMAN, D. (eds) (2002) *Heuristics and Biases: The Psychology of Intuitive Judgment*, Cambridge: Cambridge University Press.

Global Deception Research Team (2006) 'A World of Lies', *Journal of Cross-cultural Psychology*, 37(1): 60–74.

HARTWIG, M., GRANHAG, P. A., STRÖMWALL, L., and DOERING, N. (2010) 'Impression and Information Management: On the Strategic Self-regulation of Innocent and Guilty Suspects', *The Open Criminology Journal*, 3(1): 10–16.

HONTS, C. R., and KIRCHER, J. C. (1994) 'Mental and Physical Countermeasures Reduce the Accuracy of Polygraph Tests', *Journal of Applied Psychology*, 79(2): 252–59.

HONTS, C. R., DEVITT, M. K., WINBUSH, M., and KIRCHER, J. C. (1996) 'Mental and Physical Countermeasures Reduce the Accuracy of the Concealed Knowledge Test', *Psychophysiology*, 33(1): 84–92.

INBAU, F. E., REID, J. E., BUCKLEY, J. P., and JAYNE, B. C. (2013) *Criminal Interrogation and Confessions*, Burlington, MA: Jones & Bartlett.

JOHNSON, M. K. (2006) 'Memory and Reality', *American Psychologist*, 61(8): 760–71.

JOHNSON, R. R. (2006) 'Confounding Influences on Police Detection of Suspiciousness', *Journal of Criminal Justice*, 34(4): 435–42.

KASSIN, S. M., GOLDSTEIN, C. C., and SAVITSKY, K. (2003) 'Behavioral Confirmation in the Interrogation Room: On the Dangers of Presuming Guilt', *Law and Human Behavior*, 27(2): 187–203.

LEINS, D. A., FISHER, P. A., and ROSS, S. J. (2013) 'Exploring Liars' Strategies for Creating Deceptive Reports', *Legal and Criminological Psychology*, 18(1): 141–51.

LEVINE, T. R., ASADA, K. J. K., and PARK, H. S. (2006) 'The Lying Chicken and the Gaze Avoidant Egg: Eye Contact, Deception, and Causal Order', *Southern Communication Journal*, 71(4): 401–11.

LYKKEN, D. T. (1959) 'The GSR in the Detection of Guilt', *Journal of Applied Psychology*, 43(6): 385–8.

MANN, S., VRIJ, A., LEAL, S., GRANHAG, P. A., WARMELINK, L., and FORRESTER, D. (2012) 'Windows to the Soul? Deliberate Eye Contact as a Cue to Deceit', *Journal of Nonverbal Behavior*, 36(3): 205–15.

MASIP, J., SPORER, S. L., GARRIDO, E., and HERRERO, C. (2005) 'The Detection of Deception with the Reality Monitoring Approach: A Review of the Empirical Evidence', *Psychology, Crime and Law*, 11: 99–122.

MEIJER, E. H., SMULDERS, F. T., JOHNSTON, J. E., and MERCKELBACH, H. L. (2007) 'Combining Skin Conductance and Forced Choice in the Detection of Concealed Information', *Psychophysiology*, 44(5): 814–22.

NAHARI, G. (2012) 'Elaborations on Credibility Judgments by Professional Lie Detectors and Laypersons: Strategies of Judgment and Justification', *Psychology, Crime and Law*, 18: 567–77.

NAHARI, G., and BEN-SHAKHAR, G. (2011) 'Psychophysiological and Behavioral Measures for Detecting Concealed Information: The Role of Memory for Crime Details', *Psychophysiology*, 48(6): 733–44.

NAHARI, G., and BEN-SHAKHAR, G. (2013) 'Primacy Effect in Credibility Judgments: The Vulnerability of Verbal Cues to Biased Interpretations', *Applied Cognitive Psychology*, 27(2): 247–55.

NAHARI, G., and VRIJ, A. (2014) 'Are You as Good as Me at Telling a Story? Individual Differences in Interpersonal Reality-monitoring', *Psychology, Crime and Law*, 20: 573–83.

NAHARI, G., GLICKSOHN, J., and NACHSON, I. (2010) 'Credibility Judgments of Narratives: Language, Plausibility, and Absorption', *American Journal of Psychology*, 123(3): 319–35.

NAHARI, G., VRIJ, A., and FISHER, R. P. (2012) 'Does the Truth Come out in the Writing? Scan as a Lie Detection Tool'. *Law and Human Behavior*, 36(1): 68–76.

NAHARI, G., VRIJ, A., and FISHER, R. P. (2014a) 'Exploiting Liars' Verbal Strategies by Examining Unverifiable Details', *Legal and Criminological Psychology*, 19(2): 227–39.

NAHARI, G., VRIJ, A., and FISHER, R. P. (2014b) 'The Verifiability Approach: Countermeasures Facilitate Its Ability to Discriminate between Truths and Lies', *Applied Cognitive Psychology*, 28(1): 122–8.

OLSON, E. A., and CHARMAN, S. D. (2012) ' "But Can You Prove It?" Examining the Quality of Innocent Suspects' Alibis', *Psychology, Crime and Law*, 18(5): 453–71.

PORTER, S., TEN BRINKE, L., and GUSTAW, C. (2010) 'Dangerous Decisions: The Impact of First Impressions of Trustworthiness on the Evaluation of Legal Evidence and Defendant Culpability', *Psychology, Crime and Law*, 16(6): 477–91.

RASKIN, D. C. (1989) 'Polygraph Techniques for the Detection of Deception', in D. C. Raskin (ed.) *Psychological Methods in Criminal Investigation and Evidence*, New York: Springer.

ROSENFELD, J. P. (2011) 'P300 in Detecting Concealed Information', in B. Verschuere, G. Ben-Shakhar, and E. Meijer (eds) *Memory Detection: Theory and Application of the Concealed Information Test*, Cambridge: Cambridge University Press.

ROSENFELD, J. P., SOSKINS, M., BOSH, G., and RYAN, A. (2004) 'Simple, Effective Countermeasures to P300-based Tests of Detection of Concealed Information', *Psychophysiology*, 41(2): 205–19.

SAPIR, A. (2000) *The LSI Course on Scientific Content Analysis (SCAN)*, Phoenix, AZ: Laboratory for Scientific Interrogation.

SCHELLEMAN-OFFERMANS, K., and MERCKELBACH, H. (2010) 'Fantasy Proneness as a Confounder of Verbal Lie Detection Tools', *Journal of Investigative Psychology and Offender Profiling*, 7(3): 247–60.

SPORER, S. L. (2004) 'Reality Monitoring and Detection of Deception', in P. A. Granhag and L. A. Strömwall (eds) *The Detection of Deception in Forensic Contexts*, Cambridge: Cambridge University Press.

STELLER, M., and KOHNKEN, G. (1989) 'Statement Analysis: Credibility Assessment of Children's Testimonies in Sexual Abuse Cases', in D. C. Raskin (ed.) *Psychological Methods in Criminal Investigation and Evidence*, New York: Springer.

VRIJ, A. (2008) *Detecting Lies and Deceit: Pitfalls and Opportunities*, Chichester: John Wiley & Sons.

VRIJ, A., and GANIS, G. (2014) 'Theories in Deception and Lie Detection', in D. C. Raskin, C. R. Honts, and J. C. Kircher (eds) *Credibility Assessment: Scientific Research and Applications*, Kidlington, Oxford: Academic Press.

VRIJ, A., AKEHURST, L., SOUKARA, S., and BULL, R. (2004) 'Let Me Inform You How to Tell a Convincing Story: CBCA and Reality Monitoring Scores as a Function of Age, Coaching, and Deception', *Canadian Journal of Behavioural Science*, 36(2): 113–26.

VRIJ, A., GRANHAG, P. A., and PORTER, S. B. (2010) 'Pitfalls and Opportunities in Nonverbal and Verbal Lie Detection', *Psychological Science in the Public Interest*, 11(3): 89–121.

VRIJ, A., LEAL, S., MANN, S., and FISHER, R. (2012) 'Imposing Cognitive Load to Elicit Cues to Deceit: Inducing the Reverse Order Technique Naturally', *Psychology, Crime and Law*, 18(6): 579–94.

19

TOWARD RECONCILIATION OF THE TRUE AND FALSE RECOVERED MEMORY DEBATE

Robert F. Belli

Although cases of alleged historical child sexual abuse (CSA) often involve adults who report having had continuous memories of being abused, a noticeable proportion indicate that the memories of abuse are best characterized as those in which the accusers claim a point in time at which the CSA is forgotten, only to be recovered later (Connolly and Read, 2007). Since the 1980s, disagreements over the fidelity of recovered memories of CSA has led to an acrimonious debate involving professional and scientific psychologists, although there has been some degree of movement toward reconciliation in more recent years (Belli, 2012a, 2012b). Accordingly, the purpose of this chapter will be to expose (a) what is known about the occurrence of true and false recovered memories, (b) whether characteristics of memories for long-ago events are associated with fidelity, (c) how such scientific knowledge informs the wisdom of bringing cases of historical abuse to trial, given that false witness memories have led to unjustified convictions, and (d) what can be acquired from what is known about the prevalence of CSA and the science surrounding recovered memories that may lead to eventual reconciliation among those who have had contrasting points of view regarding the authenticity of recovered memories.

FALSE AND TRUE RECOVERED MEMORIES

For several decades now, psychological scientists and professionals have been aware of adults who suddenly appear to recover memories of non-recent CSA. The so-called memory wars emerged when the veracity of these recoveries became the subject of incredibly heated debate, with some providing evidence and arguments that the bulk of these recoveries are true (Freyd, 1996; Harvey and Herman, 1996; Alpert, Brown, and Courtois, 1998), while others emphasized the overall falsehood of these recoveries (Lindsay and Read, 1994; Lynn and Nash, 1994; Yapko, 1994). Although there has been some movement toward reconciliation among those who have been involved in this debate, there continue to be points over which disagreements have yet to be resolved (Belli, 2012a, 2012b; Patihis et al., 2014).

TOO OUTLANDISH TO BE TRUE

People can have such remarkable beliefs and memories that their falsehood is nearly guaranteed, including remembering alien abductions and prior lives (Persinger, 1992; Clancy, 2005; Meyersburg et al., 2009). In the realm of recovered memories of CSA, there have been claims of satanic cult rituals that, in addition to abuse, involved such horrors as torture, murder, and cannibalism. Importantly, there has not been corroboration of the existence of these extreme satanic cults (Lanning, 1992a, 1992b; Ofshe and Watters, 1994). At times, implicated in these bizarre recoveries were therapies that were designed to elicit long-repressed memories (Pendergrast, 1995). Such therapies engaged in memory work techniques that, while aimed at uncovering true events, were instead undoubtedly introducing powerful suggestions that led to false recovered memories. These memory work techniques were also associated with recoveries of less outlandish memories of CSA and other crimes, which often implicated parents as the guilty parties in legal contexts. Yet because these less outlandish memories were also elicited via suggestive therapies, their truth-value is also in doubt (Belli and Loftus, 1994; Loftus and Ketcham, 1994; Loftus, 1997).

EXPERIMENTAL EVIDENCE OF FALSE MEMORIES

For decades, experimental psychologists have been able to induce false memories in the laboratory (Laney and Loftus, 2013). For example, one aspect of the 'misinformation effect' refers to the ability to create false memories of the details of witnessed events via the mere follow-up presentation of verbal misinformation (Belli and Loftus, 1996; Zaragoza and Mitchell, 1996; Zaragoza, Belli, and Payment, 2007). The 'source monitoring' framework accounts for the creation of false memories by positing that the processes that lead to both true and false memories are largely the same (Johnson, Hashtroudi, and Lindsay, 1993; Belli and Loftus, 1994). According to this framework, determining the source of one's memories, such as whether the details one remembers were originally seen or presented as only follow-up verbal information, is an attribution that is based on the characteristics of the memory. If, for example, the memory contains perceptual visual detail, it is likely to be remembered as seen even though it was only presented verbally. Importantly, recent neuroimaging research has revealed similarities in brain activations that are associated with both true and false memories, lending credence to source monitoring processes (Mitchell and Johnson, 2009; Johnson et al., 2012).

Although much of the experimental research on false memories has examined event details, there has been work indicating that whole events can be falsely implanted in research participants. Aiming to simulate the kinds of suggestive memory work techniques that have been used in therapies that have led to recoveries of CSA, this experimental research has led to adult participants falsely remembering that, as children, they had caused major disturbances at weddings and during their schooling, among other events (Hyman, Husband and Billings, 1995; Loftus, 1997; Lindsay et al., 2004).

The typical paradigm involves presenting participants with a series of events from childhood that have been collected from family members, then asking the participants how well they remember each of these events. Unbeknown to participants, inserted into this series of events is at least one false event, created by the researchers. Not surprisingly, in their initial exposure, participants do not remember having experienced the false event. Undeterred, the experimenters instruct participants to engage in memory work activities that are similar to those used in suggestive therapies, such as imagining the events as having occurred and writing down the images that emerge. With these techniques, approximately 20 per cent of participants develop memories of the false events that include detailed perceptions. Asking participants to look at childhood photographs, which is another technique used in suggestive therapies, increases the false memory effect to approximately 50 per cent (Lindsay et al., 2004). Apparently, the additional visual cues contained in the photographs from childhood assists in the development of visual memories that become associated with the false event, which is consistent with a source-monitoring explanation.

Research indicates that some events are more difficult to implant than others. Pezdek, Finger, and Hodge (1997) discovered that whereas they could implant a false memory of being lost in a mall, they could not implant a false memory of receiving an enema during childhood. They reasoned that, because receiving an enema contains some of the same personally intimate and upsetting characteristics as being sexually abused, the false memory of being a victim of CSA would be nearly impossible to implant. More recent work, however, has shown that receiving an enema during childhood can become more plausible, and participants can be led to believe that they received an enema during childhood, if information is provided that receiving enemas during childhood is somewhat prevalent to alleviate medical conditions along with information about the procedures that happen during an enema (Hart and Schooler, 2006; Pezdek et al., 2006; Scoboria et al., 2006). Hence suggestive techniques during therapy will become more persuasive in implanting false memories of CSA if such victimization events are made more plausible by introducing notions that the experienced symptoms are consistent with CSA events that are difficult to remember and when there already exist memories of having had dysfunctional relationships with those who are later accused (Belli and Loftus, 1994; Belli et al., 1998; DePrince et al., 2012).

THEORY AND EVIDENCE FOR TRUE RECOVERIES

Recovering long-forgotten events is a commonplace occurrence: most people experience involuntary memories on a daily basis (Berntsen, 1996, 1998; Mace, 2005). Slightly more often positive than negative in valence, the exact mechanisms that lead to these involuntary recoveries is unknown, although they are often cued by a sight or a sound from the environment (Berntsen, 2007). There is also evidence that involuntary memories are usually of true rather than false events (Mace et al., 2009).

Importantly, adults have spontaneously recovered CSA memories, some of which have been corroborated (Geraerts et al., 2007).

Using a case study approach, Schooler, Bendiksen, and Ambadar (1997) suggest that a true recovery consists of an involuntary memory experience in which cues from the environment lead to an almost complete emotional unfolding of the events. Both apparent forgetting and later corroborated recovery of the abuse events also characterize the cases examined by Schooler and colleagues (1997). Other prospective research has found that the forgetting and recovery of CSA will occur among adults who have been documented to have been victimized. For example, Williams (1994, 1995) interviewed 129 adult women who had been documented, by childhood emergency room visits, as CSA victims. In these interviews, 38 per cent of the sample did not remember this specific victimization and 16 per cent reported having remembered their abuse after a period of forgetting. Taken together, these case study and prospective approaches provide evidence of both the forgetting and recovery of true CSA experiences among adults.

Betrayal trauma theory (BTT) (Freyd, 1996; DePrince et al., 2012) is a framework that accounts for the forgetting of CSA. One prediction of BTT, which has gained some measure of empirical support, is that incestuous abuse ought to be forgotten more extensively than abuse received by non-family perpetrators (Freyd, DePrince, and Zurbriggen, 2001; Freyd, Klest, and DePrince, 2010; Lindblom and Gray, 2010). Betrayal trauma theory considers trauma from CSA to exist within the context of social relationships, and CSA, especially when perpetrated by a parent, to betray the fundamental dependencies of a child for parental love and security. Despite the abuse, victims of incestuous CSA still yearn for parental love and support. Because of this conflict between the abuse and the child's needs, the child develops knowledge isolation for the abusive events. Such knowledge isolation results in complete or partial forgetting of the abuse, such as remembering one's childhood as more positive than it actually was.

EXTRAORDINARY AND ORDINARY FORGETTING MECHANISMS

Betrayal trauma theory is agnostic regarding the specific processes that lead to the forgetting of CSA. The idea of knowledge isolation can encompass extraordinary or ordinary forgetting mechanisms. On the one hand, among extraordinary memory mechanisms, the concept of repression as conceived by Freud (among others) involves a motivated unconscious that isolates emotionally traumatic events from awareness as a defence mechanism (Herman and Schatzow, 1987; Spiegel, 1997; Brown, Scheflin, and Hammond, 1998). Similarly, Brewin (2012) considers the forgetting of traumatically painful events to be a result of identity disturbances that interfere with the ability to retrieve autobiographical memories. On the other hand, because everyone experiences the forgetting of events with the passage of time (Rubin and Wenzel, 1996), it may be the case that CSA suffers from the same fate as more ordinary events.

In arguing against repression-like forgetting mechanisms, McNally (2005, 2012) posits that traumatic events, once encoded, will almost always be remembered. It may be possible to forget CSA through ordinary mechanisms, however, if the abuse occurred at a very young age or if the CSA was not originally experienced in a traumatic manner. With regard to the former, it has been empirically demonstrated that events that occur before the age of 5 are remembered less well than would be expected by forgetting as a result of the passage of time—a phenomenon known as 'childhood amnesia' (Wetzler and Sweeney, 1986). With regard to the latter, there can be little doubt that CSA will be potentially confusing, unpleasant, and uncomfortable, but such experiences are not necessarily traumatic, especially for a child who has yet to gain a deeper understanding of notions associated with sexual betrayal (McNally and Geraerts, 2009).

Unremarkably, simply not thinking about events induces them to be forgotten. In a series of experiments, Anderson and colleagues (Anderson and Green, 2001; Anderson and Levy, 2006; Anderson and Huddleston, 2012) found that instructing research participants not to think of experimental targets such as words, faces, and pictures that are accompanied by relevant cues will lead to a poorer ability to remember these 'no think' targets in comparison to cued targets that did not receive a 'no think' instruction. According to Anderson and colleagues, this ability to influence what events are remembered and forgotten by means of controlling what one thinks about is an adaptive ability that can be used to maintain functionality and emotional well-being. As a mundane example, being able to efficiently locate where one has parked one's vehicle in an often-used location is assisted by thinking about where one parked today and not thinking—that is, suppressing—where one has parked in the past. More relevant to the current discussion is the notion that remembering unpleasant events is disconcerting for all persons; hence using cognitive control to not think of unpleasant events contributes to a sense of well-being.

An effect known as the 'fading affect bias' (Walker, Vogl, and Thompson, 1997; Walker et al., 2003) supports these claims. Negative autobiographical events lose the intensity of their affect more rapidly with the passage of time in comparison to positive events and such loss of affect is correlated with poorer memory for negative events. Moreover, persons who have a weakened fading affect bias are more dysphoric than those with a normal fading affect bias, indicating that maintaining the intensity of negative affect as near equal to that of positive affect over time contributes to, or is an indication of, poorer emotional well-being. Importantly, the ability to suppress the remembering of negative events by not thinking of them may be one mechanism that contributes to the fading affect bias. Further, not thinking has been shown to be effective in reducing the retrieval of emotional stimuli (Depue, Banich, and Curran, 2006; Depue, Curran, and Banich, 2007) and autobiographical events (Noreen and MacLeod, 2013; Stephens, Braid, and Hertel, 2013), providing additional evidence of the generalizability of cognitive control mechanisms to everyday life.

Because being a victim of CSA will no doubt consist of unpleasant events, the relevance of an ordinary motivated forgetting process that moves from simply not thinking about negative events to forgetting CSA events is straightforward. Importantly, the memory suppression that results from engaging in cognitive control demystifies what has often been seen as extraordinary—that is, the forgetting of the trauma associated with CSA. Because the repression concept has often been invoked to account for the need for an extraordinary forgetting process that could be sufficiently powerful to dampen the memory of traumatic events (Herman and Schatzow, 1987; Spiegel, 1997; Brown et al., 1998), the relevance of ordinary forgetting mechanisms becomes more viable by acknowledging that CSA will be unpleasant, uncomfortable, and confusing rather than necessarily traumatic (McNally and Geraerts, 2009). Although the possibility that traumatic events may be forgotten through extraordinary forgetting mechanisms cannot be ruled out (Schooler et al., 1997; Sivers, Schooler, and Freyd, 2002; Brewin, 2012), compelling arguments can be made that only ordinary forgetting mechanisms are responsible (for example Goodyear-Smith, Laidlaw, and Large, 1998).

Although there is growing agreement among researchers of all stripes that true recoveries of CSA occur, there is disagreement about those factors that are involved in these recoveries (Belli, 2012b). Mirroring the differing perspectives regarding the forgetting of abuse, these disagreements partially reflect whether ordinary or extraordinary memory mechanisms are at play. Among explanations that appeal to ordinary processes, the 'forgot it all along (FIA) effect', a mechanism that was introduced by Schooler and colleagues (1997), is seen as a central property that governs true recovery. From their case studies, these authors noted instances in which, prior to recovery, there did exist moments of retrieval of the abuse, as revealed by persons close to the victims who were informed about the abuse. Accordingly, the FIA effect characterizes a recovery experience as not being the first occasion on which the abuse had been remembered, but rather as an occurrence in which the abuse was remembered with such surprise that an inference is drawn that the abuse had never previously been recalled. For Anderson and Huddleston (2012), prior episodes of remembering CSA events succumb to repeated suppression through the 'no think' mechanism.

McNally and Geraerts (2009) construe the FIA effect as the result of CSA victims who do not experience their abuse as traumatic at the time of its occurrence or at later rememberings, but may do so at the time of final recovery, when they realize the full nature of the sexual betrayal. In other words, it is only when one reaches adulthood and develops a more complete understanding of the complexities of human sexuality that the extent of the betrayal to one's well-being becomes realized in a final recovery.

TWO ROUTES TO RECOVERY

The notions that false recoveries are likely to be generated through powerful suggestions introduced in the course of therapeutic intervention and that true recoveries are likely to occur through the seemingly sudden spontaneous remembering of CSA events has received empirical support through the work of Geraerts and colleagues (Geraerts et al., 2007, 2009; Geraerts, 2012). This research was motivated to solve apparent inconsistencies that had been observed among individuals who had experienced recoveries of CSA. On the one hand, recovered memory participants were observed to be more suggestible than controls in the false memory Deese–Roediger–McDermott (DRM) paradigm (Roediger and McDermott, 1995), in which false memories exist in remembering having been presented with critical lure words, such as *sleep*, that were in actuality non-presented associates of words that were presented, such as *bed*, *tired* (Clancy et al., 2000). Greater suggestibility to DRM critical lures has also been found with persons who report having been abducted by aliens (Clancy et al.,

2002) and having had prior lives (Meyersburg et al., 2009), indicating that increased susceptibility to suggestion makes someone especially vulnerable to developing false memories.

On the other hand, recovered memory participants have been shown to be susceptible to the FIA effect by having forgotten prior remembering of their abuse in both anecdotal (Schooler et al., 1997) and experimental (Geraerts et al., 2006) research. Geraerts and colleagues (2007, 2009) resolved these inconsistencies by testing two samples of those who experienced recovered memories: those who had a prolonged recovery via suggestive therapy, and those who had sudden and spontaneous recovery outside of therapy. Whereas the suggestive therapy sample demonstrated higher DRM false memories in comparison to both the spontaneous sample and a continuous CSA memory sample, the spontaneous memory sample revealed higher FIA effects in comparison to the other two groups. Moreover, indicative that the suggestive sample's memories tended to be false and that the spontaneous sample's memories were likely to be true, independent corroboration rates for the suggestive group were significantly lower in comparison to the spontaneous group and a sample of participants with continuous memories of CSA (while the corroboration rates between these two latter groups did not differ).

The research of Geraerts and colleagues has several implications. By demonstrating the presence of two routes to recovery, their results open the door to a reconciliation of the heated debate that has framed the so-called memory wars by indicating that some recoveries are likely to be false, whereas others are likely to be true. In addition, their research points towards recovered memories being the result of somewhat extreme individual differences in susceptibility to either suggestibility or the FIA effect, which may explain why the great majority of individuals who report being CSA victims have continuous memories in which they never forgot about their victimization (Belli, 2012a). Their results also have forensic and legal implications, especially by pointing to the context in which the recovery occurs as a potential indicator of the veracity of what is remembered.

ADULT MEMORIES OF ALLEGED HISTORICAL ABUSE

Although the research of Geraerts and colleagues implicates the importance of the context of remembering as a valuable indicator of veracity, legal arenas pay a great deal of attention in all witness testimony—including that involving alleged historical abuse—to the characteristics of the memories.

THE CHARACTERISTICS OF WHAT IS REMEMBERED

One aspect that is taken as evidence of the veracity of memories is the extent to which the reports are detailed and vivid, as though the witness is reliving the past (Bell and Loftus, 1989). Unfortunately, providing detailed, vivid, and emotional memories has been shown not to be a reliable indicator of veracity. Conway (2013) and Howe (2013) document adult reports of historical abuse in which the memories contain vivid details that could not have been encoded, because the concepts within these details are not age-appropriate to the time at which the events allegedly occurred. For example, one adult witness remembered with which hand the perpetrator had committed CSA when dexterity would not ordinarily be a mastered concept for a child of that age; similarly, another adult witness remembered being at a vivid scene, when at the age of 2 or 3, that included 'weeds' and 'disrepair'—concepts that a person of that age would not have mastered. Clearly, these witnesses are not reporting events as they were encoded, but events as they were reconstructed and reinterpreted many years later.

Additional research demonstrating that the vividness of memories is not an indicator of accuracy involves work on 'flashbulb memories'—that is, those memories of how one first became aware of publicly disturbing events, such as political assassinations, space exploration disasters, and terrorist acts. Although people who have flashbulb memories strongly believe in their accuracy over time, there are considerable inconsistencies between immediate and later reports (McCloskey, Wible, and Cohen, 1988; Neisser and Harsch, 1992; Weaver, 1993). Moreover, in clever research, Talarico and Rubin (2003) have been able to compare the properties of flashbulb memories and everyday memories. Importantly, both types of memory deteriorate in accuracy at the same rate. Nevertheless, although belief in the accuracy of one's everyday memories and the rated vividness of everyday memories deteriorates alongside their accuracy, the belief in the accuracy of flashbulb memories and their rated vividness remain consistently high over time. Ostensibly, the detailed vividness of flashbulb memories leads one to become overly confident in their accuracy; that they are more emotional than everyday memories may also contribute to a sense of accuracy.

Focusing on the role of emotion, Sharot, Delgado, and Phelps (2004) found that heightened negative emotionality contributed to the sense of remembering photographs as having been presented regardless of whether they were shown before or not. Given this evidence, it is disturbing that the level of detail in eyewitness testimony, its congruent negative emotionality, and the confidence of the witness are considered to be the indications of accuracy of these reports among jurors and within legal systems (Bell and Loftus, 1989; Kaufmann et al., 2003).[1]

Inconsistencies in the details of abuse memories do not rule out the possibility that CSA had taken place. Fisher and colleagues (Fisher, Brewer, and Mitchell, 2009; Fisher, Vrij, and Leins, 2013) have found only weak correlations among participants who report inconsistencies in their recall of events that were taken two weeks apart and the overall accuracy of the witnesses, and it is noteworthy that defence attorneys will seek to discredit witnesses on the basis of inconsistencies in testimony. With regard to getting the details wrong, the case of John Dean is instructive. Although John Dean—once-confidant of President Nixon—was able to provide such highly detailed and convincing testimony of the Watergate scandal that he was described as a 'human tape-recorder', the details of his testimony were often revealed to be incorrect when they were compared with audio tapes of his conversations with Nixon at the White House (Neisser, 1981). Despite these inaccuracies in detail, John Dean did have

---

[1] See also *Neil v. Biggers*, 409 U.S. 188 (1972).

the gist correct, in that Nixon was guilty of criminal activity. According to 'fuzzy-trace theory' (Brainerd and Reyna, 2002), however, an overreliance on gist can support the development of false memories for details. Hence it is possible that memories of CSA that are incorrect in details may be accurate at a broader gist level.

Such dissociations between the accuracy of the details and the overall gist of memories can, however, be only cold comfort for legal systems that rely so heavily on eyewitness testimony—and the details that are provided in this testimony—in determinations of guilt and innocence. In other words, legal systems have become overly reliant on the characteristics of memories—especially their vividness, consistency, and the conveyed confidence of testimony—in their adjudication of accuracy. Unfortunately, these properties are unreliable indicators of accuracy. As outlined above, we know that, when remembering CSA events, adults will confidently add, through reconstructive processes, content that could not possibly have been originally encoded. We know that inconsistency of testimony may not be a reliable indicator of overall inaccuracy. We know that vividness and accuracy can be unrelated. We know that research participants, through suggestive techniques reminiscent of those used in some therapeutic interventions, will create whole memories of childhood events that are incorrect both in detail and gist of what is reported.

Because of the reliance of legal systems on the characteristics of witness testimony in their adjudication of guilt and innocence—which becomes so reliant without strong corroborative evidence of guilt—innocent people have been convicted of historical abuse and guilty persons have gone free, and it appears to be a matter of luck as to which of these outcomes has occurred and will again occur.

THE CONTEXT OF WHEN REMEMBERING OCCURS

As noted by Geraerts, Raymaekers, and Merckelbach (2008), recoveries that occur outside of therapy are more likely to reflect actual events in comparison to recoveries that have emerged in suggestive therapy, as indicated by the corroboration rates obtained by Geraerts and colleagues (2007) for these different groups. Hence the context in which the recoveries occur may be an important factor to consider when assessing the truth-value of these claims. Nevertheless, despite this emphasis on context, Geraerts and colleagues (2008) acknowledge that the degree of corroboration that was obtained in Geraerts and colleagues (2007) does not meet legal standards and that one should not conclude that any spontaneous recovery is genuine or that any recovery that occurs via therapy is necessarily false. They also emphasize the need to have corroborative evidence to support any claims in legal proceedings.

Additional caveats ought be included to the caution exhibited by Geraerts and colleagues (2008). We do not have sufficient scientific knowledge to determine the extent to which spontaneous recoveries are more or less likely to adequately reflect authentic abuse to justify criminal prosecution. Research by Brewin, Huntley, and Whalley (2012) has shown that involuntary memories of trauma can be false and that the heightened emotion associated with these recoveries contributes to the false sense of recollecting actual events. The FIA effect indicates that spontaneous recoveries are accompanied by prior rememberings that are subsequently forgotten, indicating that some aspect of the remembering process was sufficiently different from earlier ones to lead to an enduring recovery. It is possible that such endurance is the result of reconstructive memory processes—such as the realization that the events were sexual and/or abusive in nature—which may come at a cost of fidelity. And, as noted by Geraerts and colleagues (2008) and highlighted above, almost all memories consist of true and false—or at least biased—elements.

Another issue, raised by Raymaekers and colleagues (2012), is that the classification of recovered memories as those that were engendered in suggested therapy versus those that occurred spontaneously outside of therapy is less than clear-cut, because suggestions may have an influence outside of therapy and some individuals may have mixed memory profiles. As a related point, in their examination of historical abuse criminal court decisions in Canada, Connolly and Read (2007) found that recovery was implicated in one fifth of cases in which the accuser sought therapy, but in only 3 per cent of cases in which therapy was not sought. Although we do not know what proportion of these therapy cases included suggestive techniques, it is noteworthy that there is a strong correlation between recovery and therapy.

In conclusion, when considering the context of recovery as an indication of authenticity, one should be vigilant of (a) the potential role of suggestive therapy, (b) the possibility that suggestions can occur outside of therapy, (c) the fact that any recovery may be false, and (d) the difficulty surrounding an accurate classification of the context of recovery.

FINAL COMMENTS: TOWARD RECONCILIATION

There is convincing evidence that CSA is pervasive and tragic, and efforts should be undertaken to reduce the prevalence of its occurrence (Bolen and Scannapieco, 1999; DiLillo et al., 2006; London et al., 2007). The considerable majority of individuals who are victimized by CSA have continuous memories in which there is an ongoing awareness of the abusive events (APA Working Group, 1998). Hence the debate regarding the fidelity of recovered memories concerns a small proportion of those who claim victimization.

In attempts to seek reconciliation among the debaters, there have been meetings, presentations, and a continually developing literature among those who have held contrasting points of view (Belli 2012a, 2012b). These avenues, taken together, reveal that there is a movement toward reconciliation. Although there are continuing points of contention, there is also general agreement on the most critical issues: most would agree that both true and false memories populate a substantive proportion of recoveries, that suggestive techniques should not be used in therapy, and that recovering memories should not be a goal of trauma therapy.

One of the more contentious psychosocial issues centres on the role of the criminal courts in addressing the injustice that surrounds those who have recovered *true* memories of CSA. My own perspective is that the criminal courts are ill-prepared to correctly adjudicate cases of historical abuse that involve recovered memories.

Given the current state of scientific knowledge, it is difficult to see how, without strong corroborating evidence, any recovered memory of historic abuse could ever be 'beyond a reasonable doubt'. There is also the real danger that miscarriages of justice have occurred, and will occur, in the form of convictions of innocent persons. Such a perspective is not inconsistent with the view that those who claim victimization should be treated with compassion and respect in a manner that seeks to achieve closure. Social mechanisms other than criminal courts need to be brought into play to address the injustice that is felt among many of those who have experienced a recovery of CSA—and, similarly, to address the injustice felt by those damaged by false allegations.

REFERENCES

ALPERT, J. L., BROWN, L. S., and COURTOIS, C. A. (1998) 'Symptomatic Clients and Memories of Childhood Abuse: What the Trauma and Child Sexual Abuse Literature Tells Us', *Psychology, Public Policy, and Law*, 4(4): 941–95.

American Psychological Association (APA) Working Group (1998) 'Final conclusions of the American Psychological Association working group on Investigation of Memories of Childhood Abuse', *Psychology, Public Policy, and Law*, 4(4): 933–40.

ANDERSON, M. C., and GREEN, C. (2001) 'Suppressing Unwanted Memories by Executive Control', *Nature*, 410(6826): 366–9.

ANDERSON, M. C., and HUDDLESTON, E. (2012) 'Towards a Cognitive and Neurobiological Model of Motivated Forgetting', in R. F. Belli (ed.) *True and False Recovered Memories: Toward a Reconciliation of the Debate*, New York: Springer.

ANDERSON, M. C., and LEVY, B. J. (2006) 'Encouraging the Nascent Cognitive Neuroscience of Repression', *Behavioral and Brain Sciences*, 29(5): 511–13.

BELL, B. E., and LOFTUS, E. F. (1989) 'Trivial Persuasion in the Courtroom: The Power of (a Few) Minor Details', *Journal of Personality and Social Psychology*, 56(5): 669–79.

BELLI, R. F. (2012a) 'Epilogue: Continuing Points of Contention in the Recovered Memory Debate', in R. F. Belli (ed.) *True and False Recovered Memories: Toward a Reconciliation of the Debate*, New York: Springer.

BELLI, R. F. (2012b) 'Introduction: In the Aftermath of the So-called Memory Wars', in R. F. Belli (ed.) *True and False Recovered Memories: Toward a Reconciliation of the Debate*, New York: Springer.

BELLI, R. F., and LOFTUS, E. F. (1994) 'Recovered Memories of Childhood Abuse: A Source Monitoring Perspective', in S. J. Lynn and J. Rhue (eds) *Dissociation: Theory, Clinical, and Research Perspectives*, New York: Guilford Press.

BELLI, R. F., and LOFTUS, E. F. (1996) 'The Pliability of Autobiographical Memory: Misinformation and the False Memory Problem', in D. C. Rubin (ed.) *Remembering Our Past: Studies in Autobiographical Memory*, New York: Cambridge University Press.

BELLI, R. F., WINKIELMAN, P., READ, J. D., SCHWARZ, N., and LYNN, S. J. (1998) 'Recalling More Childhood Events Leads to Judgments of Poorer Memory: Implications for the Recovered/False Memory Debate', *Psychonomic Bulletin & Review*, 5: 318–23.

BERNTSEN, D. (1996) 'Involuntary Autobiographical Memories', *Applied Cognitive Psychology*, 10(5): 435–54.

BERNTSEN, D. (1998) 'Voluntary and Involuntary Access to Autobiographical Memory', *Memory*, 6(2): 113–41.

BERNTSEN, D. (2007) 'Involuntary Autobiographical Memories: Speculations, Findings, and an Attempt to Integrate Them', in J. H. Mace (ed.) *Involuntary Memory*, Malden, MA: Blackwell.

BOLEN, R. M., and SCANNAPIECO, M. (1999) 'Prevalence of Child Sexual Abuse: A Corrective Meta-analysis', *Social Service Review*, 73(3): 281–313.

BRAINERD, C. J., and REYNA, V. F. (2002) 'Fuzzy-trace Theory and False Memory', *Current Directions in Psychological Science*, 11(5): 164–9.

BREWIN, C. R. (2012) 'A Theoretical Framework for Understanding Recovered Memory Experiences', in R. F. Belli (ed.) *True and False Recovered Memories: Toward a Reconciliation of the Debate*, New York: Springer.

BREWIN, C. R., HUNTLEY, Z., and WHALLEY, M. G. (2012) 'Source Memory Errors Associated with Reports of Posttraumatic Flashbacks: A Proof of Concept Study', *Cognition*, 124(2): 234–8.

BROWN, D., SCHEFLIN, A. W., and HAMMOND, D. C. (1998) *Memory, Trauma Treatment, and the Law*, New York: W. W. Norton & Co.

CLANCY, S. A. (2005) *Abducted: How People Come to Believe They Were Kidnapped by Aliens*, Cambridge, MA: Harvard University Press.

CLANCY, S. A., MCNALLY, R. J., SCHACTER, D. L., LENZENWEGER, M. F., and PITMAN, R. K. (2002) 'Memory Distortion in People Reporting Abduction by Aliens', *Journal of Abnormal Psychology*, 111(3): 455–61.

CLANCY, S. A., SCHACTER, D. L., MCNALLY, R. J., and PITMAN, R. K. (2000) 'False Recognition in Women Reporting Recovered Memories of Sexual Abuse', *Psychological Science*, 11(1): 26–31.

CONNOLLY, D. A., and READ, J. D. (2007) 'Canadian Criminal Court Reports of Historic Child Sexual Abuse: Factors Associated with Delayed Prosecution and Reported Repression', in M.-E. Pipe, M. E. Lamb, Y. Orbach, and A.-C. Cederborg (eds) *Child Sexual Abuse: Disclosure, Delay, and Denial*, Mahwah, NJ: Lawrence Erlbaum.

CONWAY, M. A. (2013) 'On Being a Memory Expert Witness: Three Cases', *Memory*, 21(5): 566–75.

DEPRINCE, A. P., BROWN, L. S., CHEIT, R. E., FREYD, J. J., GOLD, S. N., PEZDEK, K., and QUINA, K. (2012) 'Motivated Forgetting and Misremembering: Perspectives from Betrayal Trauma Theory', in R. F. Belli (ed.) *True and False Recovered Memories: Toward a Reconciliation of the Debate*, New York: Springer.

DEPUE, B. E., BANICH, M. T., and CURRAN, T. (2006) 'Suppression of Emotional and Nonemotional Content in Memory: Effects of Repetition on Cognitive Control', *Psychological Science*, 17(5): 441–7.

DEPUE, B. E., CURRAN, T., and BANICH, M. T. (2007) 'Prefrontal Regions Orchestrate Suppression of Emotional Memories via a Two-phase Process', *Science*, 317(5835): 215–19.

DILILLO, D., FORTIER, M. A., HAYES, S. A., TRASK, E., PERRY, A. R., MESSMAN-MOORE, T., FAUCHIER, A., and NASH, C. (2006) 'Retrospective Assessment of Childhood Sexual and Physical Abuse: A Comparison of Scaled and Behaviorally Specific Approaches', *Assessment*, 13(3): 297–312.

FISHER, R. P., BREWER, N., and MITCHELL, G. (2009) 'The Relation between Consistency and Accuracy of Eyewitness Testimony: Legal versus Cognitive Explanations', in R. Bull, T. Valentine, and T. Williamson (eds) *Handbook of Psychology and Investigative Interviewing: Current Developments and Future Directions*, Chichester: John Wiley & Sons.

FISHER, R. P., VRIJ, A., and LEINS, D. A. (2013) 'Does Testimonial Inconsistency Indicate Memory Inaccuracy and Deception? Beliefs, Empirical Research, and Theory', in B. S. Cooper (ed.) *Applied Issues in Investigative Interviewing*, New York: Springer.

FREYD, J. J. (1996) *Betrayal Trauma: The Logic of Forgetting Childhood Abuse*, Cambridge, MA: Harvard University Press.

FREYD, J. J., DEPRINCE, A. P., and ZURBRIGGEN, E. L. (2001) 'Self-reported Memory for Abuse Depends upon Victim–Perpetrator Relationship', *Journal of Trauma & Dissociation*, 2(3): 5–17.

FREYD, J. J., KLEST, B., and DEPRINCE, A. P. (2010) 'Avoiding Awareness of Betrayal: Comment on Lindblom and Gray (2009)', *Applied Cognitive Psychology*, 24(1): 20–6.

GERAERTS, E. (2012) 'Cognitive Underpinnings of Recovered Memories of Childhood Abuse', in R. F. Belli (ed.) *True and False Recovered Memories: Toward a Reconciliation of the Debate*, New York: Springer.

GERAERTS, E., ARNOLD, M. M., LINDSAY, D. S., MERCKELBACH, H., JELICIC, M., and HAUER, B. (2006) 'Forgetting of Prior Remembering in Persons Reporting Recovered Memories of Childhood Sexual Abuse', *Psychological Science*, 17(11): 1002–8.

GERAERTS, E., LINDSAY, D. S., MERCKELBACH, H., JELICIC, M., RAYMAEKERS, L., ARNOLD, M. M., and SCHOOLER, J. S. (2009) 'Cognitive Mechanisms Underlying Recovered Memory Experiences of Childhood Sexual Abuse', *Psychological Science*, 20(1): 92–8.

GERAERTS, E., RAYMAEKERS, L., and MERCKELBACH, H. (2008) 'Recovered Memories of Childhood Sexual Abuse: Current Findings and Their Legal Implications', *Legal and Criminological Psychology*, 13(2): 165–76.

GERAERTS, E., SCHOOLER, J. W., MERCKELBACH, H., JELICIC, M., HAUER, B. J. A., and AMBADAR, Z. (2007) 'The Reality of Recovered Memories: Corroborating Continuous and Discontinuous Memories of Childhood Sexual Abuse', *Psychological Science*, 18(7): 564–7.

GOODYEAR-SMITH, F. A., LAIDLAW, T. M., and LARGE, R. G. (1998) 'In Praise of Scholarship: A Reply to McCullough', *Health Care Analysis*, 6(3): 223–6.

HART, R. E., and SCHOOLER, J. W. (2006) 'Increasing Belief in the Experience of an Invasive Procedure that Never Happened: The Role of Plausibility and Schematicity', *Applied Cognitive Psychology*, 20(5): 661–9.

HARVEY, M. R., and HERMAN, J. L. (1996) 'Amnesia, Partial Amnesia, and Delayed Recall among Adult Survivors of Childhood Trauma', in K. Pezdek and W. P. Banks (eds) *The Recovered/False Memory Debate*, San Diego, CA: Academic Press.

HERMAN, J. H., and SCHATZOW, E. (1987) 'Recovery and Verification of Memories of Childhood Sexual Trauma', *Psychoanalytic Psychology*, 4(1): 1–14.

HOWE, M. L. (2013) 'Memory Lessons from the Courtroom: Reflections on Being a Memory Expert on the Witness Stand', *Memory*, 21(5): 576–83.

HYMAN, I. E., HUSBAND, T. H., and BILLINGS, F. J. (1995) 'False Memories of Childhood Experiences', *Applied Cognitive Psychology*, 9(3): 181–97.

JOHNSON, M. K., HASHTROUDI, S., and LINDSAY, D. S. (1993) 'Source Monitoring', *Psychological Bulletin*, 114(1): 3–28.

JOHNSON, M. K., RAYE, C. L., MITCHELL, K. J., and ANKUDOWICH, E. (2012) 'The Cognitive Neuroscience of True and False Memories', in R. F. Belli (ed.) *True and False Recovered Memories: Toward a Reconciliation of the Debate*, New York: Springer.

KAUFMANN, G., DREVLAND, G. C. B., WESSEL, E., OVERSKEID, G., and MAGNUSSEN, S. (2003) 'The Importance of Being Earnest: Displayed Emotions and Witness Credibility', *Applied Cognitive Psychology*, 17(1): 21–34.

LANEY, C., and LOFTUS, E. F. (2013) 'Recent Advances in False Memory Research', *South African Journal of Psychology*, 43: 137–46.

LANNING, K. V. (1992a) *Child Sex Rings: A Behavioral Analysis*, Quantico, VA: National Center for Missing & Exploited Children.
LANNING, K. V. (1992b) *Investigator's Guide to Allegations of 'Ritual' Child Sex Abuse*, Quantico, VA: National Center for the Analysis of Violent Crime.
LINDBLOM, K. M., and GRAY, M. J. (2010) 'Relationship Closeness and Trauma Narrative Detail: A Critical Analysis of Betrayal Trauma Theory', *Applied Cognitive Psychology*, 24(1): 1–19.
LINDSAY, D. S., and READ, J. D. (1994) 'Psychotherapy and Memories of Childhood Sexual Abuse: A Cognitive Perspective', *Applied Cognitive Psychology*, 8(4): 281–338.
LINDSAY, D. S., HAGEN, L., READ, J. D., WADE, K. A., and GARRY, M. (2004) 'True Photographs and False Memories', *Psychological Science*, 15(3): 149–54.
LOFTUS, E. F. (1997) 'Dispatch from the (Un)Civil Memory Wars', in J. D. Read and D. S. Lindsay (eds) *Recollections of Trauma: Scientific Evidence and Clinical Practice*, New York: Plenum.
LOFTUS, E. F., and KETCHAM, K. (1994) *The Myth of Repressed Memory*, New York: St. Martin's.
LONDON, K., BRUCK, M., CECI, S. J., and SHUMAN, D. W. (2007) 'Disclosure of Child Sexual Abuse: A Review of the Contemporary Empirical Literature', in M.-E. Pipe, M. E. Lamb, Y. Orbach, and A.-C. Cederborg (eds) *Child Sexual Abuse: Disclosure, Delay, and Denial*, Mahwah, NJ: Laurence Erlbaum.
LYNN, S. J., and NASH, M. R. (1994) 'Truth in Memory: Ramifications for Psychotherapy and Hypnotherapy', *American Journal of Clinical Hypnosis*, 36(3): 194–208.
MACE, J. H. (2005) 'Priming Involuntary Autobiographical Memories', *Memory*, 13(8): 874–84
MACE, J. H., ATKINSON, E., MOECKEL, C. H., and TORRES, V. (2009) 'Accuracy and Perspective in Involuntary Autobiographical Memory', *Applied Cognitive Psychology*, 25(1): 20–8.
MCCLOSKEY, M., WIBLE, C. G., and COHEN, N. J. (1988) 'Is There a Special Flashbulb-memory Mechanism?', *Journal of Experimental Psychology: General*, 117(2): 171–81.
MCNALLY, R. J. (2005) 'Debunking Myths about Trauma and Memory', *Canadian Journal of Psychiatry [Revue Canadienne de Psychiatrie]*, 50(13): 817–22.
MCNALLY, R. J. (2012) 'Searching for Repressed Memory', in R. F. Belli (ed.) *True and False Recovered Memories: Toward a Reconciliation of the Debate*, New York: Springer.
MCNALLY, R. J., and GERAERTS, E. (2009) 'A New Solution to the Recovered Memory Debate', *Perspectives on Psychological Science*, 4(2): 126–34.
MEYERSBURG, C. A., BOGDAN, R., GALLO, D. A., and MCNALLY, R. J. (2009) 'False Memory Propensity in People Reporting Recovered Memories of Past Lives', *Journal of Abnormal Psychology*, 118(2): 399–404.
MITCHELL, K. J., and JOHNSON, M. K. (2009) 'Source Monitoring 15 Years Later: What Have We Learned from fMRI about the Neural Mechanisms of Source Memory?', *Psychological Bulletin*, 135(4): 638–77.
NEISSER, U. (1981) 'John Dean's Memory: A Case Study', *Cognition*, 9(1): 1–22.
NEISSER, U., and HARSCH, N. (1992) 'Phantom Flashbulbs: False Recollections of Hearing The News about Challenger', in E. Winograd and U. Neisser (eds) *Affect and Accuracy in Recall: Studies of 'Flashbulb' Memories, Vol. 4*, New York: Cambridge University Press.
NOREEN, S., and MACLEOD, M. D. (2013) 'It's All in the Detail: Intentional Forgetting of Autobiographical Memories Using the Autobiographical Think/No-Think Task', *Journal of Experimental Psychology: Learning, Memory, and Cognition*, 39(2): 375–93.
OFSHE, R., and WATTERS, E. (1994) *Making Monsters: False Memories, Psychotherapy, and Sexual Hysteria*, New York: Scribner.

PATIHIS, L., HO, L. Y., TINGEN, I. W., LILIENFELD, S. O., and LOFTUS, E. F. (2014) 'Are the "Memory Wars" over? A Scientist-Practitioner Gap in Beliefs about Repressed Memory', *Psychological Science*, 25(2): 519–30.

PENDERGRAST, M. (1995) *Victims of Memory: Sex Abuse Accusations and Shattered Lives*, Hinesburg, VT: Upper Access Books.

PERSINGER, M. A. (1992) 'Neuropsychological Profiles of Adults Who Report "Sudden Remembering" of Early Childhood Memories: Implications for Claims of Sex Abuse and Alien Visitation/Abduction Experiences', *Perceptual and Motor Skills*, 75(1): 259–66.

PEZDEK, K., BLANDON-GITLIN, I., LAM, S., HART, R. E., and SCHOOLER, J. W. (2006) 'Is Knowing Believing? The Role of Event Plausibility and Background Knowledge in Planting False Beliefs about the Personal Past', *Memory & Cognition*, 34(8): 1628–35.

PEZDEK, K., FINGER, K., and HODGE, D. (1997) 'Planting False Childhood Memories: The Role of Event Plausibility', *Psychological Science*, 8: 437–41.

RAYMAEKERS, L., SMEETS, T., PETERS, M. J. V., OTGAAR, H., and MERCKELBACH, H. (2012) 'The Classification of Recovered Memories: A Cautionary Note', *Consciousness and Cognition*, 21(4): 1640–3.

ROEDIGER, H. L. III, and MCDERMOTT, K. B. (1995) 'Creating False Memories: Remembering Words not Presented in Lists', *Journal of Experimental Psychology: Learning, Memory, and Cognition*, 21(4): 803–14.

RUBIN, D. C., and WENZEL, A. E. (1996) 'One Hundred Years of Forgetting: A Quantitative Description of Retention', *Psychological Review*, 103(4): 734–60.

SCHOOLER, J. W., BENDIKSEN, M. A., and AMBADAR, Z. (1997) 'Taking the Middle Line: Can We Accommodate Both Fabricated and Recovered Memories of Sexual Abuse?', in M. Conway (ed.) *Recovered Memories and False Memories*, Oxford: Oxford University Press.

SCOBORIA, A., MAZZONI, G., KIRSCH, I., and JIMENEZ, S. (2006) 'The Effects of Prevalence and Script Information on Plausibility, Belief, and Memory of Autobiographical Events', *Applied Cognitive Psychology*, 20: 1049–64.

SHAROT, T., DELGADO, M. R., and PHELPS, E. A. (2004) 'How Emotion Enhances the Feeling of Remembering', *Nature Neuroscience*, 7(12): 1376–80.

SIVERS, H., SCHOOLER, J., and FREYD, J. J. (2002) 'Recovered Memories', in V. S. Ramachandran (ed.) *Encyclopedia of the Human Brain, Vol. 4*, San Diego, CA: Academic Press.

SPIEGEL, D. (1997) 'Foreword', in D. Spiegel (ed.) *Repressed Memories*, Washington, DC: American Psychiatric Press.

STEPHENS, E., BRAID, A., and HERTEL, P. T. (2013) 'Suppression-induced Reduction in the Specificity of Autobiographical Memories', *Clinical Psychological Science*, 1(2): 163–9.

TALARICO, J. M., and RUBIN, D. C. (2003) 'Confidence, not Consistency, Characterizes Flashbulb Memories', *Psychological Science*, 14(5): 455–61.

WALKER, W. R., SKOWRONSKI, J. J., GIBBONS, J. A., VOGL, R. J., and THOMPSON, C. P. (2003) 'On the Emotions that Accompany Autobiographical Memories: Dysphoria Disrupts the Fading Affect Bias', *Cognition and Emotion*, 17(5): 703–23.

WALKER, W. R., VOGL, R. J., and THOMPSON, C. P. (1997) 'Autobiographical Memory: Unpleasantness Fades Faster than Pleasantness over Time', *Applied Cognitive Psychology*, 11(5): 399–413.

WEAVER, C.A. III (1993) 'Do You Need a "Flash" to Form a Flashbulb Memory?', *Journal of Experimental Psychology: General*, 122(1): 39–46.

WETZLER, S. E., and SWEENEY, J. A. (1986) 'Childhood Amnesia: An Empirical Demonstration', in D. C. Rubin (ed.) *Autobiographical Memory*, New York: Cambridge University Press.

WILLIAMS, L. M. (1994) 'Recall of Childhood Trauma: A Prospective Study of Women's Memories of Child Sexual Abuse', *Journal of Consulting and Clinical Psychology*, 62(6): 1167–76.

WILLIAMS, L. M. (1995) 'Recovered Memories of Abuse in Women with Documented Child Sexual Victimization Histories', *Journal of Traumatic Stress*, 8(4): 649–74.

YAPKO, M. D. (1994) *Suggestions of Abuse: True and False Memories of Childhood Sexual Trauma*, New York: Simon & Schuster.

ZARAGOZA, M. S., and MITCHELL, K. J. (1996) 'Repeated Exposure to Suggestion and the Creation of False Memories', *Psychological Science*, 7(5): 294–300.

ZARAGOZA, M. S., BELLI, R. F., and PAYMENT, K. E. (2007) 'Misinformation Effects and the Suggestibility of Eyewitness Memory', in M. Garry and H. Hayne (eds) *Do Justice and Let the Sky Fall: Elizabeth F. Loftus and Her Contributions to Science, Law, and Academic Freedom*, Mahwah, NJ: Lawrence Erlbaum.

20

THE DEFENDANT'S PLEA OF INNOCENT IN SEXUAL ABUSE CASES

Tim Bakken[1]

Through a new plea of 'innocent' (Bakken, 2008), this chapter focuses on a method that would introduce exonerating facts in cases in which the only substantive evidence of guilt comes from one complainant or witness. This method would alleviate the pressure on complainants to prove cases by means of their testimony only, while providing defendants with an opportunity to introduce exonerating facts and to testify truthfully without suffering adverse consequences. Thus if defendants were to plead innocent, submit to an interview with the prosecution, and allege reasonable avenues of inquiry, the government would conduct an investigation with a view toward discovering exonerating facts or help to introduce existing exonerating facts into evidence at trial. This approach is based on the unremarkable, but sometimes underappreciated, premise that no innocent person would ever be convicted if all of the facts in a case were known.

This new procedure would alleviate the inability of resource-poor people to investigate their cases and charge someone in the adversarial system with the task of trying to find the truth. If the government were to continue its prosecution, to account for the disadvantages caused by waiving the right to remain silent, defendants would be entitled to have the jury infer innocence from their behaviour. For example, in some jurisdictions, the first person to whom a complainant reports a sexual assault may testify at trial about the report to bolster the complainant's testimony, even though, normally, the first report would be inadmissible hearsay. The same rule could apply to a defendant who promptly insists on innocence following the first accusation of a sexual assault. Similarly, the jury could be instructed that the plea of innocent and waiver of the right to remain silent are indicative of innocence. In cases in which the defendant has pleaded innocent, the jury's verdict would be based on a standard of proof higher than 'beyond a reasonable doubt'.

New procedures are necessary because the adversarial system does not adequately protect innocent people. As part of the 'process that led to the creation of the modern

---

[1] The views expressed in this article are those of the author and do not reflect the official policy or position of the US government, Department of the Army, or Department of Defense.

Oxford University Press 2016

democratic states' (Langbein, 2003: 342), the adversary system arose in the eighteenth and nineteenth centuries (Vogler, 2005) to rectify the 'blunder of the Middle Ages' (Langbein, 2003: 342). According to John Langbein of Yale Law School:

> The well-meaning reforms of the eighteenth century [England] that resulted in adversary criminal trial had the effect of perpetuating the central blunder of the inherited system: the failure to develop institutions and procedures of criminal investigation and trial that would be responsible for and capable of seeking the truth.
>
> (Langbein, 2003: 343)

By privatizing the investigation process, the adversarial system requires criminal defendants, who are among the poorest and least educated members of society, to be responsible for finding evidence or proving their innocence. The system is infirm, according to Lloyd Weinreb of Harvard Law School, because:

> [I]t encourages the pursuit to the end of whatever may benefit one side or the other... All its other attributes, as we are aware elsewhere throughout our lives, are not virtues but vices, which we recognize collectively as bias.
>
> (Weinreb, 1999: 61)

One of the results of this system, according to Michael Risinger of Seton Hall Law School, was a '3.3% minimum factual *wrongful conviction* rate for capital rape-murders in the 1980s', with a possible 5 per cent wrongful conviction rate (Risinger, 2007: 778–9).

EXONERATING FACTS IN ONE-WITNESS SEXUAL OFFENCE CASES

Exonerating facts escape discovery or are not introduced into evidence because of human error, inability, or malevolence. In one-witness cases, additional substantive facts, beyond the testimony of the witness, may simply not exist. Moreover, in sexual assault cases, in recent decades, the facts that the defendant can obtain from the complainant regarding sexual history have been reduced. Also in sexual assault cases, during the middle of the twentieth century, legislatures required more evidence than a complainant's testimony to justify a conviction. In some instances, the prosecution had to show that the complainant exhibited 'utmost resistance', proof of which could be an injury. In 1903, one state supreme court in the United States approved a representative jury instruction:

> And you cannot find that such intercourse was forcible or against the will of said Ida Andrews [alleged victim] or without her consent, unless you find that she made the utmost resistance of which she was capable to prevent it.[2]

But in the latter part of the twentieth century, legislatures limited the evidence that could be introduced in sexual assault cases. The utmost resistance standard was aban-

---

[2] *State of Missouri v. Boyd*, 178 Mo. 2, 10, 76 S.W. 979, 981 (1903).

doned in the 1950s and 1960s (DelTufo, 2002), and eventually legislatures repealed the laws that required corroboration of the complainant's testimony in sexual offence cases. The UK, for example, abolished corroboration requirements in various cases in 1994[3] and specifically in sexual assault cases.[4] This decreased the number of facts that could be used by the defence, whereas the prior laws (utmost resistance) had required additional facts before a defendant could be convicted. New 'rape shield' laws limited evidence about a complainant's sexual history. The new legislation did not create a new method through which to discover additional facts nor could it: by nature and definition, other than the complainant's (and defendant's) testimony, additional facts do not exist in one-witness cases. The legislation limited the number of facts that the defence could introduce into evidence to impeach the complainant's testimony.

In effect, legislatures reconsidered what evidence is relevant. To illustrate, the US federal evidentiary rules do not permit 'evidence offered to prove that a victim engaged in other sexual behavior' or to prove 'a victim's sexual predisposition'.[5] The Criminal Code of Canada provides that:

> [E]vidence that the complainant has engaged in sexual activity, whether with the accused or with any other person, is not admissible to support an inference that, by reason of the sexual nature of that activity, the complainant (a) is more likely to have consented to the sexual activity that forms the subject-matter of the charge; or (b) is less worthy of belief.[6]

Australia's rape-shield laws are designed to:

> ...prohibit the admission of evidence of a complainant's sexual reputation; prevent the use of sexual history evidence to establish the complainant as a 'type' of person who is more likely to consent to sexual activity; and exclude the use of a complainant's sexual history as an indicator of the complainant's truthfulness.
>
> (Australian Law Reform Commission, 2005: 681–2)

In another sense, courts have allowed legislatures to limit other facts that a jury may consider in a sexual assault case. In *Maryland v. Craig*,[7] the US Supreme Court affirmed a conviction where the alleged child victim testified via closed-circuit television (CCTV), outside the presence of the defendant. The Court found that a defendant in a sexual assault case does not have a constitutional confrontation right to face a child accuser where the prosecution shows that the defendant's presence could cause the child 'severe emotional trauma'. This procedure increases the number of facts if the defendant's absence permits the child to testify more accurately and expansively, but the procedure does limit the right of confrontation, which is designed to promote truth.

Commentators have questioned whether the rape-shield laws are based on relevance in specific criminal cases or on general policy considerations. A teaching manual for a course in evidence at Harvard Law School reads:

---

[3] Criminal Justice and Public Order Act 1994, s. 33(1).
[4] Criminal Justice and Public Order Act 1994, s. 32(1)(b).
[5] US Federal Rules of Evidence, r. 412(a)(1)–(2).　　[6] Criminal Code of Canada, s. 276.
[7] *Maryland v. Craig*, 497 U.S. 836 (1990).

> The per se exclusions of the rape-shield law are predicated on assertions about relevance. There is some tendency for people to think about the concept of relevance as logical and objective. It is important, however, to recognize that concepts of relevance are very much dependent on one's point of view.
>
> (Green, Nesson, and Murray, 2000: 274)

Indeed, in contrast to laws that limit consideration of facts in sexual assault cases, legislatures found that formerly inadmissible evidence should be admissible because it is relevant. Legal relevancy can be based on legislative policy decisions, as noted above, or on scientific research, as noted below. This increase in the number of facts offered at trial had the effect of making convictions easier to obtain in sexual assault cases.

For example, legislation provided that what was formerly considered hearsay evidence could now be introduced, because it is reliable, to bolster the complainant's testimony. In New York State, the first person to whom the complainant reports a sexual assault may testify at trial about the report.[8] In other kinds of cases, this would be inadmissible hearsay,[9] which is a 'statement made outside a current trial or hearing...that a party offers in evidence to prove the truth of the matter asserted in the statement'.[10] The prosecution could argue that such an 'outcry' report is being used to show only that a complainant is not fabricating at trial, under the rationale that he or she previously made a similar statement to the outcry witness. In practice, however, jurors will probably find it difficult not to perceive the outcry witness's testimony as substantive evidence of guilt.

The rationale behind finding that certain evidence is newly relevant in sexual assault cases could be used to increase the number of facts available to defendants to prove their innocence. Under the innocence procedures, the defendant's prompt denial of sexual assault or assertion of innocence could be a basis for concluding that he or she is actually innocent, in the way that a complainant's outcry statement is used to prove that he or she was sexually assaulted. Under the rationale that most people are unlikely to make a false claim of rape, the argument is that an innocent defendant is likely to make a prompt denial of guilt immediately upon being accused, given the infamy and long prison sentences that are attached to a rape conviction.

It is particularly important to recognize relevant facts, including those not previously considered by the justice system, because sexual assault cases are more difficult to judge than other cases. They produce more defences—fabrication, misidentification, consent, and misunderstanding—than any other kind of case. First, in all kinds of cases, defendants confront complainants who fabricate, exaggerate, or lie. Similarly, *misidentification* is a common defence in all cases in which the complainant and defendant are strangers.

But the third and fourth defences are unique to sexual assault cases. Defendants may argue that complainants *consented* to physical contact. In other cases, regardless of whether the defendant and victim are strangers or acquaintances, the consent

---

[8] New York State Unified Court System, Instructions of General Applicability, 'Prompt Outcry', online at <http://www.nycourts.gov/judges/cji/1-General/CJI2d.Prompt_Outcry.pdf>
[9] US Federal Rules of Evidence, r. 802.   [10] US Federal Rules of Evidence, r. 801(c)(1)–(2).

defence is almost non-existent. It would be foolhardy for defendants charged with assault, robbery, or burglary to argue that any complainant consented to the defendant's stabbing her, taking money from her person on the street, or entering her house at midnight.

Further, in using *misunderstanding* as a defence, defendants will admit to having sexual contact with a complainant. But, in addition, the defendant will argue that even if the complainant did not subjectively consent to the contact, perhaps because of intoxication unknown to the defendant, the complainant's conduct would have led a reasonable person to believe that he or she consented. Thus sexual assault cases are more difficult to judge because, ironically, despite producing fewer facts than other cases, they produce more defences. More than in other cases, the jury depends on the testimony of complainants and defendants.

THE APPLICATION OF INNOCENCE PROCEDURES IN SEXUAL ASSAULT CASES

The focus on sexual assault complainants is especially pronounced in the adversarial system, because the accused person does not have to speak to investigators or testify at trial. This limits the facts and avenues of inquiry. An innocent person may choose not speak because his (or her) statements could support the prosecution case, such as an admission that he (or she) was near the scene of an actual crime. In these circumstances, the adversarial process has the perverse effect of preventing such an innocent person from speaking truthfully or, if he (or she) does speak, using his (or her) truthful statement to convict an innocent person. As a remedy to this problem, innocence procedures would allow innocent people to speak truthfully without placing themselves in additional jeopardy.

Especially in sexual assault cases in which consent is the defence and the defendant's testimony is the main or only defence evidence, the interrogation requirement would prevent guilty people from using innocence procedures. Even the most intelligent people have difficulty lying convincingly. Few guilty people's lies can withstand an interrogation prior to trial and the prosecution's preparation for trial based on the information it gleans from the interrogation. Having obtained information from the interrogation, prosecutors will be able to locate and question defence witnesses (although, in a one-witness case, the only witnesses will be the complainant and the defendant). Regardless, the prosecution will learn the defence and can prepare to counter it. If the prosecution proceeds to trial and the defendant testifies, the interrogation will have provided prosecutors with a rehearsal and an opportunity to impeach the defendant's trial testimony with conflicting statements that he (or she) made during the interview.

In addition, innocence procedures provide an alternative to lessen the pressure on complainants in sexual assault cases and increase the number of facts considered at trial. Consider the 'outcry' witness in sexual assault cases. An innocent defendant's post-assault conduct may reflect innocence as much as a victim's post-assault conduct may reflect an actual assault—that is, a legislature's purpose in permitting the outcry witness to testify about what the victim reported, which is normally inadmissible hearsay,[11] is to help the prosecution to prove that an assault occurred. In the US state of Texas, a child complainant's initial first report to an adult of his or her sexual assault, an 'outcry', can be introduced into evidence to show that he or she was sexually assaulted.[12] New York has a 'Prompt Outcry' jury instruction that applies to all complainants:

> The following charge should be included among the factors to consider on the credibility of a witness's testimony: You may consider whether (specify name of complainant) complained of the crime promptly or within a reasonable period of time after its alleged commission. If you find that the complaint was made promptly or within a reasonable time, you may consider whether and to what extent, if any, that fact tends to support the believability of the witness's testimony.[13]

By its terms, this jury instruction does not appear to apply to defendants' prompt cries of innocence, which may be just as reliable as a complainant's prompt outcry of assault. In addition, every US state permits expert testimony to explain complainants' behaviour in sexual assault cases to prove that a sexual assault occurred (Long, Kristiansson, and Mallios, 2013). Comparable social science research could be introduced to evaluate defendants' and other witnesses' behaviour. For example, social science findings could be introduced at trials to indicate the reliability of eyewitness identifications.[14]

Legislatures have determined that sexual assault victims and cases are unique. To the extent that social science can establish that certain behaviour among complainants is indicative of sexual assault, it is logical to conclude that certain behaviour among defendants is indicative of innocence. Indeed, courts have found that certain behaviour is indicative of guilt. In a 2013 case, *Salinas v. Texas*,[15] the US Supreme Court concluded that a defendant's silence at a moment when it might have been natural for him to issue a denial could be introduced at trial as evidence of guilt. His silence reflected an acknowledgement of guilt. It is just as logical to conclude that a defendant's assertion of innocence when it would be natural to assert innocence is evidence of innocence.

In the *Salinas* case, the police questioned a man about his knowledge of a murder of two brothers. The police did not inform him of, and he did not invoke, his constitutional right to remain silent or to be represented by an attorney. For about an hour, the suspect answered questions from the police. At one point, a police officer asked the suspect, who owned a shotgun, whether his shotgun 'would match the shells recovered at the scene of the murder'.[16] According to testimony, the suspect '[l]ooked down at the floor, shuffled his feet, bit his bottom lip, clenched his hands in his lap, [and] began to tighten up'.[17] The Court found that the prosecution could use the suspect's pre-arrest silence to prove his consciousness of guilt. The Court concluded that 'someone might decline to answer a police officer's question . . . because he is trying to think of a good lie, because he is embarrassed, or because he is protecting someone else'.[18]

---

[11] US Federal Rules of Evidence, r. 801(c)(1)–(2).   [12] Texas Code of Criminal Procedure, art. 38.072.
[13] New York State Unified Court System, Instructions of General Applicability, 'Prompt Outcry', online at <http://www.nycourts.gov/judges/cji/1-General/CJI2d.Prompt_Outcry.pdf>
[14] *New Jersey v. Henderson*, 27 A.3d 872 (2011).   [15] *Salinas v. Texas*, 133 S.Ct. 2174 (2013).
[16] *Salinas*, at 2178.   [17] *Salinas*, at 2178.   [18] *Salinas*, at 2182.

Under the same reasoning, a defendant's voluntary statement might be indicative of innocence. A new evidentiary rule that permits the defendant's prompt claim of innocence would be particularly probative because, in one-witness sexual assault cases, the only exonerating facts available to the defendant are likely to be his (or her) actions and statements, whether conducted or made prior to or at trial. Where the defendant makes a prompt pre-arrest denial of a crime, especially if the denial is similar to the denial he (or she) makes during his (or her) post-arrest interrogation, the defendant could be permitted to introduce the denial as proof of innocence. At the end of the trial, the judge could instruct the jury to the same effect. The judge could issue a similar jury instruction to credit the defendant for submitting to an interrogation by the prosecution.

The defendant's pretrial interrogation offers the prosecution a valuable new opportunity to evaluate the complainant's allegation prior to trial, as well as the defendant's defence. These evaluations would cause no trauma, no embarrassment, no public scrutiny, nor any kind of harm to an actual victim. After the prosecution questions the defendant, it could show his (or her) taped interview to the complainant. The defendant would not be present. The complainant would become aware of probable defence questions and could prepare for his or her cross-examination at trial.

Actual victims in sexual assault cases are sometimes confused by the locations of furniture and objects. They sometimes have difficulty estimating time or distance. From the defendant's recorded statement, the complainant could try to recollect time and place facts prior to his or her testimony at trial. Just as importantly, the prosecution could observe how the complainant responded to the defendant's version of events, and assess his or her accuracy and credibility in private, outside the public courtroom. The demeanour of a complainant would provide the prosecutor with significant information to determine how to try to resolve a case through a plea agreement. The entire process would provide many additional facts for the prosecution.

The defendant's recorded statement would act like a lie detector test for both the defendant and complainant. In many one-witness cases, the defence will argue that the complainant is lying. As a homicide prosecutor, I worked with a detective who was a polygraph expert. The results of polygraphs, or 'lie detector' tests, are not admissible in court. The prosecution office where we worked used polygraph results to assess the credibility of witnesses and suspects. In many cases involving internecine neighbourhood violence, a person who appears to be a witness will turn out to be a suspect and suspects will turn out to be witnesses.

While the substantive results of polygraph tests were interesting ('he's truthful or lying'), we were equally or more interested in how the witness or suspect responded when told the results. A person who is told that the 'lie detector' machine shows that he or she is lying may make additional statements. He or she will say that the machine is wrong, but might also admit that he or she was lying about some things—or even confess to a homicide or other crime. The polygraph detective said that, in his career, he had obtained more than 150 incriminating statements from suspects or witnesses through this process.

Police in the UK have used the same approach, in one instance using the results of the polygraph test to make formal post-conviction decisions. In 2011, Hertfordshire police were conducting polygraph tests on suspected first-time sex offenders 'who volunteered to cooperate'. According to a detective, the testing has helped to 'identify additional offences' (BBC News, 2011). In 2013, the police commissioner for South Yorkshire announced that he would offer lie detector tests to sex offenders who were free on bail, or on probation, or in prison to 'assess the risk they pose to the public when released' (Press Association, 2013).

Importantly for the administration of justice, the complainant will view the 'lie-detecting' recorded statement in private, outside the presence of the defendant and defence attorney, and prior to trial. When presented in this setting with an innocent defendant's truthful version of events, an exaggerating or lying complainant will be more likely to moderate or withdraw erroneous or intentionally false statements than to proceed to trial. After viewing a truthful defendant's statement, only the most malevolent lying complainant would maintain a false accusation in such a serious case. In many instances, detectives and prosecutors may recognize the falsity of this complainant's statements and end the prosecution. Absent the prosecution's recognition, any complainant with this character is likely to have exhibited significant bad behaviour in the past that would be admitted into trial through cross-examination. Just as significantly, through this viewing, an honest witness will have a basis to reconsider his or her mistaken identification of the innocent person. It will be far easier for the complainant in this private setting to admit to any doubts than to do so while testifying at trial.

EVIDENCE AND SCIENCE-BASED DECISION-MAKING

The plea of innocent creates a new truth-finding method in an unbalanced chasm of the adversarial system: the pretrial process. The innocence procedures would provide new structural and practical advantages. The plea and procedures would not be activated unless the defendant were voluntarily to plead innocent. Absent the plea, the current process would continue and nothing would be lost (or gained). By means of viewing the defendants' statements, complainants would have expanded opportunities to prepare for trial, at no emotional or resource cost to them.

Prosecutors would obtain a significant number of new facts from their interviews with defendants and the prosecutors would have an expanded opportunity to prepare for trial with complainants who observed the interviews. Prosecutors and the government would have additional responsibility to search for exonerating facts, which is a desirable outcome where defendants have limited or no resources. Any additional pretrial resource allocations to conduct an investigation would be offset by the financial and societal savings of not convicting innocent people and defending those false convictions over decades. Prosecutors would have to meet a standard higher than 'beyond a reasonable doubt', but this would be a natural and fair outcome of discovering, through the interviews with defendants, all of the facts available to the defence and, in effect, all of the defences.

In one-witness sexual assault cases now, the adversarial system's only method of resolution is to focus exclusively on the trial testimony of complainants. These relatively fact-deficient cases—in which few or no other facts exist other than those alleged in complainants' testimony—are hazardous for innocent defendants, because the only real chance for vindication is in undermining a complainant who is mistaken or lying. This method is trying for actual victims, who are, effectively, required to prove the prosecution's case, and counter the spurious defences and unfair disparagement of guilty defendants.

The justice system's dependency on complainants in one-witness cases to provide nearly 100 per cent of the evidence leads to undesirable outcomes. Jurors may be likely to convict defendants if they perceive that anyone brought to trial must be guilty of some offence. Indeed, data indicate that about 68 per cent of arrested persons are guilty of some crime (Cohen and Kyckelhahn, 2010). Actual victims may be less likely to report crimes if they know that they will have to bear the full burden of convicting guilty people. Complainants who are mistaken, exaggerating, or lying have unprecedented control over innocent defendants.

To support or counter evidentiary changes, social science research should be considered to determine whether certain statements and behaviours of complainants and defendants indicate truthfulness or the presence or absence of any crime. This research would be particularly important in sexual assault cases, in which complainants may come forward long after the alleged assaults, when statutes of limitations would normally prevent prosecutions, and in cases in which the accused persons, such as clergy, teachers, and child care workers have occupied positions of trust with the complainants, who may have been children when the alleged assaults occurred. Moreover, unlike all other cases, a single sexual assault trial may contain the testimony of many complainants about one defendant. These cases add additional layers of uniqueness beyond the defences of consent and misunderstanding. The cases involve psychological, sociological, economic, and cultural forces that exist only rarely, if ever, in other cases. The delayed or 'historical' accusation and multiple-one-witness cases are very difficult to defend for the simple reason that facts outside the statements of complainants will usually not be available.[19]

However, even if social scientists could construct experiments to test the reliability of delayed and multiple-one-witness accusations, the legal system is not yet hospitable to the introduction of the findings of social science research. In an American death penalty case from 1987, *McCleskey v. Kemp*,[20] McCleskey, a black defendant, had been found guilty and sentenced to death by a jury for killing a white police officer. On appeal and without dispute, the condemned defendant showed that a killer of a white victim is 4.3 times more likely than a killer of a black victim to receive the death penalty. Nonetheless, using largely circular reasoning, the Court found that this irrefutable social science finding was not legally relevant because this particular killer could not show, at least to the Court's satisfaction, that he suffered racial discrimination. The Court permitted McCleskey's execution. Of course, many findings and conclusions in the natural world are based on statistical correlations. In finding the killer's statistics

---

[19] In February 2014, a British actor, Bill Roache, was acquitted of allegedly assaulting five teenagers in the 1960s and 1970s. One of the complainants was aged 15 at the time of the alleged assault and testified against Roache by video-link at the age of 62 (Pidd, 2014).

[20] *McCleskey v. Kemp*, 481 U.S. 279 (1987).

insufficient, the Court simply decided not to apply social science research to an actual case.

Courts could admit into evidence scientific research regarding the reliability of delayed accusations, how witnesses in the serial one-witness cases within one trial affect each other's testimony, and how juries perceive delayed accusations and one-witness cases. In 2011, the highest court in one US state (New Jersey) took a significant first step in this direction. It concluded that social science research about the ability of eyewitnesses and the procedures surrounding their identification of suspects could be introduced into evidence through expert testimony. Based on the research and testimony, jurors would be instructed on to how to view the evidence.[21] Thus, like all scientific decisions, especially in sexual assault cases, which are unique, some legal decisions should be based on inferences that arise from research and findings generally about all cases, witnesses, and defendants.

CONCLUSION: PROTECTING INNOCENT PEOPLE AND ACTUAL VICTIMS

The innocence procedures outlined in this chapter would open new avenues of inquiry in one-witness cases. By requiring defendants who plead innocent to agree to be interviewed by the prosecution, the procedures are designed to prevent guilty defendants from using the procedures. Defendants who plead innocent and submit to an interrogation will be entitled to have the jury consider their prompt denials of guilt and to argue that innocence should be inferred from the denials, despite hearsay rules that now prohibit such prior statements. Defendants may ask judges to instruct juries that their prompt denials and submission to post-arrest interrogation are indicators of innocence. Where defendants plead innocent and comply with their obligations, juries would be required to find guilt at a standard higher than 'beyond a reasonable doubt'.

If verdicts and legal decisions are to become more reliable, courts will have to be more amenable to social science research. Legislatures and courts have determined that sexual assault complainants' prior sexual behaviour may not generally be admitted into evidence, but that their outcry statements may be admitted. The best scientific reason for excluding the sexual history and admitting the outcry would be research showing that sexual history has no bearing on whether a complainant consented and that an outcry indicates that an assault occurred. Legislatures and courts are already admitting evidence based on presumptions or research about sexual history and outcries.

Designed to protect innocent people, these procedures are similar to those designed to support actual victims. Defendants' and victims' pretrial behaviours and statements would be admitted at trial because they are reliable indicators of whether or not a sexual assault occurred. This new focus on the defendant's conduct would lessen the

[21] *State v. Henderson*, 27 A.3d 872 (2011).

pressure on actual victims to support an entire prosecution case. The additional facts produced through these procedures would ensure more accurate verdicts than are possible in the current adversarial system.

REFERENCES

Australian Law Reform Commission (2005) 'Matters outside the Uniform Evidence Acts–Rape Shield Laws', in *Uniform Evidence Law Report*, pp. 679–97 (Chapter 20). Available online at <http://www.alrc.gov.au/sites/default/files/pdfs/publications/ALRC102.pdf> [accessed October 2014].

BAKKEN, T. (2008) 'Truth and Innocence Procedures to Free Innocent Persons: Beyond the Adversarial System', *University of Michigan Journal of Law Reform*, 41: 547–83.

BBC News (2011) 'Police Trial Lie Detectors on Sex Offender Suspects', 31 December. Available online at <http://www.bbc.co.uk/news/uk-16371043> [accessed May 2016].

COHEN, T. H., and KYCKELHAHN, T. (2010) 'Felony Defendants in Large Urban Counties, 2006', *U.S. Bureau of Justice Statistics Bulletin*, May; rev'd 15 July, pp. 1–41. Available online at <http://www.bjs.gov/content/pub/pdf/fdluc06.pdf> [accessed May 2016].

DELTUFO, K. M. (2002) 'Resisting "Utmost Resistance": Using Rape Trauma Syndrome to Combat Underlying Rape Myths Influencing Acquaintance Rape Trials', *Boston College Third World Law Journal*, 22(2): 419–43.

GREEN, E. D., NESSON, C. R., and MURRAY, P. L. (2000) *Problems, Cases, and Materials on Evidence*, 3rd edn (Teacher's Manual). Available online at <http://www.law.harvard.edu/publications/evidenceiii/professorspages/tmch3d.htm> [accessed October 2014].

LANGBEIN, J. H. (2003) *The Origins of Adversary Criminal Trial*, Oxford: Oxford University Press.

LONG, J. G., KRISTIANSSON, V., and MALLIOS, C. (2013) 'When and How: Admitting Expert Testimony on Victim Behavior in Sexual Assault Cases in Pennsylvania', *Strategies in Brief*, 18. Available online at <http://www.aequitasresource.org/When-and-How-Admitting-Expert-Testimony-on-Victim-Behavior-in-PA-Issue-18.pdf> [accessed May 2016].

PIDD, H. (2014) 'Coronation Street Actor Bill Roache Cleared of Rape and Sexual Assault', *The Guardian*, 7 February. Available online at <http://www.theguardian.com/uk-news/2014/feb/06/bill-roache-cleared-rape-sexual-assault> [accessed May 2016].

Press Association (2013) 'Sex Offenders Face Lie Detector Tests before Release from Prison', *The Guardian*, 20 November. Available online at <http://www.theguardian.com/uk-news/2013/nov/20/sex-offenders-lie-detector-tests-release-prison> [accessed May 2016].

RISINGER, D. M. (2007) 'Criminal Law: Innocents Convicted—An Empirically Justified Factual Wrongful Conviction Rate', *Journal of Criminal Law and Criminology*, 97: 761–1295.

VOGLER, R. (2005) *A World View of Criminal Justice*, Aldershot: Ashgate.

WEINREB, L. W. (1999) 'Legal Ethics: The Adversary Process is not an End in Itself', *Journal of the Institute for the Study of Legal Ethics*, 2: 59–64.

21

REDUCING THE INCIDENCE AND HARMS OF WRONGFUL ALLEGATIONS OF ABUSE

Ros Burnett

> Of course the system should strive to ensure the conviction of the guilty too, but it should be borne in mind that no one, and certainly not the victims of crime, has a defensible interest in the conviction of innocent people.
>
> (Ashworth, 2006: 248)

A legal system that has traditionally served defendants well, following principles supportive of the Blackstone ratio ('better that ten guilty persons escape than that one innocent suffer'),[1] unfortunately has worked against the less powerful in society—in particular, women and children who were physically or sexually abused, but whose complaints were disbelieved. In the absence of tangible evidence, prejudice against the credibility of complainants based on their class, gender, or past conduct enabled offenders to 'get away with it', and victims were left to bear both the effects of the abuse and rejection as liars. That situation has now changed. Spurred on by victim advocacy groups, and human rights and feminist movements, recent decades have witnessed the rise of victim-focused criminal justice policies (Hoyle and Zedner, 2007), and much has been achieved to rebalance the system so that it is more attuned to the needs of victims and in order to achieve more prosecutions and convictions of the guilty.[2]

But many critics now argue that this rebalancing has gone too far, as a result of which a previous bias in favour of the more reputable accused party has switched to a bias against them. Paradoxically, the injustices that victims of abuse experienced for decades of being ignored and disbelieved are now, instead, being experienced by people wrongly accused of abuse. This final chapter offers an overview of the core obstacles and requirements in addressing the problem of wrongful allegations, drawing on the critical and constructive arguments made throughout the book. Most of the

---

[1] Derived from Blackstone (1765–69).

[2] It is clear from reports by victims' advocates that genuine victims of abuse continue to be reticent about reporting offences in case they are disbelieved and discredited. No doubt media coverage of high-profile cases in which individuals have been falsely accused act as a further disincentive. The rate of attrition between reporting such offences and achieving convictions has remained stubbornly high: see reports reviewed by Angiolini (2015).

contributors have elucidated the underlying causes and conditions that generate false reports and their acceptance as true, and they have made important observations regarding particular areas for reform. In the short space available, the following is necessarily selective and brief. Fundamentally, there is a need for (a) wrongful allegations of abuse to be officially and publicly acknowledged as a serious and rising social problem, (b) adjustments to investigative procedures, trials, and evidential standards that allow for actual innocence, and (c) transcendence of polarization and binary thinking.

ACKNOWLEDGING WRONGFUL ALLEGATIONS AS A PROBLEM

No one wants to set the clock back against the progress that has been made in advancing justice for children and women who have been sexually abused. Indeed, while that progress has been broadly welcomed, campaigners and researchers in these fields contend that more needs to be done to increase convictions for rape (Reece, 2013) and for victims of child abuse (for example Staller and Faller, 2010). Given the extent and impact of sexual offending, the drive to do more is understandable; the question is whether that prioritizing should be allowed to obscure the ever-present risk of innocent people being wrongly accused and to remove safeguards to protect innocent defendants.

HAS ONE FORM OF INSTITUTIONAL BIAS BEEN REPLACED WITH ANOTHER?

Internationally, there has been a shift driven by the child protection industry, feminism, and victims' advocates towards a doctrine of accepting self-defined victimhood and believing the victim. In England and Wales, numerous changes have been made to encourage victims of sexual abuse to report offences, including a removal of time limits for delayed prosecutions, and to make the court experience less traumatic, including guaranteed anonymity and opportunities to provide evidence via video links or from behind a screen. The extent to which revised prosecution policy has moved to presumptive guilt of the defendant in alleged sexual offences was starkly conveyed by former Director of Public Prosecutions (DPP) Sir Keir Starmer (2014), when he stressed the need for change of approach in 'assessing victim credibility in child sexual abuse cases'. He argued that:

> What is required is an attitude shift across the criminal justice system. The old tests of credibility have to go and they have to be replaced with a more sophisticated approach that starts with the assumption that the victim is telling the truth ...
>
> (Starmer, 2014: 782)

This shift to an automatic recognition of complainants as victims, followed by support and protections prior to and during court proceedings and guaranteed anonymity, is replicated in other jurisdictions and in civil proceedings. It is, for example, being extensively played out in the war against so-called rape culture across college campuses in the United States.

The contemporary justice scene across developed countries is aptly characterized by Frank Furedi, in Chapter 4, as one in which believing the victim has become a moral imperative: 'The mere allegation of victimization is all that is required to gain the designation of a victim [while the] implicit rebranding of an unproven allegation into evidence all but relieves the accuser of the burden of proof.' To make up for past errors, blanket support for self-identified victims now trumps the need for empirical truth on a case-by-case basis. Not only are evidential standards and fair trials at stake, but also the inherent danger of people being wrongly accused of abuse, with damaging consequences, applies civil settings, before and beyond criminal justice processes. In the risk-averse modern era, as Hebenton and Seddon explain in Chapter 7, the 'precautionary principle' is more concerned with anticipating risk, and therein pre-empting the need for certainty before taking preventative action. Contrary to minimizing false positives (treating innocent people as guilty), 'the logic of precaution attacks law itself' by introducing counter-law measures to restrict the liberty of suspects for the sake of saving the next potential victim.

RAISING AWARENESS OF THE PREVALENCE, CAUSES AND CONTEXT FOR WRONGFUL ALLEGATIONS

Raising the spectre of false allegations is criticized as victim-blaming and needlessly contributing to the unwillingness of victims to report abuse. Those raising these objections generally insist that the number of false allegations is miniscule compared with the sky-high incidence of abuse, and statistics from notoriously flawed studies are then cited to support that argument. Narrower conceptions of 'false' as fake, and applied to only one category of abuse (rape, child abuse) and one category of complainant (children, women), might begin to warrant arguments that such allegations are relatively 'rare'. These are a small proportion of our more broadly defined concept of wrongful allegations, which brings together mistaken and fake allegations of child abuse and sexual offences against adults; likewise those rare cases that are identified as false because there happens to be objective evidence, such as video footage or an alibi that catches the complainant in a lie or a mistake. These are the uncommon cases in which the accusers might be charged with 'wasting police time' or 'perverting the course of justice' (Levitt, 2013), the low statistics being frequently cited to support claims that untrue allegations more generally are too few to be of concern.

In a discussion of what is known about 'false allegations of rape', Candida Saunders (2012: 1169) noted the lack of an agreed definition and concluded that 'the only thing we know with any certainty about the prevalence of false allegations of rape is that we do not know how prevalent they are'. The same lacuna applies more generally to the related, but considerably broader, province of 'wrongful allegations of sexual and child abuse' in civil and criminal justice contexts. Compared with the numerous large-scale surveys conducted on the prevalence of child abuse and rape, and the inclusion of these offences in self-report crime surveys, no full-scale or rigorous survey has been conducted on the prevalence of false allegations of sexual abuse. There is a pressing need for methodologically rigorous empirical research to establish a reliable estimate of wrongful allegations of abuse. Achieving this would be a significant challenge, but should be attempted because, as Rumney (2006: 129) observed in his review of research on false allegations of rape, incorrect assumptions about false complaints are a poor basis for developing related policies.

In the absence of a representative survey on prevalence, one need only consider the multiple causal factors leading to wrongful allegations of abuse, as set out by Felicity Goodyear-Smith's typology in Chapter 8, to appreciate that wrongful allegations of abuse are far from rare, and are even likely to be multiplying throughout the current spate of inquiries and appeals for self-identified victims to come forward. Although it means raising issues that some may find morally objectionable on behalf of victims of abuse, there are moral reasons on behalf of innocent people who are wrongly accused for us all to be mindful of the ways in which victim culture is conducive to false allegations. Thus, while acknowledging the suffering of genuine victims and their entitlement to seek redress, several of the contributors discuss the compensatory benefits that might result from recognition as a victim, including sympathy, praise, a sense of self-worth, and purpose in identifying with the plight of victims and crusading against sex offenders. Such side benefits could reasonably be expected also to attract some false allegations from claimants jumping on the bandwagon, as well as the possibility of financial compensation. They too might have experienced deprived and abusive backgrounds, and may feel morally justified in accusing someone whom they wrongly suspect to be an abuser (Gunn, 2013). Alternatively, they may have persuaded themselves that have been abused by someone who is in fact innocent (Maran, 2010).

Placing this into a broader context, in Chapter 9, Barbara Hewson points towards a therapeutic and cultural climate that persuades people to attribute their adult problems to repressed experiences of child abuse and in which they are encouraged to seek closure by bringing their alleged abuser to face justice. She observes that:

> The extraordinary proliferation of historic sex abuse scandals in the UK in recent decades has also helped to forge a growing victim class, as well as an appetite on the part of the public for tales of victimhood…and a desire on the part of politicians and policymakers to garner popular support by adopting the victim cause.

Further, Hewson squares up to some unpalatable truths that most people do not have the courage to address because of the *ad hominem* attacks that are likely to follow from militant victims' advocates. One of these is that a claim for repeated sexual assault is going to get a bigger payout than a claim for an isolated case of physical chastisement.

Another unpalatable truth is that it is in the interests of professionals who counsel or represent victims for them to believe that post-traumatic stress disorder (PTSD) and lifelong damage result from sexual abuse. It provides more work for therapists, while, for personal injury lawyers, as Hewson observes, there is a 'harsh economic logic' involved: the greater the harm, the greater the damages that are potentially recoverable, with a bigger proportion in legal fees—and, in the case of multiple claims against institutions backed by insurers, the greater the pressure to settle. It is easy to see, therefore, situations in which claimants might be implicitly encouraged to exaggerate and bend the truth. David Rose is also critical, in Chapter 12, of the tactics used by personal injury solicitors that facilitate bogus complaints alongside any genuine ones. As well as advertising in prison newsletters for former care home residents to raise complaints, their meetings with groups of complainants allow collusion and their class actions against institutions mean that claimants rarely need to face cross-examination in civil trials, because such claims are normally settled out of court.

IMPROVING INVESTIGATIVE INTERVIEWING AND THE STANDARD OF EVIDENCE

It is axiomatic that someone should not be charged with a reported crime without supporting evidence. While that would leave some genuine victims without recourse to bring charges against someone, to simply ignore the need for evidence takes us into a surreal version of the justice system. The absence of evidence in sexual offences has always presented policing and the trial process with challenges. But now the 'criteria for admission of similar fact evidence [has become] much weaker' (Scott, 2015: 33). Yet the higher standard of proof ('beyond a reasonable doubt') is all-important in criminal trials for charges of sexual abuse that are proceeded against on the basis of verbal testimony, with trials for historical abuse being especially challenging. In the words of Andrew Ashworth (2006: 248):

> No jurisdiction has yet devised a form of criminal trial that can guarantee absolute accuracy in fact-finding. It is often difficult to establish the truth after the event, not least when the system depends on oral evidence given many months (sometimes years) later.

INVESTIGATOR BIAS AND FALLIBILITIES

Police are susceptible to confirmation biases just like everyone else, leading them to focus on information and beliefs that support their beliefs. In Chapter 13, Deborah Davis and Richard Leo describe the processes whereby this is played out in interrogations that lead to false confessions. Investigators ask guilt-presumptive questions and put more pressure on someone who claims innocence, who may belong to certain groups and professions now stereotyped as attracting paedophiles. The more a person protests innocence and appears to be an upright member of the community, the more he or she may be seen as hiding behind a veneer that has helped him or her to cover up wrongdoing. What investigators should be doing, of course, as Davis and Leo remind us, is leaving open the possibility that a named person may indeed be innocent. This is in line with the argument of Naughton (2013: 233) that there is a need for police officers to adopt a 'more objective approach that takes seriously the possibility that the accused or the suspect may be factually innocent'.

Despite advances in policing detection methods and interrogation procedures (Bull, 2014), investigators are fallible and have blind spots that are avoidant of cognitive dissonance (Tavris and Aronson, 2015). Suspected sex offences are particularly challenging to investigate when the only evidence is the accounts from complainant and suspect (Westera and Kebbell, 2014). David Rose points to the application of different standards in the policing of alleged sexual crimes compared to other detection work: 'The strangest thing of all is that police officers, usually so sceptical of the stories told by convicted criminals, have sometimes accepted them wholesale without conducting basic checks if they happen to concern claims of historic abuse.'

To the extent that interrogation may involve lie detection techniques, the most important point to draw from Galit Nahari's review in Chapter 18 of advances in deception research is how unreliable the outcomes of such efforts are, even when conducted by experts and with the use of tools. The results obtained are not much better than chance and practitioners are little better than laypersons at detecting deception. There are mixed findings on whether or not training improves the accuracy of deception detection (Porter, Woodworth, and Birt, 2000; Meissner and Kassin, 2002). While Nahari's chapter usefully indicates promising approaches being developed, a conclusion to be drawn is that legal professionals and juries would benefit from education about the fallibility of deception-detection methods and on how appearances can be misleading. Indeed, prior expectations and beliefs may be more relevant than actual techniques.

A MORE QUESTIONING STANCE TO THE VALIDITY OF ACCOUNTS AS EVIDENCE

Serious questions must be raised about the value of accounts as reliable testimony. In all accounts of social interactions, and especially in respect of delayed allegations of occurrences years ago, it is inevitable that details will be (re)constructed, perhaps including the salient event and inferences drawn from it. In a delayed prosecution, courts are prepared to overlook missing factual detail if they find the distress of the witness compelling and if testimony contains narrative realism (Ward, 2012). Regarding reconstruction of former events, Hacking (1998, quoted by Ward, 2012) notes that former events may be freshly experienced in the (re)telling years later at a time when the significance is likely to be understood in the light of concepts and inferences from that later period.

In Chapter 5, Mark Smith refers to the 'basic epistemological problem' in treating accounts as a 'mirror' of what happened when there is no verifying forensic evidence. It is basic social science methodology to recognize that accounts cannot be accepted on face value as evidence and that retrospective accounts are particularly prone to post hoc rationalizations. Also, a distinction should be made between 'testimony as recognition' (for recovery and giving victims a voice) and testimony as evidence. Barbara Hewson, in Chapter 9, and also Luke Gittos, in Chapter 14, describe how therapy and litigation have become dangerously intertwined when accounts elicited for therapy recovery are then used as part of class actions to gain compensation from institutions for alleged historical abuse by their (sometimes dead) former employees. Here, controversies about the value of 'recovered memories' must be confronted.

Another sensitive issue that cannot be ignored is the temptation to fabricate or exaggerate past experience in the hope of gaining compensation. To broach this may be regarded as insulting to genuine victims who are applying for compensation, although they would probably concur that bogus applicants do not help their own cases. The reality was, and is, that many complainants who report as adults that they were abused as children grew up in emotionally deprived and materially disadvantaged families, and were sent 'into care' because 'they were beyond the control of their parents or because they had become involved in youthful criminality', a background in which they 'sometimes learn that the art of deception is necessary to survival' and in which they thus 'can become skilled confabulators' (Webster, 2005: 129). As well as the resentment that may be harboured against harsh treatment by authority figures in the past, 'the potency of the compensation factor should not be underestimated' (Webster, 1998: 27). It does not take much imagination to work out that, as well as psychological factors, there would also be a financial incentive for impoverished former residents to come up with serious allegations once aware that six-figure sums could be attainable.

The chapter by David Rose, with an account of his own investigations into alleged past abuse in children's care homes, provides detailed examples of the set of conditions, identified by Webster (1998, 2005), that led to a series of miscarriages of justice circa 2000. Those incendiary conditions were regenerated (in what Rose has likened to the film *Groundhog Day*) following the eruption of the Jimmy Savile scandal in late 2012. The lessons to be drawn from Rose's chapter are similar to the recommendations that followed that earlier period and which were set out in the Home Affairs Select Committee (2002) report, *The Conduct of Investigations into Past Cases of Abuse in Children's Homes*. Regrettably, those recommendations were not acted on by the government—but the report continues to be relevant and should remain essential reading.

PROMOTING KNOWLEDGE OF HOW MEMORY WORKS

Of critical importance to the outcome of trials is the confidence placed in recovered memories of abuse and decision-makers' understanding of how memory works. In their overview of survey findings in Chapter 11, French and Ost identify the gap between memory researchers' views about how memory works and what is commonly believed by non-experts (members of the public, therapists and clinicians, and academic psychologists with other specialisms). Memory researchers accept that mildly traumatic events may be forgotten, but largely do not accept theories that traumatic memories can be repressed (with no recall) and then retrieved intact at a later stage, generally with the help of a therapist, support group, or counselling literature. Yet voluminous scientific research findings show that false memories can be induced that people come to believe as true.

Given that the non-expert groups identified in French and Ost's review include people who believe fervently in theories of repression and dissociation, often with influential roles as therapists or as jury members, Robert Belli's even-handed review in Chapter 19 of studies on true and false 'recovered memories' is important in recognizing that this highly contested area of psychology is far from resolved and in keeping open the lines of communication between those from different fields who may be called as expert witnesses. The most cogent insights are arguably that 'the living brain is dynamic, and even the most vivid traumatic memories are not literal, unchanging reproductions of what occurred' (McNally, 2005: 818), and that changing someone's memories may be similar to persuading them to changing their mind (Nash, Wheeler, and Hope, 2015). That does not override the possibility of people needing help to understand and cope with continuous memories that are painful to address, to aid their recovery; what does need to be accepted, though, is that some forms of therapy are highly dangerous in fostering false memories and influencing members of the public to believe that adult difficulties may be attributable to repressed memories of childhood abuse, resulting in wrongful convictions and broken families (Pendergrast, 1997).

THE IMPORTANCE OF CORROBORATIVE EVIDENCE

One way in which sexual offences are a *crimen exceptum* in many jurisdictions is that corroboration is no longer required for a jury to reach a guilty verdict; it is enough for the alleged victim to provide testimony of the alleged crime. While this facilitates the conviction of those who are guilty, it inevitably risks the conviction of innocent people. In Chapter 17, Steve Herman argues that strong corroboration should be required before prosecutions are brought for child sexual abuse, not least because of the harm caused to non-abused children in such cases. He holds up to the light the tendency of officials to use the term 'substantiation' as a basis for prosecution—a concept that is synonymous with corroboration in dictionary definitions, but which merely means that that a caseworker believes that a child or a parent is telling truth.

Another unsatisfactory form of evidence that passes for corroboration in trials for alleged sexual abuse is 'similar fact' evidence, whereby testimony is provided by more than one witness claiming to have been a victim. Although there is no objective proof, the claims of each person are allowed to stand as verification each for the other. Richard Webster (2002) has traced the erosion of the original legal concept of similar fact evidence, showing how a principle that was originally a safeguard to protect innocent defendants and 'an essential means of keeping prejudicial evidence out... [became] the favoured device of the prosecution, valued as an almost ever-open conduit for letting prejudicial evidence in'.

Although there had been judicial warnings that a defendant could face a number of witnesses, all of whom might be making false allegations on the basis of collusion or a contamination process, a House of Lords judgment in 1991[3] rejected the requirement for allegations to be strikingly similar and a further House of Lords judgment in 1995[4] required that 'in ruling on the admissibility of a series of similar allegations, the judge should generally assume that the allegations in question were true' (Webster, 2002). David Rose notes that restoring safeguards before accepting similar allegations as corroboration was among the recommendations of the Home Affairs Select Committee (2002) report that were not taken up by government. The dangers

---

[3] *DPP v P* [1991] 2 AC 447.   [4] *R v H* [1995] 2 AC 596.

of collusion and contamination are now much greater with the growth of Internet use and social networking.

Davis and Leo, in Chapter 13 on false confessions, draw attention to the dangers of stereotypes biasing investigators against suspects who are members of occupational groups that have become associated with forms of criminality. Those stereotypes will have also impacted on members of juries, who inevitably bring their prejudices into the courtroom. For example, it must be open to question whether an innocent priest or boarding school teacher charged with historical abuse would be given the benefit of any doubt when the 'evidence' presented amounts to what Davis and Leo call a 'contest of credibility' between the defendant and the complainant. In recognition of powerful memes about paedophile rings within certain professions, the introduction of a required judge's warning against stereotyping would be appropriate in these cases.

IMPROVE RESPONSES TO PEOPLE MAINTAINING INNOCENCE

While the human right to be presumed innocent is applicable only until 'proven guilty', it is clear from the lamentable record of miscarriages of justice on both sides of the Atlantic that a proportion of prisoners who maintain their innocence are indeed innocent. That prison and probation staff are obliged to ignore this fact, and that the system can by default extend the punishment of those who maintain innocence, adds to the profound injustice done to innocent prisoners and their families. There is therefore an urgent need for appropriate training and protocols at each stage of the criminal justice process, allowing staff to recognize the contingency of innocence, in place of a system that automatically labels those maintaining their innocence as 'in denial'.

For example, in Chapter 15, Daniel Medwed proposes that parole board members could be educated on the innocent prisoner's dilemma at different stages of the criminal process when faced with the benefits of false admission of guilt versus the hazards of maintaining innocence. Towards this, he suggests that prisoners protesting innocence could be allowed hearings to explain the basis for their claim and that parole boards could be empowered to make inquiries, 'provided that such inquiries are limited to the issue of suitability for release on parole and are not a formal determination of guilt or innocence'. Similar awareness training could be extended to all practitioners who work with prisoners and former prisoners on licence. Insofar as there are official and voluntary organizations that investigate claims of innocence, as Medwed suggests, practitioners could be enabled to refer innocence claims to them for evaluation. Innocent people condemned to remain registered as sex offenders are caught in a cruel, invidious position; probation officers could help them to endure this if they were enabled to use their own judgement once they learn more about the individual and his or her case.

With regard to the appeal process, although the Criminal Cases Review Commission (CCRC) in England and Wales is admired by, and being emulated in, other countries, a drawback for applicants convicted of sexual offences is that the CCRC will refer cases back to the Court of Appeal only if it considers there to be a 'real possibility' of the case being quashed. When a jury has reached a guilty verdict in the absence of evidence beyond a complainant's testimony, fresh evidence is unlikely to be available to applicants. In Chapter 16, Michael Zander alludes to a conundrum: jury verdicts are treated as unassailable, yet juries are fallible. He proposes that the Court of Appeal should exercise its powers to retry cases if it has doubts about a jury's decision. If that were to occur in appropriate cases, then fewer post-conviction appeals would need recourse to the CCRC. Medwed offers hope with regard to US appellate courts, which have taken note of his important research on prosecutorial susceptibility to cognitive biases (Medwed, 2012). Those biases (such as 'confirmation bias', 'status quo bias'), he argues, are likely to influence the outcome of appeals and litigation. Accordingly, he recommends 'innocence units' within prosecutors' offices, so that the original decision-maker is not involved in post-conviction reviews.

The presumption of innocence is subject to various threats (Ashworth, 2006) and has been undermined in the modern era. Ashworth (2006: 241) maintains that there has been a 'tide running in the opposite direction' in which public safety has been prioritized ahead of concerns about rights, and that '[c]riminal justice systems must strive to ensure that the public censure of a conviction, and the ensuing sentence, should not be imposed on an innocent defendant' (Ashworth, 2006: 247). In a radical suggestion towards that ideal, in Chapter 20, Timothy Bakken proposes the introduction of a 'plea of innocence'. On the basis that 'no innocent person would ever be convicted if all of the facts in a case were known', he suggests 'innocence procedures' that would place the onus on defendants, with support from an appointed official, to pursue lines of inquiry that would introduce exonerating facts in cases in which the only substantive evidence of guilt comes from one complainant or witness. Whether this speaks to an obvious path that should be taken in such cases, or whether it is an untenable proposition in a criminal justice system that does not recognize innocence as an admissible legal concept and which would require the suspension of provisions now sanctified to protect assumed victims, Bakken's focus on innocence procedures throw light on the distinct lack of fairness for innocent defendants in sexual abuse trials. It points towards the limitations on evidence that they are allowed to bring in their defence and highlights the oddity of a system that theoretically has the presumption of 'innocent until proven guilty' at its heart, but in practice is eroding that in favour of the a priori victimhood of prosecution witnesses.

REDUCING HOSTILITY AND STRIKING A BETTER BALANCE

It doubles the injustice, and adds insult to injury, that people wrongly accused of child abuse and other sexual offences are subjected to extreme verbal abuse, attacks, and harassment on social media, and sometimes hate crimes involving vandalism of their property or violent attacks. Those offering support either to people who have committed sexual offences or to people accused of sexual offences are attacked and subjected to similar abuse and harassment. These excessive responses are fuelled by the media, in which sex offenders and suspected sex offenders are typically depicted as calculating monsters, with photos or commentary that portray them in the worst possible light.

There is a need for differentiation between degrees of seriousness of same-named offences and for proportionality in responses to them. The labels 'teenager' and 'adolescent' have been replaced by the generic 'child'—and, with that, anyone attracted to a post-pubescent young person who is legally under age is now incorrectly branded as a 'paedophile'. Such is the unequivocal condemnation of sex with children that anyone suggesting that some offences are less serious than others can find themselves vilified as enabling rape and child abuse. As argued by Cameron-Blackie (2015: 32), equal censure now seems to fall on, for example, 'fooling around with a 15 year old groupie who was throwing herself at you, and actually attacking a 6 year old girl from the bushes', but to blur such distinctions 'is perverting the general public's view of what a sexual offence is and...if you pervert the general public's view you are actually perverting the jury's view'.

Prominent reportage of sexual abuse in the media needs to be balanced with continued coverage of cases that are subsequently cleared, after disconfirming evidence has been revealed. Rose gives the example of the Jersey child abuse scandal, which reported that human bones had been found, but subsequent investigation of which revealed that what was thought to be human bone was, in fact, coconut shell—and yet 'the factual corrective to Harper's narrative of Evil received only a fraction of the attention given the original, bogus allegations'. Rose points out that, since the Jimmy Savile scandal broke, such correctives have become even rarer.

TRANSCEND BINARY THINKING

A barrier to balanced debate is the polarization between advocates for victims of sexual offences and those who are focused on defendants' rights and due process for people maintaining innocence. It is inherent in the adversarial system to divide people into guilty or innocent, and victim or perpetrator. While those pure types exist, there is 'a need to move beyond monochromatic understandings of victims and offenders of sexual crime' (McAlinden, 2014: 180), to recognize that the same individuals may be both victim and offender at different times, and that, on a case-by-case basis, there are complexities and grey areas that cannot be easily shoehorned into the mould of ideal types. Further, whether someone is innocent, and whether someone is a victim, in many instances cannot be definitively established. That should not deter people from being compassionate and helpful to those who claim they are, but it is grounds for being less peremptory.

Interest groups can get their message across more starkly by using ideal types and outré examples, and by stoking public outrage to silence critics. Reece (2013) refers to training programmes aimed at dispelling stereotypes about rape, but which involve labelling as 'myth' what is actually a mixture of fact and opinion (such as the view that stranger rape is more serious than relationship rape) and promulgating the view that arguments with which they disagree are rape-supportive. 'The message of these initiatives', she suggests, 'functions to close down, not open up, the possibilities of a productive public conversation about these important and at times vexed questions' (Reece, 2013: 473).

Victims deserve compassion and sensitive treatment, but that should not exclude discussion and critical enquiry. And those who are most strident and unwilling to acknowledge the dangers of 'false positives' in the present climate should be challenged to think beyond their own interest group. After all, as Hebenton and Seddon explain in Chapter 7, 'the logic of precaution drives an inversion of the traditional criminal justice paradigm' and the priority is to eliminate 'false negatives' (letting those who might be guilty go free), whatever that takes. If we continue, as now, ratcheting up the protection for self-defined victims, and proceed on the basis that the accused are guilty on the evidence of an accusation and that those who question this are co-offenders, then we really will be back in the era, depicted in Furedi's Chapter 4, of the *Malleus Malleficarum* and Jean Bodin's logic in early modern Europe for ensuring that all accused persons are treated as guilty—a terrifying and shameful state of affairs to have reached in the twenty-first century.

A more balanced and constructive approach may lie in efforts to transcend binary thinking. Wood and Petriglieri (2005: 31) claim that 'the inherent tension leading to polarization conceals an important developmental opportunity, if we "hold" the tension long enough to permit exploration, differentiation and resolution'. They argue that, '[f]or synthesis to occur, on the other hand, some third element needs to incorporate and balance the tension of opposites, mediating and facilitating its generative function' (Wood and Petriglieri, 2005: 36). Applying such an approach to the present febrile movement to rid the world of sexual abusers and the less conspicuous, because oppressed, movement to save the innocent from wrongful convictions[5] would require substantial research funding and governmental resources to link up the specialist research areas and to unite the presently divided voluntary effort.

In the meantime, a preparedness to discuss the above-mentioned middle ground—and a willingness to share the moral high ground—could help to form a bridge between the polarity of opposites. An example of this is the concept of 'honest false testimony' elucidated by Villalobos, Davis, and Leo in their discussion, in Chapter 10, of contested rape cases. Eschewing the worst connotations, they acknowledge that 'a third possibility may be more common than previously recognized: that of genuine miscommunication and disagreements of memory between two honestly reporting parties'. That 'each party can report honestly, and yet quite falsely, what originally occurred' is applicable more widely in explaining what might have happened in disputed cases of sexual abuse, including disputes over whether the incident occurred at all. Ambiguities in verbal and non-verbal communication, the effects of alcohol or drugs, memory issues, changing perceptions, group influence processes, and, not least, the passing of time may all have a bearing on how both the accuser and the accused recall and reconstruct the reported incidents.

---

[5] See, e.g., the British False Memory Society, online <http://bfms.org.uk/>

REFERENCES

Angiolini, E. (2015) *Report of the Independent Review into the Investigation and Prosecution of Rape in London*, London: Metropolitan Police.

Ashworth, A. (2006) 'Four Threats to the Presumption of Innocence', *International Journal of Evidence and Proof*, 10(4): 241–78.

Blackstone, W. (1765–69) *Commentaries on the Laws of England*, Oxford: Clarendon Press.

Bull, R. (ed.) (2014) *Investigative Interviewing*, New York: Springer.

Cameron-Blackie, S. (2015) 'Reducing False Allegations, Reducing Their Harms: Opening Speeches', *FACTion*, 6(1): 31–5.

Gunn, B. (2013) 'The Compensation Carrot and False Allegations of Abuse', *FACTion*, 4(1): 10–12.

Hacking, I. (1998) *The Social Construction of What?* Cambridge, MA: Harvard University Press.

Home Affairs Select Committee (2002) *The Conduct of Investigations into Past Cases of Abuse in Children's Homes: Fourth Report of Session 2001–02*, London: HMSO. Available online at <http://www.publications.parliament.uk/pa/cm200102/cmselect/cmhaff/836/83602.htm> [accessed May 2016].

Hoyle, C., and Zedner, L. (2007) 'Victims, Victimisation and Criminal Justice', in M. Maguire, R. Morgan, and R. Reiner (eds) *The Oxford Handbook of Criminology*, 4th edn, Oxford: Oxford University Press.

Levitt, A. (2013) *Charging Perverting the Course of Justice and Wasting Police Time in Cases Involving Allegedly False Rape and Domestic Violence Allegations*, London: CPS.

Maran, M. (2010) *My Lie: A True Story of False Memory*, San Franscisco, CA: Jossey-Bass.

McAlinden, A. M. (2014) 'Deconstructing Victim and Offender Identities in Discourses on Child Sexual Abuse Hierarchies, Blame and the Good/Evil Dialectic', *British Journal of Criminology*, 54(2): 180–98.

McNally, R. J. (2005) 'Debunking Myths about Trauma and Memory', *Canadian Journal of Psychiatry [Revue Canadienne de Psychiatrie]*, 50(13): 817–22.

Medwed, D. S. (2012) *Prosecution Complex: America's Race to Convict, and Its Impact on the Innocent*, New York: New York University Press.

Meissner, C. A., and Kassin, S. M. (2002) ' "He's Guilty!" Investigator Bias in Judgments of Truth and Deception', *Law and Human Behavior*, 26(5): 469–80.

Nash, R. A., Wheeler, R. L., and Hope, L. (2015) 'On the Persuadability of Memory: Is Changing People's Memories No More than Changing Their Minds?', *British Journal of Psychology*, 106(2): 308–26.

Naughton, M. (2013) *The Innocent and the Criminal Justice System: A Sociological Analysis of Miscarriages of Justice*, Basingstoke: Palgrave MacMillan.

Pendergrast, M. (1997) *Victims of Memory: Incest Accusations and Shattered Lives*, London: HarperCollins.

Porter, S., Woodworth, M., and Birt, A. R. (2000) 'Truth, Lies, and Videotape: An Investigation of the Ability of Federal Parole Officers to Detect Deception', *Law and Human Behavior*, 24(6): 643–58.

Reece, H. (2013) 'Rape Myths: Is Elite Opinion Right and Popular Opinion Wrong?', *Oxford Journal of Legal Studies*, 33(3): 445–73.

Rumney, P. N. (2006) 'False Allegations of Rape', *The Cambridge Law Journal*, 65(1): 128–58.

Saunders, C. L. (2012) 'The Truth, the Half-Truth, and Nothing Like the Truth: Reconceptualizing False Allegations of Rape', *British Journal of Criminology*, 52(6): 1152–71.

SCOTT, M. (2015) 'Reducing False Allegations, Reducing Their Harms: Opening Speeches', *FACTion*, 6(1): 31–5.
STALLER, K. M., and FALLER, K. C. (eds) (2010) *Seeking Justice in Child Sexual Abuse: Shifting Burdens and Sharing Responsibilities*, New York: Columbia University Press.
STARMER, K. (2014) 'Human Rights, Victims and the Prosecution of Crime in the 21st Century', *Criminal Law Review*, 11: 777–87.
TAVRIS, C., and ARONSON, E. (2015) *Mistakes Were Made (But Not by Me): Why We Justify Foolish Beliefs, Bad Decisions, and Hurtful Acts*, rev'd edn, Boston, MA: Mariner Books.
WARD, T. (2012) 'Narrative and Historical Truth in Delayed Civil Actions for Child Abuse', in C. Gregoriou (ed.) *Constructing Crime: Discourse and Cultural Representations of Crime and Deviance*, Basingstoke: Palgrave Macmillan.
WEBSTER, R. (1998) *The Great Children's Home Panic*, Oxford: The Orwell Press.
WEBSTER, R. (2002) 'Similar Fact Evidence: The Origins and Erosion of the Modern Similar Fact Principle'. Available online at <http://www.richardwebster.net/similarfactevidence.html> [accessed January 2015].
WEBSTER, R. (2005) *The Secret of Bryn Estyn: The Making of a Modern Witch Hunt*, Oxford: The Orwell Press.
WESTERA, N. J., and KEBBELL, M. R. (2014) 'Investigative Interviewing in Suspected Sex Offences', in R. Bull (ed.) *Investigative Interviewing*, New York: Springer.
WOOD, J. D., and PETRIGLIERI, G. (2005) 'Transcending Polarization: Beyond Binary Thinking', *Transactional Analysis Journal*, 35(1): 31–9.

INDEX

Action Plan on Rape 196–7
adversarial system 271–2, 275, 273, 280–1
alcohol *see* intoxication
alibis 106–7
Allen, Woody 43, 44
All-Party Group for Abuse Investigations 160
anonymity 70, 102, 192, 232, 283
appellate system 13, 37, 215, 290–1
   Court of Appeal 215, 216–20
   Criminal Cases Review Commission (CCRC) 215, 220–2, 223
   fail-safe resorts 223
   lurking doubt test 217–19
   real possibility test 220, 221
   Runciman Royal Commission 217–18, 219, 221, 222
Ashworth, Andrew 282, 286
Association of Chief Police Officers (ACOP) 89, 161
attention-seeking 107–8

Becker, Howard 44, 51
behavioural analysis interview (BAI) 246–7
belief 54, 56
   culture of belief 100–4, 119, 121
   culture of disbelief 4–6, 121
   duty to believe 43–7
Berliner, Lucy 45
Best, Joel 50, 119
betrayal trauma theory (BTT) 258
bias
   cognitive 105–6, 208
   confirmatory 104, 209
   fading effect 259, 260, 261
   institutional 283–4
   investigative 101–6, 286–7
   judgemental 244, 250–1
   overperception 133
binary thinking 292–3
Birmingham Six 218
Blackstone ratio 86, 282
Bodin, Jean 45–6, 293
Brownmiller, Susan 66, 67, 121
Bryn Estyn 58, 62, 103, 162, 167, 169
burden of proof 43, 57, 71
Butler-Sloss, Elizabeth, Baroness Butler-Sloss 199

Cameron, David 161, 164
campus rape tribunals *see* tribunals
celebrities 5, 43, 44, 46, 47, 108, 164, 198
   victim-celebrities/celebrity-victims 123
child poverty 50
child protection 48, 56, 89, 121
child sexual abuse
   crusades against 4–6, 19, 42–51
   definitions 8
   incidence of reporting 100–1
   magnitude of the problem 228–31
   McMartin case 52–4
   moral status of the child 49–51, 61, 84
   repugnance towards 3–4
   ritual abuse 10
      historical accounts 31, 34, 35, 39–40
      metanarrative 34–9
   Rochdale 39, 196
   Rotherham 196
children's homes *see* residential child care
civil proceedings 12, 66, 67, 69, 87, 158–60, 228, 283, 285
   civil claims 156, 157–60, 165–6
      see also class actions
   civil trials 165, 192
      see also tribunals
   disciplinary hearing 19–20, 71
claims-making 50
Clancy, Susan 123, 125
class actions 157, 165, 286, 287
Clery Act 1990 (US) 74
Cleveland, UK 105
clinical psychologists *see* psychologists
cognitive bias 6, 12, 99, 105–6, 112, 204, 208, 212, 244, 291
   see also confirmation bias; status quo bias
cognitive dissonance 105, 209
college campuses 66, 68, 69, 71, 72–4, 78, 191
Community of the Wrongly Accused (COTWA) 26, 77
comparison questions technique (CQT) 247, 250
compensation
   financial 59, 108, 124, 156–62, 169, 285, 287–8
   victimization 118–19
      ideology of victim self-identification 119–23
      personal injury claims 59, 123

compensation (*cont.*)
    victim-celebrities/celebrity-victims 123
concealed information test (CIT) 247, 248, 249, 250
confessions *see* false confessions
confirmationory bias 5, 12, 104, 122, 180, 208–9, 286, 291
    idée fixe 104
    status quo bias 85, 209, 213
    tunnel vision 105
consent 11, 70, 73, 104–5, 129–31, 274
    ambiguities 131
    general interest, liking, and romantic interest vs sexual intent 133–4
    misleading sexual scripts 135
    non-verbal and indirect communication 132–3
    overperception bias 133
    token resistance 135
    memory for consent interactions 136–7
    relabeling of sexual interactions after the fact 138–9
    role of alcohol 136
contagion effect 122
content-based criterion analysis (CBCA) 233
copycat complaints 122
corroboration 227–8, 273
    importance of 233–7, 289–90
    uncorroborated reports of sexual abuse 229–31
counter-law 86–90
Court of Appeal 13, 193, 207n, 215, 216–23
crimen exceptum 3, 62, 289
Criminal Cases Review Commission (CCRC) 215, 220–2, 223, 290
criminal justice system 101–2, 112
    action plan to increase prosecution of sexual offences 195–8
    appeals *see* appellate system
    preventive action 4, 88, 92
    see also precautionary logic
criminal proceedings 12
    adversarial system 271–2, 275, 278
    defences 274–5
    erosion of safeguards 59, 86, 101, 122, 191–2, 273
    see also due process
    innocence *see* maintaining innocence
    juries 194, 271, 276
    New Zealand 102
    trial process 192–5
    victim-centred justice 101, 193, 198–200
criteria-based content analysis (CBCA) 233, 245, 250

Criminal Injuries Compensation Authority 156
cross-examination 102, 165, 277, 286
Crown Prosecution Service (CPS) 195–8
cultural values 60, 100–1, 119
custody disputes 110–11
Curtis-Thomas, Claire 160–1

damages 169
dangerousness 83, 85, 87
day care centres 31, 34, 35, 37, 38, 39
    McMartin case 32–4
    Shieldfield Nursery case 38
de Freitas, Eleanor 121–2
deception
    appearance of 178–81
    see also false memories; lie detection
Deese-Roediger-McDermott (DRM) paradigm 260, 261
defences 274–5
demons/devils 10, 32, 33, 37, 46, 56, 61, 158, 167
    see also ritual abuse
denial 54–5, 205
disclosure 86, 90
    controlled disclosure 86, 109, 111
    discretionary disclosure 86
    see also 'unstructured therapeutic disclosure'
DNA testing 26, 103–4, 110, 176, 183, 207, 209–11
Donovan Committee 217
due process 12, 69, 70–4
    evidential rules 191, 192–5
Duke Lacrosse case 72, 75, 77n
duty to believe 43–7
Dworkin, Andrea 66, 101

errors of judgment 6–7
Estrich, Susan 68
Evans, Nigel (MP) 200
event-related potential (ERP) 248
evidence 13, 26, 45, 56, 102
    available best evidence (ABE) 193
    corroboration 13, 70, 102, 108, 112, 156, 161, 165, 200, 227–8, 273
    importance of 233–7, 289–90
    uncorroborated reports of sexual abuse 194, 229–31
    DNA testing 26, 103–4, 110, 176, 183, 207, 209–11
    exculpatory evidence 4, 26
    physical evidence 5, 7, 9, 103, 176, 183–4, 209, 228, 237
    recantation evidence 208
    similar fact evidence 57, 161, 162, 286, 289

evidence-based decision making 278–80
evidential rules 191, 192–5, 272–4, 286, 287–8
evidentiary thresholds 236–7
evil 10, 31, 34, 37, 39, 56, 61–3, 167, 168
exceptional measures 3, 289
exonerating facts 272–5
exonerations 26, 103–4, 213
    National Registry of Exonerations 176n
eyewitness misidentification 104

facial emotional expressions 246
factitious disorder 111
fading affect bias 259, 260, 261
fair trial 57, 73, 193
    see also due process
false allegations *see* wrongful allegations
false confessions 12, 24, 111–12
    challenges of detection 187–8
    interrogation-induced 177
        confession 'in best interest' 181–2, 185–7
        distress intolerance 181
        enhanced likelihood, pressures, and persistence 177–8
        hopelessness 182–5
        persuasive techniques 185–7
        stereotype threat and the appearance of deception 178–81
    Mario Matthews 175–7, 183–4
false convictions 161, 162
    see also miscarriages of justice
false memories 125, 137, 139, 150, 151, 255–6, 288, 289
    criminal courts and 264–5
    Deese-Roediger-McDermott (DRM) paradigm 260, 261
    experiential evidence 256–7
    see also lie detection
false negatives 8, 86, 92, 93, 231, 235
false positives 8, 86, 92, 93, 179, 231, 235, 236, 292
false reports 228, 229, 230
false victim identities 124
fantasy 56
fear 83–6, 91–2
feminist ideology 10, 45, 48–9, 66, 101
    victim identity 120–1
    see also rape culture
financial gain 59, 108, 124
    see also compensation
forgetting mechanisms 258–60
Foucault, Michel 86
fraud 166
Frye, Marilyn 49

Gambaccini, Paul 200n
Garnier, Sir Edward (QC) 161
Garsden, Peter 157–9, 161, 163, 167, 168
Giddens, Anthony 85
Giving Victims a Voice 16, 198
Goodman, Bruce Dallas 209–11
Greenwood, David 165
Greystone Heath, Cheshire 155–7, 164
Groundhog Day 164, 165, 288
Gruber, Aya 77
guilty knowledge test (GKT) 247

Hartnett, Noel 164, 166
Haut De La Garenne 58, 168
hearsay evidence 274
Heilbron Report 192
Herman, Judith 121
historical abuse 54–5, 56, 58, 62, 63, 103, 167, 168, 191
    myths 61–3
    North Wales 57, 58, 110, 162–4
    Operation Care 158
    Operation Granite 155–7
    parliamentary inquiry into abuse investigations 57, 160–2, 288, 289
    social construction of abuse 59–61
Home Affairs Select Committee 2002 57, 160–2, 288, 289
honest false memories 139
honest false testimony 11, 105, 129–42
human rights 24, 120, 193
    Article 6, European Convention of Human Rights 193
hypnotherapists 149, 150

ideological agendas 101
    see also feminist ideology
imprisonment *see* prison
Independent Inquiry into Child Sexual Abuse (IICSA) 17, 199
innocence 12
    maintaining *see* maintaining innocence
    moral status of the child 23, 38, 49–51, 61, 84–5, 102
    plea of 13, 271
    presumption of 12, 59, 71, 73, 101, 112, 291
        see also presumption of guilt
    proving innocence 19, 26, 71, 182–5, 207–8
innocence procedures 280
    evidence and science-based decision-making 278–80
    exonerating facts 272–5
    sexual assault cases 275–8

institutional abuse 5
  historical abuse 54–5
  see also residential child care
institutional bias 283–4
interrogation 12, 13
  false confessions 177
    confession 'in best interests' 181–2, 185–7
    distress intolerance 181
    enhanced likelihood, pressures, and persistence 177–8
    hopelessness 182–5
    persuasive techniques 185–7
    stereotype threat and the appearance of deception 178–81
interviewing techniques 103, 232–3, 286–7
intoxication 11, 73, 105, 136, 139, 152, 275
investigation methods 11
investigative biases 101–6, 286–7

Janus, Eric 90–1
Jefferies, Christopher 26
Jenkins, Philip 121
Jersey 58, 168, 292
judgemental bias 244, 250–1
judges: beliefs about memory 151–2
juries 194, 271, 276, 291
  appeal against decisions see appellate system
justice system 101–2, 112, 284
  see also criminal proceedings

Kafkesque 13, 26
Kalisiak, Kelli 129–30
Keller, Fran and Dan 39
Koss, Mary 72
  one-in-four statistic 7

legislative changes 67, 68–9, 101–2, 112
Leigh, Leonard 219
Lewis, Joshua 129–30
lie detection 242–3
  interviewee-related effects 243
  judgemental biases 244
  observer-related effects 243–4
  see also false memories
lie detection tools 245
  behavioural tools: symptom validity test (SVT) 249
  general assessment 249–51
  judgemental biases 250–1
  non-verbal tools
    behavioural analysis interview (BAI) 246–7

facial emotional expressions 246
psycho-physiological methods
  comparison questions techniques (CQT) 247, 250
  concealed information test (CIT) 247, 248, 249, 250
  guilty knowledge test (GKT) 247
  neuroscience techniques 248–9
  physiological channels 247
  polygraph 90, 179, 233, 247–8, 251, 277–8
use and abuse 251
verbal tools
  criteria-based content analysis (CBCA) 245, 250
  reality monitoring (RM) 245–6, 250
  scientific content analysis (SCAN) 246
  verifiability approach 246
Lillie, Christopher 38
lurking doubt test 217–19

MacKinnon, Catherine 49, 66, 68
Macur Review 58
maintaining innocence 12–13, 16, 111, 160, 204, 206, 209–11, 213, 290–1
  Bruce Dallas Goodman 209–11
  innocent prisoner's dilemma 204–6
  parole release decision-making 204–6, 211–12
  possible reforms 211–13
  post-conviction litigation 207–9, 211–13
Marcus, Sharon 77
Matthews, Mario 175–7, 183–4
McAlpine, Alister, Baron McAlpine of West Green 4, 46–7, 108, 162–3, 167
McConville, Mike 156
McMartin case 32–4, 55, 103
media 37, 46–7, 59, 61, 91, 108, 119, 122, 163, 168, 169, 291
medical evidence 236
medical professionals and paraprofessionals (MHPs) 228, 229, 230, 231, 233, 234, 235
Megan's Law 89
memories of abuse
  false memories 125, 137, 139, 150, 151, 255–6, 288, 289
  criminal courts and 264–5
  Deese-Roedinger-McDermott (DRM) paradigm 260, 261
  experiential evidence 256–7
  see also lie detection
memory recovery techniques 109, 147, 148, 257–8, 288
memory research 11, 13, 143–5, 152, 288–9

clinicians' and therapists' beliefs about
   memory 144–5, 147–51
consent interactions 136–7
fading affect bias 259
false memories 125, 137, 139, 150, 151
forgetting mechanisms 258–60
general public's beliefs about
   memory 145–7
legal professionals' beliefs about
   memory 151–2
reconstructive processes 137–8
repressed memories 11, 109, 144–5, 146,
   147–8, 150, 151, 205
suggestive techniques 260–1
true recovered memories 255–6, 257–8
   characteristics of what is
      remembered 261–3
   context 263–4
   criminal courts and 264–5
Messham, Stephen 162–4, 167
metanarrative 34–9
miscarriages of justice 11, 13, 57, 160–1, 191,
   200, 222, 265, 272, 288
   appeals *see* appellate system
   Birmingham Six 218
misinterpretation of real events 103–4
moral crusades 4–6, 19, 42–3
   duty to believe 43–7
   historical abuse 55, 59, 103
   moral status of the child 49–51, 102
   pathologization of sexual behaviour 47–9
   rape culture 69, 71
moral entrepreneurs 43, 47, 56
moral panic 169–70
   ritual abuse 10
      historical accounts 31, 34, 35, 39–40, 103
      McMartin case 32–4
      metanarrative 34–9
moral status 42–3, 49–51, 84, 102
Mullin, Chris 160, 161
Münchausen syndrome by proxy 111
myth 34–9, 61–3, 99, 196, 292

narrative analysis 233
neoliberalism 84
Netherlands 39, 106
neuroscience techniques 248–9
New Zealand 101–2
non-verbal communication 132–3
North Wales 57, 58, 110, 162–4

objectivity 191
offenders *see* sex offenders

Okami, Paul 47–8
one-witness cases 271, 272–5, 278–80
Operation Care 158
Operation Granite 155–7
Operation Lentisk 159–60
Operation Pallial 58, 165
Operation Reno 164–6
Operation Yewtree 43, 168, 198
Orkney 55, 105–6
Oude Pekela, Netherlands 39, 106
outcry witness 274, 275
overperception bias 133

paedophile rings 5, 46, 58, 102–3, 108,
   162, 164
paedophilia 48
parental alienation syndrome 110–11
parole boards 204–6, 211–12, 290
personal injury lawyers 59, 123, 157–9, 161–2,
   167, 285–6
   civil compensation action 166
   Operation Lentisk 159–60
   Operation Reno 165
   parliamentary inquiry into abuse
      investigations 160–2
Pinker, Steven 83
polarization 292–3
police
   Association of Chief Police Officers
      (ACOP) 89, 161
   Metropolitan Police 43, 122
   police-induced false confessions
      111–12
   police records 63, 90
   police station rape suites 156
   wasting police time 7
police trawling 56–7, 103, 155, 160–2
   North Wales 162–4
   parliamentary inquiry into abuse
      investigations 160–2
political culture
   embedded suspicion 93
   neoliberal political culture 86
political thought 84
politics
   and the feminist movement 77
      see also state feminism
   German environmental politics 85
   of allegation 83
   of risk and danger 82
   'life politics' 84
polygraph 90, 179, 233, 247–8, 251, 277–8
poverty 50

precautionary logic 82–3
  counter-law 86–90
  dangerousness 83, 85, 87
  decision-making 90–2
  embedded suspicion 92–3
  'insurance-based society' 86
  perceived risk 83–6, 91–2
  technologies 89, 90
  victim-in-waiting 82, 84, 88, 89
predatory sex offenders 43, 48, 85
presumption of guilt 59, 86, 101, 122, 180
presumption of innocence 12, 59, 71, 73, 101, 112, 291
prevalence of CSA/rape 227–8, 255, 264
prevalence of wrongful allegations 9–10, 85, 284–6
preventive action/measures/orders 4, 88, 92
prison
  sentences 12, 21, 24, 31, 37, 39, 155, 205, 274
  staff 24
  vulnerable prisoners wing 22
prosecution 191
  action plan to increase prosecution of sexual offences 195–8
pseudo-victims 118, 126
psychoanalytic theory 144–5, 205
psychologists 103, 148–9, 150
psychotherapists 103, 105, 109
  beliefs about memory 144–5, 147–51
public opinion 6
public protection 82

racial discrimination 279
Radzinowicz, Sir Leon 92
rape
  consent see sexual consent
  definition 71, 101
  evidence in rape trials 192–5
  personal history and character of rape victims 192, 194, 273
  prosecutional reform 195–8
  statistics 68, 72, 78, 100, 172, 195, 284
rape culture 5, 6, 10, 66–7
  college campuses 67, 68, 69, 71, 72–4, 78, 191
  see also tribunals
  due process 69, 70–4
  international implications 70
  male-female relationships 74, 78
  men's groups and 75, 77
  national legislation 67, 68–9, 71, 74, 75, 76
  normal male behaviour 74–5
  origins of the term 66, 67–8
  Title IX 75, 78, 191n

  women as critics 77–8
  women in law 75–7
rape shield laws 70, 273
reality monitoring (RM) 245–6, 250
recantation evidence 208
recovery movement 120, 121
Reed, Dawn 38
rehabilitation 205
righteousness 5, 55, 62, 78, 158
religion 34, 47, 55, 120, 121, 158, 167, 205
repressed memories 11, 109, 144–5, 146, 147–8, 150, 151, 205
residential child care
  historical institutional abuse 54–5, 56, 58, 62, 63, 103, 168
    North Wales 57, 58, 110, 162–4
    Operation Care 158
    Operation Granite 155–7
    ritual abuse 55–7, 62
    Waterhouse Inquiry 57–9, 164
re-traumatization 43, 55
retribution 107
revenge 107
righteousness 5, 55, 62, 78, 158
  psychology of righteousness 55, 62
right to remain silent 281, 276
risk 83–6, 91–2
risk of sexual harm order 88
ritual abuse 10, 31–4, 45, 55, 62, 102–3, 105–6, 124
  historical accounts 31, 34, 35, 39–40
  McMartin case 32–4, 55
  metanarrative 34–9
  residential child care 55–7, 62, 158
Roache, William 200, 279n
Runciman Royal Commission 217–18, 219, 221, 222

satanic ritual abuse see ritual abuse
Saunders, Alison 196
Savile, Jimmy 17, 43, 46, 47, 58, 59–60, 122, 164, 166, 168, 169, 198
  Savile-effect 200
science-based decision-making 278–80
scientific content analysis (SCAN) 246
Scotland 236
secondary victimization 43, 120
self-help culture 123, 125
self-serving narratives 106–8
sex offenders
  criminal justice measures towards 4, 22, 89–90, 204–5
  repugnance towards 3–4, 22, 213, 291–2

INDEX

sex offenders register 22, 25, 90
   registration 4, 8, 89
sexual assault
   definitions 8, 70
   innocence procedures 275–8
   statistics 68–9, 72, 195, 284
      'one-in-four' 68, 72, 100
      'one-in-five' 72, 78
sexual behaviour, pathologization of
      47–9, 84–5
sexual coercion 138
sexual consent 11, 70, 73, 104–5, 129–31, 274
   ambiguities 131
      general interest, liking, and romantic
         interest vs. sexual intent 133–4
      misleading sexual scripts 135
      non-verbal and indirect
         communication 132–3
      overperception bias 133
      token resistance 135
      memory for consent interactions 136–7
      relabelling of sexual interactions after the
         fact 138–9
      role of alcohol 136
         see also intoxication
Sexual Offences (Amendment) Act 1992
      160
Sexual Offences Act 2003 88n, 89n, 196
sexual predators 43, 48, 85
sexual risk order (SRO) 89
sexual violence 85, 91
Shuttleworth, Roy 155–7
similar fact evidence 286, 289
social constructs 60, 100–1, 119
social imaginary 82
social science research 276, 279, 280
social workers 56, 63, 148, 150, 228
St Williams school 164–6
Starmer, Sir Keir 121, 126, 196, 283
state feminism 67, 69, 78
stereotypes 178–81, 184
   occupational groups 178, 290
   race-related 179
   social categories 178–9
   stepfathers 179
   stereotype threat 178–81, 290
   'woman scorned' 36
suggestive interviewing 103, 260–1
surveillance 89
survivors 118
   see also victims
sympathy 107–8
symptom validity test (SVT) 249

teachers 107
technology 89, 90
testimony 6, 12, 127, 102–3, 176–7, 183–5,
      271, 273
   expert testimony 34, 37
   eye-witness testimony 109–10, 144, 148,
      151–2
   honest false testimony 11, 105, 129–42
   testimony of recognition 120
therapeutic closure 12, 191
therapeutic tribunals 191, 198–200
therapists *see* hypnotherapists; psychologists;
      psychotherapists
Title IX *see* rape culture
trauma model 124, 125
trawling operations *see* police trawling
      operations
tribunals 10, 12, 191, 198–200
   college campuses 67, 68, 69, 71, 72–4, 78, 191
true recovered memories 255–6, 257–8
   characteristics of what is remembered
      261–3
   context 263–4
   criminal courts and 264–5
truth-telling 121
   historical and narrative truth 125

United States
   evidentiary thresholds 235, 236–7
   legislation: rape culture 67, 68–9, 71, 74,
      75, 76
   McMartin case 32–4, 55
'unstructured therapeutic disclosure' 123

veracity *see* lie detection; true recovered
      memories
verifiability approach 246
victim-blaming 43, 119, 284
victim-centred justice 101, 193, 198–200,
      273, 282
victim culture 11, 118–19
victim-in-waiting 82, 84, 88, 89
victims
   compensations of victimhood 118–19
      financial compensation 59, 124, 169
      ideology of victim self-
         identification 119–23
      personal injury claims 59, 123
      privileges of victimhood 124
      victim-celebrities/celebrity-victims 123
   contagion effect 122
   copycat complaints 122
   cross-examination 102

victims (*cont.*)
   disbelief in 4, 5
   duty to believe 43–7, 121
   false victim identities 124
   gender and victim identity 118–19
   lifelong damage 123
   moral status 42–3, 49–51, 84
   motivations 10–11, 59, 61, 99, 100
   pseudo-victims 118, 126
   recovery movement 120, 121
   secondary victimization 43, 120
   self-help culture 123, 125
   survivors 118
   testimony as recognition 120
   therapeutic closure 12, 191
   trauma model 124, 125
   truth-telling 121
      historical and narrative truth 125
   victim-blaming 43, 119, 284
Victims' Code 197
victims' perspectives 16–17, 55, 60–1
video-recorded interviews 232
violence 83, 85
   violent assault 8
   violent environments 73
   violent offenders 83
Violence Against Women Act (VAWA) (US) 67, 68–9, 71, 74, 75, 76
vulnerability 83, 84, 86
vulnerable adults 4

Walton, Sir John 216
Waterhouse Inquiry 57–9, 103, 163, 164
Waterhouse, Sir Ronald 57, 163
Webster, Richard 58, 63, 125, 155, 161, 167, 169
Werther effect 122
witch hunts 31, 33, 35, 45–6, 56, 61–2, 167
Wolmar, Christian 58
Woodiwiss, Jo 125
Woolf, Fiona, Dame Woolf 199

Woolf, Harry, Lord Woolf 160
wrongful allegations
   consequences for the accused 4, 9, 16–26, 227
      employment 16, 25
      families 16, 19–20, 21, 23
      health 16
      imprisonment 16, 21, 22, 24
      injustice and betrayal 18–19, 24, 25–6
      Kafkaesque 13, 26,
      labelled as sexual offender 186, 292
      reputation 16
      stigma 26, 38
      suicide, thoughts of 18, 20, 21, 38, 227
      trauma 17–19, 20, 21
   corroboration *see* corroboration
   definitions 7–8, 99, 100
   errors of judgement 6–7
   investigation bias 101–6
   miscommunications regarding consent *see* sexual consent
   misinterpretation of real events 103–4
   motivations 10–11, 59, 99, 100, 112
      factitious disorder and Münchausen syndrome by proxy 111
      false confessions 12, 24, 111–12
      honest false testimony 11
      parental alienation syndrome and custody disputes 110–11
      partly true allegations 109–10
      self-serving narratives of abuse 106–8
      sincerely believed false allegations 109
   prevalence 9, 10, 85, 284–6
   reducing the incidence and harms of 232–3, 282–93
   suggestive interviewing 103
   true cases and 232
wrongful convictions
      see appellate system; miscarriages of justice
Wyre, Ray 55